ABORTION

AN ETERNAL
SOCIAL AND
MORAL ISSUE

ISSN 1538-6643

ABORTION

AN ETERNAL SOCIAL AND MORAL ISSUE

Sandra M. Alters

INFORMATION PLUS® REFERENCE SERIES
Formerly Published by Information Plus, Wylie, Texas

GALE
CENGAGE Learning™

Detroit • New York • San Francisco • New Haven, Conn • Waterville, Maine • London

Abortion: An Eternal Social and Moral Issue

Sandra M. Alters

Kepos Media, Inc.: Paula Kepos and Janice Jorgensen, Series Editors

Project Editors: Elizabeth Manar, Kathleen J. Edgar

Rights Acquisition and Management: Jermaine Bobbitt, Tracie Richardson

Composition: Evi Abou-El-Seoud, Mary Beth Trimper

Manufacturing: Cynde Lentz

For product information and technology assistance, contact us at **Gale Customer Support, 1-800-877-4253.** For permission to use material from this text or product, submit all requests online at **www.cengage.com/permissions.** Further permissions questions can be e-mailed to **permissionrequest@cengage.com**

Cover photograph: Contemplation of Justice statue, U.S. Supreme Court Building, Image copyright Tim Mainiero, 2009. Used under license from Shutterstock.com.

While every effort has been made to ensure the reliability of the information presented in this publication, Gale, a part of Cengage Learning, does not guarantee the accuracy of the data contained herein. Gale accepts no payment for listing; and inclusion in the publication of any organization, agency, institution, publication, service, or individual does not imply endorsement of the editors or publisher. Errors brought to the attention of the publisher and verified to the satisfaction of the publisher will be corrected in future editions.

Gale
27500 Drake Rd.
Farmington Hills, MI 48331-3535

ISBN-13: 978-0-7876-5103-9 (set)   ISBN-10: 0-7876-5103-6 (set)
ISBN-13: 978-1-4144-4112-2   ISBN-10: 1-4144-4112-6

ISSN 1538-6643

This title is also available as an e-book.
ISBN-13: 978-1-4144-7002-3 (set)
ISBN-10: 1-4144-7002-9 (set)
Contact your Gale sales representative for ordering information.

Printed in the United States of America
1 2 3 4 5 6 7 14 13 12 11 10

TABLE OF CONTENTS

123056

includes comments on the April 2007 Supreme Court ruling that the federal Partial-Birth Abortion Ban Act of 2003 is constitutional. Chapter 13 provides counterarguments.

This chapter includes statements through 2009 from political, medical, and judicial figures who argue that partial-birth abortion should not be banned, especially when the life of the mother is at risk. The chapter includes comments on the April 2007 Supreme Court ruling that the federal Partial-Birth Abortion Ban Act of 2003 is constitutional. Chapter 12 provides counterarguments.

PREFACE

Abortion: An Eternal Social and Moral Issue is part of the *Information Plus Reference Series*. The purpose of each volume of the series is to present the latest facts on a topic of pressing concern in modern American life. These topics include the most controversial and studied social issues in the 21st century: capital punishment, care for senior citizens, crime, the environment, health care, immigration, minorities, national security, social welfare, women, youth, and many more. Even though this series is written especially for high school and undergraduate students, it is an excellent resource for anyone in need of factual information on current affairs.

By presenting the facts, it is the intention of Gale, Cengage Learning to provide its readers with everything they need to reach an informed opinion on current issues. To that end, there is a particular emphasis in this series on the presentation of scientific studies, surveys, and statistics. These data are generally presented in the form of tables, charts, and other graphics placed within the text of each book. Every graphic is directly referred to and carefully explained in the text. The source of each graphic is presented within the graphic itself. The data used in these graphics are drawn from the most reputable and reliable sources, such as from the various branches of the U.S. government and from major independent polling organizations. Every effort has been made to secure the most recent information available. Readers should bear in mind that many major studies take years to conduct and that additional years often pass before the data from these studies are made available to the public. Therefore, in many cases the most recent information available in 2010 is dated from 2005 to 2009. In the case of abortion statistics, and in particular worldwide abortion statistics, the data are sometimes older. Older statistics are sometimes presented in this series if they are of particular interest and no more-recent information exists.

Even though statistics are a major focus of the *Information Plus Reference Series*, they are by no means its only content. Each book also presents the widely held positions and important ideas that shape how the book's subject is discussed in the United States. These positions are explained in detail and, where possible, in the words of their proponents. Some of the other material to be found in these books includes historical background, descriptions of major events related to the subject, relevant laws and court cases, and examples of how these issues play out in American life. Some books also feature primary documents or have pro and con debate sections that provide the words and opinions of prominent Americans on both sides of a controversial topic. All material is presented in an even-handed and unbiased manner; readers will never be encouraged to accept one view of an issue over another.

HOW TO USE THIS BOOK

Few topics rouse as much dissension and disagreement as the topic of abortion. Some people assert that it is a woman's right to choose to have an abortion, whereas others assert that abortion is tantamount to murder. This book attempts to provide both sides of the divisive argument. Also included is information on the number and types of abortions performed in the United States, abortion clinics, teen pregnancy and abortion, views of abortion from around the world, religious thoughts on abortion, and legal rulings pertaining to abortion.

Abortion: An Eternal Social and Moral Issue consists of 13 chapters and 3 appendixes. Each chapter is devoted to a particular aspect of abortion. For a summary of the information covered in each chapter, please see the synopses provided in the Table of Contents at the front of the book. Chapters generally begin with an overview of the basic facts and background information on the chapter's topic, then proceed to examine subtopics of particular interest. For example, Chapter 4: Abortion in the United States: A Statistical Study, begins with a discussion of the major sources for abortion statistics in the United States: the Centers for Disease Control and Prevention, a government agency, and the Guttmacher Institute, a private organization that studies reproductive health issues. The chapter then compares data from both sources on the number of abortions performed in the United States. A discussion of the characteristics of women seeking abortions and their reasons for pursuing this course of action follows. Next, the chapter examines the statistics of out-of-state versus in-state abortions, including a discussion of why some women travel out of state for this type of medical care and the availability of abortion providers and their training. The remainder of the chapter is devoted to an examination of abortion methods, including women's perceptions of them, the percentage of each used, when they are performed, their cost, and their safety. Readers can find their way through a chapter by looking for the section and subsection headings, which are clearly set off from the text. They can also refer to the book's extensive index if they already know what they are looking for.

Statistical Information

The tables and figures featured throughout *Abortion: An Eternal Social and Moral Issue* will be of particular use to readers in learning about this issue. These tables and figures represent an extensive collection of the most recent and important statistics on abortion and related issues—for example, graphics cover the chronology of major abortion cases, the major political parties' positions on abortion, reported numbers of legal abortions in the United States, teenage birth rates, the number of incidents of violence at abortion clinics, the number of legal and illegal abortions worldwide, and public opinion on whether abortion should be legal. Gale, Cengage Learning believes that making this information available to readers is the most important way to fulfill the goal of this book: to help readers understand the issues and controversies surrounding abortion in the United States and to reach their own conclusions.

Each table or figure has a unique identifier appearing above it for ease of identification and reference. Titles for the tables and figures explain their purpose. At the end of each table or figure, the original source of the data is provided.

To help readers understand these often complicated statistics, all tables and figures are explained in the text. References in the text direct readers to the relevant statistics. Furthermore, the contents of all tables and figures are fully indexed. Please see the opening section of the index at the back of this volume for a description of how to find tables and figures within it.

Appendixes

Besides the main body text and images, *Abortion: An Eternal Social and Moral Issue* has three appendixes. The first is the Important Names and Addresses directory. Here, readers will find contact information for a number of government and private organizations that can provide further information on abortion. The second appendix is the Resources section, which can also assist readers in conducting their own research. In this section, the author and editors of *Abortion: An Eternal Social and Moral Issue* describe some of the sources that were most useful during the compilation of this book. The final appendix is the detailed index, which facilitates reader access to specific topics in this book.

ADVISORY BOARD CONTRIBUTIONS

The staff of Information Plus would like to extend its heartfelt appreciation to the Information Plus Advisory Board. This dedicated group of media professionals provides feedback on the series on an ongoing basis. Their comments allow the editorial staff who work on the project to make the series better and more user-friendly. The staff's top priority is to produce the highest-quality and most useful books possible, and the Information Plus Advisory Board's contributions to this process are invaluable.

The members of the Information Plus Advisory Board are:

- Kathleen R. Bonn, Librarian, Newbury Park High School, Newbury Park, California
- Madelyn Garner, Librarian, San Jacinto College, North Campus, Houston, Texas
- Anne Oxenrider, Media Specialist, Dundee High School, Dundee, Michigan
- Charles R. Rodgers, Director of Libraries, Pasco-Hernando Community College, Dade City, Florida
- James N. Zitzelsberger, Library Media Department Chairman, Oshkosh West High School, Oshkosh, Wisconsin

COMMENTS AND SUGGESTIONS

The editors of the *Information Plus Reference Series* welcome your feedback on *Abortion: An Eternal Social and Moral Issue*. Please direct all correspondence to:

Editors
Information Plus Reference Series
27500 Drake Rd.
Farmington Hills, MI 48331-3535

CHAPTER 1

ABORTION: AN ETERNAL SOCIAL AND MORAL ISSUE

WHAT IS ABORTION?

An abortion—which is also called induced abortion—is a procedure performed to end a pregnancy before birth occurs. This is not the same as a spontaneous abortion, a process that occurs when a fetus or embryo dies in the mother's uterus and is expelled by the body. Spontaneous abortion is also called a miscarriage.

The length of a pregnancy is measured in weeks from the first day of a woman's last menstrual period. A normal human pregnancy lasts about 40 weeks. Pregnancy can also be described in trimesters. There are three trimesters in a pregnancy, and each trimester is about three months long.

According to Sonya B. Gamble et al. of the Centers for Disease Control and Prevention, in "Abortion Surveillance—United States, 2005" (*Morbidity and Mortality Weekly Report*, vol. 57, no. SS-13, November 28, 2008), 88% of induced abortions in 2005 were reported to have been performed during the first 12 weeks, or first trimester, of pregnancy—the time of least risk to the health of the mother. Few abortions were reported to have been provided after 15 weeks, which is about four months of pregnancy: 3.7% were obtained at 16 to 20 weeks and 1.3% at 21 weeks or later. Gestational age was not reported for the remainder of abortions, so percentages in one or more of these categories may vary from what was reported.

Induced abortion can be accomplished in several ways, using surgery or medications. (See Table 1.1.) Early surgical and medical abortions can be done safely in a physician's office or clinic. Later abortions are often performed in hospitals or in special clinics.

The type of abortion a woman has depends on her choice, health, and how long she has been pregnant. It also depends on the legality of the procedure. In *Gonzales v. Carhart* (550 U.S. 124 [2007]), the U.S. Supreme Court ruled that the Partial-Birth Abortion Ban Act is constitutional, thus making illegal the intact dilation and extraction procedure.

Abortions have been performed since the beginning of recorded history. There have always been women who, for a variety of reasons, wanted to terminate their pregnancies. In the 21st century the abortion issue has developed into a conflict about whether an embryo or fetus is entitled to legal rights, and whether a woman's right to control her life and body includes the right to end an unwanted pregnancy. Even though abortion has been debated for centuries, motivations to condemn or support it have varied with changing political and social conditions.

ANCIENT TIMES

Abortion is mentioned in the ancient Code of Assyria (in Mesopotamia) of the 12th century BC. Provision 53 explicitly ordered that any woman who had an abortion should be impaled on stakes without the dignity of burial. If the woman did not survive the abortion, her body was to be similarly impaled, again without burial. Likewise, ancient Jewish law strictly forbade abortion as a method of avoiding childbirth, although it allowed the sacrifice of the fetus to save the life of the mother.

Conversely, in ancient Greece and Rome abortion was often used to limit family size. It was socially acceptable, as was the practice of disposing of deformed and weak infants through exposure (abandoning babies outdoors with the intent that they die). Males were favored; parents who did not want to have the expense of raising a female infant labeled her as "weak" and resorted to exposure.

The Greek philosophers Plato (428–348 BC) and Aristotle (384–322 BC) both approved of abortion as a means of population control. They also advocated exposure in the belief that it would ensure the best possible offspring.

TABLE 1.1

Methods of abortion, 2009

Medical abortion

For a medical abortion, a combination of drugs is taken to end a pregnancy. A medical abortion does not require surgery and can be performed during the first or second trimester. The medications considered "standard practice" in 2009 for medical abortions were:
• Mifepristone/misoprostol—Mifepristone is an anti-progesterone, formerly known as RU486. Misoprostol is a synthetic prostaglandin and is the prostaglandin that is generally used. These two drugs are used in the following way: First, mifepristone terminates a pregnancy by blocking the action of progesterone in the pregnant woman's body. Progesterone helps maintain the uterine lining, which is necessary for a pregnancy to be sustained. Thus the embryo/fetus detaches from the uterine wall when mifepristone is taken. Second, a synthetic prostaglandin (usually misoprostol) is administered orally or vaginally one to two days later. This drug causes the uterus to contract and expel its contents.

Surgical abortion

Surgical abortions remove the contents of the uterus. They are performed in a few ways, with the procedure depending on the length of the pregnancy:
• Suction curettage (vacuum aspiration)—Suction curettage can be performed during the first trimester—up to 12 weeks—of pregnancy. First, the opening of the uterus (the cervix) is widened, or dilated, by the insertion of small rods or sponges. A thin plastic tube is then inserted through the dilated cervix and into the uterus. The tube is attached to a pump that suctions out uterine contents. After the suctioning, it is sometimes necessary to use a curette (a sharp, spoon-like instrument) to gently scrape the walls of the uterus to be certain that all the fragments of the fetus and placenta have been removed.
• Dilation and Evacuation (D&E)—D&E is generally performed during the second trimester—from 12 to 24 weeks—of pregnancy. The procedure is similar to suction curettage, but the cervix is dilated more. In addition, forceps may be used to grasp larger pieces of tissue.
• Induction—For abortions in the second or, more generally, the third trimester, labor may be started (induced) with drugs. Drugs may be put in the vagina, injected into the uterus, or given intravenously (IV) to start contractions that will expel the fetus. Alternatively, salt water or urea may be injected into the amniotic sac surrounding the fetus. This stops the pregnancy and starts uterine contractions. Taking a large amount of fluid out of the amniotic sac may also be used to stop the pregnancy and start contractions. Some drugs may be given directly to the fetus.
• Intact dilation and extraction (IDX or intact D&X or [colloquially] partial birth abortion)—This abortion technique became illegal in the United States as of April 18, 2007, when the Supreme Court ruled that the Partial Birth Abortion Ban Act was constitutional. The procedure was used for abortions at 21 weeks or more of pregnancy. Two days before the fetus was aborted, dilation of the cervix began. After the water broke, the physician grasped the fetus' developing leg with forceps and turned it to the breech position (hind end first). The fetus was pulled down the birth canal to expose the developing feet, legs, arms, and shoulders. The developing head was generally too large to pass, so an incision was made in the back of the skull and the cranial contents were removed by aspiration. After the skull collapsed, the rest of the fetus passed.

SOURCE: Created by Sandra Alters for Gale, 2009

Plato wrote in *The Republic* that any woman older than 40 years (an age when the rate of birth defects increases sharply) should be compelled to abort a pregnancy.

Scholars who credit the Greek mathematician and physician Hippocrates (c. 460–c. 377 BC) with the Hippocratic Oath claim that he opposed abortion. (In its early form, the Hippocratic Oath prohibited abortion. It has been modified for modern use to be a medical code of ethics that states "First do no harm.") Others claim that this prohibition was a reflection of the Pythagorean teaching opposing abortion and that physicians in ancient times generally did not follow this oath.

The consequences of adultery or prostitution were compelling reasons for a woman or her family to end her pregnancy. In the ancient Roman household the father was the judge when it came to the ethical life of the family. He alone had the authority to order or forbid an abortion. When abortions were performed, Romans were not concerned with the life of the child but with the health of the mother, because some women were poisoned accidentally by improper mixtures of abortion-inducing drugs. Thus, fathers usually opted for infanticide (killing an infant after birth) rather than for abortion.

THE CHRISTIAN POSITION ON ABORTION

Christianity is a system of beliefs and practices founded in Palestine by the followers of Jesus (4? BC–AD 29?) approximately 2,000 years ago and is based on the Old and New Testament of the Bible. There are a variety of Christian religions, including Catholicism and a variety of Protestant denominations. Catholicism has existed since the earliest days of Christianity. Protestantism, however, dates back only to the Reformation, a 16th-century movement in western Europe that aimed at reforming some doctrines and practices of the Catholic Church and resulted in the establishment of the Protestant churches. There is disagreement as to which religions the term *protestant* encompasses. One organizational structure of religious preferences, using 13 religious groupings, is shown in Table 1.2. This table is from the *American Religious Identification Survey* (*ARIS* 2008; March 2009, http://www.americanreligionsurvey-aris.org/reports/ARIS_Report_2008.pdf), which was conducted by Barry A. Kosmin and Ariela Keysar of Trinity College in Hartford, Connecticut.

Table 1.2 was devised to categorize religions in the United States for research purposes. However, more than 1,000 denominations of Protestantism exist in the 21st century. In Table 1.2 the category "mainline Christian" is a group of Protestant religions, as are the categories "Pentecostal/Charismatic" and "Protestant Denominations." The Baptist religion is considered by some to be Protestant; others do not consider it Protestant because it did not arise through the Protestant Reformation.

As Table 1.2 shows, the United States is a country with a predominantly Christian population. In 2008, 25.1% of U.S. adults considered themselves to be Catholic, 15.8% to be Baptist, and 33.7% to belong to another type of Protestant denomination. Thus, 74.6% of American adults were Christian. Mormons made up 1.4% of the U.S. adult population,

TABLE 1.2

Self-identification of U.S. adult population by religious tradition, 1990, 2001, 2008

Religious tradition	1990 Estimate	%	2001 Estimate	%	2008 Estimate	%
Catholic	46,004,000	26.2	50,873,000	24.5	57,199,000	25.1
Baptist	33,964,000	19.3	33,820,000	16.3	36,148,000	15.8
Mainline Christian	32,784,000	18.7	35,788,000	17.2	29,375,000	12.9
Methodist	14,174,000	8.0	14,039,000	6.8	11,366,000	5.0
Lutheran	9,110,000	5.2	9,580,000	4.6	8,674,000	3.8
Presbyterian	4,985,000	2.8	5,596,000	2.7	4,723,000	2.1
Episcopalian/Anglican	3,043,000	1.7	3,451,000	1.7	2,405,000	1.1
United Church of Christ	438,000	0.2	1,378,000	0.7	736,000	0.3
Christian generic	25,980,000	14.8	22,546,000	10.8	32,441,000	14.2
Christian unspecified	8,073,000	4.6	14,190,000	6.8	16,834,000	7.4
Non-denom. Christian	194,000	0.1	2,489,000	1.2	8,032,000	3.5
Protestant unspecified	17,214,000	9.8	4,647,000	2.2	5,187,000	2.3
Evangelical/born again	546,000	0.3	1,088,000	0.5	2,154,000	0.9
Pentecostal/charismatic	5,647,000	3.2	7,831,000	3.8	7,948,000	3.5
Pentecostal unspecified	3,116,000	1.8	4,407,000	2.1	5,416,000	2.4
Assemblies of God	617,000	0.4	1,105,000	0.5	810,000	0.4
Church of God	590,000	0.4	943,000	0.5	663,000	0.3
Protestant denominations	4,630,000	2.6	5,949,000	2.9	7,131,000	3.1
Churches of Christ	1,769,000	1.0	2,593,000	1.2	1,921,000	0.8
Jehovah's Witness	1,381,000	0.8	1,331,000	0.6	1,914,000	0.8
Seventh Day Adventist	668,000	0.4	724,000	0.3	938,000	0.4
Mormon/Latter Day Saints	2,487,000	1.4	2,697,000	1.3	3,158,000	1.4
Jewish[a]	3,137,000	1.8	2,837,000	1.4	2,680,000	1.2
Eastern religions	687,000	0.4	2,020,000	1.0	1,961,000	0.9
Buddhist	404,000	0.2	1,082,000	0.5	1,189,000	0.5
Muslim	527,000	0.3	1,104,000	0.5	1,349,000	0.6
NRMs[b] & other religions	1,296,000	0.8	1,770,000	0.9	2,804,000	1.2
Nones/no religion	14,331,000	8.2	29,481,000	14.1	34,169,000	15.0
Agnostic	1,186,000[c]	0.7	991,000	0.5	1,985,000	0.9
Atheist	N/A	N/A	902,000	0.4	1,621,000	0.7
DK/refused	4,031,000	2.3	11,300,000	5.4	11,815,000	5.2
Total	175,440,000	100	207,983,000	100	228,182,000	100

[a]This refers only to Jews by religion and not to the total Jewish ethnic population.
[b]New religious movements.
[c]Agnostics and atheists were combined in NSRI 1990.

SOURCE: Barry A. Kosmin and Ariela Keysar, "Table 3. Self-Identification of U.S. Adult Population by Religious Tradition 1990, 2001, 2008," in *American Religious Identification Survey (ARIS 2008): Summary Report*, Trinity College, Hartford, CT March 2009, http://www.americanreligionsurvey-aris.org/reports/ARIS_Report_2008.pdf (accessed May 18, 2009)

and Jews 1.2%. Agnostics and atheists made up 15% of the population—a group that had nearly doubled in its percentage since 1990, whereas the Christian and Jewish populations had declined slightly. The Muslim population in the United States had doubled since 1990, but Muslims still made up less than 1% of the U.S. adult population in 2008.

In *U.S. Religious Landscape Survey—Religious Affiliation: Diverse and Dynamic* (February 2008, http://religions.pewforum.org/pdf/report-religious-landscape-study-full.pdf), the Pew Forum on Religion and Public Life finds similar results. The Pew results show that in 2008 Catholics made up 23.9% of the U.S. population, whereas *ARIS* shows 25.1%. Pew results show all Protestant religions made up 51.3% of the U.S. population, whereas *ARIS* shows 49.5%; both included Baptist religions in this group. The Pew

results show the unaffiliated category, which included atheists, agnostics, and "nothing in particular," encompassed 16.1% of the U.S. population, whereas *ARIS* shows this group accounted for 15%. Other results are similar as well, with both surveys agreeing that a growing proportion of Americans said they are not affiliated with any religion, that Protestantism is declining in the United States even though evangelical Protestantism is increasing, and that an increasing proportion of Americans—although a very small proportion—identify themselves as being Muslim, Hindu, or Buddhist.

Early Christian Position on Abortion

The first written works of Christianity hardly mention abortion. The earliest known Christian document that declared abortion a sin was the *Didache*, which was written in about AD 100. *Didache* 2:2 states, "You shall not kill the embryo by abortion and shall not cause the newborn to perish." The early church leaders agreed that if an abortion was performed to hide the consequences of fornication and adultery, then it was a sin that required penance. This sparked the debate whether abortion was murder.

The Roman Catholic Position on Abortion

During the first six centuries of the Roman Catholic Church, theologians theorized and debated about the starting point of human life. St. Augustine (354–430), whose teachings helped establish the church's theological foundation, taught that abortion is not the murder of an infant (infanticide). He wrote, "The law does not provide that the act [abortion] pertains to homicide, for there cannot yet be said to be a live soul in a body that lacks sensation when it is not formed in flesh and so is not endowed with sense." Reflecting a similar viewpoint, the *Irish Canons* (c. AD 675) noted that the penalty for illicit intercourse (a minimum of seven years on bread and water) was far more severe than the penance for abortion (three and a half years on the same diet).

The Catholic theologian St. Thomas Aquinas (1225?–1274) developed the concept of hylomorphism, which defines a human being as the unity of body and soul. This resulted in the belief that there could be no human being without the presence of both elements. In other words, the soul can exist only in a fully formed body, which he noted did not occur until the fifth or sixth month of fetal development. In *Summa Theologica* (part 1, question 90, article 4), Thomas Aquinas wrote, "The soul, as a part of human nature, has its natural perfection only as united to the body."

However, not all Catholic theologians agreed with Thomas Aquinas's position. Some theologians taught that hominization (the point at which a fetus acquires a soul and becomes a human being) occurred at 40 days (slightly more than one month) after conception for males and 80 days (not quite three months) for females. This was also referred to as the "ensoulment" of the fetus.

In 1312, at the Council of Vienne, the Catholic Church officially adopted Thomas Aquinas's hylomorphic theory of human life and upheld this traditional doctrine through the 16th century. Nonetheless, even though the church endorsed Thomas Aquinas's theory, theological discussions on abortion and the fetus continued. From the 12th through the 16th centuries various popes issued differing pronouncements on abortion and the fetal status, depending on their personal beliefs about the moment of ensoulment. In some cases they imposed excommunication (exclusion from church membership) as a penalty for purposefully aborting a fetus.

In *Apostolicae Sedis* (1869) Pope Pius IX (1792–1878) declared abortion a homicide and, therefore, was grounds for excommunication. This decision was reaffirmed in 1917 with the issuance of *Code of Canon Law*. Canon 2350, Paragraph 1, states, "Persons who procure abortion, mothers not excepted, automatically incur excommunication reserved to the Ordinary at the moment the crime takes effect: if they are clerics, they shall also be deposed." Recent popes have firmly upheld this canon. Pope Pius XII (1876–1958), who was deeply concerned about abortion, wrote in *Allocution to Midwives* (October 29, 1951, http://www.ewtn.com/library/PAPALDOC/P511029.HTM): "Every human being, even the child in the womb, has the right to life directly from God and not from his parents, not from any society or human authority. Therefore, there is no man, no human authority, no science, no 'indication' at all—whether it be medical, eugenic, social, economic, or moral—that may offer or give a valid judicial title for a direct deliberate disposal of an innocent human life, that is, a disposal which aims at its destruction, whether as an end in itself or as a means to achieve the end, perhaps in no way at all illicit."

The Second Vatican Council (1962–1965), the largest Roman Catholic Church gathering in Christian history, declared in *Gaudium Et Spes* (December 7, 1965, http://www.vatican.va/archive/hist_councils/ii_vatican_council/documents/vat-ii_cons_19651207_gaudium-et-spes_en.html) that abortion is a "supreme dishonor to the Creator." The council further observed that "from the moment of its conception life must be guarded with the greatest care while abortion and infanticide are unspeakable crimes."

In *Humane Vitae* (July 25, 1968, http://www.vatican.va/holy_father/paul_vi/encyclicals/documents/hf_p-vi_enc_25071968_humanae-vitae_en.html, 1968), Pope Paul VI (1897–1978) stated, "We are obliged once more to declare that the direct interruption of the generative process already begun and, above all, all direct abortion, even for therapeutic reasons, are to be absolutely excluded as lawful means of regulating the number of children."

Pope John Paul II (1920–2005) proclaimed his firm stance against contraception, abortion, and euthanasia (mercy killing) in *Evangelium Vitae* (March 25, 1995, http://www.vatican.va/holy_father/john_paul_ii/encyclicals/documents/hf_jp-ii_enc_25031995_evange lium-vitae_en.html). He claimed that modern society promoted a "culture of death." In 1998 the National Conference of Catholic Bishops of the United States issued "Living the Gospel of Life: A Challenge to American Catholics" (http://www.usccb.org/prolife/gospel.shtml). The conference stated that "direct abortion is *never* a morally tolerable option. It is *always* a grave act of violence against a woman and her unborn child. This is so even when a woman does not see the truth because of the pressures she may be subjected to, often by the child's father, her parents or friends."

The successor of Pope John Paul II, Pope Benedict XVI (Joseph Cardinal Ratzinger; 1927–), stated shortly after assuming the papacy that he and the Catholic Church would continue to stand firmly against abortion. This statement was in keeping with Ratzinger's earlier stance as evidenced in *Donum Vitae* (February 22, 1987, http://www.cin.org/vatcong/donumvit.html), which was issued by the Congregation for the Doctrine of the Faith (CDF) and which Ratzinger signed. *Donum Vitae* focused on biomedical techniques such as in vitro fertilization; the embryo and fetus were once again affirmed to be "a person from the first instant of his existence." Ratzinger, as Pope Benedict XVI, and the CDF issued an update of *Donum Vitae* in 2008. *Instruction Dignitas Personae: On Certain Bioethical Questions* (December 12, 2008, http://www.usccb.org/comm/Dignitaspersonae/Dignitas_Personae.pdf) stated that "the human being is to be respected and treated as a person from the moment of conception."

The Protestant Position on Abortion

Until the late 1960s almost all Protestant churches opposed abortion. However, the changing social climate, as well as the U.S. Supreme Court decision in *Roe v. Wade* (410 U.S. 113 [1973]), which legalized abortion in the United States, spurred a change in Protestant positions on abortion.

Since 1970 the Presbyterian Church has supported free and open access to abortion without legal restriction. At about the same time, the United Methodists, the Lutheran Church in America, the United Church of Christ, the Disciples of Christ, and the Southern Baptist Convention adopted policies allowing abortion as a decision of the woman or the couple. In 1980 the Southern Baptist Convention began to reverse its stance, first by opposing the use of tax money to fund abortions. By the late 1980s the Southern Baptist Convention made its opposition to abortion, except to prevent the death of the mother, a firm policy. It reaffirmed this policy in 2003 on the 30th anniversary of the *Roe v. Wade* decision. Many evangelical, fundamentalist, and independent Bible churches are also against abortion. However, many Protestant denominations still support open access to abortion.

THE ISLAMIC POSITION ON ABORTION

Islam has more than 1 billion followers worldwide, but as Table 1.2 shows, in 2008 it had only 1.3 million followers in the United States, accounting for only 0.6% of the adult population. The Koran, which Muslims believe to contain God's revelations to Muhammad (c. 570–632), the historical founder of the religion of Islam, describes the development of the fetus, "O Mankind! If ye are in doubt concerning the Resurrection, then lo! We have created you from dust, then from a drop of seed, then from a clot, then from a little lump of flesh shapely and shapeless, that We may make [it] clear for you. And We cause what We will to remain in the wombs for an appointed time, and afterward We bring you forth as infants" (Koran 22:5, as translated by Mohammed Marmaduke Pickthall, in *The Meaning of the Glorious Quran*, 1938).

The Koran teaches that fetal development is divided into three 40-day stages. At the end of the third stage, the soul enters the fetus. Muslims, who belong to various groups, differ in their beliefs as to when—or if—abortion is allowed. Some sects believe it is permissible to have an abortion before ensoulment, whereas others argue that God forbids the killing of both the born and unborn, even those who have not received a soul. They claim the Koran (6:140) specifically teaches, "They are losers who besottedly have slain their children without knowledge, and have forbidden that which Allah bestowed upon them." However, Muslims generally agree that abortion is acceptable to save the mother's life.

THE JEWISH POSITION ON ABORTION

Table 1.2 shows that in 2008 Jewish-Americans made up 1.2% of the U.S. population. Like Islam, Judaism has no one position on abortion. In the United States most Jews belong to one of three groups: Orthodox, Conservative, or Reform Judaism. Reform and Conservative Jews generally believe that abortion is the choice of the woman. Jewish law does not recognize a fetus, or even an infant younger than 30 days old, as having legal rights. The laws of mourning do not apply to an expelled fetus or a child who does not survive to his 30th day. The biblical text that is the basis for this states, "If a man strikes and wounds a pregnant woman so that her fruit be expelled, but no harm befall her, then he shall be fined as her husband shall assess, and the matter placed before the judges. But if harm befall her, then thou shalt give life for life" (Exodus 21:22).

The Mishnah is the code of Jewish law that forms the basis of the Talmud, the most definitive statement of Jewish law. The Mishnah, which dates back to the second century BC, states, "If a woman is having difficulty in giving birth, it is permitted to cut up the child in her womb and take it out limb by limb because her life takes precedence. However, if the greater part of the child has come out, it must not be touched, because one life must not be taken to save another."

The Jewish philosopher Maimonides (1135–1204) wrote that abortion was permitted if it would ease a mother's illness, even if the illness was not life threatening. Other scholars, however, have differed, saying abortion was permitted only to save the mother's life. During the Holocaust (1938–1945) Jewish women who became pregnant were encouraged by their rabbis to abort because the Germans had declared that all pregnant Jewish women would be killed.

Orthodox Judaism takes a restrictive position on abortion, teaching that a fetus is an organic part of the mother and, as such, does not have legal status. Nonetheless, termination of a pregnancy is strongly condemned on moral grounds. Even though a mother's life takes precedence over the unborn, Orthodox Jews believe that the fetus, particularly after the 40th day from conception, has a right to life that cannot be denied. Cases of rape or fetal deformity do not give a mother permission to terminate a pregnancy unless they are a threat to her mental health (e.g., if the mother becomes suicidal as a result of the pregnancy).

THE MORMON POSITION ON ABORTION

The Church of Jesus Christ of the Latter-day Saints (LDS, the Mormon Church) had its beginnings in 1820 with the founder Joseph Smith Jr. (1805–1844). Section 59:6 of *The Doctrine and Covenants of the Church of Jesus Christ of Latter-day Saints* (1996) states, "Thou shalt not steal; neither commit adultery, nor kill, nor do anything like unto it." This statement translates into an LDS position that abortion is wrong and that a person should not only avoid abortion but also not take part in arranging, paying for, or providing one. Exceptions can be made, such as when the life or health of the mother is in jeopardy or if the pregnancy is the result of incest or rape.

THE AMERICAN EXPERIENCE

Roots in the British Tradition

The U.S. legal tradition developed from the British tradition. Until England broke away from the Roman Catholic Church in the 16th century, it had observed the church's laws. Henry de Bracton (c. 1210–1268), the father of English common law, was the first to mention abortion in English common law. (The English common law was a body of laws based on judicial precedents, or court decisions and opinions, rather than on written laws.) Greatly influenced by church law and theologians, Bracton wrote in *De Legibus et Consuetudinibus Angliae* (c. 1235), "If there be anyone who strikes a pregnant woman or gives her a poison whereby he causes an abortion, if the foetus be already formed or animated, and especially if it be animated, he commits homicide."

When the English jurist Sir Edward Coke (1552–1634) wrote *The Institutes of the Laws of England* (1628) 400 years later, the law had changed. "If a woman be quick with child," Coke wrote, "and by a potion or otherwise killeth it in her womb; or if a man beat her, whereby the child dieth in her body, and she is delivered of a dead child, this is a great misprision [misdemeanor], but no murder; but if the child be born alive, and dieth of the potion, battery, or other cause, this is murder." The term *quickening* refers to the first time the mother feels the fetus moving in the womb. It often occurs during the 16th to 18th week of pregnancy.

A century later the English jurist and professor Sir William Blackstone (1723–1780) upheld in *Commentaries on the Laws of England* (1765–1769) Coke's interpretation that it was a serious misdemeanor if the child was killed in the womb and murder if it was killed after birth. Despite the observations of Coke and Blackstone, abortion was not a criminal offense in England between 1327 and 1803.

After 1803, however, British law prohibited abortion. The first written statute in England against abortion was the Miscarriage of Women Act of 1803 (also known as Lord Ellenborough's Act), which affirmed punishment for the administration of drugs to induce abortion. The punishment for abortion before quickening included exile, whipping, or imprisonment. The punishment for abortion after quickening was death. However, after the death penalty was abolished in 1837, abortion both before and after quickening was considered a felony with similar punishments. (Britain legalized abortion through 24 weeks of gestation in 1968.)

The First Abortion Laws in the United States

The first abortion laws in the United States were based on English common law as described by Coke and Blackstone. In 1821 Connecticut passed the first abortion law. Even though it was patterned after the British 1803 Miscarriage of Women Act, which addressed all forms of abortion, the Connecticut statute addressed postquickening abortion only, declaring it to be a felony.

In 1828 New York passed a statute with two provisions. The first provision imposed a second-degree manslaughter penalty for a postquickening abortion. A prequickening abortion was considered a misdemeanor. The second provision contained an exception clause permitting "therapeutic" abortion if "necessary to preserve the life of such a mother or shall have been advised by two physicians to be necessary for such a purpose." This New York law served as a model for many state statutes prohibiting abortion.

Despite these state statutes regulating abortion, the sale of abortion-inducing drugs continued during the first half of the 19th century. The newspapers regularly advertised "monthly pills" and new methods to relieve "obstructions of the womb."

In 1871 the *New York Times* called abortion "The Evil of the Age" (August 23, 1871). The newspaper article stated, "The enormous amount of medical malpractice [a euphemism for abortion] that exists and flourishes, almost unchecked, in the City of New York, is a theme for most serious consideration. Thousands of human beings are thus murdered before they have seen the light of this world."

The American Medical Association

The American Medical Association (AMA), which was founded in 1847, initially campaigned against abortion. At that time women did not regularly turn to physicians for questions on childbirth and "women problems"; instead, they went to people who had little medical training, such as midwives and pharmacists. In addition, women also saw "quacks," people with no medical training, but who advertised expertise and offered their "services" to women. The AMA was concerned about the dangers that abortions posed for the women who received them. In addition, the association argued that abortion providers ignored the portion of the Hippocratic Oath that stated, "I will not give a lethal drug to anyone if I am asked, nor will I advise such a plan; and similarly I will not give a woman a pessary to cause an abortion."

The simplest solution to this difficult situation was to make abortion illegal. The medical profession saw this as an opportunity to drive the quacks out of the field and to bolster their own professional image. In addition, medical science had recently recognized that life existed in the fetus before quickening, and many physicians were morally offended by the act of aborting a live fetus.

The AMA was not motivated to criminalize abortion for moral or professional reasons alone. Physicians were swept up by the growing anti-immigrant sentiments of the time. There were concerns that, because of the uncontrolled use of abortion, the proportion of "good Anglo-Saxon stock" was diminishing in the face of increasing immigration, which was predominantly Catholic at the time.

Antiabortion Laws

Because of the intense lobbying by the AMA, the period from 1860 to 1880 produced the most important proliferation of antiabortion legislation in U.S. history. States and territories enacted more than 40 antiabortion statutes. Of these, 13 outlawed abortion for the first time and 21 revised old antiabortion laws by making them more stringent. In 1873 Congress passed the Comstock Law (named after its chief supporter, the American morals crusader Anthony Comstock [1844–1915]). Primarily intended to ban the dissemination of pornography and birth control devices, this legislation also prohibited the use of abortion devices.

Abortion continued despite the laws that banned it. Frederick Joseph Taussig states in *Abortion, Spontaneous, and Induced* (1936) that in the early 20th century as many as one out of three pregnancies was terminated. (Other forms of birth control were either unreliable or difficult to obtain.) Wealthy women generally found physicians who lent their own interpretations to the allowable exceptions for therapeutic (medically necessary) abortions. Poor women, however, usually had to resort to self-induced or illegal abortions, which resulted in countless mutilations and deaths.

In 1934 Congress held hearings to amend the Comstock Law to allow doctors to provide birth control information and prescribe contraceptive devices. However, support was strong for the Comstock Law; defenders of the law held that allowing doctors to provide birth control information was tantamount to the government supporting population control. The Comstock Law remained in effect for nearly four more decades. On January 8, 1971, President Richard M. Nixon (1913–1994) signed a law overturning the 98-year-old federal anticontraception law.

CHANGING ATTITUDES

Over time, advances in medicine enabled most women to carry their pregnancies to term uneventfully. Doctors became hard-pressed to diagnose life-threatening complications so that they might prescribe therapeutic abortions. In 1959 the American Law Institute proposed a revised Model Penal Code that gave physicians guidelines with which to work. The code proposed that physicians be permitted to terminate a pregnancy if one of the following conditions was met:

- The pregnancy threatened the life of the mother or would critically impair the mother's physical or mental condition.
- The child would be born with a grave physical or mental defect.
- The pregnancy resulted from rape or incest.

The need for the abortion had to be approved by two physicians. The inclusion of the mother's mental condition became a factor for doctors because the definition of health was beginning to include mental health at that time.

By the 1960s all 50 states and the District of Columbia allowed therapeutic abortions to save the life of the mother. Colorado and New Mexico also permitted abortions to prevent serious irreparable harm to the mother. Alabama, Oregon, Massachusetts, and the District of Columbia allowed abortions simply to protect the health of the mother.

Thalidomide and Rubella

No sooner were these laws adopted than their restrictions were tested by events that occurred in the early 1960s. In 1962 Sherri Finkbine of Arizona found out that thalidomide, a drug she had been taking to treat morning sickness during her pregnancy, may have caused deformities in the child she was carrying. European women who used the drug were reported to be delivering severely deformed babies. Finkbine decided, on her physician's advice, to have a legal abortion.

After Finkbine publicized her dilemma to warn others of the effects of thalidomide, the hospital refused to perform the abortion for fear of criminal liability. An appeal to the Arizona Supreme Court was unsuccessful, so the Finkbines flew to Sweden, where the abortion was performed. The Swedish doctor confirmed that the embryo was deformed.

During the early 1960s a rubella (German measles) epidemic swept the United States. Many women who had contracted measles during early pregnancy obtained legal abortions because they thought their fetuses might have birth defects. Many others could not have abortions (legal or illegal), either because of legal restrictions or a lack of funds. Consequently, many women delivered their children with a greater risk of disabilities.

In 1967 the AMA called for the liberalization of abortion laws and in 1970 urged that abortion be limited only by the "sound clinical judgment" of a physician.

WOMEN SPEAK OUT

The thalidomide and rubella episodes stimulated interest in the abortion issue and created empathy for the mothers-to-be who had found themselves in these difficult situations. Furthermore, the 1960s were a period of change— a time when many people questioned accepted beliefs. Americans were discussing human sexuality more openly, which made it easier to talk about abortion. Many sought to put a stop to the deaths and mutilations brought on by unqualified abortionists.

The Laws Begin to Change

Increased interest in the abortion issue caused many states to reform their laws, using the Model Penal Code as a guide. In 1967 Colorado, California, and North Carolina became the first states to liberalize their statutes. By 1973 a total of 13 states had enacted this type of legislation.

In 1970 Alaska, Hawaii, New York, and Washington chose the radical alternative of legalizing all abortions performed by a physician—up to a legally determined time in the pregnancy. Alaska, Hawaii, and Washington also established state residency requirements and shorter time periods during which women could have an abortion on demand. By one vote, New York passed the most liberal law of the four states. It permitted abortion for any reason up to 24 weeks of pregnancy. Beyond that point, an abortion could only be performed to save the mother's life.

In 1972 the American Bar Association approved the Uniform Abortion Act as a model for all state statutes. It was based on the New York law. That same year the President's Commission on Population Growth and the American Future, headed by the philanthropist John D. Rockefeller III (1906–1978), released its final report, which recommended that "present state laws restricting abortion be liberalized along the lines of the New York statute."

Meanwhile, as legislatures continued to reexamine their state abortion laws, state and federal courts were beginning to declare some states' abortion laws unconstitutional because they were vague and interfered with a woman's right to privacy. Many thousands of women traveled to states where abortion had become legal to obtain an abortion. According to John W. Klotz, in *A Christian View of Abortion* (1973), the New York State Department of Health reported that 278,122 legal abortions were performed between July 1, 1970, and December 31, 1971. Furthermore, the department noted that 40% of the women who had these abortions were from out of state. Many states watched to see what would happen in New York, Alaska, Hawaii, and Washington and awaited the legal clarification that inevitably would have to come from the U.S. Supreme Court. It came on January 22, 1973, in the historic *Roe v. Wade* decision, which is discussed in the next chapter along with other important Supreme Court decisions on abortion.

CHAPTER 2
U.S. SUPREME COURT DECISIONS

Abortion is an issue that is divisive and about which many people feel passionate. Those who call themselves pro-choice believe that women should be able to control their own bodies and reproductive decisions. These abortion rights proponents believe that abortion is about reproductive choice and a constitutional right to privacy. Those on the antiabortion side of the issue, who call themselves pro-life, believe that fetuses have a right to life and that no one should have the legal right to destroy a life after it is conceived, even if that pre-born person is still in the womb.

The abortion issue affects not only women in their reproductive years but also potential fathers and other family members, as well as those who are involved in the debate on moral, ethical, philosophical, and legal grounds. Thus, abortion is a national issue and one that is governed in the United States by federal law.

The federal court system is divided into three major types of courts: district courts, circuit courts of appeals, and the U.S. Supreme Court. There is at least one district court in each state; they serve as trial courts for lawsuits pertaining to federal law that arise in that state. Circuit courts of appeals reconsider rulings from the district courts, usually by a three-judge panel. Federal lawsuits that have passed through the district courts and circuit courts of appeals may then be appealed to the Supreme Court, which is the ultimate authority on interpreting federal law.

State laws can modify federal laws somewhat, but state abortion laws that contradict federal law cannot be enforced. The Supreme Court, being the highest federal court in the country, becomes the ultimate battleground in the debate over abortion.

ROE V. WADE

On January 22, 1973, the Supreme Court handed down a landmark decision in the now-famous *Roe v. Wade* (410 U.S. 113) legal battle. This ruling made it legal for a woman and her doctor to choose abortion without restrictions in the earlier months of pregnancy and with restrictions in the later months. The lawsuit was filed on behalf of Norma McCorvey (1947–), who used the alias Jane Roe. Her attorneys alleged that the abortion law in Texas (the state in which she lived) violated her constitutional rights and the rights of other women. The defendant was Henry Menasco Wade (1914–2001), the district attorney of Dallas County, Texas.

Now, more than three decades and many dozens of court decisions later, the essential tenet of the *Roe v. Wade* decision—that abortion is a constitutional liberty—has not been overturned. However, several court decisions have permitted increasing restrictions and preconditions on a woman's right to an abortion. This chapter will examine the major steps in the Supreme Court's interpretation of the *Roe v. Wade* decision from 1973 through mid-2009. The cases are presented by issue. A chronology and a brief explanation of major abortion cases can be found in Table 2.1. The citations, such as 410 U.S. 113, refer to the volume (first number) and page (last number) of the series of bound volumes titled *United States Reports*, which contain the hard copies of final, official judicial decisions of the U.S. Supreme Court.

Table 2.1 shows that the last Supreme Court decision on abortion as of mid-2009 was *Gonzales v. Carhart* (550 U.S. 124 [2007]), which ruled that the Partial-Birth Abortion Ban Act of 2003 was constitutional. At the state level, however, there was much judicial activity after that ruling. NARAL Pro-Choice America notes in "*Roe v. Wade* and the Right to Choose" (January 2009, http://www.prochoiceamerica.org/assets/files/Courts-SCOTUS-Roe.pdf) that 16 anti-choice legislative measures were enacted by states in 2008. In addition, the organization states that "in 2008 alone, legislators in 12 states considered 22 near-total bans on abortion care, and 15 states have not repealed their existing bans, some of which could become enforceable if *Roe* falls."

TABLE 2.1

Chronology of major Supreme Court decisions on abortion, 1973–2007

Roe v. Wade—1973, 410 U.S. 113

Found abortion legal and established the trimester approach of unrestricted abortion in the first trimester, reasonably regulated abortion in relation to the woman's health in the second trimester, and permitted states to prohibit abortion in the third trimester, except when necessary to preserve the woman's life or health.

Doe v. Bolton—1973, 410 U.S. 179

Held unconstitutional Georgia's statute requiring performance of abortions in hospitals, approval by hospital abortion committee, confirmation by two consulting physicians, and restriction to state residents.

Bigelow v. Virginia—1975, 421 U.S. 809

Made invalid the application of a Virginia statute that prohibited the advertisement of abortion services.

Connecticut v. Menillo—1975, 423 U.S. 9

Ruled that states may require that abortions must be performed by physicians. This case was an appeal of a conviction of a nonphysician for performing abortions.

Planned Parenthood of Central Missouri v. Danforth—1976, 428 U.S. 52

Ruled that a state may not require the written permission of a spouse or the consent of a parent, in the case of a minor, for an abortion. Further ruled that the state could not prohibit the use of saline injection abortions, and found the provision requiring the physician to preserve the life of the fetus "unconstitutionally overbroad."

Maher v. Roe—1977, 432 U.S. 464; **Beal v. Doe**—432 U.S. 438; **Poelker v. Doe**—432 U.S. 519

Ruled that, although the state could not ban abortion, it was under no legal obligation to fund nontherapeutic abortions or provide the public facilities for such abortions.

Colautti v. Franklin—1979, 439 U.S. 379

Overturned a Pennsylvania law that required physicians to try to save the fetus even if the fetus was less than six months developed and not yet viable.

Bellotti v. Baird—1979, 443 U.S. 622

Found that a statute requiring a minor to get her parents' consent or to obtain judicial approval following parental notification unconstitutionally burdened the minor's right to an abortion.

Harris v. McRae—1980, 448 U.S. 297

Found that the Hyde Amendment did not impinge on a woman's freedom to terminate a pregnancy but, rather, encouraged alternatives deemed to be in the public interest. This ruling also permitted use of federal Medicaid funds only for abortions necessary to save the life of the pregnant woman.

Williams v. Zbaraz—1980, 448 U.S. 358

Ruled that states do not have to pay for medically necessary abortions for women on Medicaid (as in *Harris* v. *McRae*). This case was a challenge to a version of the Hyde Amendment in Illinois.

H.L. v. Matheson—1981, 450 U.S. 398

Upheld a Utah statute requiring a physician to notify a minor's parents of their daughter's intention to obtain an abortion.

Planned Parenthood of Kansas City, Missouri v. Ashcroft—1983, 462 U.S. 476

Found unconstitutional that all abortions after 12 weeks of pregnancy be performed in a hospital, but upheld a provision requiring pathology reports for every abortion, the presence of a second physician for abortions performed after viability, and parental consent or judicial bypass for minors.

City of Akron v. Akron Center for Reproductive Health, Inc.—1983, 462 U.S. 416

Held unconstitutional the following requirements: that all abortions after the first trimester be performed in a hospital, parental consent or judicial order be required for all minors under 15 years of age, specific information designed to dissuade a woman from abortion be presented, a 24-hour waiting period be observed, and methods for the disposal of fetal tissue be established.

Simopoulos v. Virginia—1983, 462 U.S. 506

Upheld Virginia hospitalization requirement that included outpatient clinics. This case was an appeal of a criminal conviction of a physician for violating a Virginia law that requires all post-first-trimester abortions to be performed in hospitals. Virginia law provides for licensing of freestanding ambulatory surgical facilities as "hospitals." If Dr. Simopoulos's clinic had been licensed, criminal prosecution could have been avoided. The Virginia law is constitutional and not as restrictive as the laws struck down in **City of Akron v. Akron Center for Reproductive Health, Inc.** (1983) and **Planned Parenthood of Kansas City, Missouri v. Ashcroft** (1983)

Thornburgh v. American College of Obstetricians and Gynecologists—1986, 476 U.S. 747

Ruled that the information required under "informed consent," public reports, and disclosure of detailed information about abortions performed were not reasonably related to protecting a woman's health.

Webster v. Reproductive Health Services—1989, 492 U.S. 490

Upheld the Missouri law stating that "the life of each human being begins at conception." Also ruled that the state had the right to require physicians to perform viability tests on any fetus believed to be 20 or more weeks old, to forbid the use of public employees and facilities to perform abortions not necessary to save a woman's life, and to prohibit the use of public funds, employees, or facilities to counsel a woman to have an abortion not necessary to save her life.

Hodgson v. Minnesota—1990, 497 U.S. 417

Upheld a law requiring minors to notify both parents of an abortion decision because there was a provision for judicial bypass within the law.

Ohio v. Akron Center for Reproductive Health, Inc.—1990, 497 U.S. 502

Upheld ruling requiring one-parent notification plus judicial bypass. Also upheld a requirement that the physician personally notify the parent and ruled that states need not guarantee absolute anonymity to the minor seeking bypass.

Rust v. Sullivan—1991, 500 U.S. 173

Prohibited clinics that used Title X funds from counseling regarding abortion or giving abortion referrals.

Planned Parenthood of Southeastern Pennsylvania v. Casey—1992, 505 U.S. 833

Stopping just short of overturning **Roe v. Wade**, this ruling dropped the trimester framework and adopted an "undue burden" standard. Specifically, it upheld informed consent, a 24-hour waiting period, parental consent, and reporting and recordkeeping requirements. It rejected a requirement for spousal consent.

History of *Roe v. Wade*

Texas's abortion law had been in place since 1857, and it permitted abortion only when the mother's life was endangered. McCorvey, a pregnant single woman, challenged the constitutionality of this law in 1969, using the pseudonym Jane Roe to protect her privacy.

TABLE 2.1

Bray v. Alexandria Women's Health Clinic—1993, 506 U.S. 263

Found that the anti-abortion protests outside of clinics could not be interpreted as a violation of the Civil Rights Act. Women seeking abortions were not a class of persons qualifying for protection under the law and the protesters' behavior did not show class-based discriminatory ill will against women.

National Organization for Women v. Scheidler—1994, 510 U.S. 249

Ruled that the Racketeer-Influenced and Corrupt Organizations Act did not have to include an economic motive and could be used to prosecute the protest activities of anti-abortion groups and any other groups that seek to prevent the operation of legitimate businesses.

Madsen v. Women's Health Center—1994, 512 U.S. 753

Upheld an injunction forbidding anti-abortion protesters from entering a 36-foot fixed buffer zone in front of an abortion clinic, and upheld noise restrictions, which prevented the use of bullhorns and shouting. The Court did not uphold the injunction preventing protesters from approaching patients and staff workers in a 300-foot buffer zone around clinics and staff residences or the prohibition against nonthreatening posters and signs in the 36-foot buffer zone.

Schenck v. Pro-Choice Network of Western New York—1997, 117 519 U.S. 357

Upheld an injunction forbidding anti-abortion protesters from entering a 15-foot fixed buffer zone in front of an abortion clinic. Also upheld the provision of "cease and desist," whereby two protesters at a time could perform "sidewalk counseling." However, the protesters had to stop counseling and leave the buffer zone on request. The Court did not uphold the injunction preventing protesters from coming within a 15-foot floating buffer zone of people entering or leaving an abortion clinic.

Hill v. Colorado—2000, 530 U.S. 703

Ruled that a Colorado statute does not violate the First Amendment by forbidding anyone from knowingly approaching closer than within eight feet of another person who is within 100 feet of the entrance of a health care facility, without that person's consent, to give them a leaflet, display a sign, or engage in protest, education, or counseling. It was found not to violate the First Amendment because it does not regulate speech on the basis of content or viewpoint.

Stenberg v. Carhart—2000, 530 U.S. 914

Upheld by a narrow margin (5–4) the Eighth Circuit Court of Appeals' decision that made Nebraska's ban on "partial-birth" abortion invalid. The court ruled on two components of Nebraska's ban, including the lack of a health exception and the undue burden on a woman's right to abortion created by broad language of the ban.

Scheidler v. NOW—2003, 537 U.S. 393

Held that anti-abortion groups could not be sued for extortion under racketeering laws intended to combat organized crime.
Ruled that the Partial-Birth Abortion Ban Act of 2003 was unconstitutional in three ways: it places an undue burden on women seeking abortions, its language is vague, and it lacks a required exception for medical actions needed to preserve the woman's health.

Scheidler v. NOW—2006, 547 U.S. 9

Ruled 8-0 that the physical violence that occurred outside of abortion clinics was not punishable under the Hobbs Act. This ruling appears to have ended a case that was fought for twenty years.

Ayotte v. Planned Parenthood of Northern New England—2006, 546 U.S. 320

Let stand a New Hampshire parental notification law that requires a forty-eight hour prior notification of parents before an abortion is performed on their minor child, even if the delay puts the health of the child at risk. The high court ruled that lower court decisions of unconstitutionality of the law were in error, and it returned the case to lower courts and to the state legislature to consider other remedies for the lack of a health exception.

Gonzales v. Carhart—2007, 550 U.S. 124

Ruled that the Partial-Birth Abortion Ban Act of 2003 is constitutional. This is the first time the U.S. Supreme Court has upheld an abortion restriction without requiring an exception to protect the health of the mother, and it is the first time the High Court has approved a ban on a specific medical procedure. The Partial-Birth Abortion Ban Act disallows abortion by the intact dilation and extraction (IDX or intact D&X) procedure, which is generally used for abortions at 21 weeks or more of pregnancy.

SOURCE: Created by Sandra Alters for Gale, 2009

In a 7-2 decision in *Roe v. Wade*, the Supreme Court found that a law that prohibited abortion, except to save the life of the mother and without regard for the state of the pregnancy, violated the due process clause of the Fifth Amendment. The due process clause of the Fifth Amendment, ratified in 1791, is the U.S. Constitution's guarantee that no level of government can arbitrarily or unfairly deprive individuals of their basic constitutional rights to life, liberty, and property. The 14th Amendment takes this guarantee one step further by ensuring protection against infringement (taking away rights) by state governments. The high court said the 14th Amendment protects the right to privacy against state action, including a woman's right to terminate her pregnancy. The court based this right to privacy on the 1942 case *Skinner v. Oklahoma* (316 U.S. 535), which struck down a state law that called for sterilizing people who have been convicted two or more times of "felonies involving moral turpitude" (immoral acts).

In the *Roe v. Wade* decision, however, the court noted that, even though the right to abortion is guaranteed, the state has legitimate interests in protecting the health of the pregnant woman and the potentiality of human life. The weight given to each of these interests changes as the pregnancy develops.

The court divided a normal pregnancy into three-month stages (trimesters):

- First trimester—during approximately the first three months the decision to abort must be left up to the woman and her physician.

- Second trimester—after the first trimester of pregnancy the state may regulate the abortion procedure in ways necessary to promote the mother's health.

- Third trimester—after the fetus is viable (able to survive outside the womb) the state, to protect the potential life of the fetus, may regulate and even forbid abortion, except where necessary to preserve the life or health of the mother.

Doe v. Bolton Expands *Roe v. Wade*

On the same day that the Supreme Court decided *Roe v. Wade*, it expanded the ruling with *Doe v. Bolton* (410 U.S. 179 [1973]), a lawsuit brought against the attorney general of Georgia by a pregnant woman using the pseudonym Mary Doe and 23 others. Doe had applied for a therapeutic (medically necessary) abortion under Georgia law and had been turned down. While reiterating its *Roe v. Wade* ruling that states may not prevent abortion by making it a crime, the high court observed that states are not allowed to make abortions hard to obtain by imposing complicated procedural conditions. The court found unconstitutional the following state requirements:

- All abortions must take place in hospitals accredited by the Joint Committee on Accreditation of Hospitals.

- Abortions must be approved by a hospital abortion committee.

- Two consulting physicians must confirm the judgment of the performing physician.

GOVERNMENT SUPPORT OR NONSUPPORT OF ABORTION
Public Funding of Nontherapeutic Abortions

On June 20, 1977, the Supreme Court ruled on three cases concerning women too poor to afford an abortion. One case involved the Connecticut Welfare Department, which had issued regulations limiting state Medicaid benefits for first-trimester abortions to those that were medically necessary. An indigent (poor) woman, using the pseudonym Susan Roe, challenged the regulations and sued Edward Maher, the commissioner of social services in Connecticut. In *Maher v. Roe* (432 U.S. 464), the court held that the 14th Amendment does not require a state participating in Medicaid to pay for needy women's expenses arising out of nontherapeutic (not medically necessary) abortions simply because it pays childbirth expenses. The court observed that a state may choose to favor childbirth over abortion and is under no obligation to show why it chooses to do so.

The second case, which was similar to *Maher v. Roe*, involved the Pennsylvania Department of Public Welfare. A Pennsylvania law restricted Medicaid-funded abortions to indigent women, allowing them only in situations deemed medically necessary by a physician. In *Beal v. Doe* (432 U.S. 438), the Supreme Court found that states could exclude nontherapeutic abortions from coverage under their Medicaid programs.

The third case involved a St. Louis, Missouri, policy that prohibited nontherapeutic abortions in the city's two publicly run hospitals. In *Poelker v. Doe* (432 U.S. 519),

the high court ruled that St. Louis could refuse to provide publicly financed hospitals for nontherapeutic abortions even though it provided facilities for childbirth. Because the policy did not deny women the right to have an abortion, it was consistent with the U.S. Constitution. In summary, the Supreme Court found with these three cases that even though the state cannot ban abortions, it is under no legal obligation to fund nontherapeutic abortions or to provide public facilities for such abortions.

Abortion Funding Restrictions of the Hyde Amendment—Constitutional or Not?

The Hyde Amendment was passed by Congress in 1976 and excludes abortion from the comprehensive health care services provided to low-income people by the federal government through Medicaid. The cases of *Maher*, *Beal*, and *Poelker* did not address the issue of whether federal law, such as the Hyde Amendment, or state laws with similar provisions were constitutional. Because most federal funding for abortion was done through Medicaid, cutting federal monies mostly affected the poor. Not surprisingly, the issue of the constitutionality of the Hyde Amendment soon made its way into the nation's courts.

In June 1980, in a 5-4 decision, the Supreme Court held in *Harris v. McRae* (448 U.S. 297) that the Hyde Amendment is constitutional. The court ruled that the funding restrictions of the Hyde Amendment do not infringe on a woman's right to terminate her pregnancy as held in *Roe v. Wade*. The court stated, "It simply does not follow that a woman's freedom of choice carries with it a constitutional entitlement to the financial resources to avail herself of the full range of protected choices....Although government may not place obstacles in the path of a woman's exercise of her freedom of choice, it need not remove those not of its own creation."

PUBLIC FUNDING OF THERAPEUTIC ABORTIONS. In *Harris v. McRae*, the high court further ruled that a state that participates in the Medicaid program is not required to fund therapeutic abortions if federal reimbursement has been withdrawn under the Hyde Amendment. On that same day the Supreme Court, in three related cases—*Williams v. Zbaraz*, *Miller v. Zbaraz*, and *United States v. Zbaraz* (448 U.S. 358)—held that an Illinois law, with similar funding restrictions as the Hyde Amendment, did not violate the 14th Amendment.

FEDERALLY FUNDED CLINICS CANNOT COUNSEL ABOUT ABORTION AS AN OPTION. The central question of *Rust v. Sullivan* (500 U.S. 173 [1991]) was whether government regulations violate the First Amendment if they prohibit federally funded projects from engaging in counseling concerning referrals for activities advocating abortion as a means of family planning. In May 1991 the Supreme Court ruled that providing information was included in this prohibition and that rights provided by the First Amendment (free speech) and Fifth Amendment (preventing government from depriving individuals of their basic constitutional rights) were not infringed on by this prohibition.

STATE RESTRICTIONS ON ABORTION

Since *Roe v. Wade*, abortion laws generally have been modified by the continual addition of restrictions on the ability to obtain an abortion. Over the years many states have passed statutes stretching the limits of the law, mainly in the areas of informed consent, waiting periods, spousal or parental consent, parental notice, and place of abortions, as well as fetal viability and the disposal of the fetus.

Figure 2.1 shows the states that had abortion bans as of January 2009. Fifteen states outlawed abortion throughout pregnancy as of that date. According to NARAL Pro-Choice America, in *Who Decides? The Status of Women's Reproductive Rights in the United States* (January 2009, http://www.prochoiceamerica.org/choice-action-center/in _your _state/who-decides/introduction/whodecides2009.pdf), these bans contradicted federal law in place at the time, so they were considered unconstitutional and unenforceable.

Informed Consent and Spousal/Parental Consent

Planned Parenthood of Central Missouri v. Danforth (428 U.S. 52 [1976]) was the first case heard before the Supreme Court that confronted *Roe v. Wade* and *Doe v. Bolton*. Two Missouri-licensed physicians challenged several restrictions of the Missouri Code, which required the following:

- A woman must sign a written consent to the abortion and certify that "her consent is informed and freely given and is not the result of coercion."

- A woman must get a written consent from her husband for the abortion.

- The attending physician must exercise professional care to preserve the fetus's life and health, failing which he or she would be held guilty of manslaughter and liable for damages.

- An unmarried woman under 18 must get the written consent of a parent or person in the place of a parent to permit abortion.

The Supreme Court ruled in *Planned Parenthood v. Danforth* that during the first 12 weeks of pregnancy an abortion was a matter of interest only to the woman and her physician. The state cannot "delegate to a spouse a veto power which the state itself is absolutely and totally prohibited from exercising during the first trimester of pregnancy," as ruled in *Roe v. Wade*. Similarly, the court struck down the parental consent requirement. The court found the provision requiring the physician to preserve the life and health of the fetus "unconstitutionally overbroad," especially because it covered the first three months of pregnancy, when the fetus is not able to survive outside the womb. In addition, the majority also ruled that the state could not prohibit the use of any safe abortion method.

PARENTAL CONSENT. In 1979 a Massachusetts law required parental consent for an abortion to be performed on an unmarried woman under the age of 18. However, if either or both of the parents refused, a judge of the superior court could rule on the issue. The *Bellotti v. Baird* (443 U.S. 622 [1979]) case asked whether the law unconstitutionally restricted the right of a minor to have an abortion. In an 8-1 ruling the Supreme Court observed, "A child, merely on account of his minority, is not beyond the protection of the Constitution." The court declared that the Massachusetts statute was unconstitutional on two grounds: "First, it permits judicial authorization for an abortion to be withheld from a minor who is found by the superior court to be mature and fully competent to make this decision independently. Second, it requires parental consultation or notification in every instance, whether or not in the pregnant minor's best interests, without affording her an opportunity to receive an independent judicial determination that she is mature enough to consent or that an abortion would be in her best interests."

Parental Notification

Two years later the Supreme Court ruled again on whether a minor, who was fully dependent on her parents, had to inform her parents of her decision to have an abortion (i.e., to notify them, not to obtain their consent). Referring to *Bellotti v. Baird*, the court noted in *H. L. v. Matheson* (450 U.S. 398 [1981]), "A statute setting out a mere requirement of parental notice when possible does not violate the constitutional rights of an immature, dependent minor...whether or not to bear a child...is a grave decision, and a girl of tender years, under emotional stress, may be ill-equipped to make it without mature advice and emotional support."

Similarly, in 1990 the Supreme Court upheld in *Ohio v. Akron Center for Reproductive Health* (497 U.S. 502) a 1985 Ohio statute that required a physician performing an abortion on a minor to give 24-hour prior notice to at least one parent or guardian. The law provided the minor with a way to bypass her parents (called a judicial bypass) by asking the juvenile court to issue an order that would authorize her to give her own consent. In upholding this part of the statute, the Supreme Court also ruled that states need not guarantee absolute anonymity to the minor seeking judicial bypass.

In 1981 Minnesota passed a law (Subdivision 2 of Minn. Stat. 144.343) requiring a minor to inform both parents 48 hours before having an abortion, even if the

FIGURE 2.1

State near-total abortion bans, January 2009

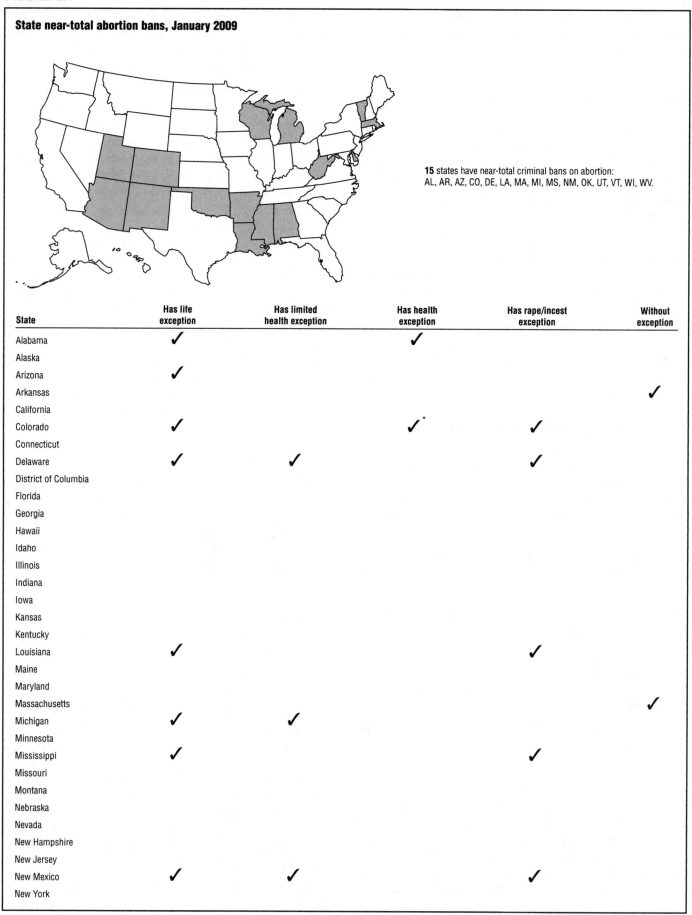

15 states have near-total criminal bans on abortion: AL, AR, AZ, CO, DE, LA, MA, MI, MS, NM, OK, UT, VT, WI, WV.

State	Has life exception	Has limited health exception	Has health exception	Has rape/incest exception	Without exception
Alabama	✓		✓		
Alaska					
Arizona	✓				
Arkansas					✓
California					
Colorado	✓		✓*	✓	
Connecticut					
Delaware	✓	✓		✓	
District of Columbia					
Florida					
Georgia					
Hawaii					
Idaho					
Illinois					
Indiana					
Iowa					
Kansas					
Kentucky					
Louisiana	✓			✓	
Maine					
Maryland					
Massachusetts					✓
Michigan	✓	✓			
Minnesota					
Mississippi	✓			✓	
Missouri					
Montana					
Nebraska					
Nevada					
New Hampshire					
New Jersey					
New Mexico	✓	✓		✓	
New York					

FIGURE 2.1

State near-total abortion bans, January 2009 [CONTINUED]

State	Has life exception	Has limited health exception	Has health exception	Has rape/incest exception	Without exception
North Carolina					
North Dakota					
Ohio					
Oklahoma	✓				
Oregon					
Pennsylvania					
Rhode Island					
South Carolina					
South Dakota					
Tennessee					
Texas					
Utah	✓	✓		✓	
Vermont	✓				
Virginia					
Washington					
West Virginia	✓				
Wisconsin	✓				
Wyoming					
Totals	**13**	**4**	**2**	**6**	**2**

*Law contains a full health exception, but requires approval from a three-physician panel.

SOURCE: "Near-Total Abortion Bans," in *Who Decides? The Status of Women's Reproductive Rights in the United States*, NARAL Pro-Choice America and NARAL Pro-Choice America Foundation, January 1, 2009, http://www.prochoiceamerica.org/choice-action-center/in_your_state/who-decides/maps-and-charts/map.jsp?mapID=26 (accessed May 5, 2009)

parents were no longer married and one parent had little or nothing to do with the minor's upbringing. Subdivision 2 was mandatory except in cases of parental abuse or neglect. The law also created a judicial bypass procedure. Subdivision 6 allowed a minor who did not want to inform either parent to go to court, be supplied with counsel, and be judged whether she was mature enough to make the decision alone or if an abortion was in her best interest.

The Supreme Court upheld the Minnesota law in *Hodgson v. Minnesota* (497 U.S. 417 [1990]) because it provided a provision for judicial bypass. The high court ruled that "the constitutional objection to the two-parent notice requirement is removed by the judicial bypass option provided in Subdivision 6 of the Minnesota statute." The decision, however, was divided, with several justices agreeing with some parts of the decision but not others.

In 2003 Planned Parenthood of Northern New England sought a ruling against a 2003 New Hampshire law that required written parental notification 48 hours before any abortion was provided to a minor unless "the attending abortion provider certifies in the pregnant minor's medical record that the abortion is necessary to prevent the minor's death and there is insufficient time to provide the required notice." There was also a provision for judicial bypass within the law. In *Planned Parenthood of Northern New England et al. v. Peter Heed, Attorney General of the State of New Hampshire* (No. 04-1161), the district court found the law unconstitutional because it lacked an explicit exception to protect the health of the pregnant minor and because the exception for abortions necessary to prevent the minor's death was too narrow. An appeals court upheld this ruling in 2004.

The Supreme Court heard this case in November 2005 and ruled in January 2006. In *Ayotte v. Planned Parenthood of Northern New England* (546 U.S. 320), the high court did not agree that the law was unconstitutional and returned the case to the lower courts and state legislature to reconsider whether there might be other remedies for the lack of a health exception.

In *Who Decides?*, NARAL Pro-Choice America indicates that in January 2009, 28 states had laws requiring parental consent and another 16 required parental notification before a minor had an abortion. (See Figure 2.2.) Seven of these state laws—those in Alaska, California, Illinois,

FIGURE 2.2

State restrictions on minors' access to abortion, January 2009

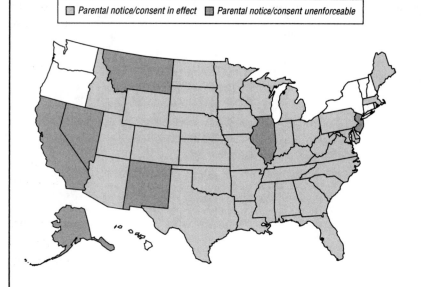

☐ Parental notice/consent in effect   ☐ Parental notice/consent unenforceable

28 states restrict young women's access to abortion by requiring parental consent: AK, AL, AR, AZ, CA, ID, IN, KY, LA, MA, ME, MI, MO, MS, NC, ND, NM, OH, OK, PA, RI, SC, TN, TX, UT, VA, WI, WY

16 states restrict young women's access to abortion by requiring parental notice: CO, DE, FL, GA, IA, IL, KS, MD, MN, MT, NE, NJ, NV, OK, SD, WV

State	State mandates		Consent/notice required from	
	Parental consent	**Parental notice**	**One parent**	**Two parents**
Alabama	✓		✓	
Alaska	✓		✓	
Arizona	✓		✓	
Arkansas	✓		✓	
California	✓		✓	
Colorado		✓		✓
Connecticut				
Delaware		✓	✓	
District of Columbia				
Florida		✓	✓	
Georgia		✓	✓	
Hawaii				
Idaho	✓		✓	
Illinois		✓	✓	
Indiana	✓		✓	
Iowa		✓	✓	
Kansas		✓	✓	
Kentucky	✓		✓	
Louisiana	✓		✓	
Maine	✓		✓	
Maryland	✓	✓	✓	
Massachusetts	✓			✓*
Michigan	✓		✓	
Minnesota		✓		✓
Mississippi	✓			✓
Missouri	✓		✓	
Montana		✓	✓	
Nebraska		✓	✓	

FIGURE 2.2

State restrictions on minors' access to abortion, January 2009 [CONTINUED]

State	State mandates		Consent/notice required from	
	Parental consent	Parental notice	One parent	Two parents
Nevada		✓	✓	
New Hampshire				
New Jersey		✓	✓	
New Mexico	✓		✓	
New York				
North Carolina	✓		✓	
North Dakota	✓			✓
Ohio	✓		✓	
Oklahoma	✓	✓	✓	
Oregon				
Pennsylvania	✓		✓	
Rhode Island	✓		✓	
South Carolina	✓		✓	
South Dakota		✓	✓	
Tennessee	✓		✓	
Texas	✓		✓	
Utah	✓		✓	
Vermont				
Virginia	✓		✓	
Washington				
West Virginia		✓	✓	
Wisconsin	✓		✓	
Wyoming	✓		✓	
Totals	**28**	**16**	**38**	**5**

Note: Some states allow additional exceptions to these restrictions not included in this chart. Please refer to detailed summaries at http://www.prochoice.org for this information.
*This statute requires two-parent consent, but a court has issued an order that the law be enforced as requiring the consent of one parent.

SOURCE: Adapted from "Restrictions on Young Women's Access to Abortion," in *Who Decides? The Status of Women's Reproductive Rights in the United States*, NARAL Pro-Choice America and NARAL Pro-Choice America Foundation, January 1, 2009, http://www.prochoiceamerica.org/choice-action-center/in_your_state/who-decides/maps-and-charts/map.jsp?mapID=12 (accessed May 6, 2009)

Montana, Nevada, New Jersey, and New Mexico—contradicted federal law, so they were considered unconstitutional and unenforceable.

Place Restriction, Fetal Development and Viability Discussion, and Fetal Disposal

In 1975 the Supreme Court ruled in *Connecticut v. Menillo* (423 U.S. 9) that a state may require that abortions be performed only by physicians. Such restrictions continued in 1978, when the city of Akron, Ohio, enacted the ordinance Regulations of Abortions, which determined how abortions should be performed in the city. Among the restrictions on abortions were the following:

- All abortions performed after the first trimester of pregnancy had to be done in a hospital.

- The attending physician must inform the patient of the status of her pregnancy; the development of the fetus; the date of possible fetal viability; the physical and emotional complications that may result from an abortion; and the availability of agencies to provide her with assistance and information regarding birth control, childbirth, and adoption. The physician must also tell the patient about the particular risks associated with her pregnancy and the abortion method to be used.

- Physicians performing abortions must ensure that fetal remains were disposed of in a "humane and sanitary manner."

Violation of any provision constituted a criminal misdemeanor. Many antiabortion groups considered the Akron ordinances model legislation to be followed by other communities wishing to regulate abortion within their jurisdictions.

After mixed rulings in the federal district court and in the federal court of appeals, the case was argued before the Supreme Court. In a 6-3 decision in *City of Akron v. Akron*

Center for Reproductive Health, Inc. (462 U.S. 416 [1983]), the Supreme Court upheld its earlier ruling in *Roe v. Wade.*

Noting the significant medical improvements in abortion procedures and the concurrent sharp decrease in the number of deaths resulting from late-term abortions, the high court ruled that it was not necessary to have all second trimester abortions performed in a hospital.

The court also ruled that the provision regarding what information the physician must give the woman before abortion was unconstitutional: "By insisting upon recitation of a lengthy and inflexible list of information, Akron unreasonably has placed 'obstacles in the path of the doctor upon whom [the woman is] entitled to rely for advice in connection with her decision.'"

Finally, the Supreme Court invalidated the provision requiring a "humane and sanitary" disposal of the fetal remains. Even though Akron claimed the purpose of this provision was to prevent the disposal of aborted fetuses in garbage piles, the city was not clear that this alone was the main reason for the provision. The high court agreed with the appellate court that the provision suggested a possible regulation on "some sort of 'decent burial' of an embryo at the earliest stages of formation." The court concluded that this unclear provision is "fatal" where a physician could be criminally held liable for disposing of the fetal remains.

A case in 1983 further challenged such restrictions on abortion. The case of *Planned Parenthood of Kansas City, Missouri v. Ashcroft* (462 U.S. 476) concerned a Missouri law requiring the following:

- All abortions after the first trimester must be performed in a hospital.

- Minors must have parental consent or judicial authorization for their abortions.

- Two doctors must be present at the abortion.

- A pathologist's report must be obtained for every abortion.

The court found the hospitalization requirement to be unconstitutional for the same reasons stated in *Akron v. Akron Center for Reproductive Health, Inc.*, but the court found the other restrictions constitutional.

Late-Term Abortions

STATE PARTIAL-BIRTH ABORTION LAWS. Table 2.2 shows that as of May 1, 2009, 31 states had adopted laws banning partial-birth abortions. The term *partial-birth abortion* is favored by those who oppose the procedure and is the common name for the medical procedure known as intact dilation and extraction (intact D&X), which can be used to end pregnancies in the second or third trimester, generally after 20 weeks of gestation. (See Table 1.1 in Chapter 1.) Sonya B. Gamble et al. of the Centers for Disease Control and Prevention report in

"Abortion Surveillance—United States, 2005" (*Morbidity and Mortality Weekly Report*, vol. 57, no. SS-13, November 28, 2008) that 820,151 abortions were performed in 2005. Of these abortions, only 1.3% were performed after 20 weeks of pregnancy.

Nebraska's partial-birth abortion law was the first to reach the Supreme Court. In June 2000 the court struck down in *Stenberg v. Carhart* (530 U.S. 914) Nebraska's partial-birth abortion ban by a narrow margin of 5-4, saying it was unconstitutional because it did not have an exception for protecting a woman's health.

Even though the term *partial-birth abortion* generally refers to the intact D&X procedure, the legal definition varies among states. This phrase is defined in the Nebraska statute as "an abortion procedure in which the person performing the abortion partially delivers vaginally a living unborn child before killing the unborn child and completing the delivery. For purposes of this subdivision, the term 'partially delivers vaginally a living unborn child before killing the unborn child' means deliberately and intentionally delivering into the vagina a living unborn child, or a substantial portion thereof, for the purpose of performing a procedure that the person performing such procedure knows will kill the unborn child and does kill the unborn child."

Attorneys challenging the law as unconstitutional had three arguments:

- These bans are deceptive measures designed to outlaw virtually every type of abortion procedure.

- These laws are unconstitutional because they have no exceptions for women's health, and they criminalize doctors for providing the safest medical care.

- These laws are unconstitutional because they unduly burden a woman's right to choose, thus violating standards set in *Roe v. Wade* and *Planned Parenthood of Southeastern Pennsylvania v. Casey* (505 U.S. 833 [1992]).

The court ruled on the last two points: the lack of a health exception (allowing an abortion when "necessary, in appropriate medical judgment, for the preservation of the life or health of the mother") and the undue burden on a woman's right to abortion (created by broad language of the ban, which makes it unclear which methods of abortion are banned). For the majority, Justice Stephen G. Breyer (1938–) wrote, "Taking account of these virtually irreconcilable points of view, aware that constitutional law must govern a society whose different members sincerely hold directly opposing views, and considering the matter in light of the Constitution's guarantees of fundamental individual liberty, this Court, in the course of a generation, has determined and then redetermined that the Constitution offers basic protection to the woman's right to choose."

TABLE 2.2

State bans on "partial-birth" abortion, May 2009

State	Status of law	Definition		Exceptions		
		Mirrors federal definition	State definition	Broad health	Narrow health	Life only
Alabama	▼		▼			▼
Alaska	▼		▼			▼
Arizona	▼		▼			▼
Arkansas	X	X	▼			X
Florida	▼		▼			▼
Georgia	X*		X*	X*		
Idaho	▼		▼			▼
Illinois	▼		▼			
Indiana	†		†			†
Iowa	▼		▼			▼
Kansas	X*		X*	X*		
Kentucky	▼		▼			▼
Louisiana	X	X				X
Michigan	▼		▼			▼
Mississippi	†		†			†
Missouri	§	§				§
Montana	†*		†*			†*
Nebraska	▼		▼			▼
New Jersey	▼		▼			▼
New Mexico	X*		X*		X*	
North Dakota	X	X				X
Ohio	X	X			X	
Oklahoma	†		†			X
Rhode Island	▼		▼			▼
South Carolina	†		†			†
South Dakota	†		†			†
Tennessee	†		†			†
Utah	X	X				X
Virginia	X	X				X
West Virginia	▼		▼			▼
Wisconsin	▼		▼			▼
Total	**16**	**6**	**10**	**2**	**2**	**11**

▼ Enforcement permanently enjoined (prohibited) by court order; policy not in effect.
§ This law is temporarily enjoined pending a final decision in the courts.
X Policy is currently in effect.
† This policy is presumably unenforceable under the terms set out in Stenberg v. Carhart; however, it has not been challenged in court.
*Law applies post-viability only.

SOURCE: Guttmacher Institute, Community Health Centers and Family Planning, "Bans on 'Partial Birth' Abortion," in *State Policies in Brief: Bans on "Partial-Birth" Abortion*, New York: Guttmacher, May 1, 2009, http://www.guttmacher.org/statecenter/spibs/spib_BPBA.pdf (accessed May 7, 2009)

For the minority, Justice Clarence Thomas (1948–) wrote:

> *Casey* itself noted that States may "express profound respect for the life of the unborn".... States may, without a doubt, express this profound respect by prohibiting a procedure that approaches infanticide, and thereby dehumanizes the fetus and trivializes human life. The AMA [in the American Medical Association Board of Trustees "Factsheet" on H.R. 1122, June 1997] has recognized that this procedure is "ethically different from other destructive abortion techniques because the fetus, normally twenty weeks or longer in gestation, is killed outside the womb. The 'partial birth' gives the fetus an autonomy which separates it from the right of the woman to choose treatments for her own body."

FEDERAL PARTIAL-BIRTH ABORTION LAWS. In 1995 Congress passed the Partial-Birth Abortion Ban Act, which was vetoed by President Bill Clinton (1946–) in 1996. In 1997 Congress once again passed the Partial-Birth Abortion Ban Act, which was once again vetoed by President Clinton that same year. Congress then passed the Partial-Birth Abortion Ban Act of 2003. On November 5, 2003, President George W. Bush (1946–) signed it into law, becoming the first U.S. president to ever place a federal ban on abortion. However, within hours of Bush's signing the bill, a federal judge in Nebraska granted a temporary restraining order, making the law ineffective until its constitutionality—according to the 2000 *Stenberg v. Carhart* decision—could be determined.

Lawsuits challenging the constitutionality of the Partial-Birth Abortion Ban Act of 2003 were brought in three states: Nebraska, New York, and California. The federal judge in San Francisco, the first to render a decision, ruled that the Partial-Birth Abortion Ban Act of 2003 was unconstitutional in three ways: it places an undue burden on women seeking abortions, its language is vague, and it lacks a required exception for medical actions needed to preserve the woman's health. In 2004 federal judges in all three states ruled the legislation as unconstitutional. In July 2005 a federal appeals court in St. Louis upheld the Nebraska ruling.

THE FEDERAL PARTIAL-BIRTH ABORTION BAN ACT OF 2003 DECLARED CONSTITUTIONAL. The constitutionality of the 2003 Partial-Birth Abortion Ban Act was heard in the Supreme Court as *Gonzales v. Carhart*. In April 2007 the high court ruled in a 5-4 decision that the federal Partial-Birth Abortion Ban Act of 2003 was constitutional. The act imposes civil and criminal penalties on physicians who knowingly perform the intact D&X abortion procedure, which is called the intact D&E in the act and in the court ruling because it is a variation of the dilation and evacuation (D&E) procedure. (See Table 1.1 in Chapter 1 for descriptions of abortion procedures.) The intact D&X (intact D&E) had been used for abortions at 21 or more weeks of gestation.

Justice Anthony M. Kennedy (1936–) delivered the opinion of the court. He was joined in this opinion by Chief Justice John G. Roberts Jr. (1955–) and Justices Samuel A. Alito Jr. (1950–), Antonin Scalia (1936–), and Thomas. The long opinion includes the following: "The Act's ban on abortions that involve partial delivery of a living fetus furthers the Government's objectives. No one would dispute that, for many, D&E is a procedure itself laden with the power to devalue human life. Congress could nonetheless conclude that the type of abortion proscribed by the Act requires specific regulation because it implicates additional ethical and moral concerns that justify a special prohibition. Congress determined that the abortion methods it proscribed had a 'disturbing similarity to the killing of a newborn infant.'"

This decision opened the door to reviving state bans on late-term abortion procedures previously blocked by the courts. Those who applauded the high court's decision in upholding the federal Partial-Birth Abortion Ban Act not only expected state late-term abortion bans to be revived but also saw the possibility of adding more restrictions on late-term abortion procedures.

Justice Ruth Bader Ginsburg's (1933–) dissenting opinion, joined by Justices John Paul Stevens (1920–), David H. Souter (1939–), and Breyer, included the following: "Today's decision is alarming.... It tolerates, indeed applauds, federal intervention to ban nationwide a procedure found necessary and proper in certain cases by the American College of Obstetricians and Gynecologists (ACOG).... For the first time since *Roe*, the Court blesses a prohibition with no exception safeguarding a woman's health."

Ginsburg ended her dissent with the following concern about a future attack on the *Roe v. Wade* decision and a woman's right to choose abortion: "In sum, the notion that the Partial-Birth Abortion Ban Act furthers any legitimate governmental interest is, quite simply, irrational. The

court's defense of the statute provides no saving explanation. In candor, the Act, and the court's defense of it, cannot be understood as anything other than an effort to chip away at a right declared again and again by this Court—and with increasing comprehension of its centrality to women's lives."

LATER-TERM ABORTIONS. The majority of states restrict later-term abortions, and the meaning of *later-term* varies among states. Table 2.3 shows state policies on later-term abortions and that the threshold for later-term ranges from viability to the third trimester. Viability varies among fetuses. However, the lower limit appears to be about 21 to 22 weeks of gestation, or between five and six months, which is the last portion of the second trimester.

PROTESTERS AT ABORTION CLINICS

In the more than 30 years since the *Roe v. Wade* decision, reproductive health clinics and health care providers across the United States and Canada have been under attack by antiabortion protesters. Physicians and clinic workers have been shot; clinics have been bombed, burned down, invaded, and blockaded; and patients have been abused and intimidated. In 1993 the protests turned deadly for the first time when the physician David Gunn (1946–1993) was fatally shot by Michael Griffin (1961–), an antiabortion protester, in Pensacola, Florida.

Also in 1993 the Supreme Court heard *Bray v. Alexandria Women's Health Clinic* (506 U.S. 263), a case in which antiabortion protesters challenged an injunction (ban) against their activities, which included blocking access to health care facilities in the Washington, D.C., area. The injunction being challenged was based on an 1871 civil rights statute that provided protection against private conspiracies, such as the Ku Klux Klan preventing blacks from exercising their freedoms. In this case it was argued that antiabortion activists were preventing women from exercising their freedoms. The judges found that antiabortion protests outside of an abortion clinic were not in violation of the Civil Rights Act because "women seeking abortions" were not a "class of persons seeking protection under the law" and protesters do not show class-based discrimination toward women.

In 1994, to help prevent clinic violence, Congress overwhelmingly passed the Freedom of Access to Clinic Entrances Act (FACE), which was signed into law by President Clinton. FACE is designed to protect both those providing and those receiving reproductive health care services. It forbids the use of "force," "threat of force," or "physical obstruction" to prevent someone from providing or receiving reproductive health services. There are criminal and civil penalties for those who break the law. It is clear that the law has had an effect on certain

TABLE 2.3

State policies on later-term abortions, May 2009

State	Threshold for later-term abortions	Later-term abortion permitted when threat to woman's:			When a later-term abortion is performed a second physician must	
		Life and health	Life and physical health	Life	Attend	Approve
Alabama	Viability		X			X
Arizona	Viability	X			X	
Arkansas	Viability	X^a			X	
California	Viability	X				
Connecticut	Viability	X				
Delaware	▼			▼		
Florida	24 weeks	X				X
Georgia	3rd trimester	X				X
Idaho	Viability			X		X
Illinois	Viability	X			X	
Indiana	Viability		X		X	
Iowa	3rd trimester	X				
Kansas	Viability	X				X
Kentucky	Viability	X				
Louisiana	Viability	X			X	
Maine	Viability	X				
Maryland	Viability	X^b				
Massachusetts	24 weeks	X				
Michigan	Viability			X		
Minnesota	▼	▼			▼	
Missouri	Viability	X			X	
Montana	Viability		X			X
Nebraska	Viability	X				
Nevada	24 weeks	X				
New York	24 weeks			X	X	
North Carolina	20 weeks	X				
North Dakota	Viability	X				X
Ohio	▼		▼		▼	▼
Oklahoma	Viability	X			X	
Pennsylvania	24 weeks		X		X	X
Rhode Island	24 weeks			X		
South Carolina	3rd trimester	X^c				X
South Dakota	24 weeks	X				
Tennessee	Viability	X				
Texas	3rd trimester	X				
Utah	Viability	X^a, b				
Virginia	3rd trimester	X				X
Washington	Viability	X				
Wisconsin	Viability	X				
Wyoming	Viability	X				
Total	**37**	**29**	**4**	**4**	**9**	**10**

▼ Enforcement permanently enjoined (prohibited) by a court order; policy not in effect.
X Policy is currently in effect.
^a Also permitted in case of rape or incest.
^b Also permitted in case of fetal abnormality, in Utah the law applies to a lethal abnormality.
^c If done for mental health reasons, must have the certification of an independent psychiatrist.

SOURCE: Guttmacher Institute, Community Health Centers and Family Planning, "State Policies on Later-Term Abortions," in *State Policies in Brief: State Policies on Later-Term Abortions*, New York: Guttmacher, May 1, 2009, http://www.guttmacher.org/statecenter/spibs/spib_PLTA.pdf (accessed May 7, 2009)

types of clinic violence (see Chapter 6). However, violence does continue.

Other Supreme Court cases provide for the constitutionality of buffer zones between protesters and patients and clinic employees. For instance, in *Madsen v. Women's Health Center* (512 U.S. 753 [1994]) the court upheld an injunction that forbade protesters from entering a 36-foot (11-m) buffer zone in front of an abortion clinic and upheld noise restrictions. (However, the court did not uphold an injunction that prevented protesters from getting within 300 feet [91.4 m] of a clinic or staff residence to approach clinic staff and patients. Also, nonthreatening posters within the 36-foot buffer zone were allowed.)

In 1997 the court upheld in *Schenck et al. v. Pro-Choice Network of Western New York* (519 U.S. 357) an injunction that forbade antiabortion protesters from entering a 15-foot (4.6 m) fixed buffer zone in front of an abortion clinic. The protesters had argued that their right to free speech was being violated, but the high court ruled that their free speech was ensured because they could be heard from a distance. Also, the court allowed "cease and desist" counseling. This meant that as many as two protesters at a time could perform "sidewalk counseling" within the buffer zone, but if the counselors were asked to stop (to "cease and desist"), they had to honor that request and leave the buffer zone. (The court did not uphold the injunction preventing protesters from coming within a 15-foot floating buffer zone of people entering or leaving an abortion clinic. A floating buffer zone around a person moves as the person moves.)

In 2000 in *Hill v. Colorado* (530 U.S. 703), the court ruled that a Colorado statute does not violate the First Amendment (free speech) and the right to a free press. The statute forbids anyone to knowingly come closer than 8 feet (2.4 m) to anyone who is within 100 feet (30.5 m) of the entrance of a health care facility without that person's consent, for the purpose of giving the person a leaflet, offering education or counseling, displaying a sign, or otherwise engaging in protest. The court concluded that the statute "is a regulation of the places where some speech may occur."

National Organization for Women v. Scheidler: A 20-Year-Long Case

In 2003 the seventeen-year-old *National Organization for Women v. Scheidler* case was decided, but the case would not be over until 2006. The parties to the case were the National Organization for Women (NOW) and Joseph Scheidler of the Pro-Life Action League.

In June 1986 NOW and two abortion clinics in Delaware filed a complaint in federal court against Scheidler and the Pro-Life Direct Action League, alleging violations of the Sherman and Clayton antitrust laws that are intended to prevent the formation of monopolies. In 1989 NOW added charges that individuals and organizations that oppose legal abortion violated the Racketeer Influenced and Corrupt Organizations Act (RICO) by engaging in a nationwide conspiracy to shut down abortion clinics through "a pattern of racketeering activity" that included acts of extortion in violation of the Hobbs Act.

In 1991 the case was dismissed on the grounds that the RICO law requires the defendants to have an economic motive for their crimes, and an appeal by NOW was unsuccessful. In 1992 NOW asked the Supreme Court for a ruling on the use of the RICO statute. In 1994 the high court ruled in favor of NOW, allowing it to use federal antiracketeering laws against antiabortion activists who organize others for terrorist activities, such as bombing and forcefully blocking abortion clinics. RICO cannot be used against those engaging in peaceful protests.

After many delays, the *NOW v. Scheidler* trial took place in 1998. The jury found that the defendants were guilty of racketeering and engaged in a nationwide conspiracy to deny women access to medical facilities. However, in 2002 Scheidler asked the Supreme Court to review the decision. In February 2003 the Supreme Court

decided 8-1 in *Scheidler v. NOW* (537 U.S. 393) that the RICO statute was used improperly against Scheidler and other antiabortion activists, meaning that these groups could not be sued for extortion under racketeering laws intended to combat organized crime. Thus, the prior guilty verdict against Scheidler and his codefendants was overturned.

NOW claimed that the 2003 decision did not address the question of whether physical violence outside of clinics might still be punished under the Hobbs Act. In February 2006 the Supreme Court ruled 8-0 (Justice Alito did not take part in the consideration or decision of this case because he had been officially nominated to the court only a month before) on this issue in favor of Scheidler in *Scheidler v. National Organization for Women Inc.* (No. 04-1244), stating that the charge of extortion could not be applied to pro-life demonstrations outside abortion facilities. Physical violence outside of clinics was not punishable under the Hobbs Act.

Antiabortion advocates (and others such as labor union supporters) hailed the decision as one that supported the right of people to protest for social change. Pro-choice advocates saw the ruling as a statement that the Supreme Court was no longer going to protect abortion clinics and women attending those clinics against the violence of antiabortion protesters. In "Supreme Court Ends Protection against Abortion Clinic Violence" (February 28, 2006, http://www.now.org/press/02-06/02-28.html), Kim Gandy, the president of NOW, speaks against this decision, "Without strong protections against clinic assaults, the legal right to abortion could become meaningless. If women are too terrified to walk into clinics and healthcare providers are too terrified to keep their doors open, then we will have lost the fight for reproductive freedom even with *Roe v. Wade* still on the books."

RULINGS ON THE FETUS
Saving a "Viable Fetus"

In January 1979, almost six years after the landmark *Roe v. Wade* decision, the issue of the legal identity of the fetus first reached the Supreme Court. In *Colautti v. Franklin* (439 U.S. 379) the plaintiff (the person who brings an action in a court of law) challenged the provisions of a Pennsylvania law that gave the state the power to protect an unborn child beginning in the sixth month of pregnancy.

This law required physicians performing abortions to save the fetus if they had grounds to believe that the fetus "may be viable." The Supreme Court held that the provisions of the law were "void for vagueness" because the meanings of the terms *viable* and *may be viable* were unclear and because these provisions interfered with the physicians' proper exercise of judgment. The court also found the law unconstitutional because it could impose criminal liability on physicians if they were thought to have failed to take proper action.

Ruling That Life Begins at Conception

In 1986 Missouri passed legislation amending a number of laws concerning unborn children and abortion. It placed a number of restrictions on abortions. The new law:

- Declared that life begins at conception.

- Required physicians to perform tests to determine the viability of fetuses after 20 weeks of gestational age.

- Forbade the use of public employees and facilities for abortions not necessary to save the mother's life.

- Prohibited the use of public funds, employees, or facilities for the purpose of counseling a woman to have an abortion not necessary to save her life.

Lower courts struck down these restrictions, but the Supreme Court did not. In 1989 the court upheld the Missouri law in *Webster v. Reproductive Health Services* (492 U.S. 490). This ruling was the first case in which a majority of the justices generally opposed abortion, and it revealed the court's willingness to adopt a more lenient attitude toward state limitations on abortions.

Writing for the 5-4 majority, Chief Justice William H. Rehnquist (1924–2005), who was joined by Justices Byron R. White (1917–2002) and Kennedy, found nothing wrong with the preamble of the Missouri law, which stated that "the life of each human being begins at conception." The court observed that *Roe v. Wade* "implies no limitation on a State's authority to make a value judgment favoring childbirth over abortion.... The preamble can be read simply to express that sort of value judgment." The court chose not to rule on the constitutionality of the law's preamble because it considered the preamble to be merely an abstract proposition.

Relying on *Maher*, *Poelker*, and *McRae*, the court ruled that "a government's decision to favor childbirth over abortion through the allocation of public funds does not violate *Roe v. Wade*." In addition, "Missouri's decision to use public facilities and employees to encourage childbirth over abortion places no governmental obstacle in the path of a woman who chooses to terminate her pregnancy, but leaves her with the same choices as if the State had decided not to operate any hospitals at all."

Perhaps the most controversial aspect of the Missouri law was the requirement that a physician had to determine the viability of the fetus if the physician thought the fetus might be 20 or more weeks old. There was no debate over whether a fetus is viable at 20 weeks, because the earliest that a fetus is viable is at 21 to 22 weeks of gestational life. However, there could be a four-week error in estimating gestational age. The court ruled that the testing for fetal viability was constitutional because it furthered Missouri's interest in protecting potential human life.

Chief Justice Rehnquist thought the "rigid" trimester system outlined in *Roe v. Wade* was no longer useful, if it ever was. He felt the *Roe v. Wade* framework, which contains specific elements such as trimesters and viability, was not consistent with the concept of a constitution that deals in general principles.

Even though they came close, the majority did not overturn *Roe v. Wade*. While respecting the preamble of the Missouri law, Rehnquist concluded that even though the state's interest had been moved back well into the second trimester of pregnancy, *Webster* did not revisit the *Roe v. Wade* rulings.

Scalia, however, believed *Roe v. Wade* should have been overturned in this case because most of the justices thought the *Roe v. Wade* decision was wrong. He stated, "It thus appears that the mansion of constitutionalized abortion law, constructed overnight in *Roe v. Wade*, must be disassembled doorjamb by doorjamb, and never entirely brought down, no matter how wrong it may be."

Justice Harry A. Blackmun (1908–1999), who wrote the *Roe v. Wade* decision, was equally angry but for the opposite reason. In a dissent joined by Justices William J. Brennan Jr. (1906–1997) and Thurgood Marshall (1908–1993), Blackmun observed that "the fundamental constitutional right of women to decide whether to terminate a pregnancy, survive but are not secure."

Even though it did not overturn *Roe v. Wade*, *Webster* did mark a significant change in the legal landscape related to abortion. It gave the states more latitude in placing restrictions on abortion and weakened the viability and trimester framework that had previously been used to help determine the legality of terminating a pregnancy.

ROE V. WADE IS NOT OVERTURNED

From the Trimester Framework to Undue Burden

Pennsylvania has had a long history of trying to pass restrictive abortion statutes, which began with the Abortion Control Act of 1974. In 1989, having seen how in *Webster* a more conservative Supreme Court seemed ready to overturn decisions made by an earlier, more liberal court, the Pennsylvania legislature passed a new Abortion Control Act, which was an amended version of the 1974 abortion law.

Before the Abortion Control Act took effect, five abortion clinics and one physician (representing himself and a group of physicians who provided abortion services) sued the state of Pennsylvania, which was represented by Governor Robert P. Casey (1932–2000). The resulting case was *Planned Parenthood of Southeastern Pennsylvania v. Casey* (505 U.S. 833 [1992]).

The Supreme Court ruling on *Casey* was a 5-4 split decision, with the majority opinion written by Justices Sandra Day O'Connor (1930–), Kennedy, and Souter and joined in part by Justices Stevens and Blackmun. The majority reaffirmed the essential holding in *Roe v. Wade*, "A recognition of a woman's right to choose to have an abortion before fetal viability and to obtain it without undue interference from the State." After viability, however, the state may prohibit abortion but only if it provides exceptions for pregnancies that may endanger the woman's life or health.

In addition, the court rejected the trimester framework, which had strictly limited the state from regulating abortion during early pregnancy, and replaced it with the undue burden standard. Under the undue burden standard states may put restrictions on the abortion process (throughout the whole pregnancy) as long as they do not have "the purpose or effect of placing a substantial obstacle in the path of a woman seeking an abortion of a nonviable fetus."

The justices upheld Pennsylvania's proposed restrictions—a 24-hour waiting period, informed consent, parental consent, and reporting and record-keeping requirements—except for the spousal-consent requirement. Chief Justice Rehnquist and Justices Thomas, White, and Scalia agreed with the provisions upheld by the majority decision, but they felt the decision did not go far enough. They proposed that requiring spousal consent was a rational attempt to encourage communication between spouses and should be upheld. Furthermore, they felt that a woman's liberty to abort her unborn child is not a right protected by the Constitution and that the *Roe v. Wade* decision had been a mistake.

Stevens, however, wrote an opinion supporting the *Roe v. Wade* decision and rejecting the 24-hour waiting period and the "biased" informed-consent provision (which required pro-life information to be given to the woman seeking an abortion). Blackmun rejected all the provisions of the Pennsylvania law and reaffirmed the constitutionality of the *Roe v. Wade* decision.

THE BASIS FOR MAINTAINING *ROE V. WADE*. Even though conceding that people differ in their beliefs about the morality of terminating a pregnancy, the justices explained that they upheld *Roe v. Wade*'s essential holding because their duty is "to define the liberty of all," not to impose their own moral standards: "These matters, involving the most intimate and personal choices a person may make in a lifetime, choices central to personal dignity and autonomy, are central to the liberty protected by the Fourteenth Amendment. At the heart of liberty is the right to define one's own concept of existence, of meaning, of the universe, and of the mystery of human life. Beliefs about these matters could not define the attributes of personhood were they formed under compulsion of the State."

The justices also maintained:

Though abortion is conduct, it does not follow that the State is entitled to proscribe it in all instances. That is because the liberty of the woman is at stake in a sense unique to the human condition, and so, unique to the law. The mother who carries a child to full term is subject to anxieties, to physical constraints, to pain that only she must bear. That these sacrifices have from the beginning of the human race been endured by woman with a pride that ennobles her in the eyes of others and gives to the infant a bond of love cannot alone be grounds for the State to insist she make the sacrifice. Her suffering is too intimate and personal for the State to insist, without more, upon its own vision of the woman's role, however dominant that vision has been in the course of our history and our culture. The destiny of the woman must be shaped to a large extent on her own conception of her spiritual imperatives and her place in society.

The court also upheld the right to abortion because of its obligation to follow precedent. Under the doctrine of stare decisis (literally, to stand by things decided), which requires courts to reach consistent conclusions in cases that raise the same factual and legal issues, a majority of the court could not justify overthrowing the findings of *Roe v. Wade*.

CHAPTER 3
ABORTION: A MAJOR POLITICAL ISSUE

A DEFINITION OF POLITICS

Merriam-Webster's Collegiate Dictionary (11th edition) defines the term *politics* as "the art or science concerned with guiding or influencing governmental policy." This chapter examines those who make the policy (the laws)—Congress and state legislatures—and those who rule on the constitutionality of those laws—the state-level federal courts and the U.S. Supreme Court—to examine major factors in the politics of abortion. In addition, the president plays an important role in the politics of abortion, because he nominates federal judges, even though these nominees must pass through a process of U.S. Senate confirmation.

JUDICIAL APPOINTMENTS AND POLITICS

When the president and most of the Senate are of the same political party, and when they are in agreement about the direction public policy should take, confirmation of a judicial nominee is relatively easy. The opposition party, however, is sometimes able to use procedural practices, such as filibusters (prolonged speeches), to delay or prevent the confirmation vote.

Federal judges are appointed for life, so each appointment has a long-lasting influence on the court system and on the lives of Americans. Because the judges are appointed by the president, the nominees usually hold political views that are similar to the president's. Thus, if a president is opposed to abortion, it is likely that he or she will appoint federal judges who are known to be conservative on this issue.

Jeffrey A. Segal, the coauthor of *Advice and Consent: The Politics of Judicial Appointments* (2005), notes that "most justices appointed by conservative presidents cast a high percentage of conservative votes.... Likewise, most justices appointed by liberal presidents cast a higher percentage of left-of-center votes than their colleagues seated by more conservative presidents."

However, Segal's coauthor Lee Epstein adds, "During the first four years of justices' tenure, their voting behavior correlates at a rather high level with their appointing president's ideology, but for justices with ten or more years of service, that relationship drops precipitously. In other words, liberal presidents appoint liberal justices who continue to take liberal positions for a while, and the same holds true for conservatives. But as new issues come to the Court, or as the justice for whatever reason makes adjustments in his or her political outlook, the president's influence wanes."

Given their prominent role in interpreting the country's laws, federal judges have had a tremendous impact on the issue of abortion. Nowhere is this more true than in the numerous Supreme Court rulings that have dealt with this topic since the 1970s (see Chapter 2) and in the Supreme Court justices who were appointed in 2005 and 2006 during the administration of George W. Bush (1946–) and in 2009 during the administration of Barack Obama (1961–).

Bush Court Nominees

When Bush was elected in 2000, liberal politicians were afraid that he would appoint many conservative judges to the federal courts during his presidential term, which began in January 2001. In an effort to control the situation, Senate Democrats, who held the majority in that branch of Congress during the first two years of the Bush presidency, delayed in the Senate Judiciary Committee highly conservative Bush nominees from confirmation to lower-court federal judgeships.

After the 2002 midterm elections, Republicans regained control of the Senate and Democrats were no longer able to delay Bush judicial nominees in committee, so Democrats used the filibuster as an alternate delay tactic. In 2004 President Bush was reelected, and Senate Republicans threatened to change the Senate rules to eliminate the use of the filibuster to delay confirmation of judicial nominees.

A bipartisan (two-party) agreement was struck between seven moderate Senate Democrats and seven moderate Senate Republicans (called the Gang of 14) to avoid continued filibuster yet not to change Senate rules. This bipartisan group also became active in trying to advise President Bush on acceptable Supreme Court nominees to replace Justice Sandra Day O'Connor (1930–), who was retiring.

In July 2005 President Bush nominated John G. Roberts Jr. (1955–) to replace O'Connor. However, in September 2005—before Roberts could be confirmed by the Senate—Chief Justice William H. Rehnquist (1924–2005) of the Supreme Court passed away. Bush took this opportunity to renominate Roberts for the chief justice position, and Roberts was confirmed in September 2005. Then in November 2005 Bush nominated Samuel A. Alito Jr. (1950–) to replace O'Connor. Alito was confirmed in January 2006.

Obama Court Nominee

On May 1, 2009, President Obama announced that Justice David H. Souter (1939–) would retire at the end of the Supreme Court term in June 2009. Even though Souter had been appointed by President George H. W. Bush (1924–), a Republican conservative, he had liberal leanings and wrote (with Justices Anthony M. Kennedy [1936–] and O'Connor) in the 1992 decision of *Planned Parenthood of Southeastern Pennsylvania v. Casey* (505 U.S. 833) that "the essential holding of *Roe v. Wade* should be retained and once again reaffirmed."

On May 26, 2009, President Obama announced his choice for Souter's replacement: federal appeals court judge Sonia Sotomayor (1954–). Her views on abortion and *Roe v. Wade* (410 U.S. 113 [1973]) were largely unknown at the time of her nomination, and her related decisions told only that she based her judicial decisions on constitutional law. Nonetheless, Robert Barnes and Michael D. Shear report in "Abortion Rights Backers Get Assurances on Nominee" (*Washington Post*, May 29, 2009) that a few days after Sotomayor's nomination Robert Gibbs (1971–), the White House press secretary, assured pro-choice supporters that Sotomayo believed in "constitutional protections for a woman's right to [abortion]." She was officially confirmed by the Senate on August 6, 2009, and thus became the first Hispanic justice and only the third female justice of the Supreme Court.

Should Potential Judges' Positions on Abortion Be a Key Issue in Their Nominations?

In May 2009 Quinnipiac University conducted a national poll on the various aspects of Sotomayor's nomination, and the results were published in the press release "U.S. Voters Approve 2-1 of Obama's Sotomayor Pick, Quinnipiac University National Poll Finds; Legal Skill More Important Than Diversity, Most Say" (May 29, 2009, http://www.quinnipiac.edu/x1295.xml?ReleaseID=1306). When

TABLE 3.1

Public opinion on whether senators should consider Supreme Court justice nominee Sotomayor's views on controversial issues such as abortion during confirmation proceedings, 2009

	Total	Republican	Democrat	Independent	Men	Women
Only qualifications	47%	33%	56%	47%	50%	44%
Consider views	43	58	32	45	41	45
Don't know/NA	10	9	12	8	10	11

Note: The margin of sampling error for this poll was +/−2.6 percentage points.

SOURCE: "8. Should Senators Support or Oppose Sonia Sotomayor's Nomination to the Supreme Court Based Only on Whether She Is Qualified to Be a Justice, or Should They Also Consider Her Views on Controversial Issues Like Abortion and Affirmative Action?" in *U.S. Voters Approve 2–1 of Obama's Sotomayor Pick, Quinnipiac University National Poll Finds; Legal Skill More Important Than Diversity, Most Say*, May 29, 2009, Quinnipiac University, http://www.quinnipiac.edu/x1295.xml?ReleaseID=1306 (accessed June 1, 2009)

asked whether senators should support or oppose Sotomayor's nomination based on her qualifications alone, or whether they should also consider her views on controversial issues such as abortion, 47% of respondents said qualifications were all that mattered. (See Table 3.1.) Forty-three percent thought her views on controversial issues such as abortion should be considered. Separating Republican respondents from Democrats yielded slightly different results. A higher percentage of Republicans (58%) than Democrats (32%) thought senators should consider Sotomayor's views. Conversely, a higher percentage of Democrats (56%) than Republicans (33%) thought that only her qualifications should be considered.

During Roberts's nomination, Quinnipiac University had conducted a national poll in July 2005 that asked the same question regarding the consideration of his nomination. In the press release "Supreme Court Nominee Should Speak up on Abortion, U.S. Voters Tell Quinnipiac University National Poll; Bush Approval Drops to New Low" (July 27, 2005, http://www.quinnipiac.edu/x1295.xml?ReleaseID=820), the university notes that in 2005, 56% of respondents thought that views on controversial issues such as abortion should be considered. Quinnipiac pollsters also asked if Roberts should reveal his position on abortion during his Senate confirmation hearings. Sixty-one percent believed Roberts should reveal his position, whereas 32% believed he should not. The poll found that voters were split on whether Roberts should be confirmed if he did not speak publicly about his views on the subject.

According to Denis Steven Rutkus of the Congressional Research Service (CRS), in *Proper Scope of Questioning of Supreme Court Nominees: The Current Debate* (September 1, 2005, http://digital.library.unt.edu/govdocs/crs/permalink/meta-crs-7899:1), during Roberts's nomination the Senate Republican Policy Committee did not agree that judicial nominees should be coerced to reveal their positions on particular issues. In July 2005 the committee issued the statement "The Proper Scope of Questioning for Judicial Nominees," in which the committee noted that "no judicial nominee should be compelled to answer any question that would force him or her to prejudge or signal future conclusions regarding any case or issue." Furthermore, the committee suggested that this practice turns "judicial nominees into mere 'candidates' who must make political promises in order to be confirmed."

WHAT ROBERTS AND ALITO SAID AS CANDIDATES AND HOW THEY SUBSEQUENTLY VOTED. During the Senate confirmation hearings, Roberts would not say whether he would reverse the long-standing *Roe v. Wade* decision legalizing abortion, but he did say he believed the U.S. Constitution provided a right to privacy—a key foundational point of *Roe v. Wade*. Alito, during his Senate confirmation hearings, said he would approach any Supreme Court case on abortion with an open mind. Both were confirmed, and in November 2006 both faced the process of rendering a Supreme Court judgment on the constitutionality of the Partial-Birth Abortion Ban Act of 2003 in *Gonzales v. Carhart* (550 U.S. 124 [2007]). Roberts and Alito voted with Justices Antonin Scalia (1936–), Anthony M. Kennedy (1936–), and Clarence Thomas (1948–) that the act was constitutional—this majority thus overturned many previous lower court rulings that the act was unconstitutional. Chapter 2 contains a more detailed discussion of the history of the Partial-Birth Abortion Ban Act and this Supreme Court decision.

STATE GOVERNMENTS AND LEGISLATURES ON ABORTION

In January 1973 the Supreme Court legalized abortion with the *Roe v. Wade* decision, setting the stage for this politically sensitive issue to become a continuing topic of debate in Congress and in state legislatures. In general, the Democratic Party supports a woman's right to choose abortion, whereas the Republican Party does not.

The *Roe v. Wade* decision was a catalyst for the pro-life movement, which had its beginnings in the late 1960s. Pro-life groups (called antiabortion or antichoice groups by their opponents) consider the *Roe v. Wade* decision to be government-sanctioned mass killing of the unborn. Following the landmark decision, antiabortion activists supported constitutional amendments to overturn the *Roe v. Wade* ruling, but none were passed. A constitutional amendment requires two-thirds approval of each house of Congress and ratification by three-quarters of the state legislatures. Since then, antiabortion groups have attempted to limit aspects of the *Roe v. Wade* decision, not only by influencing the appointment of lower-court and Supreme Court judges but also by restricting the rights to abortion conferred by the *Roe v. Wade* ruling. Pro-choice groups suggest that other anti-

choice legislative measures—such as recognizing the embryo and fetus as a person for legal purposes, mandating a waiting period and counseling requirements, and restricting minors' access to abortion—are also attempts to chip away at the *Roe v. Wade* decision.

Figure 3.1 shows the states that enacted legislation in 2008 that placed greater limits on a woman's right to choose abortion. According to NARAL Pro-Choice America, in *Who Decides? The Status of Women's Reproductive Rights in the United States* (January 2009, http://www.prochoiceamerica.org/choice-action-center/in_your_state/who-decides/introduction/whodecides2009.pdf), in 2008 a total of 502 antiabortion measures were introduced in state legislatures, and 24 were enacted in 16 states; 459 pro-choice measures were introduced in state legislatures, and 39 were enacted in 23 states. The antichoice legislative measures most frequently considered by states in 2008 were increased counseling (giving pro-life information to a woman seeking an abortion) and mandatory delay requirements, mandatory ultrasounds, abortion bans, restrictions on young women's access to reproductive health services, and targeted regulation of abortion providers. (See Figure 3.2.)

Figure 3.3 shows the choice positions of state governments. To be considered either pro-choice or antichoice in this analysis, both most of the legislature and the governor of the state must hold this position. Figure 3.4 and Table 3.2 separate the two. Figure 3.4 shows each governor's position (as well as the president and vice president) as of January 1, 2009. Table 3.2 shows each state legislature's position on choice.

State restrictions on abortion are varied and numerous. Table 3.3 shows an overview of state abortion laws. The most common restrictions in effect are parental notification or consent requirements for minors, state-sponsored abortion-alternative counseling, waiting periods before receiving an abortion, and limitations on public funding.

HOMICIDE LAWS AND FETUSES

As of June 2008, 35 states had homicide laws that recognize unborn fetuses as victims at some point before birth. (See Figure 3.5.) The Unborn Victims of Violence Act of 2004 covers unborn victims of federal and military crimes; it does not, however, override existing state laws. The legislation states that anyone who causes the death or bodily injury of a fetus is "guilty of a separate offense" and that "the punishment for that separate offense is the same as the punishment provided for that conduct under Federal law had that injury or death occurred to the unborn child's mother." The law makes exceptions for legal medical procedures, including abortion, and acts on behalf of a pregnant woman. However, opponents of the law consider it a sneak attack on abortion rights because, in effect, it considers a fetus to be a person. They also state that pro-life groups are attempting to label the fetus as a person to change public perception about the nature of abortion.

FIGURE 3.1

States that enacted anti-choice legislation in 2008

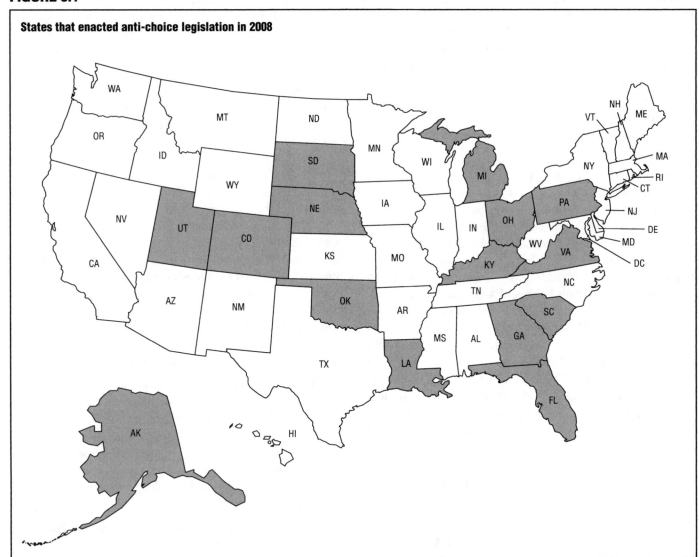

SOURCE: "States That Enacted Anti-Choice Legislation in 2008," in *Who Decides? The Status of Women's Reproductive Rights in the United States*, NARAL Pro-Choice America and NARAL Pro-Choice America Foundation, January 2009, http://www.prochoiceamerica.org/assets/graphics/whodecides/2009/enacted-anti-leg-big.png (accessed May 6, 2009)

FEDERAL FUNDING AND ABORTION

The federal government established the Medicaid program in 1965 to pay for medical care for the nation's needy through a federal-state cost-sharing arrangement. During the administration of Richard M. Nixon (1913–1994), the U.S. Department of Health, Education, and Welfare (HEW; now the U.S. Department of Health and Human Services) reimbursed states for abortions for poor women. Following the *Roe v. Wade* decision in 1973, HEW considered abortion a medical procedure funded by Medicaid, so a cost-sharing arrangement went into effect.

Sonya B. Gamble et al. of the Centers for Disease Control and Prevention indicate in "Abortion Surveillance—United States, 2005" (*Morbidity and Mortality Weekly Report*, vol. 57, no. SS-13, November 28, 2008) that after *Roe v. Wade* the number of abortions increased rapidly until by 1977 almost 1 million abortions were being performed annually. Antiabortion supporters were angered by what they considered a mass slaughter being partially financed with tax dollars, and they responded by lobbying their senators and representatives to end this practice.

The Hyde Amendment

In 1976 Representative Henry J. Hyde (1924–2007; R-IL) introduced an abortion rider to the HEW-Labor appropriations bill. The 1976 rider, since known as the Hyde Amendment, has become the subject of an annual battle in Congress. Hyde originally proposed that no federal funding could be used for abortion. Following considerable debate, Congress settled on a compromise, which stated that none of the funds contained in the appropriations bill would be used to perform abortions except:

FIGURE 3.2

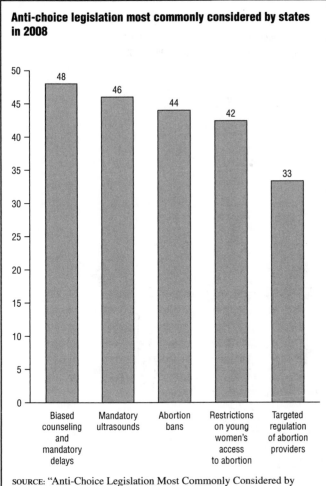

Anti-choice legislation most commonly considered by states in 2008

SOURCE: "Anti-Choice Legislation Most Commonly Considered by States in 2008," in *Who Decides? The Status of Women's Reproductive Rights in the United States*, NARAL Pro-Choice America and NARAL Pro-Choice America Foundation, January 2009, http://www .prochoiceamerica.org/assets/graphics/whodecides/2009/anti-leg-considered-big.png (accessed May 6, 2009)

- For victims of rape or incest if the occurrence was reported promptly to the proper authorities.

- If justified to save the mother's life.

- In instances where two doctors determined that "severe and long-lasting physical health damage to the mother" may result.

The Departments of Labor and Health, Education, and Welfare Appropriations Act, which included the abortion provision, became law in September 1976 and went into effect in August 1977. Beginning in 1979 the physical health provision of the Hyde Amendment was removed, and in 1981 the rape and incest provision was removed. Thus, federal funding could be used for abortion services only to save the mother's life. In 1980 the Supreme Court ruled in *Harris v. McRae* (448 U.S. 297) that the Hyde Amendment and its restrictions were constitutional (see Chapter 2). In 1993 Congress rewrote the Hyde Amendment to once again include federal funding of abortions for pregnancies that resulted

from rape or incest, and that form of the amendment was in force through mid-2009.

STATE FUNDING AND ABORTION

Medicaid is a federal assistance program for low-income people. Medicaid is implemented by the states, but with federal funds and guidelines. Thus, states must cover the cost of abortions for low-income women when their pregnancies result from rape or incest, or if the continued pregnancy endangers the life of the mother.

As of May 2009, 32 states plus the District of Columbia restricted the funding of abortion under Medicaid except in cases of life endangerment, rape, and incest. (See Table 3.4.) South Dakota, in violation of federal law, provided Medicaid funding for abortion only if a woman's life was in danger. Seventeen states funded abortion in all or most circumstances, using state funds when Medicaid would not pay.

Abortion Funding and Managed Care

In 1996, for the first time since the *Roe v. Wade* decision, congressional elections resulted in a pro-life majority in both the U.S. House of Representatives and the Senate. Pro-life lawmakers pointed out that, because states are increasingly contracting with managed-care organizations to provide Medicaid recipients with health services, the Hyde Amendment had to be revised. Representative Hyde sought to forbid health plans from offering abortion coverage when they contracted with states under Medicaid. He claimed that in cases where states used their own funds to pay for abortions beyond the federally mandated cases of rape, incest, and life endangerment, purchasing a health plan using a "co-mingling" of federal and state monies presented the possibility of an indirect federal abortion subsidy.

Hyde's proposed change was met with opposition from pro-choice Democrats. They protested that the new law would negatively affect privately insured women whose insurance companies contracted with the states. It would also affect Medicaid recipients in those states where abortions were subsidized. The revised version eventually passed with the provision that federal funds would not be used to purchase managed-care packages that included coverage of abortion. States that covered abortion with their own funds would be able to continue doing so under a separate program. In November 1997 President Bill Clinton (1946–) signed the Departments of Labor, Health and Human Services, and Education, and Related Agencies Appropriations Act of 1998 with the abortion provision.

Abortion Funding and the State Children's Health Insurance Program

In August 1997 the Balanced Budget Act amended the Social Security Act by adding Title XXI (State Children's Health Insurance Program, or CHIP) to allocate funds to states to provide child health assistance to uninsured, low-income children who are not eligible for Medicaid. Under

FIGURE 3.3

Pro-choice and anti-choice state governments, January 2009

There are seven states with pro-choice governments (both a majority of the legislature and the governor are pro-choice): IA, ME, MA, NH, NJ, OR, WA.

There are 10 states with anti-choice governments (both a majority of the legislature and the governor are anti-choice): AL, ID, LA, MS, NE, ND, RI, SD, TX, UT.

	Choice positions in the states		
	Pro-choice	Mixed-choice	Anti-choice
Governor	19	13	18
Senate	17*	13	21
House	16	10	23

*And the District of Columbia.

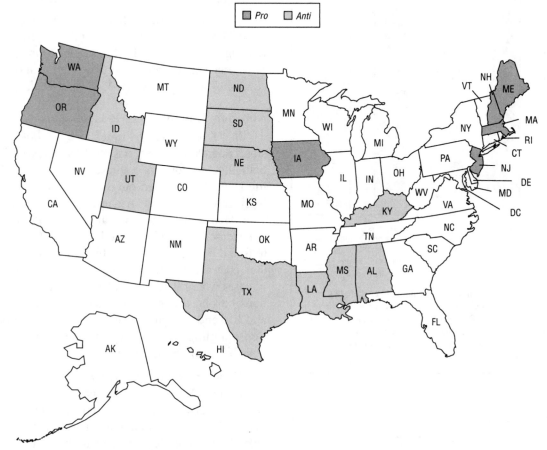

SOURCE: "Key Findings: Political Findings: Choice Positions of State Governments," in *Who Decides? The Status of Women's Reproductive Rights in the United States*, NARAL Pro-Choice America & NARAL Pro-Choice America Foundation, January 1, 2009, http://www.prochoiceamerica.org/choice-action-center/in_your_state/who-decides/introduction/key-findings-political.html (accessed May 6, 2009)

CHIP state funds may be used for abortion only to save the life of the mother or if the pregnancy resulted from rape or incest.

How Much Do States Pay?

In *Public Funding for Family Planning, Sterilization, and Abortion Services, FY 1980–2006* (2008, http://www.guttmacher.org/pubs/2008/01/28/or38.pdf), Adam Sonfield, Casey Alrich, and Rachel Benson Gold of the Guttmacher Institute, a nonprofit organization that engages in reproductive health research, policy analysis, and public education, report that in 2006 about 177,404 abortions were paid for with public,

mainly state, funds. The researchers note that, among the abortions paid for with public funds, state governments reported spending $88.8 million in 2006 to provide 177,213 abortion procedures. The federal government spent $183,000 for 191 abortion procedures. The 17 states with nonrestrictive policies were where virtually all publicly funded abortion procedures occurred.

Table 3.4 shows the states that voluntarily funded abortions in 2009 for low-income women, those that were under court order to do so, and those that had restrictive funding policies.

FIGURE 3.4

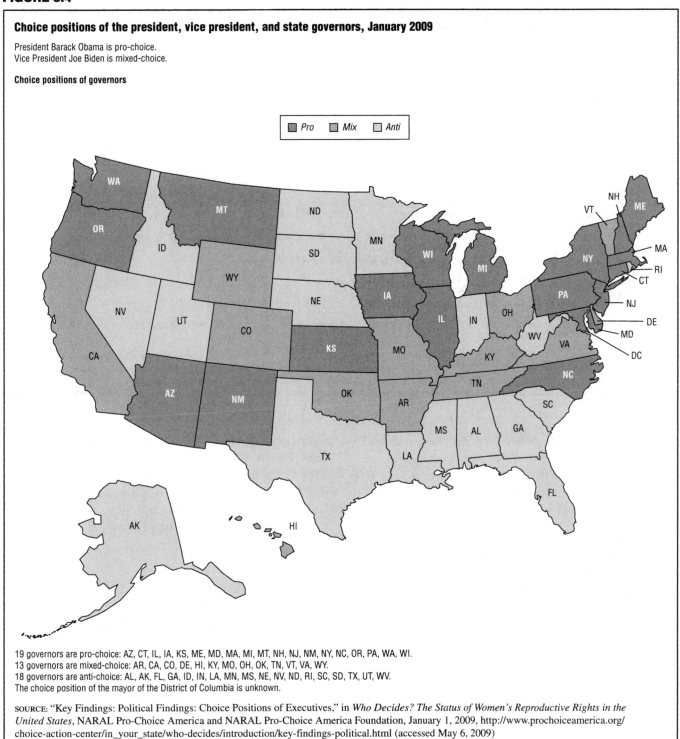

Choice positions of the president, vice president, and state governors, January 2009

President Barack Obama is pro-choice.
Vice President Joe Biden is mixed-choice.

Choice positions of governors

Pro   Mix   Anti

19 governors are pro-choice: AZ, CT, IL, IA, KS, ME, MD, MA, MI, MT, NH, NJ, NM, NY, NC, OR, PA, WA, WI.
13 governors are mixed-choice: AR, CA, CO, DE, HI, KY, MO, OH, OK, TN, VT, VA, WY.
18 governors are anti-choice: AL, AK, FL, GA, ID, IN, LA, MN, MS, NE, NV, ND, RI, SC, SD, TX, UT, WV.
The choice position of the mayor of the District of Columbia is unknown.

SOURCE: "Key Findings: Political Findings: Choice Positions of Executives," in *Who Decides? The Status of Women's Reproductive Rights in the United States*, NARAL Pro-Choice America and NARAL Pro-Choice America Foundation, January 1, 2009, http://www.prochoiceamerica.org/choice-action-center/in_your_state/who-decides/introduction/key-findings-political.html (accessed May 6, 2009)

ABORTION SERVICES FOR MILITARY PERSONNEL

David F. Burrelli of the CRS notes in *Abortion Services and Military Medical Facilities* (April 24, 2002, http://digital.library.unt.edu/govdocs/crs/permalink/meta-crs-2404:1) that before 1970 the U.S. armed forces did not have any official policy regarding the provision of abortion. Individual commanders had unwritten policies that lower-rank personnel followed. Military medical facilities followed the laws in the states in which they were located, and it was up to individual physicians whether to offer abortion services.

In 1970 the U.S. Department of Defense (DOD) issued an order that abortions in the military should be performed only when medically necessary or when the mental health of the mother was in danger. After the 1973 Supreme Court decision in *Roe v. Wade*, the DOD funded

TABLE 3.2

Choice positions of the federal and state legislatures, January 2009

U.S. Congress

The choice composition of the U.S. Senate is:
• 40 pro-choice senators
• 19 mixed-choice senators
• 41 anti-choice senators

The choice composition of the U.S. House is:

• 185 pro-choice members
• 45 mixed-choice members
• 205 anti-choice members

State Legislatures*

Anti-choice legislatures that are solidly anti-choice still outnumber solidly pro-choice legislatures:
• 12 states and the District of Columbia have pro-choice legislatures (both the house and senate are pro-choice): CA, CO, DE, DC (Council), HI, IA, ME, MA, NH, NJ, OR, VT, WA.
• 19 states have anti-choice legislatures (both the house and senate are anti-choice): AL, AZ, AR, ID, KY, LA, MI, MS, MO, NE, ND, OH, PA, RI, SD, TN, TX, UT, WV.
Choice composition of state senates:
• 15 states have a pro-choice senate (and the District of Columbia Council is pro-choice): CA, CO, CT, DE, DC, HI, IA, ME, MA, MN, NH, NJ, OR, VT, WA, WI.
• 14 states have a mixed-choice senate: AK, FL, GA, IL, MD, MT, NV, NM, NY, NC, SC, VA, WV, WY.
• 21 states have an anti-choice senate: AL, AZ, AR, ID, IN, KS, KY, LA, MI, MS, MO, NE, ND, OH, OK, PA, RI, SD, TN, TX, UT.
Choice composition of state houses:
• 15 states have a pro-choice house: CA, CO, DE, HI, IA, ME, MD, MA, NH, NJ, NM, NY, OR, VT, WA.
• 11 states have a mixed-choice house: CT, IL, IN, MN, MT, NV, NC, OH, SC, WV, WI.
• 23 states have an anti-choice house: AL, AK, AZ, AR, FL, GA, ID, KS, KY, LA, MI, MS, MO, ND, OK, PA, RI, SD, TN, TX, UT, VA, WY.

*The terms "house" and "senate" include the equivalent bodies in states that have different titles for their state legislative bodies. Nebraska has a unicameral body that is counted as a senate.

SOURCE: "Key Findings: Political Findings: Choice Positions of Legislatures, " in *Who Decides? The Status of Women's Reproductive Rights in the United States*, NARAL Pro-Choice America and NARAL Pro-Choice America Foundation, January 1, 2009, http://www.prochoiceamerica.org/choice-action-center/in_your_state/who-decides/introduction/key-findings-political.html (accessed May 6, 2009)

abortions for women eligible for military health care. To perform an abortion, Burrelli explains, two physicians had to satisfy the stipulation of medical necessity or risk to mental health. In addition, the funding had to fall within the state regulations concerning abortions.

By 1981 abortion was allowed only to save the life of the mother. In 1988 the DOD began banning all abortions at military medical facilities overseas, even if the woman was willing to pay for the procedure herself. Burrelli notes that in 1993 President Clinton issued a memorandum to "permit abortion services to be provided [at U.S. military facilities], if paid for entirely with non-DOD funds." However, in 1996, after Republicans took control of Congress, the National Defense Authorization Act again banned the performance of abortions in U.S. military medical facilities, even if privately funded, except in cases of endangerment to the mother's life, rape, or incest.

During subsequent sessions of Congress, proposed amendments to the 1996 National Defense Authorization Act, such as allowing privately paid abortions, were defeated. According to NARAL Pro-Choice America, in "Lift the Ban on Privately Funded Abortion Services for Military Women Overseas" (January 28, 2009, http://www.prochoiceamerica.org/assets/files/Abortion-Access-to-Abortion-Women-Government-Military-Private-Funding.pdf), as of January 2009 the ban on privately funded abortion services for military women overseas was still not repealed. Thus, women in the U.S. armed forces wanting an abortion

had to return to the United States or had to have the procedure performed at a private overseas facility, which was difficult or impossible, depending on where the woman was stationed. Furthermore, as she waited to return to the United States or travel to a safe facility overseas, the pregnancy progressed and the health risks of abortion likely increased.

ABORTION SERVICES FOR INCARCERATED WOMEN

In "Incarcerated Women and Abortion Provision: A Survey of Correctional Health Providers" (*Perspectives on Sexual and Reproductive Health*, vol. 41, no. 1, March 2009), Carolyn B. Sufrin, Mitchell D. Creinin, and Judy C. Chang reveal that the incidence of pregnancy among incarcerated women in U.S. jails and prisons ranges from 6% to 10%. Approximately 1,400 women per year give birth while incarcerated.

Even though no data exist on the percentage of unwanted pregnancies in the population of incarcerated women, the Guttmacher Institute reports in *In Brief: Facts on Induced Abortion in the United States* (July 2008, http://www.guttmacher.org/pubs/fb_induced_abortion.html) that 22% of all pregnancies (not including miscarriages) in the general population of American women are terminated by abortion. Thus, it is reasonable to assume that a similar percentage of pregnant, incarcerated women would choose to terminate their pregnancies.

TABLE 3.3

Overview of state abortion laws, May 2009

State	Must be performed by a licensed physician	Must be performed in a hospital if at:	Second physician must participate if at:	Prohibited except in cases of life or health endangerment if at:	"Partial-birth" abortion banned	Public funding of abortion		Private insurance coverage limited to life endangerment
						Funds all or most medically necessary abortions	Funds limited to life endangerment, rape and incest	
AL	X	Viability	Viability	Viability[a]	□		X	
AK	X				□	X		
AZ			Viability	Viability	□	X		
AR	X		Viability	Viability	X		X	
CA	X			Viability		X		
CO	X						X	
CT	X	Viability		Viability		X		
DE				□[c]			X	
DC							X	
FL	X		24 weeks	24 weeks	□		X	
GA	X		3rd trimester	3rd trimester	Postviability		X	
HI	X					X		
ID	X	Viability	3rd trimester	Viability[c]	□		X	X
IL	X		Viability	Viability	□	X		
IN	X	2nd trimester	Viability	Viability[a]	X		X[a]	
IA	X			3rd trimester	□		X[d]	
KS			Viability	Viability	Postviability		X	
KY		2nd trimester		Viability	□		X	X
LA	X		Viability	Viability	X		X	
ME	X			Viability			X	
MD	X			Viability[d]		X		
MA	X	12 weeks		24 weeks		X		
MI	X			Viability[c]	□		X	
MN	X	2nd trimester	□	□		X		
MS	X				X		X[d]	
MO	X	Viability	Viability	Viability	□		X	X
MT			Viability	Viability[a]	Postviability	X		
NE	X			Viability	□		X	
NV	X	24 weeks		24 weeks			X	
NH							X	
NJ	X	14 weeks			□	X		
NM					Postviability	X		
NY			24 weeks	24 weeks[c]		X		
NC	X	20 weeks		20 weeks			X	
ND	X	12 weeks	12 weeks	Viability	X		X	X
OH	X		□	□[a]	X		X	
OK	X	2nd trimester	Viability	Viability	X		X	
OR						X		
PA	X	Viability	Viability	24 weeks[a]			X	
RI	X			24 weeks[c]	□		X	□
SC	X	3rd trimester	3rd trimester	3rd trimester	X		X	
SD	X	24 weeks		24 weeks	X		Life only	
TN	X			Viability	X		X	
TX	X			3rd trimester			X	
UT	X	90 days		Viability[b, d]	X		X[a, d]	
VT						X		
VA	X	2nd trimester	Viability	3rd trimester	X		X[d]	
WA				Viability		X		
WV					□	X		
WI	X	12 weeks		Viability	□		X[a]	
WY	X			Viability			X	
Total	**38**	**19**	**18**	**37**	**16**	**17**	**32+DC**	**4**

□ Permanently enjoined (prohibited) by a court order; law not in effect.
[a]Exception in case of threat to the woman's physical health.
[b]Exception in case of rape or incest.
[c]Exception in case of life endangerment only.
[d]Exception in case of fetal abnormality.

Sufrin, Creinin, and Chang note that "the Eighth Amendment, which prohibits cruel and unusual punishment, guarantees all prisoners the right to health care; the Fourteenth Amendment, which prohibits states from depriving a person privacy without due process of the law, protects women's right to choose abortion regardless of incarceration. Nevertheless ... the thicket of abortion politics can limit prisoners' access to health services." This idea is borne out in Table 3.5, which shows the percentage of correctional health providers reporting selected abortion services between 2006 and 2007 by the majority party of the legislature in the provider's home state. These data show that abortion services are more available to women incarcerated in states with Democratic-controlled

TABLE 3.3

Overview of state abortion laws, May 2009 [CONTINUED]

State	Providers may refuse to participate		Mandated counseling includes information on:				Waiting period (in hours) after counseling	Parental involvement required for minors
	Individual	Institution	Breast cancer link	Fetal pain	Negative psychological effects	Ultrasound services		
AL							24	Consent
AK	X	Private	X	X				□
AZ	X	X						Consent
AR	X	X		X			Day Before	Consent
CA	X	Religious						□
CO	X	X						Notice
CT	X							
DE	X	X					□	Notice^e
DC								
FL	X	X						Notice
GA	X	X			X	X	24	Notice
HI	X	X						
ID	X	X					24	Consent
IL	X	Private						□
IN	X	Private				X	18	Consent
IA	X	Private						Notice
KS	X	X	X				24	Notice
KY	X	X					24	Consent
LA	X	X		X			24	Consent
ME	X	X						
MD	X	X						
MA	X	X					□	Consent
MI	X	X			X	X	24	Consent
MN	X	Private		X			24	Notice^f
MS	X	X	X				24	Consent^f
MO	X	X					24	Consent
MT	X	Private					□	□
NE	X	X			X		24	Notice
NV	X	Private						□
NH								
NJ	X	Private						□
NM	X	X						□
NY	X							
NC	X	X						Consent
ND	X	X					24	Consent^f
OH	X	X					24	Consent
OK	X	Private	X	X		X	24	Consent and Notice
OR	X	Private						
PA	X	Private					24	Consent
RI	X							Consent
SC	X	Private			X		1	Consent
SD	X	X		X	X		24	Notice
TN	X	X					□	Consent
TX	X	Private	X	X	X		24	Consent
UT	X	Private			X	X	24^g	Consent and Notice
VT								
VA	X	X					24	Consent
WA	X	X						
WV			X		X		24	Notice^e
WI	X	X				X	24	Consent^e
WY	X	Private						Consent
Total	**46**	**43**	**6**	**8**	**7**	**6**	**24**	**34**

□ Permanently enjoined (prohibited) by a court order; law not in effect.

X Policy is currently in effect.

^e Specified health professionals may waive parental involvement in certain circumstances.

^f Both parents must consent to the abortion.

^g The waiting period requirement is waived if the pregnancy is the result of rape or incest, the fetus has grave defects or the patient is younger than 15.

SOURCE: Guttmacher Institute, Community Health Centers and Family Planning, "Overview of State Abortion Law," in *State Policies in Brief: An Overview of Abortion Laws*, New York: Guttmacher, May 1, 2009, http://www.guttmacher.org/statecenter/spibs/spib_OAL.pdf (accessed May 6, 2009)

or bipartisan legislatures than with Republican-controlled legislatures. In states with Democratic legislatures, 78% of correctional health providers reported that incarcerated women could obtain abortions, compared with 72% in states with bipartisan legislatures and 50% in states with Republican legislatures.

AVOIDING ABORTION: FUNDING THROUGH TITLE X FOR FAMILY PLANNING/CONTRACEPTION

In 1970, with broad bipartisan support, Congress enacted Title X (Family Planning Program) of the Public Health Service Act, which provides federal assistance to

FIGURE 3.5

State laws regarding fetuses as victims, June 2008

These states have homicide laws that regard fetuses as victims at any stage of prenatal development. Includes Alaska.

These states have homicide laws that regard fetuses as victims but only at certain stages of prenatal development.

These states do not recognize the killing of an unborn child as homicide. Includes Hawaii.

New York has conflicting laws. One statute dictates that the killing of a fetus after 24 weeks of pregnancy is homicide. Yet a different statute defines a "person" as "a human being who has been born and is alive."

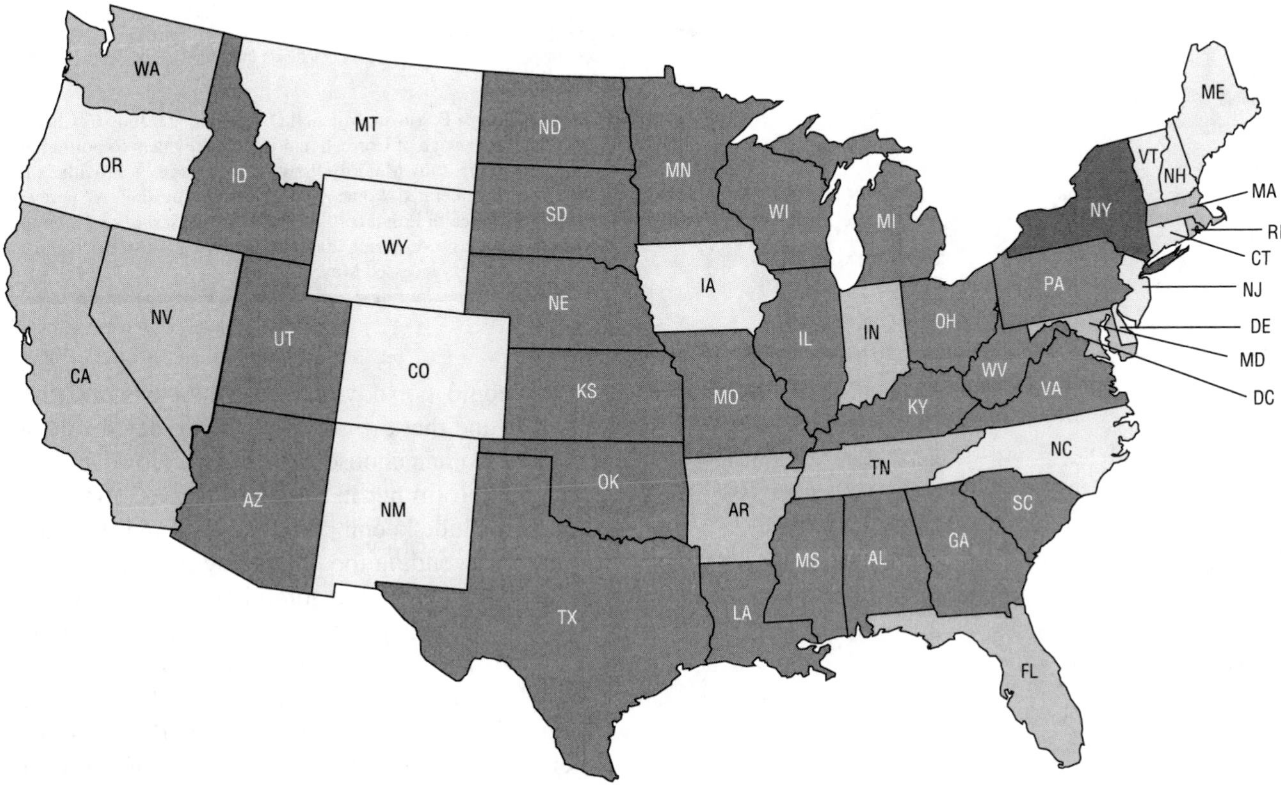

SOURCE: Adapted from "Full-Coverage Unborn Victim States," "Partial-Coverage Unborn Victim States," and "Conflicting Statutes," in *State Homicide Laws That Recognize Unborn Victims*, National Right to Life Committee, June 25, 2008, http://www.nrlc.org/Unborn_Victims/Statehomicidelaws092302.html (accessed May 8, 2009)

family planning clinics for contraception, infertility, and basic gynecologic services. The law specifically prohibits abortion as a method of family planning and forbids the use of any program monies to perform or advocate abortion. The program is intended to primarily benefit low-income women and adolescents.

According to Rachel Benson Gold et al. of the Guttmacher Institute, in *Next Steps for America's Family Planning Program: Leveraging the Potential of Medicaid and Title X in an Evolving Health Care System* (2009, http://www.guttmacher.org/pubs/NextSteps.pdf), 4,300 family planning centers across the United States received Title X funding in 2006. These centers provided health care services to approximately 4.8 million women in that year. In *Family Planning Annual Report: 2004 Summary* (July 2005, http://www.guttmacher.org/pubs/FPAR2004.pdf), the

Guttmacher Institute notes that of women using Title X–funded clinics in 2004, 73% were 20 years and older and 64% were white. Approximately 68% had incomes at or below the federal poverty level (which means they earned less than $15,020 per year for a family of three). The institute estimates that these clinics were the only source of family planning services for more than 80% of the women they served. The National Abortion Federation explains in the fact sheet "Abortion and Title X: What Health Care Providers Need to Know" (August 2007, http://www.prochoice.org/about_abortion/facts/abortion_title_x.html) that fewer than 5% of Title X–funded recipients are abortion providers.

Gold et al. indicate that Title X–supported clinics enable nearly 1 million women each year to avoid unintended pregnancy. The researchers note that without the services

TABLE 3.4

State funding of abortion under Medicaid, May 2009

State	Generally follows the federal standard, funds in cases of:		Funds all or most medically necessary abortions
	Life endangerment, rape and incest	Other exceptions	
Alabama	X		
Alaska			Court order
Arizona			Court order
Arkansas	X		
California			Court order
Colorado	X		
Connecticut			Court order
Delaware	X		
Dist. of Columbia	X		
Florida	X		
Georgia	X		
Hawaii			Voluntarily
Idaho	X		
Illinois			Court order
Indiana	X	Physical health	
Iowa	X	Fetal abnormality	
Kansas	X		
Kentucky	X		
Louisiana	X		
Maine	X		
Maryland			Voluntarily
Massachusetts			Court order
Michigan	X		
Minnesota			Court order
Mississippi	X	Fetal abnormality	
Missouri	X		
Montana			Court order
Nebraska	X		
Nevada	X		
New Hampshire	X		
New Jersey			Court order
New Mexico			Court order
New York			Voluntarily
North Carolina	X		
North Dakota	X		
Ohio	X		
Oklahoma	X		
Oregon			Court order
Pennsylvania	X		
Rhode Island	X		
South Carolina	X		
South Dakota	*		
Tennessee	X		
Texas	X		
Utah	X	Physical health/ fetal abnormality	
Vermont			Court order
Virginia	X	Fetal abnormality	
Washington			Voluntarily
West Virginia			Court order
Wisconsin	X	Physical health	
Wyoming	X		
Total	**32 + DC**		**17**

*State only pays for abortions when necessary to protect the woman's life.

SOURCE: Guttmacher Institute, Community Health Centers and Family Planning, "State Funding of Abortion under Medicaid," in *State Policies in Brief: State Funding of Abortion under Medicaid*, New York: Guttmacher, May 1, 2009, http://www.guttmacher.org/statecenter/spibs/spib_SFAM.pdf (accessed May 7, 2009)

TABLE 3.5

Percentage of correctional health providers reporting abortion services, by majority party of legislature in provider's home state, 2006–07

Service	Republican (N=91)	Democratic (N=119)	Bipartisan (N=72)
Abortion is allowed	50	78	72
Provider arranges appointments	40	62	50
Provider arranges transportation	77	95	87

Notes: Sixteen states have predominantly Republican legislatures, 22 states predominantly Democratic legislatures and 11 states bipartisan legislatures; in Nebraska, legislators do not identify themselves or run as members of a particular party. This analysis excludes four respondents—three who did not indicate their state of origin and one who was from Nebraska.

SOURCE: Carolyn B. Sufrin, Mitchell D. Creinin, and Judy C. Chang, "Table 2. Percentage of Correctional Health Providers Reporting Selected Abortion Services, by Majority Party of Legislature in Provider's Home State," in "Incarcerated Women and Abortion Provision: A Survey of Correctional Health Providers," *Perspectives on Sexual and Reproductive Health*, vol. 41, no. 1, March 2009, http://www.guttmacher.org/pubs/psrh/full/4100609.pdf (accessed May 15, 2009)

clinics could not advise a pregnant woman to have an abortion and that the clinic could not pay for the abortion should a woman choose to have one. However, the clinics "are to" inform her in a "nondirective" manner that her options include keeping the baby, giving the child up for adoption, or ending the pregnancy by having an abortion. In September 1986 the administration of Ronald Reagan (1911–2004) changed the wording in the guidelines from "are to"—which implied a mandatory requirement—to "may"—which was subject to individual judgment. Should the woman want an abortion, the federally funded agency had to provide her with a list of abortion clinics that operated without federal funding.

Male Involvement in Family Planning

In "Title X Male Involvement Prevention Services" (November 13, 2007, http://www.hhs.gov/opa/familyplanning/grantees/maleinvolvement/index.html), the U.S. Department of Health and Human Services (HHS) notes that since 1997 the Title X program has provided additional funds for an adolescent male initiative that employs male high school students as interns in the clinics. The students receive training in clinic operation and peer education, assistance in identifying possible careers in health and health-related occupations, and use of services in a family planning setting. The program has also awarded research grants to organizations that include social and educational services to males, enabling these organizations to evaluate the addition of reproductive health and family planning services to their existing program. In spite of these incentives to draw men into Title X clinics, Gold et al. report that in 2006 Title X–supported clinics served only 272,000 male contraceptive clients.

provided in Title X–funded clinics, the number of unintended pregnancies per year would be increased by 31%.

Guidelines instituted during the administration of Jimmy Carter (1924–) indicated that federally funded

Confidential Family Planning Services for Adolescents

Christine Cadena notes in "Title X of the Public Health Service Act: Impact on Family Planning, Abortion, and Teen Services" (*Associated Content*, August 31, 2007) that teens make up about one-third of family planning clients in many Title X–funded clinics. The law requires Title X clinics to encourage parental participation in teenage reproductive health decisions, but under federal law clinics have to respect a teenager's wish not to involve his or her parents. Courts have recognized the importance of confidential services for teenagers. In *Planned Parenthood Association of Utah v. Matheson* (582 F. Supp. 1001, 1009 [D. Utah 1983]), a district federal court prohibited a "blanket parental notification requirement" for minors seeking contraceptives. The court observed that adolescents who seek contraceptives are usually already sexually active. Therefore, these same adolescents would continue engaging in sexual activity even if they could not obtain contraceptives, thereby exposing themselves to "the health risks of early pregnancy and venereal disease."

Laws vary among the states as to whether minors can consent to their own health care. Table 3.6 shows that 21 states plus the District of Columbia allow minors to consent to contraceptive health care services. Some states allow minors to give consent only if their health is in danger or if they are married, a parent, or are pregnant or have been pregnant. As with a variety of issues, state laws and federal law are not always the same. However, the Guttmacher Institute points out in *State Policies in Brief: Minors' Access to Contraceptive Services* (August 1, 2009, http://www.guttmacher.org/statecenter/spibs/spib_MACS.pdf) that over the past 30 years state laws have come to more closely reflect federal law, which has upheld a minor's right to privacy in obtaining contraceptives.

Funding for Private Family Planning Clinics

In "Family Planning" (October 25, 2007, http://www.hhs.gov/opa/familyplanning/index.html), the HHS indicates that besides providing monies to family planning clinics run by state and local governments, Title X also awards grants to private nonprofit groups that offer family planning services. In 1988 the HHS, acting on President Reagan's recommendation, issued regulations revising its interpretation of Section 1008, the long-standing statutory prohibition against using Title X funds to "promote abortion." The guidelines reaffirmed that Congress intended Title X funds "to be used only to support preventive family planning services."

The Reagan administration further prohibited counselors at federally funded clinics from discussing abortion as an alternative in an unintended pregnancy and from referring pregnant women to an abortion provider even if patients ask for such assistance and it is paid for with private funds. This prohibition against discussing abortion in Title X clinics became known as the gag rule.

TITLE X CLINICS AND THE GAG RULE. About 36 state health departments and 78 national organizations opposed the gag rule because they said it violated the clinics' First Amendment right to free speech and infringed on the doctor-patient relationship. In a 5-4 decision in *Rust v. Sullivan* (500 U.S. 173 [1991]), the Supreme Court upheld the gag rule.

The American Medical Association attacked the ruling, not only because it interfered with the doctor-patient relationship but also because it exposed doctors to the risk of medical malpractice lawsuits for not informing a woman with a high-risk pregnancy of all her options. Pregnancy can be a risk to the health of a woman with diabetes, cancer, acquired immunodeficiency syndrome (AIDS), hypertension, renal (kidney) disease, sickle cell anemia, malnutrition, or other serious illnesses. Some of these diseases particularly affect African-American women who, because of their greater rates of poverty, are more likely than white women to use federally funded clinics for health care.

Some federally funded clinics, including the Planned Parenthood Federation of America, chose, at the risk of having to close, to turn down federal support rather than comply with the gag rule. William R. Archer (1928–), the deputy assistant secretary of the HHS, responded that if clinics did not comply, the HHS would simply find other clinics to replace them. However, there were areas of the country where there were no other existing health care providers ready to step in, leaving women who depended on subsidized health care with no source for prenatal care and contraceptive services.

Those in Congress who opposed *Rust v. Sullivan* fought to overturn the Title X gag rule by placing a rider blocking it on an HHS appropriations bill. In November 1991, when President George H. W. Bush received the appropriations bill, he vetoed it because of the rider.

Supporters of the bill tried to garner the two-thirds majority in Congress needed to overturn the presidential veto but failed. In August 1992 a federal appeals court ruled that the HHS could move forward with implementation of the regulations. On January 22, 1993, two days after President Clinton took the oath of office and on the 20th anniversary of *Roe v. Wade*, Clinton repealed the gag rule.

In 2003 Title X regulations were adopted that mandated that pregnant women at Title X–funded clinics be told all their legal medical options—including termination of pregnancy—in a factual and accurate manner, without encouraging abortion. The clinics could provide a referral for abortion services if requested, but the clinics

TABLE 3.6

State policies on minors' access to contraceptive services, June 2009

State	Explicitly allows all minors to consent to services	Explicitly allows certain minors may consent to services					No explicit policy
		Health	Married	Parent	Pregnant or ever pregnant	Other	
Alabama			X[a]	X[a]	X[a]	HS graduate[a] or 14 years[a]	
Alaska	X						
Arizona	X						
Arkansas	X						
California	X						
Colorado	X						
Connecticut			X[b]				
Delaware						12 years[c]	
Dist. of Columbia	X						
Florida		X	X	X	X		
Georgia	X						
Hawaii						14 years[c]	
Idaho	X						
Illinois		X	X	X	X	Referral	
Indiana			X[b]				
Iowa	X						
Kansas						Mature minor	
Kentucky	X[c]						
Louisiana			X[b]				
Maine		X	X	X			
Maryland	X[c]						
Massachusetts	X[d]						
Michigan			X[b]				
Minnesota	X[c]						
Mississippi			X	X		Referral	
Missouri			X[b]				
Montana	X[c]						
Nebraska			X[b]				
Nevada			X[b]	X[a]		Mature minor[a]	
New Hampshire						Mature minor[a]	
New Jersey			X[a]		X[a]		
New Mexico	X						
New York	X[d]						
North Carolina	X						
North Dakota							X
Ohio							X
Oklahoma			X[c]		X[c]		
Oregon	X[c]						
Pennsylvania			X[a]		X[a]	HS graduate[a]	
Rhode Island							X
South Carolina			X[b]			16 years or Mature minor	
South Dakota			X[b]				
Tennessee	X						
Texas			X[b]			e	
Utah			X[b]			e	
Vermont			X[b]				
Virginia[b]	X						
Washington	X						
West Virginia			X[b]			Mature Minor	
Wisconsin							X
Wyoming	X						
Total	**21 + DC**	**3**	**21**	**6**	**6**	**11**	**4**

[a]State policy does not specifically address contraceptive services but applies to medical care in general.
[b]State law confers the rights and responsibilities of adulthood to minors who are married.
[c]Physician may, but is not required to, inform the minor's parents.
[d]The state funds a statewide program that gives minors access to confidential contraceptive care.
[e]State funds may not be used to provide minors with confidential contraceptive services.

SOURCE: Guttmacher Institute, Community Health Centers and Family Planning, "Minors' Access to Contraceptive Services," in *State Policies in Brief: Minors' Access to Contraceptive Services*, New York: Guttmacher, June 1, 2009, http://www.guttmacher.org/statecenter/spibs/spib_MACS.pdf (accessed June 2, 2009)

could not provide abortion services themselves. As of mid-2009, these regulations were still in effect.

The Adequacy of Title X Funding

Even though the authorizing law for the Title X family planning program expired on September 30, 1985, annual appropriations legislation has continued its funding. During the Reagan (1981–1989) and Bush (1989–1993) administrations, funding was less than it was in 1980. (See Table 3.7.) Funding rose dramatically during the Clinton administration (1993–2001). In Clinton's last year in office, almost $254 million in Title X funds were appropriated. Funding had also

TABLE 3.7

Funding for the Office of Family Planning, fiscal years 1971–2008

Fiscal year	Office of Family Planning total funds appropriated
2008	299,981,000
2007	283,146,000
2006	283,103,000
2005	285,977,000
2004	278,348,000
2003	273,350,000
2002	265,000,000
2001	253,932,000
2000	238,885,000
1999	215,000,000
1998	203,452,000
1997	198,452,000
1996	192,592,000
1995	193,349,000
1994	180,918,000
1993	173,418,000
1992	149,585,000
1991	144,311,000
1990	139,135,000
1989	138,320,000
1988	139,663,000
1987	142,500,000
1986	136,372,000
1985	142,500,000
1984	140,000,000
1983	124,088,000
1982	124,176,000
1981	161,671,000
1980	162,000,000
1979	135,000,000
1978	135,000,000
1977	113,000,000
1976	100,615,000
1975	100,615,000
1974	100,615,000
1973	100,615,000
1972	61,815,000
1971	6,000,000

SOURCE: Adapted from "Funding History," in *Budget*, U.S. Department of Health and Human Services, Office of Population Affairs, Office of Family Planning, 2009, http://www.hhs.gov/opa/about/budget/ (accessed May 6, 2009)

increased during the administration of George W. Bush (2001–2009). In 2006 over $283 million was funded, and in 2008 nearly $300 million was funded. Nevertheless, the National Family Planning and Reproductive Health Association (NFPRHA) states in "History of Title X" (August 5, 2009, http://www.nfprha.org/main/about_us.cfm?Category= Title_X&Section=Main) that Title X funding "has languished" and that if it had kept up with medical inflation since 1980 "it would have been funded at more than $725 million instead of the FY 2007 level of $283 million."

ATTEMPTS TO "DEFUND" TITLE X. Each year antiabortion lawmakers try to "defund," or eliminate, federal monies from the Title X program. Even though the law prohibits Title X funds from being used for abortion, opponents of Title X argue that organizations such as the Planned Parenthood Federation of America, which provides abortions, should not receive Title X funds. They believe clinic clients might think abortion is a method of family planning. In addition,

critics feel that instead of preventing teen pregnancy by providing adolescents with contraceptives, more efforts should be made in encouraging abstinence before marriage.

ABSTINENCE-ONLY EDUCATION. Title X clinics do offer adolescents abstinence counseling and education. However, in *The Content of Federally Funded Abstinence-Only Education Programs* (December 2004, http://oversight.house .gov/documents/20041201102153-50247.pdf), the House of Representatives Committee on Government Reform finds that "over 80% of the abstinence-only curricula ... contain false, misleading, or distorted information about reproductive health." Moreover, the committee notes, the government spent twice as much on abstinence-only education in 2005 (about $170 million) than in 2001, and this educational program does not teach basic facts about contraception.

Besides providing teens with erroneous information, abstinence-only education programs do not appear to help teens abstain from sex. Christopher Trenholm et al. find in "Impacts of Abstinence Education on Teen Sexual Activity, Risk of Pregnancy, and Risk of Sexually Transmitted Diseases" (*Journal of Policy Analysis and Management*, vol. 27, no. 2, 2008), a study on the effectiveness of four well-implemented abstinence-only education programs, that abstinence-only education did not reduce teen sexual activity. Conversely, the programs did not put students at a higher risk for teen pregnancy or sexually transmitted diseases as some had feared.

In the press release "President Obama's FY 2010 Budget Takes Positive Steps, but More Investment in Common-Sense Solutions Is Needed" (May 7, 2009, http://www.nfprha.org/ main/media_detail.cfm?ID=119), the NFPRHA indicates that the Obama administration's 2010 budget eliminated funding of abstinence-only education and increased funding for Title X by $10 million. Furthermore, the HHS highlights in "A New Era of Responsibility" (February 2009, http://www.whitehouse.gov/omb/assets/fy2010_new _era/Department_of_Health_and_Human_Services1.pdf) that the abstinence-only programs were being replaced with evidence-based programs that "stress the importance of abstinence while providing medically-accurate and age-appropriate information to youth who have already become sexually active."

INTERNATIONAL U.S. AID FOR FAMILY PLANNING AND CONTRACEPTION

Foreign Assistance Act

In 1961 Congress passed the Foreign Assistance Act (FAA), which reorganized the U.S. foreign assistance programs and mandated the creation of an agency to administer them—the U.S. Agency for International Development (USAID). USAID offered direct support to the developing nations of the world.

The FAA had few restrictions on how assistance was to be provided and contained only general guidelines on the kinds of factors to be taken into account before providing assistance. In 1973 Congress amended the FAA with the Helms Amendment, which forbid the use of U.S. foreign aid funding "to pay for the performance of abortions as a method of family planning or to motivate or coerce any person to practice abortions."

The Mexico City Policy/Global Gag Rule

At the United Nations (UN) population conference in Mexico City, Mexico, in 1984, President Reagan announced that the United States would no longer support overseas private family planning groups that, with their own funds, performed or promoted abortion. He indicated that the United States would provide monies to organizations that advocated only "natural" or noncontraceptive methods of family planning.

When the International Planned Parenthood Federation (IPPF) refused to implement the Reagan family planning restriction on its affiliates in developing countries, the administration withdrew U.S. funds from the IPPF. The IPPF took USAID to court and lost. In June 1991 the Supreme Court upheld the policy by refusing to hear the case *Planned Parenthood Federation of America v. Agency for International Development* (cert. denied, 498 U.S. 933). Even though the Reagan restriction was never enacted into law, it was enforced as an executive order for almost a decade.

In 1985 the Reagan administration also withheld $10 million in aid from the UN Fund for Population Activities (UNFPA; now the UN Population Fund). The UNFPA was dedicated to limiting the world's population increase. The Reagan administration charged the UNFPA with helping the government of the People's Republic of China to carry out forced abortions and sterilizations. The $10 million was roughly equal to the UNFPA's annual spending in the People's Republic of China. Funding for the UNFPA has been debated in Congress every year since 1985.

The Reagan administration's Mexico City Policy was retained by the subsequent administration of George H. W. Bush. However, when President Clinton took office in January 1993, he revoked the Mexico City Policy (which also became known as the global gag rule) and restored the U.S. contribution to the UNFPA. He also revoked the domestic gag rule.

Since 1994 antiabortion advocates have introduced abortion-related clauses to a number of foreign aid measures. These lawmakers, led by Representative Christopher H. Smith (1953–; R-NJ), have sought to restrict U.S. aid to family planning groups that provide legal abortion services or advocate abortion rights in their countries.

For the first time, the global gag rule was written into law in the omnibus appropriations bill for fiscal year 2000. (An omnibus appropriations bill authorizes the government to spend money on a variety of things.) In exchange for the release by Congress of $926 million in dues owed the UN, President Clinton agreed to restrictions on the $385 million appropriated for international family planning. Private organizations that performed or promoted abortion could not receive U.S. funds, as was the case under the Mexico City Policy.

On January 22, 2001, on the first day of President George W. Bush's presidency and the 28th anniversary of *Roe v. Wade*, the new president issued a memorandum reinstating the Mexico City Policy, which had been rescinded since January 22, 1993.

Even though the reinstated global gag rule was identical to the one implemented two decades earlier, the trend in abortion law worldwide had been toward making laws less strict. Between 1985 (when the global gag rule was first implemented) and 2009, 39 countries had made their abortion laws less strict, and 7 countries had tightened their laws. (See Table 3.8.) In May 2008, 40% of all women worldwide lived in countries where abortion is legal without restriction. (See Figure 3.6.) Another 34% lived in countries where abortion is legal with restriction. With the more recent implementation of the global gag rule, the possibility of conflict arose because more coun-

TABLE 3.8

Countries changing their abortion laws since the initial imposition of the "global gag rule," 1985–2009

39 countries have liberalized their abortion laws since the initial imposition of the global gag rule

Albania	1991, 1996	India	2002
Algeria	1985	Iran	2005
Australia	2002	Malaysia	1989
Belgium	1990	Mali	2002
Bhutan	2004	Mongolia	1989
Botswana	1991	Nepal	2002
Benin	2003	Niger	2006
Bulgaria	1990	Pakistan	1990
Burkina Faso	1996	Portugal	2007
Cambodia	1997	Romania	1989
Canada	1988	Saint Lucia	2004
Chad	2002	Slovakia	1986
Columbia	2006	South Africa	1996, 2004
Czech Republic	1986	Spain	1985
Denmark	2003	Swaziland	2005
Ethiopia	2005	Sweden	2007
France	2001	Switzerland	2002
Ghana	1985	Tasmania	2001
Greece	1986	Thailand	2005
Guinea	2000		

7 countries have tightened their laws

El Salvador	1998	Poland	1997
Hungary	2000	Russian Federation	2003
Latvia	2002, 2003	United States	2003, 2007
Nicaragua	2006		

SOURCE: Created by Sandra Alters for Gale, 2009

FIGURE 3.6

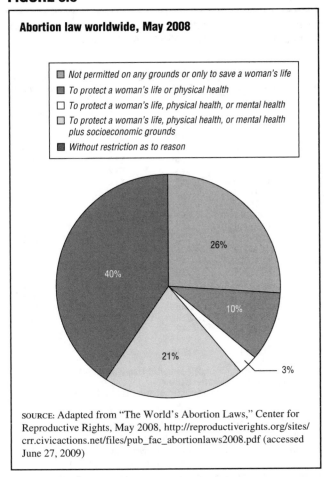

Abortion law worldwide, May 2008

- ■ Not permitted on any grounds or only to save a woman's life
- ■ To protect a woman's life or physical health
- □ To protect a woman's life, physical health, or mental health
- □ To protect a woman's life, physical health, or mental health plus socioeconomic grounds
- ■ Without restriction as to reason

26%

40%

10%

21%

3%

SOURCE: Adapted from "The World's Abortion Laws," Center for Reproductive Rights, May 2008, http://reproductiverights.org/sites/crr.civicactions.net/files/pub_fac_abortionlaws2008.pdf (accessed June 27, 2009)

When President Obama took office on January 20, 2009, one of his first presidential acts was to repeal the global gag rule and restore funding to international health groups that perform or promote abortions. The Guttmacher Institute reports in the press release "President Obama's 2010 Budget: A Decidedly Mixed Bag" (May 8, 2009, http://www.guttmacher.org/media/inthenews/2009/05/08/index.html) that:

> funding for international family planning and reproductive health programs would increase to $543 million—$48 million more than current levels. Additionally, the president is recommending a $50 million contribution to the United Nations Population Fund (UNFPA), the same amount as this year. The budget does propose deleting all the limitations on the U.S. contribution to UNFPA, including one that prevents any U.S. funds from being used in UNFPA's China program and another that deducts from the annual U.S. contribution the amount that UNFPA spends in China that same year. If approved by Congress, the overall amount proposed for international family planning and reproductive health programs—$593 million—would represent the highest level ever from the U.S. government.

NONMARITAL CHILDBEARING, WELFARE REFORM, AND ABORTION

In 1995, as Congress worked to overhaul the nation's welfare system, the legislators were split on issues concerning teen pregnancy and abortion. Some believed that discontinuing federal cash assistance to the needy would help discourage nonmarital childbearing. According to Lisa Kaeser of the Guttmacher Institute, in "Washington Memo" (August 7, 1996), these members regarded out-of-wedlock births, especially among adolescents, as "both a central cause of welfare dependency and a direct result of the 'culture' it creates." Others feared that limiting welfare cash benefits would lead poor women to choose abortion.

In 1996 the 60-year-old federal cash assistance program, Aid to Families with Dependent Children, was eliminated, and President Clinton signed the new welfare reform law, the Personal Responsibility and Work Opportunity Reconciliation Act of 1998, which created the Temporary Assistance for Needy Families (TANF) program. TANF provides assistance and work opportunities to needy families by granting states the federal funds and wide flexibility to develop and implement their own welfare programs.

The new welfare reform law outlined specific provisions for reducing nonmarital and teen pregnancies. It allowed states to spend a portion of their TANF funds on "prepregnancy family services," but prohibited funding of other medical services, such as abortions.

Even though most nonmarital births were to women not on welfare, Congress used the welfare reform law to stress the issue of "illegitimacy." To encourage the states

tries that receive U.S. population assistance allowed abortions than during the past implementation.

In September 2003 President Bush issued an executive order preventing the U.S. Department of State from giving family planning grants to international groups that provide abortion-related counseling, effectively extending the global gag rule, which previously applied only to USAID. However, the new order exempted agencies in Africa and the Caribbean that would benefit from President Bush's five-year, $15 billion global AIDS initiative.

In April 2005 the Senate passed an amendment to the Foreign Affairs Authorization Act brought forward by Senators Barbara Boxer (1940–; D-CA) and Olympia J. Snowe (1947–; R-ME) that would repeal the global gag rule. In a House-Senate conference committee meeting during which House-Senate differences in the act were being negotiated, the Boxer-Snowe amendment was dropped. In November 2005 President Bush signed the act without the amendment. In 2007 another Boxer-Snowe amendment to repeal the global gag rule passed in the Senate. However, the bill was dropped and never passed into law due to the threat of a presidential veto during budget negotiations.

to develop effective solutions for reducing out-of-wedlock births, the act provided for a performance incentive called "Bonus to Reward Decrease in Illegitimacy Ratio." Under the new law the federal government awarded up to $100 million annually each year from 1996 to 2003 to a maximum of five states that reduced nonmarital births while decreasing their abortion rates below 1995 levels.

Table 3.9 shows the number, rate, and percentage of births to unmarried women for 1980 and 1985 to 2006. In spite of the government's incentives, the rate of out-of-wedlock births (the number of births for every 1,000 unmarried women) did not decrease during the years of the reward act (1996 to 2003) but remained relatively stable. In addition, during the years of the reward act the population increased and the rate of marriage declined. This decline was documented by National Marriage Project researchers at Rutgers University in *The State of Our Unions 2008: The Social Health of Marriage in America* (February 2009, http://marriage.rutgers.edu/Publications/SOOU/2008update.pdf). An increase in the population and a decline in the rate of marriage resulted in an increase in the population of unmarried women. The stable rate of out-of-wedlock births in a larger population of unmarried women resulted in a rise in the number and percent of births to unmarried women.

This pattern of stability in the birthrate to unmarried women from 1996 to 2003 can also be seen in Figure 3.7. Notice that in Table 3.9 the birthrate for unmarried

TABLE 3.9

Number, rate, and percentage of births to unmarried women, and birth rate for married women, 1980 and 1985–2006

Year	Births to unmarried women			Birthrate for married women[c]
	Number	Rate[a]	Percent[b]	
2006	1,641,946	50.6	38.5	88.0
2005	1,527,034	47.5	36.9	87.3
2004	1,470,189	46.1	35.8	87.6
2003	1,415,995	44.9	34.6	88.1
2002	1,365,966	43.7	34.0	86.3
2001	1,349,249	43.8	33.5	86.7
2000	1,347,043	44.1	33.2	87.4
1999	1,308,560	43.3	33.0	84.8
1998	1,293,567	43.3	32.8	84.2
1997	1,257,444	42.9	32.4	82.7
1996	1,260,306	43.8	32.4	82.3
1995	1,253,976	44.3	32.2	82.6
1994	1,289,592	46.2	32.6	82.9
1993	1,240,172	44.8	31.0	86.1
1992	1,224,876	44.9	30.1	88.5
1991	1,213,769	45.0	29.5	89.6
1990	1,165,384	43.8	28.0	93.2
1989	1,094,169	41.6	27.1	91.9
1988	1,005,299	38.5	25.7	90.8
1987	933,013	36.0	24.5	90.0
1986	878,477	34.2	23.4	90.7
1985	828,174	32.8	22.0	93.3
1980	665,747	29.4	18.4	97.0

[a]Births to unmarried women per 1,000 unmarried women aged 15–44 years.
[b]Percentage of all births to unmarried women.
[c]Births to married women per 1,000 married women aged 15–44 years.

SOURCE: Joyce A. Martin et al., "Table D. Number, Rate, and Percentage of Births to Unmarried Women and Birth Rate for Married Women: United States, 1980 and 1985–2006," in "Births: Final Data for 2006," *National Vital Statistics Reports*, vol. 57, no. 7, January 7, 2009, http://www.cdc.gov/nchs/data/nvsr/nvsr57/nvsr57_07.pdf (accessed May 8, 2009)

FIGURE 3.7

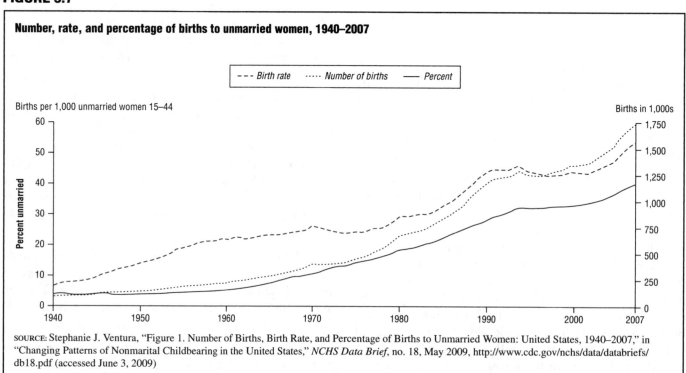

Number, rate, and percentage of births to unmarried women, 1940–2007

SOURCE: Stephanie J. Ventura, "Figure 1. Number of Births, Birth Rate, and Percentage of Births to Unmarried Women: United States, 1940–2007," in "Changing Patterns of Nonmarital Childbearing in the United States," *NCHS Data Brief*, no. 18, May 2009, http://www.cdc.gov/nchs/data/databriefs/db18.pdf (accessed June 3, 2009)

women was 43.8 births for every 1,000 unmarried women in 1996, and was slightly below or above this rate from 1996 to 2003, with no upward trend. The funding of the reward act ended before the end of the calendar year in 2003 because the government's fiscal year runs from October 1 to September 30, which may account for some of the rise in the birthrate to unmarried women in that year. After the program ended, birthrates to unmarried women increased through 2006.

A Changing Pattern of Nonmarital Childbearing

Figure 3.8 shows the birthrates for unmarried women by age in 1980, 1990, 2002, and 2006. The rate of nonmarital births to young women aged 15 to 17 declined in 2002 and 2006 from a high in 1990, and the rate for young women aged 18 to 19 was relatively stable during those years after a sharp increase between 1980 and 1990. The rates of nonmarital births for mothers in age categories 20 to 24 and older increased between 1980 and 2006. Thus, Figure 3.8 shows a changing pattern of childbearing in unmarried women by age in the United States over the past nearly three decades: the birthrate for older unmarried women has increased, whereas the birthrate for younger unmarried teens has decreased, and the birthrate for older unmarried teens has stabilized.

Over the past decades the concept of out-of-wedlock births has changed both socially and demographically. The term *out-of-wedlock*, which had negative implications and usually referred to an unplanned teenage pregnancy, has been replaced in many instances with the term *nonmarital childbearing*. It has also become more socially acceptable for single women to give birth to children and to plan their nonmarital childbearing. In addition, many couples choose to not marry, and women in these relationships are included in the statistics of births to unmarried women. In *State of Our Unions 2008*, the National Marriage Project shows the decline in the rate of marriage in the United States since 1970. In that year there were 76.5 marriages for every 1,000 unmarried women aged 15 and older. By 1990 the rate had declined to 54.5, and by 2007 it had dropped even further to 39.2.

Stephanie J. Ventura of the National Center for Health Statistics explains in "Changing Patterns of Nonmarital Childbearing in the United States" (*NCHS Data Brief*, no. 18, May 2009) that in the 1990s and prior, out-of-wedlock births were considered negative because of their impact on family structure, the economic security of children, and the health of the child. In recent years, because of the change in family structure and the prevalence of a variety of family

FIGURE 3.8

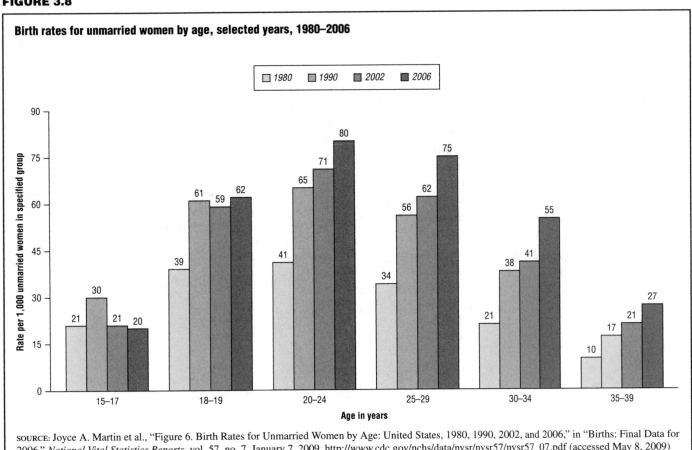

Birth rates for unmarried women by age, selected years, 1980–2006

SOURCE: Joyce A. Martin et al., "Figure 6. Birth Rates for Unmarried Women by Age: United States, 1980, 1990, 2002, and 2006," in "Births: Final Data for 2006," *National Vital Statistics Reports*, vol. 57, no. 7, January 7, 2009, http://www.cdc.gov/nchs/data/nvsr/nvsr57/nvsr57_07.pdf (accessed May 8, 2009)

FIGURE 3.9

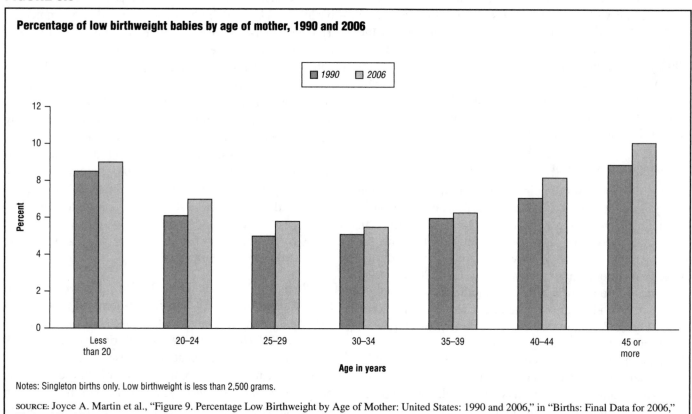

Percentage of low birthweight babies by age of mother, 1990 and 2006

Notes: Singleton births only. Low birthweight is less than 2,500 grams.

SOURCE: Joyce A. Martin et al., "Figure 9. Percentage Low Birthweight by Age of Mother: United States: 1990 and 2006," in "Births: Final Data for 2006," *National Vital Statistics Reports*, vol. 57, no. 7, January 7, 2009, http://www.cdc.gov/nchs/data/nvsr/nvsr57/nvsr57_07.pdf (accessed May 8, 2009)

structures, economic and health issues are what remain when considering births to unmarried women.

Economic issues are of high concern with unmarried teenage mothers because they have not yet entered the workforce and established a stable career and, in many cases, have not yet completed their schooling. Health issues are of concern as well because low birth weight babies are born in higher percentages to women at either end of their childbearing years. (See Figure 3.9.) Thus, unmarried teens have a high percentage of low birth weight babies and are less likely than older women to be able to economically support a child and provide appropriate health care.

The birthrate for this high-risk group (unmarried teens) declined between 1990 and 2006. (See Figure 3.8.) Conversely, the birthrate for the less-at-risk group (older unmarried women) rose over the past three decades, as did the birthrate to unmarried women in general (aged 15 to 44) since 2003. (See Figure 3.7 and Table 3.9.) Consonant with the birthrate difference between these groups is a difference in the proportion of abortions. Abortions to teens made up only 16.6% of all reported legal abortions in 2005, whereas abortions to unmarried women in general made up 83.4% of all abortions. (See Table 3.10.) According to the National Abortion Federation, in "Women Who Have Abortions" (2003, http://www.prochoice.org/pubs_research/publications/downloads/about_abortion/women_who_have_abortions.pdf), the most common reason women terminate their pregnancies is that the pregnancies are unplanned and are coupled with a "lack of money and/or unreadiness to start or expand their families due to existing responsibilities. Many feel that the most responsible course of action is to wait until their situation is more suited to childrearing." Chapter 4 provides a more detailed look at these and other abortion statistics.

TABLE 3.10

Legal abortions by race, age, and marital status, selected states, 2005

| | Race | | | | | | Total | |
| | White | | Black | | Other | | | |
Characteristic	No.	(%)	No.	(%)	No.	(%)	No.	(%)
Age group (years)								
<15	1,258	(0.4)	1,561	(0.8)	134	(0.3)	2,953	(0.6)
15–19	47,797	(16.4)	31,701	(16.1)	5,013	(13.1)	84,511	(16.0)
20–24	98,832	(33.9)	63,788	(32.3)	10,959	(28.5)	173,579	(32.9)
25–29	66,074	(22.7)	50,528	(25.6)	9,237	(24.1)	125,839	(23.9)
30–34	40,895	(14.0)	30,314	(15.4)	6,795	(17.7)	78,004	(14.8)
35–39	26,290	(9.0)	14,972	(7.6)	4,449	(11.6)	45,711	(8.7)
≥40	10,312	(3.5)	4,608	(2.3)	1,812	(4.7)	16,732	(3.2)
Total[a]	**291,458**	**(100.0)**	**197,472**	**(100.0)**	**38,399**	**(100.0)**	**527,329**	**(100.0)**
Marital status								
Married	52,441	(18.5)	20,526	(11.0)	12,381	(33.9)	85,348	(16.9)
Unmarried	230,529	(81.5)	165,968	(89.0)	24,139	(66.1)	420,636	(83.1)
Total[b]	**282,970**	**(100.0)**	**186,494**	**(100.0)**	**36,520**	**(100.0)**	**505,984**	**(100.0)**

[a]Data from 36 states, the District of Columbia, and New York City; excludes eight states (Arizona, Nebraska, Nevada, New Mexico, New York Upstate, Utah, Washington, and Wyoming) in which race was reported as unknown for >15% of women. Percentages might not add to 100.0 because of rounding.
[b]Data from 35 states, the District of Columbia, and New York City; excludes seven states (Arizona, Arkansas, Nebraska, Nevada, New Mexico, Utah, and Wyoming) in which race or marital status was reported as unknown for >15% of women.

SOURCE: Sonya B. Gamble et al., "Table 14. Reported Legal Abortions, by Known Race, Age Group, and Marital Status of Women Who Obtained an Abortion—Selected States, United States, 2005," in "Abortion Surveillance—United States, 2005," *Morbidity and Mortality Weekly Report*, vol. 57, no. SS-13, November 28, 2008, http://www.cdc.gov/mmwr/PDF/ss/ss5713.pdf (accessed May 8, 2009)

CHAPTER 4

ABORTION IN THE UNITED STATES:
A STATISTICAL STUDY

WHO COLLECTS ABORTION DATA?

There are two major sources for abortion statistics. The Centers for Disease Control and Prevention (CDC) collects abortion statistics for the U.S. government. The Guttmacher Institute, a private organization that studies reproductive health issues and strongly supports the position that abortion is an acceptable option, conducts periodic surveys of abortions performed in the United States and throughout the world.

The CDC compiles abortion information collected by state health departments, hospitals, and other medical facilities. These data come from 52 reporting areas—the 50 states, the District of Columbia, and New York City. By contrast, the Guttmacher Institute directly contacts all known abortion providers for its periodic surveys and follows up its inquiries by letter and telephone. Thus, the Guttmacher Institute data are considered to be the most accurate data available.

The total number of abortions reported to the CDC by the individual states is generally lower than that collected by the Guttmacher Institute. The CDC believes that the number of abortions performed in physicians' offices is probably underreported more often than are those done in hospitals and other medical facilities. Because most abortions in physicians' offices are usually performed in the early stages of pregnancy, the CDC's early abortion counts are likely less than the actual numbers.

HOW MANY ABORTIONS?
CDC Data

As of August 2009, the most recent CDC survey data of legally induced abortions were compiled in "Abortion Surveillance—United States, 2005" (*Morbidity and Mortality Weekly Report*, vol. 57, no. SS-13, November 28, 2008) by Sonya B. Gamble et al. of the CDC. There has been a seemingly consistent decrease in the number of abortions per year since 1996, with the exception of 2002, but it is difficult to accurately compare annual data from years 1995 to 2005

with years before 1995, because the more recent data lack information from certain states. For 2005, 820,151 abortions were reported. (See Figure 4.1 and Table 4.1.)

The CDC began its abortion surveillance in 1969, two years after Colorado became the first state to liberalize its abortion statute. From 1970 through 1982 the reported number of abortions increased each year, with the largest percentage of increase occurring between 1970 and 1971. (See Figure 4.1 and Table 4.1.) From 1976 through 1982 the annual increase slowed and then dropped slightly in 1983. From 1983 through 1990 the number of abortions increased again, with year-to-year fluctuations of 5% or less. The annual number of abortions has decreased since 1990 (the year in which the number of abortions was the highest reported by Gamble et al.).

The abortion ratio is the number of legal abortions for every 1,000 live births in a given year. In 2005 the abortion ratio was 233 legal abortions per 1,000 live births, or about 1 abortion for every 4 births. (See Table 4.1.)

The abortion ratio increased steadily from 1970 through 1980 and then remained somewhat stable for most of the next decade. Gamble et al. report that the highest ratio was 364 per 1,000 live births in 1984. (See Figure 4.1 and Table 4.1.) Since 1987 the abortion ratio has declined. The ratio for 2005 was the lowest recorded since 1973.

The overall abortion rate refers to the number of abortions performed per 1,000 women aged 15 to 44 years (the primary childbearing years). The abortion rate rose from 5 abortions per 1,000 women in 1970 to 25 per 1,000 in 1980. (See Figure 4.1 and Table 4.1.) From 1981 through 1993 the rate remained stable at 23 to 24 abortions per 1,000 women. The abortion rate declined to 21 in 1994 and remained stable at 20 to 21 abortions per 1,000 women through 1997. Since then the abortion rate declined further to 17 in 1998 and 1999, to 16 from 2000 to 2004, and to 15 in 2005 in all reporting areas.

FIGURE 4.1

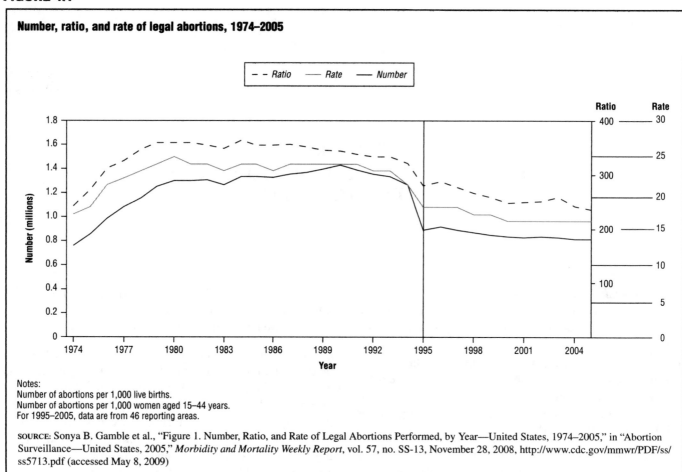

Number, ratio, and rate of legal abortions, 1974–2005

Notes:
Number of abortions per 1,000 live births.
Number of abortions per 1,000 women aged 15–44 years.
For 1995–2005, data are from 46 reporting areas.

SOURCE: Sonya B. Gamble et al., "Figure 1. Number, Ratio, and Rate of Legal Abortions Performed, by Year—United States, 1974–2005," in "Abortion Surveillance—United States, 2005," *Morbidity and Mortality Weekly Report*, vol. 57, no. SS-13, November 28, 2008, http://www.cdc.gov/mmwr/PDF/ss/ss5713.pdf (accessed May 8, 2009)

Rachel K. Jones et al. of the Guttmacher Institute suggest in "Abortion in the United States: Incidence and Access to Services, 2005" (*Perspectives on Sexual and Reproductive Health*, vol. 40, no. 1, March 2008) that the overall decreasing abortion rates may be the result of several factors:

- Changes in birth control practices, including an increased and better use of contraception.

- A decreased number of unplanned pregnancies.

- An increase in women carrying unintended pregnancy to term.

- Reduced access to abortion services.

Guttmacher Institute Data

The Guttmacher Institute started collecting data on abortion in 1973, the year of the *Roe v. Wade* (410 U.S. 113) ruling. Because the Guttmacher Institute directly surveys abortion providers, its abortion counts and rates are generally higher than those reported by the CDC. For instance, the abortion rate reported by the CDC in 1997 was nearly 9% lower than the rate Guttmacher Institute reported. (See Table 4.1 and Figure 4.2.) According to the Guttmacher Institute, the abortion rate for women aged 15

to 44 years was 21.1 in 2001 and 19.4 in 2005. By contrast, the CDC's data for 2001 to 2005 calculated the annual rate at 16 abortions per 1,000 women in the same age group, and at 15 abortions per 1,000 women from all reporting areas.

CHARACTERISTICS OF WOMEN SEEKING ABORTION

According to Gamble et al., half (49.9%) of the women who had abortions in 2005 were younger than 25 years of age. (See Table 4.2.) Most were white (55.1%), unmarried (83.1%), and in the first two months of pregnancy (62.1%). Only 1.4% were 21 or more weeks into their pregnancy.

Age

According to Gamble et al., women in the 20- to 24-year-old age group obtained the greatest proportion of abortions in 2005—one-third (32.9%) of the total. Nearly one-quarter (23.9%) were obtained by those aged 25 to 29 years, and slightly less than one-sixth (16%) were obtained by women aged 15 to 19 years. Less than 1% were obtained by women younger than 15 years. Women aged 30 to 34 years had 14.8% of abortions in 2005, and women 35 years and older had 11.9%.

TABLE 4.1

Number, ratio, and rate of legal abortions, 1970–2005

Year	Number of legal abortions	Ratio[a]	Rate[b]	Number of areas reporting Central health agency[c]	Number of areas reporting Hospitals/facilities[d]
All reporting areas					
1970	193,491	52	5	8	7
1971	485,816	137	11	19	7
1972	586,760	180	13	21	8
1973	615,831	196	14	26	26
1974	763,476	242	17	37	15
1975	854,853	272	18	39	13
1976	988,267	312	21	41	11
1977	1,079,430	325	22	46	6
1978	1,157,776	347	23	48	4
1979	1,251,921	358	24	47	5
1980	1,297,606	359	25	47	5
1981	1,300,760	358	24	46	6
1982	1,303,980	354	24	46	6
1983	1,268,987	349	23	46	6
1984	1,333,521	364	24	44	8
1985	1,328,570	354	24	44	8
1986	1,328,112	354	23	43	9
1987	1,353,671	356	24	45	7
1988	1,371,285	352	24	45	7
1989	1,396,658	346	24	45	7
1990	1,429,247	344	24	46	6
1991	1,388,937	338	24	47	5
1992	1,359,146	334	23	47	5
1993	1,330,414	333	23	47	5
1994	1,267,415	321	21	47	5
1995	1,210,883	311	20	48	4
1996	1,225,937	315[e]	21	48	4
1997	1,186,039	306	20	48	4
1998[f]	884,273	264	17	48	0
1999[f]	861,789	256	17	48	0
2000[g]	857,475	245	16	49	0
2001[g]	853,485	246	16	49	0
2002[g]	854,122	246	16	49	0
2003[h]	848,163	241	16	49	0
2004[h]	839,226	238	16	49	0
2005[i]	820,151	233	15	49	0
46 reporting areas[j]					
1995	894,086	280	18	45	1
1996	920,214	288[e]	18	45	1
1997	885,624	277	18	44	2
1998	870,184	267	17	46	0
1999	847,283	258	17	46	0
2000	836,360	249	16	46	0
2001	833,183	250	16	46	0
2002	835,122	251	16	46	0
2003	829,071	258	16	46	0
2004	819,353	241	16	46	0
2005	809,881	236	16	46	0

[a]Number of abortions per 1,000 live births.
[b]Number of abortions per 1,000 women aged 15–44 years.
[c]State health departments and the health departments of New York City and the District of Columbia.
[d]Hospitals or other medical facilities in state.
[e]Beginning in 1996, the ratio was based on births reported by the National Center for Health Statistics, Centers for Disease Control and Prevention (CDC).
[f]Without estimates for Alaska, California, New Hampshire, and Oklahoma, which did not report number of legal abortions for 1998–1999.
[g]Without estimates for Alaska, California, and New Hampshire, which did not report number of legal abortions for 1998–2002.
[h]Without estimates for California, New Hampshire, and West Virginia, which did not report number of legal abortions for 2003 and 2004.
[i]Without estimates for California, New Hampshire, and Louisiana, which did not report for 2005.
[j]Without estimates for Alaska, which did not report number of legal abortions for 1998–2002; for California and New Hampshire, which did not report for 1998–2004; for Oklahoma, which did not report for 1998–1999; for West Virginia, which did not report for 2003–2004; and for Louisiana, which did not report for 2005.

SOURCE: Sonya B. Gamble et al., "Table 2. Number, Ratio, and Rate of Legal Abortions and Source of Reporting for All Reporting Areas and for the 46 Areas That Reported in 1998–2005, by Year—United States, 1970–2005," in "Abortion Surveillance—United States, 2005," *Morbidity and Mortality Weekly Report* vol. 57, no. SS-13, November 28, 2008, http://www.cdc.gov/mmwr/PDF/ss/ss5713.pdf (accessed May 8, 2009)

As mentioned previously, in 2005 most abortions (62.1%) were early abortions—those obtained during the first eight weeks of pregnancy. (See Table 4.2.)

The percentage of early abortions had grown rather steadily over the previous 32 years, from 36.1% in 1973. As Figure 4.3 shows, the percentage of women

FIGURE 4.2

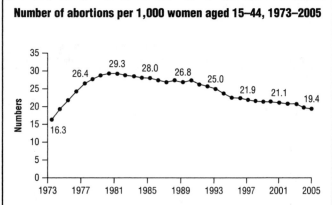

Number of abortions per 1,000 women aged 15–44, 1973–2005

SOURCE: Guttmacher Institute, Community Health Centers and Family Planning, "Number of Abortions per 1,000 Women Aged 15–44, by Year," in *In Brief: Facts on Induced Abortion in the United States*, New York: Guttmacher, July 2008, http://www.guttmacher.org/pubs/fb_induced_abortion.pdf (accessed May 9, 2009)

who obtained an early abortion in 2005 increased with age until age 30.

Gamble et al. indicate that even though less than 1% of all abortions in 2005 were obtained by teenagers younger than 15 years of age, their abortion ratio (number of abortions per 1,000 live births) was, by far, the highest. (See Figure 4.4.) Put simply, within this age group the percentage of abortions was small, but of those adolescents who got pregnant, most chose abortion.

In 2005 the abortion ratio was lowest for women aged 30 to 34 years (140 per 1,000 live births). (See Table 4.3.) Women aged 35 to 39 and 25 to 29 had the second- and third-lowest ratio of abortions to live births (168 and 187 per 1,000 live births, respectively).

Except for the 35- to 39-year-old age group, the abortion ratio increased from 1974 through the early 1980s. (See Figure 4.5.) It declined thereafter, especially for the youngest and oldest groups, with abortion ratios for the 20- to 34-year-old age group remaining relatively stable since the mid-1980s.

Race and Ethnicity

In 2005 slightly more than half (53%) of women in the United States who had an abortion were white, about one-third (35.5%) were African-American, and 7.7% were of other races. (See Table 4.4.) However, the abortion ratio for African-American women (467 per 1,000 live births) was approximately three times the ratio for white women (158 per 1,000 live births). Similarly, the abortion rate for African-American women (28 per 1,000 women) was also approximately three times the rate for white women (9 per 1,000 women).

The abortion ratio for Hispanic women in 2005 was only slightly lower than that for non-Hispanic women (205 per 1,000 versus 223 per 1,000 live births). (See Table 4.5.) However, the abortion rate for Hispanic women was considerably higher than that for non-Hispanic women (21 per 1,000 Hispanic women versus 14 per 1,000 non-Hispanic women).

For women in all age groups, with the exception of the category "some other race alone," in June 2006 fertility was higher for Hispanic women of any race at 74.4 births per 1,000 women than for Native American or Alaskan Native (67.5), African-American (58), Asian-American (54), white alone (51.9), and non-Hispanic white (49.5) women. (See Table 4.6.)

Marital Status

In 2005, as in past years, unmarried women (divorced, widowed, or never married) accounted for the greatest proportion of those who had an abortion (83.1%). (See Table 4.2.) Married women, including those who are separated from their husbands, made up only 16.9% of those who had an abortion in 2005.

Contraceptive Use before Pregnancy

Nathalie Bajos et al. examine in "Contraception at the Time of Abortion: High-Risk Time or High-Risk Women?" (*Human Reproduction*, vol. 21, no. 11, November 2006) the contraceptive use of women who had an abortion compared with women who had not had an abortion. One purpose of their study was to determine if women who had an abortion used less effective contraceptive methods than those who did not have an abortion. Bajos et al. find that women who had an abortion were less likely to use contraception than women who had not had an abortion. In addition, they were much less likely to use "the pill" or an intrauterine device (IUD) for contraception before their abortion than women who had not had an abortion. Conversely, women who had an abortion were more likely than women who had not had an abortion to use condoms and natural methods of birth control, which are less effective contraceptive methods than the pill or IUD. Study results show that the percentage of women who used these more effective means of birth control rose after an abortion.

Previous Live Births and Previous Abortions

According to Gamble et al., 53.5% of all women who had an abortion in 2005 had never obtained one before, whereas 25.2% had obtained one previous abortion and 18.8% had obtained two or more abortions. The number of previous induced abortions was unknown for 2.6% of women obtaining an abortion in that year.

WHY DO WOMEN HAVE ABORTIONS?

In *In Brief: Facts on Induced Abortion in the United States* (July 2008, http://www.guttmacher.org/pubs/fb_indu ced_abortion.html), the Guttmacher Insti-

TABLE 4.2

Characteristics of women who obtained legal abortions, selected years, 1973–2005

Characteristics	1973	1974	1975	1976	1977	1978	1979	1980	1981	1982	1983
Reported no. of legal abortions	615,831	763,476	854,853	988,267	1,079,430	1,157,776	1,251,921	1,297,606	1,300,760	1,303,980	1,268,987
Residence						Percent distribution[b]					
In-state/area	74.8	86.6	89.2	90.0	90.0	89.3	90.0	92.6	92.5	92.9	93.3
Out-of-state/area	25.2	13.4	10.8	10.0	10.0	10.7	10.0	7.4	7.5	7.1	6.7
Age (yrs)											
≤19	32.7	32.6	33.1	32.1	30.8	30.0	30.0	29.2	28.0	27.1	27.1
20–24	32.0	31.8	31.9	33.3	34.5	35.0	35.4	35.5	35.3	35.1	34.7
≥25	35.3	35.6	35.0	34.6	34.7	35.0	34.6	35.3	36.7	37.8	38.2
Race[c]											
White	72.5	69.7	67.8	66.6	66.4	67.0	68.9	69.9	69.9	68.5	67.6
Black	27.5	30.3	32.2	33.4	33.6	33.0	31.1	30.1	30.1	31.5	32.4
Other[d]	—[tt]	—	—	—	—	—	—	—	—	—	—
Ethnicity											
Hispanic	—	—	—	—	—	—	—	—	—	—	—
Non-Hispanic	—	—	—	—	—	—	—	—	—	—	—
Marital status											
Married	27.4	27.4	26.1	24.6	24.3	26.4	24.7	23.1	22.1	22.0	21.4
Unmarried	72.6	72.6	73.9	75.4	75.7	73.6	75.3	76.9	77.9	78.0	78.6
No. of live births[f]											
0	48.6	47.9	47.1	47.7	53.4	56.6	58.1	58.4	58.3	57.8	57.1
1	18.8	19.6	20.2	20.7	19.0	19.2	19.1	19.4	19.7	20.3	20.7
2	14.2	14.8	15.5	15.4	14.4	14.1	13.8	13.7	13.7	13.9	14.2
3	8.7	8.7	8.7	8.3	7.0	5.9	5.5	5.3	5.3	5.1	5.2
≥4	9.7	9.0	8.5	7.9	6.2	4.2	3.5	3.2	3.0	2.9	2.8
Type of procedure											
Curettage	88.4	89.7	91.0	92.8	93.7	94.6	95.0	95.5	96.1	96.5	96.8
Suction curettage	74.9	77.4	82.6	82.6	90.7	90.2	91.3	89.8	90.4	90.7	91.1
Sharp curettage	13.5	12.3	8.4	10.2	3.0	4.4	3.7	5.7	5.7	5.8	5.7
Intrauterine instillation	10.3	7.8	6.2	6.0	5.4	3.9	3.3	3.1	2.8	2.5	2.1
Hysterotomy/ hysterectomy[g]	0.7	0.6	0.4	0.3	0.2	0.1	0.1	0.1	0.1	0.0	0.0
Other[g]	0.6	1.9	2.4	0.9	0.7	1.4	1.6	1.3	1.0	1.0	1.1
Weeks of gestation											
≤8	36.1	42.6	44.6	47.0	51.1	52.2	52.1	51.7	51.2	50.6	49.7
≤6	—	—	—	—	—	—	—	—	—	—	—
7	—	—	—	—	—	—	—	—	—	—	—
8	—	—	—	—	—	—	—	—	—	—	—
9–10	29.4	28.7	28.4	28.1	27.2	26.9	26.9	26.2	26.8	26.7	26.8
11–12	17.9	15.4	14.9	14.4	13.1	12.3	12.5	12.2	12.1	12.4	12.8
13–15	6.9	5.5	5.0	4.5	3.4	4.0	4.2	5.1	5.2	5.3	5.8
16–20	8.0	6.6	6.1	5.1	4.3	3.7	3.4	3.9	3.7	3.9	3.9
≥21	1.7	1.2	1.0	0.9	0.9	0.9	0.9	0.9	1.0	1.1	1.0

	1984	1985	1986	1987	1988	1989	1990	1991	1992	1993	1994
Reported no. of legal abortions	1,333,521	1,328,570	1,328,112	1,353,671	1,371,285	1,396,658	1,429,247	1,388,937	1,359,146	1,330,414	1,267,415
Residence						Percent distribution[b]					
In-state/area	92.0	92.4	92.4	91.7	91.4	91.0	91.8	91.7	92.1	91.4	91.5
Out-of-state/area	8.0	7.6	7.6	8.3	8.6	9.0	8.2	8.3	7.9	8.6	8.5
Age (yrs)											
≤19	26.4	26.3	25.3	25.8	25.3	24.2	22.4	21.0	20.1	20.0	20.2
20–24	35.3	34.7	34.0	33.4	32.8	32.6	33.2	34.4	34.5	34.4	33.5
≥25	38.3	39.0	40.7	40.8	41.9	43.2	44.4	44.6	45.4	45.6	46.3

tute notes that each year almost half of all pregnancies in the United States are unplanned. Four out of 10 women with unplanned pregnancies obtain an abortion, resulting in approximately 22% of all pregnancies (with the exception of miscarriages) ending in abortion. The most common reasons that women give for choosing abortion are:

- Three-quarters say that having a baby would interfere with their school, work, or other responsibilities, including responsibilities to other individuals.

- Three-quarters say they cannot afford a child.

- Half say they do not want to be a single parent or are having problems with their husband or partner.

TABLE 4.2

Characteristics of women who obtained legal abortions, selected years, 1973–2005 [CONTINUED]

Characteristics	1984	1985	1986	1987	1988	1989	1990	1991	1992	1993	1994
Race[c]											
White	67.4	66.7	67.0	66.4	64.4	64.2	64.8	63.9	61.6	60.9	60.6
Black	32.6	29.8	28.7	29.3	31.1	31.2	31.9	32.5	33.9	34.9	34.7
Other[d]	—[e]	3.5	4.3	4.3	4.5	4.6	3.3	3.6	4.5	4.2	4.7
Ethnicity											
Hispanic	—	—	—	—	—	—	11.4	13.2	15.0	14.5	14.1
Non-Hispanic	—	—	—	—	—	—	88.6	86.8	85.0	85.5	85.9
Marital status											
Married	20.5	19.3	20.2	20.8	20.3	20.1	21.7	21.4	20.8	20.4	19.9
Unmarried	79.5	80.7	79.8	79.2	79.7	79.9	78.3	78.6	79.2	79.6	80.1
No. of live births[f]											
0	57.0	56.3	55.1	53.6	52.4	52.2	49.1	47.8	45.9	46.5	46.2
1	20.9	21.6	22.1	22.8	23.4	23.6	24.4	25.3	25.9	25.8	25.9
2	14.4	14.5	14.9	15.5	16.0	15.9	17.0	17.5	18.0	17.8	17.8
3	5.1	5.1	5.3	5.5	5.6	5.7	6.1	6.4	6.7	6.6	6.7
≥4	2.6	2.5	2.6	2.6	2.6	2.6	3.4	3.0	3.5	3.3	3.4
Type of procedure											
Curettage	96.8	97.5	97.0	97.2	98.6	98.8	98.9	99.0	98.9	99.1	99.1
Suction curettage	93.1	94.6	94.5	93.4	95.1	97.1	97.2	96.5	95.7	95.5	96.5
Sharp curettage	3.7	2.9	2.5	3.8	3.5	1.7	1.7	2.5	3.2	3.6	2.6
Intrauterine instillation	1.9	1.7	1.4	1.3	1.1	0.9	0.8	0.6	0.7	0.6	0.5
Other[g]	1.3	0.8	1.6	1.5	0.3	0.3	0.3	0.4	0.4	0.3	0.4
Weeks of gestation											
≤8	50.5	50.3	51.0	50.4	48.7	49.8	51.6	52.4	52.1	52.3	53.7
≤6	—	—	—	—	—	—	—	—	14.3[h]	14.7[i]	15.7[j]
7	—	—	—	—	—	—	—	—	15.6[h,k]	16.2[i]	16.5[j]
8	—	—	—	—	—	—	—	—	22.2[h]	21.6[i]	21.6
9–10	26.4	26.6	25.8	26.0	26.4	25.8	25.3	25.1	24.2	24.4	23.5
11–12	12.6	12.5	12.2	12.4	12.7	12.6	11.7	11.5	12.1	11.6	10.9
13–15	5.8	5.9	6.1	6.2	6.6	6.6	6.4	6.1	6.0	6.3	6.3
16–20	3.9	3.9	4.1	4.2	4.5	4.2	4.0	3.8	4.2	4.1	4.3
≥21	0.8	0.8	0.8	0.8	1.1	1.0	1.0	1.1	1.4	1.3	1.3

Characteristics	1995	1996	1997	1998	1999	2000	2001	2002	2003	2004	2005
Reported no. of legal abortions	1,210,883	1,225,937	1,186,039	884,273	861,789	857,475	853,485	854,122	848,163	839,226	820,151
Reported no. of legal abortions excluding AK, CA, LA, H, OK, WV[a]	905,577	932,079	897,363	881,535	859,291	847,744	844,115	845,573	839,713	830,577	809,881
Residence					Percent distribution[b]						
In-state/area	91.5	91.7	91.8	91.4	91.2	91.3	91.3	91.2	91.5	92.1	91.7
Out-of-state/area	8.5	8.3	8.2	8.6	8.8	8.7	8.7	8.8	8.5	7.9	8.3
Age (yrs)											
≤19	20.1	20.3	20.1	19.8	19.2	18.8	18.1	17.5	17.4	17.4	17.1
20–24	32.5	31.8	31.7	31.8	32.2	32.8	33.4	33.4	33.5	32.8	32.8
≥25	47.4	47.9	48.2	48.4	48.6	48.4	48.5	49.1	49.1	49.8	50.1
Race[c]											
White	59.6	59.1	58.4	58.7	56.2	56.6	55.4	55.5	55.0	54.1	55.1
Black	35.0	35.3	35.9	35.4	37.3	36.3	36.6	36.6	37.1	38.2	36.9
Other**	5.4	5.6	5.7	5.9	6.5	7.1	8.0	7.9	7.9	7.7	8.0
Ethnicity											
Hispanic	15.1	15.7	15.6	17.1	17.3	17.2	17.1	18.2	18.1	21.5	20.3
Non-Hispanic	84.9	84.3	84.4	82.9	82.7	82.8	82.9	81.8	81.9	78.5	79.7

OUT-OF-STATE VERSUS IN-STATE ABORTIONS

Table 4.7 presents abortion data by the state of residence of women obtaining abortions in 2005, the number of abortions that occurred in that state in that year, and the percent of legal abortions obtained by out-of-state residents. In 2005, as in previous years, the largest reported numbers of abortions were performed in New York (124,849), Florida (92,513), and Texas (77,108).

The fewest abortions in 2005 were performed in South Dakota (805) and Idaho (1,099).

Abortion rates by state of occurrence do not necessarily reflect the number of abortions obtained by residents. Many women travel out of state for abortions because of a lack of providers or because of restrictive laws, such as required parental notification and consent

TABLE 4.2

Characteristics of women who obtained legal abortions, selected years, 1973–2005 [CONTINUED]

Characteristics	1995	1996	1997	1998	1999	2000	2001	2002	2003	2004	2005
Marital status											
Married	19.7	19.6	19.0	18.9	19.2	18.7	18.4	18.1	17.9	17.2	16.9
Unmarried	80.3	80.4	81.0	81.1	80.8	81.3	81.6	81.9	82.1	82.8	83.1
No. of live births[f]											
0	45.2	44.2	42.2	41.1	40.6	40.0	45.2	40.0	40.2	41.0	41.0
1	26.5	26.8	27.6	27.9	27.9	27.7	25.2	27.3	27.1	26.8	26.6
2	18.0	18.4	19.1	19.6	19.8	20.1	18.4	20.2	20.1	19.7	19.8
3	6.8	7.0	7.3	7.5	7.7	7.9	7.3	8.2	8.2	8.1	8.2
≥4	3.5	3.6	3.8	3.9	4.0	4.3	3.9	4.3	4.4	4.5	4.4
Type of procedure											
Curettage	98.9	98.8	98.3	98.3	98.2	97.9	95.5	92.4	90.0	88.6	87.1
Suction curettage	96.6	96.5	97.3	96.8	96.0	95.6	92.8	90.0	88.3	87.4	86.2
Sharp curettage	2.3	2.3	1.0	1.5	2.2	2.3	2.7	2.4	1.7	1.2	0.9
Intrauterine instillation	0.5	0.4	0.4	0.3	0.2	0.4	0.6	0.8	0.9	0.6	0.8
Other[g]	0.6	0.8	1.3	1.4	1.6	1.7	3.9	6.8	9.1	10.8	12.1
Weeks of gestation											
≤8	54.0	54.6	55.4	55.7	57.6	58.1	59.1	60.5	60.5	61.4	62.1
≤6	15.7[i]	16.3[j]	17.6[l]	19.2[m]	21.9[n]	23.3[n]	24.9[l]	27.1[m]	26.9[m]	28.1[o]	29.6[p]
7	17.1[i]	17.4[j]	18.1[l]	17.8[m]	17.6[n]	17.8[n]	17.9[l]	17.8[m]	18.1[m]	18.1[o]	18.1[p]
8	21.2[i]	21.0[j]	19.6[l]	18.8[m]	18.2[n]	17.1[n]	16.4[l]	15.6[m]	15.5[m]	15.2[o]	14.6[p]
9–10	23.1	22.6	22.0	21.5	20.2	19.8	19.0	18.4	18.0	17.6	17.1
11–12	10.9	11.0	10.7	10.9	10.2	10.2	10.0	9.6	9.7	9.3	9.3
13–15	6.3	6.0	6.2	6.4	6.2	6.2	6.2	6.0	6.2	6.3	6.3
16–20	4.3	4.3	4.3	4.1	4.3	4.3	4.3	4.1	4.2	4.0	3.8
≥21	1.4	1.5	1.4	1.4	1.5	1.4	1.4	1.4	1.4	1.4	1.4

[a]With two exceptions (i.e., Louisiana and West Virginia), no characteristics were available for the excluded states in years before 1998. Alaska data were available for 2004; Oklahoma for 2000–2003; West Virginia for 1995–2002; and Louisiana data not available for 2005.

[b]Based on known values in data from all areas reporting a given characteristic with ≤15% unknowns. The number of areas adequately reporting a given characteristic varied. For 2005, the number of areas included for residence was 47; age, 48; race, 38; ethnicity, 30; marital status, 43; number of previous live births, 40; number of previous induced abortions, 42; type of procedure, 45; and weeks of gestation, 42. Early numbers might differ (by 0.1%) from numbers previously published because of adjusting percentages to total 100.0%.

[c]Black race reported as black and other races through 1984. For 1990–1997, one state included "other" races with blacks.

[d]Includes all other races.

[e]Not available.

[f]For 1973–1977, data indicate number of living children.

[g]Hysterotomy and hysterectomy included in "other" beginning in 1984. "Other" also included procedures reported as "other" and medical (nonsurgical) procedures beginning in 1996. For 2005, the number of medical (nonsurgical) procedures reported was 66,487.

[h]Data for 36 of 39 areas reporting weeks of gestation.

[i]Data for 38 of 41 areas reporting weeks of gestation.

[j]Data for 38 of 40 areas reporting weeks of gestation.

[k]Data for 37 of 40 areas reporting weeks of gestation.

[l]Data for 40 of 42 areas reporting weeks of gestation.

[m]Data for 42 of 44 areas reporting weeks of gestation.

[n]Data for 41 of 43 areas reporting weeks of gestation.

[o]Data for 41 of 44 areas reporting weeks of gestation.

[p]Data for 39 of 40 areas reporting weeks of gestation.

SOURCE: Sonya B. Gamble et al., "Table 1. Characteristics of Women Who Obtained Legal Abortions—United States, 1973–2005," in "Abortion Surveillance—United States, 2005," *Morbidity and Mortality Weekly Report*, vol. 57, no. SS-13, November 28, 2008, http://www.cdc.gov/mmwr/PDF/ss/ss5713.pdf (accessed May 8, 2009)

(see Chapters 2, 11, and 12), waiting periods, and required counseling that involves more than one visit to the provider. Figure 4.6 lists the states that require a waiting period before an abortion can be obtained and those that require biased counseling.

Biased counseling means that the woman is counseled in a way that promotes choices other than abortion. Theodore J. Joyce et al. of the Guttmacher Institute find in *The Impact of State Mandatory Counseling and Waiting Period Laws on Abortion: A Literature Review* (April 2009, http://www.guttmacher.org/pubs/MandatoryCounseling.pdf) that if the counseling was delivered over the Internet, by mail, or by telephone it made no measurable impact on choice but might postpone the abortion. If the

counseling required an additional in-person visit before the procedure, it, too, made no impact on choice but placed extra burdens on women regarding the costs of childcare, time from work, or extra travel.

For women obtaining an abortion in 2005 whose state of residence was reported, 91.7% had their abortion in the state where they lived. (See Table 4.7.) That is, 8.3% of reported abortions were obtained by out-of-state residents, with a wide range from 0.3% in Alaska to 50.7% in the District of Columbia.

AVAILABILITY OF ABORTION PROVIDERS

Jones et al. note that in 2005, 87% of U.S. counties had no abortion providers, up from 77% in 1978. (See Table 4.8.)

FIGURE 4.3

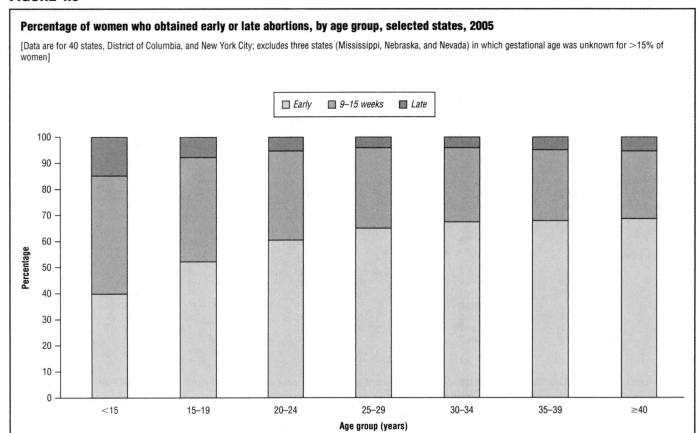

Percentage of women who obtained early or late abortions, by age group, selected states, 2005

[Data are for 40 states, District of Columbia, and New York City; excludes three states (Mississippi, Nebraska, and Nevada) in which gestational age was unknown for >15% of women]

Notes: Percentage based on total known weeks of gestation. Early is defined as less than or equal to 8 weeks' gestation. Late is defined as greater than or equal to 16 weeks' gestation.

SOURCE: Sonya B. Gamble et al., "Figure 4. Percentage of Women Who Obtained Early or Late Abortions, by Age Group—Selected States, United States, 2005," in "Abortion Surveillance—United States, 2005," *Morbidity and Mortality Weekly Report*, vol. 57, no. SS-13, November 28, 2008, http://www.cdc.gov/mmwr/PDF/ss/ss5713.pdf (accessed May 8, 2009)

Slightly over one-third (35%) of women of childbearing age (15 to 44 years old) lived in counties with no known providers. The states with the highest percentage of women in counties with no abortion providers were Wyoming (96%), Mississippi (91%), West Virginia (84%), Arkansas (79%), South Dakota (78%), Kentucky (77%), North Dakota (75%), and South Carolina (72%). Jones et al. indicate that over two-thirds (69%) of the country's metropolitan areas lacked abortion services, as did 97% of nonmetropolitan counties. For many women in rural areas, obtaining an abortion entailed traveling hundreds of miles from their residence.

Table 4.8 also shows that the number of abortion providers in the United States had decreased from 2,380 in 1992 to 1,787 in 2005, a decrease of 25%. During this same period three states had an increase in the number of providers (Connecticut [43 to 52], South Dakota [1 to 2], and Delaware [8 to 9]), two states had no change in the number of providers (North Dakota [1] and Utah [6]), and forty-five states and the District of Columbia saw a decrease.

Jones et al. suggest that the use of medical abortion (abortion pills) "has become more integrated into abor-

tion services." The researchers note that this type of abortion service requires less training and equipment, and is more easily provided by clinics and physician's offices than are surgical abortions. Furthermore, Jones et al. report that of the 1,787 providers in 2005, 45% were clinics, 34% were hospitals, and 21% were physician's offices. However, 95% of abortions were performed in clinics and physician's offices, and only 5% were performed in hospitals.

Abortion Medical Training

In "Abortion Training in United States Obstetrics and Gynecology Residency Programs" (*Obstetrics and Gynecology*, vol. 108, no. 2, August 2006), Katherine L. Eastwood et al. discuss the questionnaire they designed to identify characteristics of the programs that provide abortion training, to verify the numbers of procedures learned in these programs, and to determine the availability of abortion training. The questionnaire was mailed to directors of physician residency programs in the United States.

Eastwood et al. reveal that larger residency programs were more likely than smaller residency programs to

FIGURE 4.4

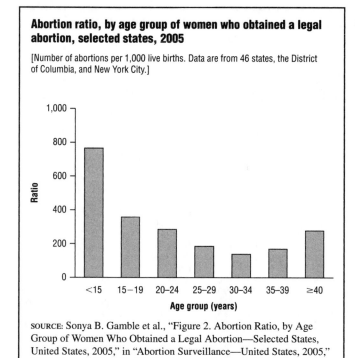

Abortion ratio, by age group of women who obtained a legal abortion, selected states, 2005

[Number of abortions per 1,000 live births. Data are from 46 states, the District of Columbia, and New York City.]

SOURCE: Sonya B. Gamble et al., "Figure 2. Abortion Ratio, by Age Group of Women Who Obtained a Legal Abortion—Selected States, United States, 2005," in "Abortion Surveillance—United States, 2005," *Morbidity and Mortality Weekly Report*, vol. 57, no. SS-13, November 28, 2008, http://www.cdc.gov/mmwr/PDF/ss/ss5713.pdf (accessed May 8, 2009)

rics and gynecology in various techniques of elective abortion and the management of complications associated with the various procedures used."

The American Academy of Family Physicians (AAFP) holds in "Reproductive Decisions" (2009, http://www.aafp.org/online/en/home/policy/policies/r/reproductdecisions.html) that physicians should work toward decreasing the number of unwanted pregnancies by providing patient education and counseling. If a woman becomes pregnant, the AAFP believes that it is her legal right to make reproductive decisions. However, the AAFP also states that "no physician shall be compelled to perform any act which violates his/her good judgment or personally held moral principles." Furthermore, the AAFP states that abortion should be performed only by a "duly-licensed physician in conformance with standards of good medical practice as determined by the laws and regulations governing the practice of medicine in that locale."

In "Training in Reproductive Decisions" (2009, http://www.aafp.org/online/en/home/policy/policies/r/trainreproductdecisions.html), the AAFP recommends that medical students and family practice residents be trained in counseling and referral skills regarding all options available to pregnant women. This would include contraceptive methods (including sterilization), adoption services, abortion services, financial assistance, and other assistance available to the mother or the child. It also calls for providing opportunities for residents to learn skills they think will be part of their future practices.

include abortion techniques in physician routine training, rather than include it as optional training. Nearly three-quarters of large programs included routine training in abortion techniques, whereas slightly less than half of medium and small programs did. Only 8% to 14% of all programs excluded abortion training altogether. Catholic-affiliated (12%) and Protestant-affiliated (33%) programs were less likely than other types of programs (nonreligious, 55%; Jewish, 58%; and other programs, 89%) to offer routine training in abortion techniques.

Using data gathered by the Guttmacher Institute along with their own survey data, Eastman et al. determine trends in abortion training in residency programs from 1985 through 2004. Routine training increased from 23% in 1985 to 51% in 2004, whereas optional training decreased from 50% in 1985 to 39% in 2004. The incidence of no training decreased as well, from 28% in 1985 to 10% in 2004.

Eastwood et al. note that physicians' training in abortion techniques is extremely important because abortion is one of the most common medical procedures performed in the United States. They state, "Women seeking such care [abortions], the majority of whom are poor, require access to treatment by well-qualified providers, and if complications arise, need appropriate and compassionate care. Continued abortion provision necessitates ongoing training of new providers, a task that can largely be accomplished by educating residents in obstet-

HOW MUCH DOES AN ABORTION COST?

Abortion fees vary, depending on the stage of pregnancy, where the abortion is performed, the kind of procedure, and the anesthetic used. There may be other costs if the abortion cannot be done locally. Expenses might include travel costs, costs for overnight stays, or lost wages in states that require a waiting period between counseling and the abortion.

Jones et al. indicate that in 2006 the mean (average) charge for an abortion performed at 10 weeks of pregnancy in an abortion clinic was $415. The fees generally covered the examination, laboratory tests, local anesthesia, the procedure, and the follow-up visit. In nonspecialized clinics the average cost was $463, and in physician's offices was $705.

The cost of an abortion increases after the first trimester because the procedure becomes more complex, takes more time, and requires the provider to have a higher level of training. In 2006 the mean charge for an abortion performed at 20 weeks of pregnancy in an abortion clinic was $1,432, in a nonspecialized clinic was $1,337, and in a physician's office was $1,245.

TABLE 4.3

Reported legal abortions, by age group of women who obtained an abortion and state of occurrence, selected states, 2005

[Data from 46 states, the District of Columbia, and New York City]

	Age group (years)																
	<15		15–19		20–24		25–29		30–34		35–39		≥40		Unknown		Total	
State/area	No.	(%)	No.	(%)	No.	(%)	No.	(%)	No.	(%)	No.	(%)	No.	(%)	No.	(%)	No.	(%)[a]
Alabama	97	(0.9)	1,992	(17.8)	3,917	(34.9)	2,575	(23.0)	1,577	(14.1)	788	(7.0)	260	(2.3)	5	(0.0)	11,211	(100.0)
Alaska	12	(0.6)	374	(19.1)	679	(34.7)	421	(21.5)	242	(12.4)	146	(7.5)	77	(3.9)	4	(0.2)	1,955	(100.0)
Arizona	55	(0.5)	1,868	(17.4)	3,582	(33.4)	2,267	(21.1)	1,372	(12.8)	822	(7.7)	317	(3.0)	440	(4.1)	10,723	(100.0)
Arkansas	45	(1.0)	740	(15.8)	1,588	(33.8)	1,070	(22.8)	727	(15.5)	395	(8.4)	129	(2.7)	1	(0.0)	4,695	(100.0)
Colorado	79	(0.7)	2,077	(17.8)	3,911	(33.5)	2,475	(21.2)	1,614	(13.8)	1,038	(8.9)	447	(3.8)	41	(0.4)	11,682	(100.0)
Connecticut	87	(0.7)	2,216	(18.3)	3,942	(32.6)	2,749	(22.7)	1,602	(13.2)	1,019	(8.4)	340	(2.8)	155	(1.3)	12,110	(100.0)
Delaware[b]	20	(0.7)	555	(18.3)	1,082	(35.7)	685	(22.6)	371	(12.2)	242	(8.0)	76	(2.5)	0	(0.0)	3,031	(100.0)
Dist. of Columbia	25	(1.0)	433	(17.2)	785	(31.2)	628	(24.9)	368	(14.6)	204	(8.1)	75	(3.0)	0	(0.0)	2,518	(100.0)
Georgia	246	(0.8)	4,656	(14.7)	10,048	(31.7)	7,927	(25.0)	5,103	(16.1)	2,796	(8.8)	904	(2.9)	0	(0.0)	31,680	(100.0)
Hawaii	19	(0.5)	678	(19.1)	1,173	(33.1)	771	(21.7)	472	(13.3)	303	(8.5)	127	(3.6)	5	(0.1)	3,548	(100.0)
Idaho[b]	6	(0.5)	208	(18.9)	330	(30.0)	267	(24.3)	138	(12.6)	107	(9.7)	43	(3.9)	0	(0.0)	1,099	(100.0)
Illinois[b,c]	237	(0.6)	6,672	(17.5)	11,753	(30.8)	9,103	(23.9)	5,810	(15.2)	3,400	(8.9)	1,178	(3.1)	0	(0.0)	38,153	(100.0)
Indiana	41	(0.4)	1,716	(16.1)	3,676	(34.4)	2,476	(23.2)	1,519	(14.2)	844	(7.9)	297	(2.8)	117	(1.1)	10,686	(100.0)
Iowa	32	(0.5)	1,055	(17.9)	2,051	(34.9)	1,311	(22.3)	779	(13.2)	455	(7.7)	179	(3.0)	19	(0.3)	5,881	(100.0)
Kansas	56	(0.5)	1,771	(16.9)	3,614	(34.5)	2,457	(23.5)	1,419	(13.6)	842	(8.0)	303	(2.9)	0	(0.0)	10,462	(100.0)
Kentucky	23	(0.6)	543	(14.4)	1,276	(33.8)	863	(22.9)	554	(14.7)	363	(9.6)	124	(3.3)	30	(0.8)	3,776	(100.0)
Maine	12	(0.5)	510	(19.2)	863	(32.5)	569	(21.4)	329	(12.4)	201	(7.6)	91	(3.4)	78	(2.9)	2,653	(100.0)
Maryland[b]	43	(0.5)	1,276	(13.9)	2,900	(31.5)	2,370	(25.8)	1,455	(15.8)	877	(9.5)	277	(3.0)	0	(0.0)	9,198	(100.0)
Massachusetts	100	(0.4)	3,709	(15.9)	7,547	(32.4)	5,136	(22.1)	3,366	(14.5)	2,455	(10.6)	932	(4.0)	23	(0.1)	23,268	(100.0)
Michigan	175	(0.7)	4,497	(17.8)	8,259	(32.8)	5,676	(22.5)	3,697	(14.7)	2,174	(8.6)	712	(2.8)	19	(0.1)	25,209	(100.0)
Minnesota	50	(0.4)	1,975	(14.8)	4,569	(34.2)	3,198	(23.9)	1,905	(14.3)	1,229	(9.2)	436	(3.3)	0	(0.0)	13,362	(100.0)
Mississippi	35	(1.2)	469	(15.4)	1,144	(37.6)	760	(25.0)	397	(13.1)	162	(5.3)	70	(2.3)	4	(0.1)	3,041	(100.0)
Missouri	55	(0.7)	1,230	(15.4)	2,709	(34.0)	1,824	(22.9)	1,142	(14.3)	721	(9.0)	296	(3.7)	0	(0.0)	7,977	(100.0)
Montana	7	(0.3)	467	(21.7)	737	(34.2)	412	(19.1)	289	(13.4)	170	(7.9)	72	(3.3)	1	(0.0)	2,155	(100.0)
Nebraska	17	(0.5)	532	(16.8)	1,105	(34.8)	706	(22.3)	427	(13.5)	279	(8.8)	107	(3.4)	0	(0.0)	3,173	(100.0)
Nevada	36	(0.3)	1,696	(16.1)	3,155	(29.9)	2,349	(22.2)	1,545	(14.6)	998	(9.4)	365	(3.5)	421	(4.0)	10,565	(100.0)
New Jersey[d]	184	(0.6)	5,593	(17.9)	9,591	(30.7)	7,650	(24.5)	4,460	(14.3)	2,692	(8.8)	1,055	(3.4)	5	(0.0)	31,230	(100.0)
New Mexico	32	(0.5)	1,126	(19.0)	2,099	(35.4)	1,306	(22.0)	702	(11.8)	403	(6.8)	190	(3.2)	76	(1.3)	5,934	(100.0)
New York	751	(0.6)	22,012	(17.6)	37,806	(30.3)	29,031	(23.3)	18,601	(14.9)	11,741	(9.4)	4,497	(3.6)	410	(0.3)	124,849	(100.0)
City	524	(0.6)	14,838	(16.7)	25,905	(29.1)	21,483	(24.2)	14,036	(15.8)	8,594	(9.7)	3,156	(3.6)	355	(0.4)	88,891	(100.0)
State	227	(0.6)	7,174	(20.0)	11,901	(33.1)	7,548	(21.0)	4,565	(12.7)	3,147	(8.8)	1,341	(3.7)	55	(0.2)	35,958	(100.0)
North Carolina	235	(0.7)	4,815	(14.9)	10,533	(32.6)	7,595	(23.5)	4,678	(14.5)	2,496	(7.7)	834	(2.6)	1,149	(3.6)	32,335	(100.0)
North Dakota[e]	—	—	255	(20.7)	447	(36.3)	262	(21.3)	137	(11.1)	90	(7.3)	38	(3.1)	—	—	1,231	(100.0)
Ohio	240	(0.7)	5,817	(17.0)	11,502	(33.7)	7,968	(23.3)	4,687	(13.7)	2,708	(7.9)	947	(2.8)	259	(0.8)	34,128	(100.0)
Oklahoma	34	(0.5)	1,099	(16.5)	2,312	(34.8)	1,524	(22.9)	930	(14.0)	523	(7.9)	181	(2.7)	38	(0.6)	6,641	(100.0)
Oregon	48	(0.4)	1,899	(16.4)	3,759	(32.4)	2,672	(23.0)	1,686	(14.5)	1,061	(9.1)	449	(3.9)	28	(0.2)	11,602	(100.0)
Pennsylvania	226	(0.6)	5,760	(16.5)	11,714	(33.6)	7,903	(22.6)	5,028	(14.4)	3,105	(8.9)	1,172	(3.4)	1	(0.0)	34,909	(100.0)
Rhode Island	19	(0.4)	868	(17.0)	1,712	(33.6)	1,132	(22.2)	717	(14.1)	398	(7.8)	185	(3.6)	60	(1.2)	5,091	(100.0)
South Carolina	43	(0.6)	1,218	(18.1)	2,132	(31.7)	1,509	(22.5)	1,044	(15.5)	571	(8.5)	199	(3.0)	0	(0.0)	6,716	(100.0)
South Dakota[e]	—	—	135	(16.8)	281	(34.9)	179	(22.2)	116	(14.4)	68	(8.4)	25	(3.1)	—	—	805	(100.0)
Tennessee	126	(0.8)	2,495	(15.4)	5,548	(34.3)	3,918	(24.2)	2,381	(14.7)	1,284	(7.9)	373	(2.3)	53	(0.3)	16,178	(100.0)
Texas	208	(0.3)	9,911	(12.9)	26,264	(34.1)	19,654	(25.5)	11,790	(15.3)	6,720	(8.7)	2,558	(3.3)	3	(0.0)	77,108	(100.0)
Utah	14	(0.4)	569	(16.0)	1,139	(32.0)	842	(23.7)	495	(13.9)	332	(9.3)	103	(2.9)	62	(1.7)	3,556	(100.0)
Vermont	7	(0.4)	326	(20.1)	570	(35.2)	342	(21.1)	176	(10.9)	130	(8.0)	68	(4.2)	1	(0.1)	1,620	(100.0)
Virginia	118	(0.4)	3,938	(15.0)	8,980	(34.1)	6,198	(23.6)	3,767	(14.3)	2,283	(8.7)	875	(3.3)	150	(0.6)	26,309	(100.0)

WHEN ARE ABORTIONS PERFORMED?

Table 4.2 (from Gamble et al.) shows that in 2005 close to two-thirds (62.1%) of abortions were performed at eight weeks or less of development. Figure 4.7 (from the Guttmacher Institute) shows that in 2004 about the same percentage (61.3%) of abortions were performed at nine weeks or less. Both sources also show that fewer than 5% of abortions were performed after 15 weeks of gestation.

As in past years, in 2005 a larger percentage of women aged 19 years and younger obtained abortions later in pregnancy than did older women. (See Table 4.9.) In addition, a larger percentage of African-American women obtained abortions later in pregnancy (between nine and 15 weeks) than did white women and women of other races.

White women had the lowest percentage of abortions at 16 to 20 weeks or later in their pregnancies.

ABORTION METHODS

Abortion can be performed using surgical or medical (drug) methods. Surgical abortions are performed in a few ways, depending on the length of the pregnancy, and have been available in the United States for decades. Medical abortions, which are performed with the drugs mifepristone and misoprostol, have been available in this country only since the U.S. Food and Drug Administration approval of mifepristone in 2000. Mifepristone is the drug that terminates the pregnancy and misoprostol helps evacuate the uterus. Methods of abortion are described in

TABLE 4.3

Reported legal abortions, by age group of women who obtained an abortion and state of occurrence, selected states, 2005 [CONTINUED]

[Data from 46 states, the District of Columbia, and New York City]

| State/area | Age group (years) | | | | | | | | | | | | | | | | Total | |
| | <15 | | 15–19 | | 20–24 | | 25–29 | | 30–34 | | 35–39 | | ≥40 | | Unknown | | | |
	No.	(%)	No.	(%)	No.	(%)	No.	(%)	No.	(%)	No.	(%)	No.	(%)	No.	(%)	No.	(%)[a]
Washington	132	(0.5)	4,404	(18.3)	8,055	(33.4)	5,294	(22.0)	3,277	(13.6)	2,106	(8.7)	833	(3.5)	7	(0.0)	24,108	(100.0)
West Virginia	5	(0.3)	303	(18.1)	567	(33.9)	413	(24.7)	233	(13.9)	114	(6.8)	37	(2.2)	2	(0.1)	1,674	(100.0)
Wisconsin[b]	53	(0.6)	1,673	(17.5)	3,341	(34.9)	2,083	(21.8)	1,309	(13.7)	791	(8.3)	316	(3.3)	0	(0.0)	9,566	(100.0)
Wyoming[e]	—	—	—	—	—	—	—	—	—	—	—	—	—	—	—	—	14	(100.0)
Total[f]	**4,085**	**(0.6)**	**118,131**	**(16.4)**	**234,747**	**(32.6)**	**168,520**	**(23.4)**	**104,433**	**(14.5)**	**62,646**	**(8.7)**	**23,169**	**(3.2)**	**3,667**	**(0.5)**	**719,415**	**(100.0)**
Abortion ratio[g]	764		358		283		187		140		168		278				219	
Abortion rate[h]	1		14		29		22		13		8		3				14	

[a]Percentages might not add to 100.0 because of rounding.
[b]Includes residents only.
[c]Number of procedures for the ≥45 years age group are included with those of the unknown age group because data were not available separately (data have been <0.2% in previous years). The category of ≥40 years, therefore, represents the 40–44 years group for Illinois.
[d]Numbers do not include private physicians' procedures.
[e]Cell details not displayed because of small numbers.
[f]Totals do not include small numbers.
[g]Calculated as the number of legal abortions obtained by women in a given age group per 1,000 live births to women in the same age group for these states. For each state, data for women of unknown age were distributed according to the known age distribution for that state.
[h]Calculated as the number of legal abortions obtained by women in a given age group per 1,000 women in the same age group for these states. Women aged 13–14 years were used for the denominator for the <15 years age group, women aged 40–44 years were used for the denominator for the ≥40 years age group, and women aged 15–44 years were used for the denominator for the total rate. For each state, data for women of unknown age were distributed according to the known age distribution for that state.

SOURCE: Sonya B. Gamble et al., "Table 4. Reported Legal Abortions, by Age Group of Women Who Obtained an Abortion and State of Occurrence—Selected States, United States, 2005," in "Abortion Surveillance—United States, 2005," *Morbidity and Mortality Weekly Report*, vol. 57, no. SS-13, November 28, 2008, http://www.cdc.gov/mmwr/PDF/ss/ss5713.pdf (accessed May 8, 2009)

FIGURE 4.5

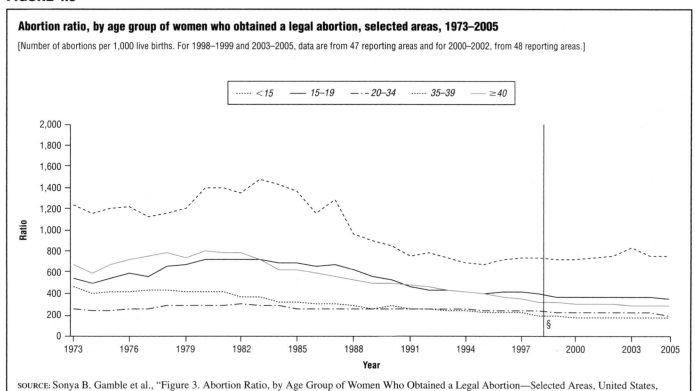

Abortion ratio, by age group of women who obtained a legal abortion, selected areas, 1973–2005

[Number of abortions per 1,000 live births. For 1998–1999 and 2003–2005, data are from 47 reporting areas and for 2000–2002, from 48 reporting areas.]

SOURCE: Sonya B. Gamble et al., "Figure 3. Abortion Ratio, by Age Group of Women Who Obtained a Legal Abortion—Selected Areas, United States, 1973–2005," in "Abortion Surveillance—United States, 2005," *Morbidity and Mortality Weekly Report*, vol. 57, no. SS-13, November 28, 2008, http://www.cdc.gov/mmwr/PDF/ss/ss5713.pdf (accessed May 8, 2009)

more detail in Table 1.1 in Chapter 1. The type of abortion a woman obtains depends on her choice of method, her health, and the gestational age of the fetus.

Percentages of Methods Used

The CDC has collected data since 1973 on the types of procedures used each year to perform abortions and has

TABLE 4.4

Legal abortions, by race of women and state of occurrence, selected areas 2005

	Race								Total	
	White		Black		Other		Unknown			
State/area	Number	(%)	Number	(%)	Number	(%)	Number	(%)	Number	(%)[a]
Alabama	4,788	(42.7)	6,127	(54.7)	238	(2.1)	58	(0.5)	11,211	(100.0)
Alaska	1,162	(59.4)	131	(6.7)	592	(30.3)	70	(3.6)	1,955	(100.0)
Arkansas	2,837	(60.4)	1,493	(31.8)	326	(6.9)	39	(0.8)	4,695	(100.0)
Colorado	8,383	(71.8)	771	(6.6)	1,529	(13.1)	999	(8.6)	11,682	(100.0)
Delaware[b]	1,630	(53.8)	1,274	(42.0)	127	(4.2)	0	(0.0)	3,031	(100.0)
District of Columbia	512	(20.3)	1,243	(49.4)	741	(29.4)	22	(0.9)	2,518	(100.0)
Georgia	11,853	(37.4)	18,325	(57.8)	1,502	(4.7)	0	(0.0)	31,680	(100.0)
Hawaii	906	(25.5)	101	(2.8)	2,275	(64.1)	266	(7.5)	3,548	(100.0)
Idaho	1,018	(92.6)	16	(1.5)	55	(5.0)	10	(0.9)	1,099	(100.0)
Indiana	6,898	(64.6)	3,084	(28.9)	326	(3.1)	378	(3.5)	10,686	(100.0)
Iowa[b]	4,684	(79.6)	540	(9.2)	564	(9.6)	93	(1.6)	5,881	(100.0)
Kansas	6,974	(66.7)	2,336	(22.3)	1,120	(10.7)	32	(0.3)	10,462	(100.0)
Kentucky	2,602	(68.9)	733	(19.4)	285	(7.5)	156	(4.1)	3,776	(100.0)
Maine	2,277	(85.8)	61	(2.3)	259	(9.8)	56	(2.1)	2,653	(100.0)
Maryland[b]	2,108	(22.9)	6,019	(65.4)	976	(10.6)	95	(1.0)	9,198	(100.0)
Massachusetts	11,619	(49.9)	4,491	(19.3)	4,948	(21.3)	2,210	(9.5)	23,268	(100.0)
Michigan	14,088	(55.9)	9,336	(37.0)	991	(3.9)	794	(3.1)	25,209	(100.0)
Minnesota	8,529	(63.8)	2,831	(21.2)	1,683	(12.6)	319	(2.4)	13,362	(100.0)
Mississippi	672	(22.1)	2,348	(77.2)	8	(0.3)	13	(0.4)	3,041	(100.0)
Missouri	4,492	(56.3)	3,091	(38.7)	371	(4.7)	23	(0.3)	7,977	(100.0)
Montana	1,764	(81.9)	17	(0.8)	280	(13.0)	94	(4.4)	2,155	(100.0)
New Jersey[c]	9,861	(31.6)	13,979	(44.8)	7,216	(23.1)	174	(0.6)	31,230	(100.0)
New York City	34,701	(39.0)	41,953	(47.2)	5,083	(5.7)	7,154	(8.0)	88,891	(100.0)
North Carolina	13,426	(41.5)	14,304	(44.2)	1,495	(4.6)	3,110	(9.6)	32,335	(100.0)
North Dakota	990	(80.4)	31	(2.5)	202	(16.4)	8	(0.6)	1,231	(100.0)
Ohio	19,673	(57.6)	12,070	(35.4)	799	(2.3)	1,586	(4.6)	34,128	(100.0)
Oklahoma	4,781	(72.0)	1,277	(19.2)	583	(8.8)	0	(0.0)	6,641	(100.0)
Oregon	9,677	(83.4)	707	(6.1)	1,090	(9.4)	128	(1.1)	11,602	(100.0)
Pennsylvania	19,837	(56.8)	13,260	(38.0)	1,791	(5.1)	21	(0.1)	34,909	(100.0)
Rhode Island	3,313	(65.1)	776	(15.2)	348	(6.8)	654	(12.8)	5,091	(100.0)
South Carolina	3,965	(59.0)	2,560	(38.1)	188	(2.8)	3	(0.0)	6,716	(100.0)
South Dakota	640	(79.5)	46	(5.7)	118	(14.7)	1	(0.1)	805	(100.0)
Tennessee	8,289	(51.2)	7,269	(44.9)	407	(2.5)	213	(1.3)	16,178	(100.0)
Texas	54,643	(70.9)	17,955	(23.3)	3,391	(4.4)	1,119	(1.5)	77,108	(100.0)
Vermont	1,543	(95.2)	28	(1.7)	49	(3.0)	0	(0.0)	1,620	(100.0)
Virginia	11,398	(43.3)	10,940	(41.6)	2,251	(8.6)	1,720	(6.5)	26,309	(100.0)
West Virginia	1,454	(86.9)	183	(10.9)	28	(1.7)	9	(0.5)	1,674	(100.0)
Wisconsin[b]	6,615	(69.2)	2,285	(23.9)	0[d]	(0.0)[e]	666[f]	(7.0)[f]	9,566	(100.0)
Total	**304,602**	**(53.0)**	**203,991**	**(35.5)**	**44,235**	**(7.7)**	**22,293**	**(3.9)**	**575,121**	**(100.0)**
Abortion ratio[g]	158		467		319				220	
Abortion rate[h]	9		28		18				13	

Note: Data from 36 states, the District of Columbia, and New York City; excludes eight states (Arizona, Nebraska, Nevada, New Mexico, New York Upstate, Utah, Washington, and Wyoming) in which race was reported as unknown for >15% of women.
[a]Percentages might not add to 100.0 because of rounding.
[b]Includes residents only.
[c]Numbers do not include private physicians' procedures.
[d]"Other" included with "unknown."
[e]Not applicable.
[f]Includes "other."
[g]Calculated as the number of legal abortions obtained by women of a given race per 1,000 live births to women of the same race for these states. For each state, data for women of unknown race were distributed according to the known racial distribution for that state.
[h]Calculated as the number of legal abortions obtained by women of a given race per 1,000 women aged 15–44 years of the same race for these states. For each state, data for women of unknown race were distributed according to the known racial distribution for that state. New York City data were excluded because separate population data were not readily available for New York City.

SOURCE: Sonya B. Gamble et al.,"Table 9. Reported Legal Abortions, by Race of Women Who Obtained an Abortion and State of Occurrence—Selected Areas, United States, 2005," in "Abortion Surveillance—United States, 2005," *Morbidity and Mortality Weekly Report*, vol. 57, no. SS-13, November 28, 2008, http://www.cdc.gov/mmwr/PDF/ss/ss5713.pdf (accessed May 8, 2009)

determined that there has been a shift in the proportion of which procedures are used. From 1973 to 1991 the percentage of abortions performed by curettage (gentle scraping with a spoon-like instrument, which here includes dilation of the cervix and evacuation of the uterus by aspiration) increased from 88.4% to 99%. (See Table 4.2.) The percentage then dropped slightly during the late 1990s, and more sharply to 97.9% in 2000 and then to 87.1% in 2005. The 2005 decline brought the percentage of curettage performed below the 1973 level for the first time since that year. The percentage of abortions performed by intrauterine instillation (induction) declined sharply from 10.3% in 1973 to 0.8% in 2005. This procedure has been used in less than 1% of all abortions since 1989. Medical (nonsurgical)

TABLE 4.5

Legal abortions, by ethnicity of women and state of occurrence, selected states, 2005

State/area	Hispanic No.	Hispanic (%)	Non-Hispanic No.	Non-Hispanic (%)	Unknown No.	Unknown (%)	Total No.	Total (%)[a]
Alabama	309	(2.8)	10,866	(96.9)	36	(0.3)	11,211	(100.0)
Arizona	4,097	(38.2)	6,014	(56.1)	612	(5.7)	10,723	(100.0)
Arkansas	199	(4.2)	4,474	(95.3)	22	(0.5)	4,695	(100.0)
Colorado	2,457	(21.0)	7,660	(65.6)	1,565	(13.4)	11,682	(100.0)
Delaware[b]	277	(9.1)	2,711	(89.4)	43	(1.4)	3,031	(100.0)
Dist. of Columbia	359	(14.3)	2,143	(85.1)	16	(0.6)	2,518	(100.0)
Hawaii	221	(6.2)	3,077	(86.7)	250	(7.0)	3,548	(100.0)
Idaho	133	(12.1)	959	(87.3)	7	(0.6)	1,099	(100.0)
Indiana	745	(7.0)	8,532	(79.8)	1,409	(13.2)	10,686	(100.0)
Kansas	1,049	(10.0)	9,193	(87.9)	220	(2.1)	10,462	(100.0)
Maine	53	(2.0)	2,246	(84.7)	354	(13.3)	2,653	(100.0)
Minnesota	747	(5.6)	12,498	(93.5)	117	(0.9)	13,362	(100.0)
Mississippi	16	(0.5)	3,020	(99.3)	5	(0.2)	3,041	(100.0)
Missouri	187	(2.3)	7,764	(97.3)	26	(0.3)	7,977	(100.0)
New Jersey[c]	7,436	(23.8)	23,401	(74.9)	393	(1.3)	31,230	(100.0)
New Mexico	3,114	(52.5)	2,235	(37.7)	585	(9.9)	5,934	(100.0)
New York	31,727	(25.4)	81,092	(65.0)	12,030	(9.6)	124,849	(100.0)
City	27,210	(30.6)	54,926	(61.8)	6,755	(7.6)	88,891	(100.0)
State	4,517	(12.6)	26,166	(72.8)	5,275	(14.7)	35,958	(100.0)
Ohio	1,118	(3.3)	32,618	(95.6)	392	(1.1)	34,128	(100.0)
Oregon	1,291	(11.1)	10,288	(88.7)	23	(0.2)	11,602	(100.0)
Pennsylvania	2,218	(6.4)	32,677	(93.6)	14	(0.0)	34,909	(100.0)
South Carolina	317	(4.7)	6,397	(95.3)	2	(0.0)	6,716	(100.0)
South Dakota	44	(5.5)	761	(94.5)	0	(0.0)	805	(100.0)
Tennessee	728	(4.5)	15,153	(93.7)	297	(1.8)	16,178	(100.0)
Texas	28,006	(36.3)	47,983	(62.2)	1,119	(1.5)	77,108	(100.0)
Utah	702	(19.7)	2,550	(71.7)	304	(8.5)	3,556	(100.0)
Vermont	28	(1.7)	1,587	(98.0)	5	(0.3)	1,620	(100.0)
West Virginia	10	(0.6)	1,659	(99.1)	5	(0.3)	1,674	(100.0)
Wisconsin[b]	868	(9.1)	8,698	(90.9)	0	(0.0)	9,566	(100.0)
Wyoming[d]	—	—	11	(78.6)	—	—	14	(100.0)
Total[e]	**88,456**	**(19.4)**	**348,267**	**(76.3)**	**19,851**	**(4.3)**	**456,577**	**(100.0)**
Abortion ratio[f]	205		223				219	
Abortion rate[g]	21		14				15	

Note: Data from 28 states, the District of Columbia, and New York City; excludes 12 states (Alaska, Georgia, Massachusetts, Montana, Nebraska, Nevada, North Carolina, North Dakota, Oklahoma, Rhode Island, Virginia, and Washington) in which ethnicity was reported as unknown for >15% of women.

[a]Percentages might not add to 100.0 because of rounding.
[b]Includes residents only.
[c]Numbers do not include private physicians' procedures.
[d]Cell details not displayed because of small numbers.
[e]Totals do not include small numbers.
[f]Calculated as the number of legal abortions obtained by women of a given ethnicity per 1,000 live births to women of the same ethnicity for these states. For each state, data for women of unknown ethnicity were distributed according to the known ethnicity distribution for that state.
[g]Calculated as the number of legal abortions obtained by women of a given ethnicity per 1,000 women aged 15–44 years of the same ethnicity for these states. For each state, data for women of unknown ethnicity were distributed according to the known ethnicity distribution for that state.

SOURCE: Sonya B. Gamble et al., "Table 10. Reported Legal Abortions, by Ethnicity of Women Who Obtained an Abortion and State of Occurrence—Selected States, United States, 2005," in "Abortion Surveillance—United States, 2005," *Morbidity and Mortality Weekly Report*, vol. 57, no. SS-13, November 28, 2008, http://www.cdc.gov/mmwr/PDF/ss/ss5713.pdf (accessed May 8, 2009).

procedures are included in the "other" procedure category, which has risen dramatically in recent years, from 1.7% in 2000 to 12.1% in 2005.

Women's Perceptions of Abortion Methods

Pak Chung Ho of the University of Hong Kong notes in the review article "Women's Perceptions on Medical Abortion" (*Contraception*, vol. 74, no. 1, July 2006) that the most common reasons women of various nationalities chose a medical rather than a surgical abortion were fear of surgery or general anesthesia, perception of greater safety with a medical abortion, perception of greater naturalness of a medical abortion, avoidance of pain in coun-

tries (such as China) where little or no anesthesia is used with a surgical abortion, ability to have the abortion before seven weeks' gestation, and privacy. The most common reasons women chose a surgical rather than a medical abortion were the quickness of the procedure, no extra visits to the doctor (as with a medical abortion), ability to be anesthetized and unaware of the procedure, wariness of new medications, and fear of side effects of medications.

In his review study, Ho compares the research on the acceptability of medical abortion by women in various countries. He reports that "the results showed that, despite the wide geographical distribution of the studies, over 80% of women were satisfied with medical abortion. A similar

TABLE 4.6

Fertility indicators for women aged 15–44, by age, race, and Hispanic origin, June 2006

| Characteristic | Number of women Estimate | Women who had a birth in the last 12 months | | |
		Total Estimate	Percent distribution Estimate	Births per 1,000 women Estimate
Total	76,172,507	4,182,942	100.0	54.9
Age				
15 to 19 years	10,551,372	278,445	6.7	26.4
20 to 24 years	10,134,195	935,039	22.4	92.3
25 to 29 years	9,976,440	1,173,652	28.1	117.6
30 to 34 years	9,679,647	987,324	23.6	102.0
35 to 39 years	10,559,537	583,591	14.0	55.3
40 to 44 years	11,384,220	170,791	4.1	15.0
45 to 50 years	13,887,096	54,100	1.3	3.9
Marital status				
Married	35,225,985	2,698,790	64.5	76.6
Widowed	719,572	13,541	0.3	18.8
Divorced	7,378,966	167,767	4.0	22.7
Separated	2,317,577	113,275	2.7	48.9
Never married	30,530,407	1,189,569	28.4	39.0
Cohabitation status				
Not married[a]	40,946,522	1,484,152	35.5	36.2
Living with an unmarried partner	2,742,042	199,051	4.8	72.6
Not living with an unmarried partner	38,204,480	1,285,101	30.7	33.6
Nativity and citizenship				
Native	64,375,416	3,347,731	80.0	52.0
Foreign born	11,797,091	835,211	20.0	70.8
Naturalized citizen	4,293,664	210,880	5.0	49.1
Not a citizen	7,503,427	624,331	14.9	83.2
Race and Hispanic origin				
White alone	54,423,321	2,826,551	67.6	51.9
White alone, non-Hispanic	48,410,876	2,394,767	57.3	49.5
Black alone	10,431,264	605,433	14.5	58.0
American Indian or Alaska Native alone	654,150	44,148	1.1	67.5
Asian alone	3,879,167	209,615	5.0	54.0
Native Hawaiian and other Pacific Islander alone	125,034	7,676	0.2	61.4
Some other race alone	5,262,240	407,992	9.8	77.5
Two or more races	1,397,331	81,527	1.9	58.3
Hispanic (any race)	11,739,015	873,368	20.9	74.4
Educational attainment				
Not a high school graduate	14,581,563	746,907	17.9	51.2
High school, 4 years	19,704,046	1,133,009	27.1	57.5
College, 1 or more years	41,886,898	2,303,026	55.1	55.0
Some college or associate's degree	23,475,815	1,171,936	28.0	49.9
Bachelor's degree	12,908,885	763,260	18.2	59.1
Graduate or professional degree	5,502,198	367,830	8.8	66.9
Labor force status				
In labor force[b]	53,071,870	2,397,953	57.3	45.2
Employed	49,115,747	2,109,291	50.4	42.9
Unemployed	3,956,123	288,662	6.9	73.0
Not in labor force	20,983,532	1,774,412	42.4	84.6

percentage of women would choose the method again if they needed an abortion in the future or would recommend medical abortion to their friends. All these data show that medical abortion is highly acceptable to women who chose the method after counseling." Ho also notes that most women who had experienced both surgical and medical abortion found medical abortion to be a better choice.

Deaths from Abortion

As Table 4.10 shows, the fatality rate from abortion procedures has dropped from 4.1 deaths per 100,000 reported legal induced abortions in 1972 to a low point of 0.3 deaths per 100,000 in 1995. In 1997 the rate was 0.6. Fatality rates are not shown from 1998 to 2004 because of missing data. Melonie Heron et al. of the CDC report in "Deaths: Final Data for 2006" (*National Vital Statistics Reports*, vol. 57, no. 14, April 2009) that in 2006 the number of maternal deaths because of medical abortion was zero and for other types of induced abortion was zero. Even though induced abortion–related deaths are rare, medical and surgical abortions are procedures that entail some risk. In general, early abortions are safer than later abortions, and abortions performed at or before eight weeks of pregnancy are considered to be the safest.

TABLE 4.6

Fertility indicators for women aged 15–44, by age, race, and Hispanic origin, June 2006 [CONTINUED]

| | | Women who had a birth in the last 12 months | | |
Characteristic	Number of women Estimate	Total Estimate	Percent distribution Estimate	Births per 1,000 women Estimate
Annual family income				
Less than $10,000	15,889,965	526,785	12.6	33.2
$10,000 to $14,999	2,308,705	206,620	4.9	89.5
$15,000 to $24,999	5,324,892	453,454	10.8	85.2
$25,000 to $34,999	5,864,945	438,014	10.5	74.7
$35,000 to $49,999	8,599,979	552,125	13.2	64.2
$50,000 to $74,999	13,215,740	779,033	18.6	58.9
$75,000 to $99,999	9,647,862	500,678	12.0	51.9
$100,000 to $149,999	9,444,088	454,476	10.9	48.1
$150,000 to $199,999	3,105,652	145,109	3.5	46.7
$200,000 or more	2,770,679	126,648	3.0	45.7
Poverty status[c]				
Below 100 percent of poverty in the past 12 months	11,521,336	1,053,398	25.2	91.4
100 percent to 199 percent of poverty in the past 12 months	12,967,105	876,609	21.2	67.6
200 percent of poverty or above in the past 12 months	50,155,075	2,235,862	53.2	44.5
Public assistance				
Receiving public assistance	1,742,895	269,300	6.4	154.5
Not receiving public assistance	74,429,612	3,913,642	93.6	52.6

[a]Includes separated, widowed, divorced, and never-married women.
[b]Labor force status is only determined for the population 16 years old and over.
[c]For whom poverty status is determined.
Note: Births per 1,000 shows the likelihood that a given group of women will have a birth.

SOURCE: Jane Lawler Dye, "Table 1. Fertility Indicators for Women 15 to 44 Years Old by Age and Race and Hispanic Origin: June 2006," in *Fertility of American Women: 2006*, U.S. Department of Commerce, Economics and Statistics Administration, U.S. Census Bureau, August 2008, http://www.census.gov/prod/2008pubs/p20–558.pdf (accessed May 9, 2009)

TABLE 4.7

Number[a], ratio[b], and rate[c] of legal abortions by state, and percentage of legal abortions obtained by out-of-state residents[d], 2005

State/area	Residence			Occurrence			% of legal abortions obtained by out-of-state residents
	Number of legal abortions	Ratio	Rate	Number of legal abortions	Ratio	Rate	
Alabama	9,905	164	11	11,211	185	12	16.8
Alaska	2,207	211	15	1,955	187	14	0.3
Arizona[e]	10,786	112	9	10,723	111	9	3.1
Arkansas	4,862	124	9	4,695	120	8	13.5
California[f]	—[g]	—	—	—	—	—	—
Colorado	10,636	154	11	11,682	169	12	9.7
Connecticut	12,501	300	17	12,110	290	17	3.1
Delaware[h]	3,275	281	18	4,148	356	23	26.9
Dist. of Columbia	2,181	274	15	2,518	316	17	50.7
Florida[i]	—	—	—	92,513	409	27	—
Georgia	28,440	200	14	31,680	223	16	11.6
Hawaii	3,538	197	14	3,548	198	14	0.5
Idaho	1,843	80	6	1,099	48	4	3.1
Illinois	39,317	220	15	43,409	242	16	7.9
Indiana	11,741	135	9	10,686	123	8	3.9
Iowa[h]	5,672	144	10	5,881	150	10	11.3
Kansas	5,643	141	10	10,462	262	19	47.0
Kentucky	2,594	46	3	3,776	67	4	—
Louisiana[f]	—	—	—	—	—	—	—
Maine	2,535	180	10	2,653	188	10	5.2
Maryland[h]	10,875	145	9	10,797	144	9	14.7
Massachusetts[e]	23,219	302	17	23,268	303	17	4.3
Michigan	24,938	195	12	25,209	197	12	2.8
Minnesota	12,840	181	12	13,362	188	12	7.9
Mississippi	6,286	148	10	3,041	72	5	2.8
Missouri	13,968	178	12	7,977	101	7	8.2
Montana	2,021	174	11	2,155	186	12	8.1
Nebraska	2,810	107	8	3,173	121	9	14.7
Nevada	9,949	267	20	10,565	283	21	6.3
New Hampshire[f]	—	—	—	—	—	—	—
New Jersey[j]	31,590	278	18	31,230	274	17	5.5
New Mexico	6,273	218	16	5,934	206	15	5.6
New York	118,861	482	29	124,849	507	30	—
City	82,925	706	—	88,891[k]	756	—	7.1[l]
State	35,936[m]	279	—	35,958	279	—	6.8[l]
North Carolina	27,521	224	15	32,335	263	18	16.9
North Dakota	882	105	7	1,231	147	10	36.8
Ohio	32,019	216	14	34,128	230	15	8.1
Oklahoma	7,018	135	10	6,641	128	9	4.0
Oregon	10,432	227	14	11,602	253	16	12.3
Pennsylvania	36,852	253	15	34,909	240	14	4.1
Rhode Island	4,035	318	18	5,091	401	22	23.0
South Carolina	12,278	213	14	6,716	116	8	3.9
South Dakota	916	80	6	805	70	5	18.3
Tennessee	13,850	169	11	16,178	198	13	21.3
Texas	74,569	193	15	77,108	200	15	3.5
Utah	3,445	67	6	3,556	69	6	7.8
Vermont	1,466	233	12	1,620	257	13	10.6
Virginia	27,576	264	17	26,309	252	16	4.7

TABLE 4.7

Number[a], ratio[b], and rate[c] of legal abortions by state, and percentage of legal abortions obtained by out-of-state residents[d], 2005

[CONTINUED]

State/area	Residence			Occurrence			% of legal abortions obtained by out-of-state residents
	Number of legal abortions	Ratio	Rate	Number of legal abortions	Ratio	Rate	
Washington	24,242	293	18	24,108	292	18	5.0
West Virginia[f]	2,089	100	6	1,674	80	5	13.3
Wisconsin[h]	10,798	152	10	9,817	138	9	2.6
Wyoming	904	125	9	14	2[n]	0[n]	0.0
Other residence[o]	2,759	—	—	NA[p]	NA	NA	NA
Total known	**716,496**			**820,151**	**233**	**15**	**8.3**
Unknown residence[q]	6,901						
Not reported by residence[r]	96,754						
Total	**820,151**	**233**	**15**				

[a]Abortion data reported by central health agencies.

[b]Number of abortions per 1,000 live births. Number of live births obtained. Source: Martin JA, Hamilton BE, Sutton PD, Ventura SJ, Menacker F, Kirmeyer S. Births: final data for 2004. Atlanta, GA: US Department of Health and Human Services, CDC, National Center for Health Statistics; 2006. (National Vital Statistics Reports; vol. 55, no. 1).

[c]Number of abortions per 1,000 women aged 15–44 years. Source: US Bureau of the Census, Population Estimates Branch, state estimates by demographic characteristics, 6 face group, Released August 4, 2006. Available at http://www.census.gov/popest/states/ASRH/files/SC_EST2005_alldata6.txt.

[d]Based on number of abortions for which residence of women were known.

[e]Reported numbers of abortions for in-state residents without detailed information regarding out-of-state residents.

[f]State did not report abortions.

[g]Not available.

[h]Reported for own residents only.

[i]State reported abortions by occurrence only.

[j]Numbers do not include private physicians' procedures.

[k]Reported by the New York City Department of Health.

[l]Percentage based on number of abortions reported as "out-of-reporting area."

[m]Abortions for women whose state of residence was listed as "New York."

[n]Ratio and rate not provided because of small numbers.

[o]Women whose residence was listed as Canada, Mexico, or "other."

[p]Not applicable.

[q]Reported as unknown residence (6,901) or out-of-state residence, but not specified (2,759).

[r]Total for states that did not report abortions by residence.

SOURCE: Sonya B. Gamble et al., "Table 3. Reported Number, Ratio, and Rate of Legal Abortions by Residence and Occurrence, and Percentage of Abortions Obtained by Out-Of-State Residents, by State of Occurrence—United States, 2005," in "Abortion Surveillance—United States, 2005," *Morbidity and Mortality Weekly Report*, vol. 57, no. SS-13, November 28, 2008, http://www.cdc.gov/mmwr/PDF/ss/ss5713.pdf (accessed May 8, 2009)

FIGURE 4.6

Mandatory state waiting periods and biased counseling for abortion, January 2009

☐ Has biased counseling and mandatory delay law   ☐ Biased counseling and mandatory delay law unenforceable

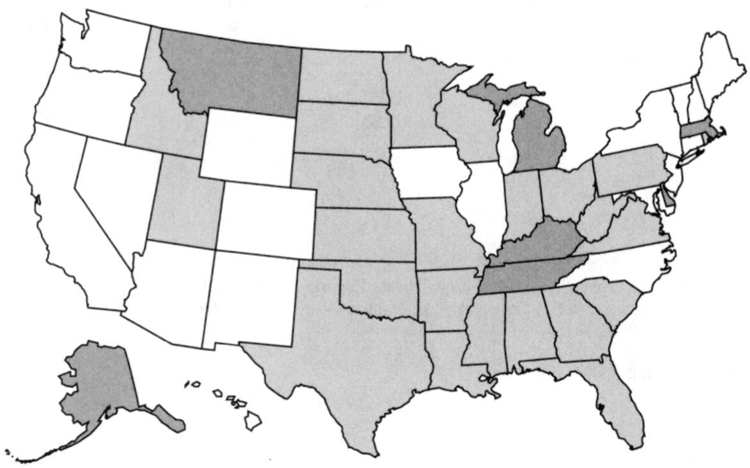

31 states have laws subjecting women seeking abortions to biased counseling and/or mandatory delays: AK, AL, AR, DE, FL, GA, ID, IN, KS, KY, LA, MA, MI, MN, MO, MS, MT, ND, NE, OH, OK, PA, RI, SC, SD, TN, TX, UT, VA, WI, WV.

State	State subjects women seeking abortion to:	
	Biased counseling	**Mandatory delay**
Alabama	✓	✓
Alaska	✓	
Arizona		
Arkansas	✓	✓
California		
Colorado		
Connecticut		
Delaware	✓	✓[a]
District of Columbia		
Florida	✓	
Georgia	✓	✓
Hawaii		
Idaho	✓	✓
Illinois		
Indiana	✓	✓
Iowa		
Kansas	✓	✓
Kentucky	✓[b]	✓
Louisiana	✓	✓
Maine		
Maryland		✓[a]
Massachusetts	✓	✓
Michigan	✓	✓
Minnesota	✓	✓
Mississippi	✓	✓
Missouri	✓	✓
Montana	✓	✓
Nebraska	✓	✓

FIGURE 4.6

Mandatory state waiting periods and biased counseling for abortion, January 2009 [CONTINUED]

State	State subjects women seeking abortion to:	
	Biased counseling	Mandatory delay
Nevada		
New Hampshire		
New Jersey		
New Mexico		
New York		
North Carolina		
North Dakota	✓	✓
Ohio	✓	✓
Oklahoma	✓	✓
Oregon		
Pennsylvania	✓	✓
Rhode Island	✓	
South Carolina	✓	✓
South Dakota	✓	✓
Tennessee	✓	✓
Texas	✓	✓
Utah	✓	✓
Vermont		✓
Virginia	✓	✓
Washington		
West Virginia	✓	✓
Wisconsin	✓	✓
Wyoming		
Totals	**31**	**28**

[a]The law is unconstitutional & unenforceable only with respect to the mandatory delay.
[b]The law is unconstitutional & unenforceable only with respect to the in-person receipt of the state-mandated information and materials provision.

SOURCE: Adapted from "Biased Counseling & Mandatory Delay," in *Who Decides? The Status of Women's Reproductive Rights in the United States*, NARAL Pro-Choice America and NARAL Pro-Choice America Foundation, January 2009, http://www.prochoiceamerica.org/choice-action-center/in_your_state/who-decides/maps-and-charts/map.jsp?mapID=14 (accessed May 8, 2009)

TABLE 4.8

Number of abortion providers and counties with no provider, selected years 1992–2005

Region and state	Providers					Counties, 2005		% of women in counties with no provider*
	1992	1996	2000	2005	% change, 2000–2005	Total	% with no provider	
U.S. total	2,380	2,042	1,819	1,787	−2	3,141	87	35
Northeast	620	562	536	541	1	217	51	17
Connecticut	43	40	50	52	4	8	25	10
Maine	17	16	15	13	−13	16	63	46
Massachusetts	64	51	47	45	−4	14	14	7
New Hampshire	16	16	14	13	−7	10	50	19
New Jersey	88	94	86	85	−1	21	19	10
New York	289	266	234	261	12	62	40	7
Pennsylvania	81	61	73	56	−23	67	78	40
Rhode Island	6	5	6	4	−33	5	80	39
Vermont	16	13	11	12	9	14	43	24
Midwest	260	212	188	183	23	1,055	94	50
Illinois	47	38	37	38	3	102	92	34
Indiana	19	16	15	15	0	92	93	63
Iowa	11	8	8	9	13	99	93	56
Kansas	15	10	7	7	0	105	96	57
Michigan	70	59	50	51	2	83	83	33
Minnesota	14	13	11	11	0	87	95	62
Missouri	12	10	6	7	17	115	96	68
Nebraska	9	8	5	6	20	93	97	45
North Dakota	1	1	2	1	−50	53	98	75
Ohio	45	37	35	27	−23	88	90	51
South Dakota	1	1	2	2	0	66	98	78
Wisconsin	16	11	10	9	−10	72	93	63
South	620	505	442	405	28	1,423	91	47
Alabama	20	14	14	13	−7	67	93	61
Arkansas	8	6	7	3	−57	75	97	79
Delaware	8	7	9	9	0	3	33	18
District of Columbia	15	18	15	12	−20	1	0	0
Florida	133	114	108	103	−5	67	69	20
Georgia	55	41	26	34	31	159	92	62
Kentucky	9	8	3	3	0	120	98	77
Louisiana	17	15	13	9	−31	64	92	62
Maryland	51	47	42	41	−2	24	58	19
Mississippi	8	6	4	2	−50	82	99	91
North Carolina	86	59	55	37	−33	100	83	48
Oklahoma	11	11	6	6	0	77	96	57
South Carolina	18	14	10	6	−40	46	91	72
Tennessee	33	20	16	13	−19	95	94	59
Texas	79	64	65	64	−2	254	93	35
Virginia	64	57	46	46	0	134	86	57
West Virginia	5	4	3	4	33	55	96	84
West	880	763	653	658	1	446	78	15
Alaska	13	8	7	9	29	27	81	23
Arizona	28	24	21	19	−10	15	73	16
California	554	492	400	424	6	58	41	4
Colorado	59	47	40	43	8	64	78	23
Hawaii	52	44	51	39	−24	5	20	0
Idaho	9	7	7	7	0	44	93	68
Montana	12	11	9	8	−11	56	91	49
Nevada	17	14	13	8	−38	17	88	12
New Mexico	20	13	11	12	9	33	88	47
Oregon	40	35	34	32	−6	36	78	26
Utah	6	7	4	6	50	29	93	55
Washington	65	57	53	49	−8	39	67	14
Wyoming	5	4	3	2	−33	23	96	96

*Population counts are for April 1, 2005.

SOURCE: Rachel K. Jones et al., "Table 3. Number of Abortion Providers, Selected Years, and Percentage Change between 2000 and 2005; Number of Counties and Percentage with No Provider, 2005; and Percentage of Women Aged 15–44 Living in Counties with No Provider, 2005—All by Region and State," in "Abortion in the United States: Incidence and Access to Services, 2005," *Perspectives on Sexual and Reproductive Health*, vol. 40, no. 1, 2008, http://www.guttmacher.org/pubs/journals/4000608.pdf (accessed June 4, 2009)

FIGURE 4.7

Timing of abortions, 2004

[In weeks from last menstrual period]

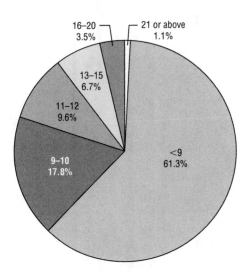

Note: Eighty-nine percent of abortions occur in the first 12 weeks of pregnancy.

SOURCE: Guttmacher Institute, Community Health Centers and Family Planning, "When Women Have Abortions," in *In Brief: Facts on Induced Abortion in the United States*, New York: Guttmacher, July 2008, http://www.guttmacher.org/pubs/fb_induced_abortion.pdf (accessed May 9, 2009)

TABLE 4.9

Legal abortions, by length of gestation, and demographic characteristics of women who obtained abortions, selected states, 2005

Characteristic	Weeks of gestation												Total	
	≤8		9–10		11–12		13–15		16–20		≥21			
	No.	(%)	No.	(%)	No.	(%)	No.	(%)	No.	(%)	No.	(%)	No.	(%)[a]
Age group (years)														
<15	1,366	(39.9)	706	(20.6)	448	(13.1)	397	(11.6)	322	(9.4)	187	(5.5)	3,426	(100.0)
15–19	51,670	(52.2)	19,496	(19.7)	11,712	(11.8)	8,506	(8.6)	5,420	(5.5)	2,217	(2.2)	99,021	(100.0)
20–24	120,240	(60.6)	35,121	(17.7)	19,734	(9.9)	13,254	(6.7)	7,477	(3.8)	2,564	(1.3)	198,390	(100.0)
25–29	92,458	(65.2)	23,485	(16.6)	12,121	(8.5)	7,769	(5.5)	4,428	(3.1)	1,540	(1.1)	141,801	(100.0)
30–34	59,285	(67.6)	13,627	(15.5)	6,708	(7.7)	4,404	(5.0)	2,647	(3.0)	1,010	(1.2)	87,681	(100.0)
35–39	35,278	(67.8)	7,966	(15.3)	3,766	(7.2)	2,507	(4.8)	1,872	(3.6)	679	(1.3)	52,068	(100.0)
≥40	13,312	(68.7)	2,810	(14.5)	1,355	(7.0)	914	(4.7)	748	(3.9)	248	(1.3)	19,387	(100.0)
Total[b]	**373,609**	**(62.1)**	**103,211**	**(17.2)**	**55,844**	**(9.3)**	**37,751**	**(6.3)**	**22,914**	**(3.8)**	**8,445**	**(1.4)**	**601,774**	**(100.0)**
Race														
White	186,265	(66.5)	43,578	(15.5)	22,990	(8.2)	15,426	(5.5)	8,864	(3.2)	3,165	(1.1)	280,288	(100.0)
Black	107,121	(58.1)	34,400	(18.7)	19,377	(10.5)	13,336	(7.2)	7,802	(4.2)	2,408	(1.3)	184,444	(100.0)
Other	25,191	(67.7)	5,311	(14.3)	2,587	(6.9)	2,089	(5.6)	1,549	(4.2)	498	(1.3)	37,225	(100.0)
Total[c]	**318,577**	**(63.5)**	**83,289**	**(16.6)**	**44,954**	**(9.0)**	**30,851**	**(6.1)**	**18,215**	**(3.6)**	**6,071**	**(1.2)**	**501,957**	**(100.0)**
Ethnicity														
Hispanic	55,297	(64.2)	13,761	(16.0)	6,983	(8.1)	5,798	(6.7)	3,217	(3.7)	1,126	(1.3)	86,182	(100.0)
Non-Hispanic	205,265	(62.1)	57,103	(17.3)	30,843	(9.3)	20,429	(6.2)	12,625	(3.8)	4,423	(1.3)	330,688	(100.0)
Total[d]	**260,562**	**(62.5)**	**70,864**	**(17.0)**	**37,826**	**(9.1)**	**26,227**	**(6.3)**	**15,842**	**(3.8)**	**5,549**	**(1.3)**	**416,870**	**(100.0)**

[a]Percentages might not add to 100.0 because of rounding.
[b]Data from 40 states, the District of Columbia, and New York City; excludes three states (Mississippi, Nebraska, and Nevada) in which weeks of gestation was reported as unknown for >15% of women.
[c]Data from 33 states, the District of Columbia, and New York City; excludes nine states (Arizona, Mississippi, Nebraska, Nevada, New Mexico, New York Upstate, Utah, Washington, and Wyoming) in which race or weeks of gestation was reported as unknown for >15% of women.
[d]Data from 27 states, the District of Columbia, and New York City; excludes 12 states (Alaska, Georgia, Mississippi, Montana, Nebraska, Nevada, North Carolina, North Dakota, Oklahoma, Rhode Island, Virginia, and Washington) in which ethnicity or weeks of gestation was reported as unknown for >15% of women.

SOURCE: Sonya B. Gamble et al., "Table 16. Reported Legal Abortions, by Known Weeks of Gestation, Age Group, Race, and Ethnicity of Women Who Obtained an Abortion—Selected States, United States, 2005," in "Abortion Surveillance—United States, 2005," *Morbidity and Mortality Weekly Report*, vol. 57, no. SS-13, November 28, 2008, http://www.cdc.gov/mmwr/PDF/ss/ss5713.pdf (accessed May 8, 2009)

TABLE 4.10

Number of deaths and fatality rates for abortion-related deaths reported to the Centers for Disease Control (CDC), by type of abortion, 1972–2004

Year	Type of abortion — Induced — Legal	Type of abortion — Induced — Illegal	Unknown[b]	Total	Case-fatality rate[a]
1972	24	39	2	65	4.1
1973	25	19	3	47	4.1
1974	26	6	1	33	3.4
1975	29	4	1	34	3.4
1976	11	2	1	14	1.1
1977	17	4	0	21	1.6
1978	9	7	0	16	0.8
1979	22	0	0	22	1.8
1980	9	1	2	12	0.7
1981	8	1	0	9	0.6
1982	11	1	0	12	0.8
1983	11	1	0	12	0.9
1984	12	0	0	12	0.9
1985	11	1	1	13	0.8
1986	11	0	2	13	0.8
1987	7	2	0	9	0.5
1988	16	0	0	16	1.2
1989	12	1	0	13	0.9
1990	9	0	0	9	0.6
1991	11	1	0	12	0.8
1992	10	0	0	10	0.7
1993	6	1	2	9	0.5
1994	10	2	0	12	0.8
1995	4	0	0	4	0.3
1996	9	0	0	9	0.7
1997	7	0	0	7	0.6
1998	10	0	0	10	—[c]
1999	4	0	0	4	—[c]
2000	11	0	0	11	—[c]
2001	6	1	0	7	—[c]
2002	9	0	0	9	—[c]
2003	10	0	0	10	—[c]
2004	7	1	0	8	—[c]
Total	**393**	**95**	**15**	**504**	**1.1[d]**

[a]Legal induced abortion-related deaths per 100,000 reported legal induced abortions for the United States.
[b]Unknown whether induced or spontaneous abortions.
[c]Case-fatality rates for 1998–2004 cannot be calculated because a substantial number of abortions occurred in the nonreporting states/areas, and the total number of abortions (the denominator) is unknown.
[d]Case-fatality rate computed for 1972–1997 only.
Note: Certain numbers might differ from those in previously published reports because additional information has been supplied to Center for Disease Control (CDC).

SOURCE: Sonya B. Gamble et al., "Table 19. Number of Deaths and Case-Fatality Rates for Abortion-Related Deaths Reported to CDC, by Type of Abortion—United States, 1972–2004," in "Abortion Surveillance—United States, 2005," *Morbidity and Mortality Weekly Report*, vol. 57, no. SS-13, November 28, 2008, http://www.cdc.gov/mmwr/PDF/ss/ss5713.pdf (accessed May 8, 2009)

CHAPTER 5
TEEN PREGNANCY AND ABORTION

TEEN PREGNANCY

Teen pregnancy is a serious concern in the United States. According to the Centers for Disease Control and Prevention (CDC), 745,000 teens became pregnant in 2004. (See Figure 5.1.) Sixty-four percent were 18 to 19 years of age, 34% were teens aged 15 to 17, and 2% were adolescents under 15 years of age.

According to the CDC, in *Preventing Teen Pregnancy: An Update in 2009* (March 2009, http://www.cdc.gov/repro ductivehealth/AdolescentReproHealth/PDF/ARH-Update 2008FactSheet.pdf), the United States has higher rates of teen pregnancies, births, and abortions than most other industrialized countries. For example, Table 8.4 in Chapter 8 shows that in 2003 women aged 19 and younger in the United States had an abortion rate of 22 abortions for every 1,000 women. This rate was higher in 2003 than for most other countries shown on the list; countries with higher teen abortion rates in 2003 were New Zealand, Sweden, Estonia, England and Wales, and the Russian Federation. The United States has made progress in the teen abortion rate, however. In 1996 the rate was 29 abortions per 1,000 women aged 19 and younger. The only industrialized countries shown in Table 8.4 with higher teen abortion rates in that year were Estonia, the Russian Federation, and Hungary.

International comparative statistics are usually difficult and time consuming to compile, so they are often dated. As of mid-2009, the most recent comparative compilation of pregnancy, birth, and abortion rates among teenagers in the United States and other developed countries from the Guttmacher Institute used data from the mid-1990s. In *Teenage Sexual and Reproductive Behavior in Developed Countries: Can More Progress Be Made? Executive Summary* (November 2001, http://www.guttmacher.org/pubs/ summaries/euroteens_summ.pdf), the Guttmacher Institute uses these data to show that the United States in the mid-1990s had the highest rates of teen pregnancies, births, and

abortions among Western industrialized countries in general, and had higher rates than Sweden, France, Canada, and Great Britain in particular.

The Guttmacher Institute reported these figures as part of a study conducted to see what the United States could learn from countries with lower teen pregnancy rates. In *Teenage Sexual and Reproductive Behavior in Developed Countries*, the Guttmacher Institute reveals that sexually active teens in the United States were less likely to use contraceptives, especially highly effective ones such as hormonal methods, primarily because they tended to have shorter sexually intimate relationships than did teens in other developed countries. American teens were also more likely to have multiple sex partners (more than four) than teens in the other study countries: Sweden, France, Canada, and Great Britain.

The Guttmacher Institute suggests that the U.S. approach to reducing teen pregnancy focuses on telling teens that it is wrong to start childbearing early and that this pronouncement is not a great enough deterrent to teens. In addition, the Guttmacher Institute indicates that the United States does not provide sufficient resources to help teens make responsible choices. The study attributes the other countries' lower rates of teenage pregnancy to parental and governmental support of teenagers by providing information about and access to effective contraception and adequate health services. In addition, the Guttmacher Institute finds that government agencies and parents in these countries help teenagers make responsible decisions about sexual relationships, the use of birth control, and the prevention of sexually transmitted diseases (STDs).

A Decline in Teen Pregnancy Rates

Figure 5.2 and Figure 5.3 show that pregnancy rates rose for teens from 1976 through 1990 for teens aged 15 to 17 and 1991 for teens aged 18 to 19. The rates then

FIGURE 5.1

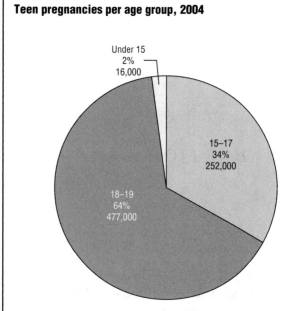

Teen pregnancies per age group, 2004

Under 15
2%
16,000

15–17
34%
252,000

18–19
64%
477,000

SOURCE: Adapted from Stephanie J. Ventura et al., "Table 3. Number and Percent Distribution of Pregnancies by Outcome of Pregnancy by Age, Race, and Hispanic Origin of Woman: United States, 1990 and 2004," in "Estimated Pregnancy Rates by Outcome for the United States, 1990–2004," *National Vital Statistics Reports*, vol. 56, no. 15, April 14, 2008, http://www.cdc.gov/nchs/data/nvsr/nvsr56/nvsr56_15.pdf (accessed June 5, 2009)

FIGURE 5.2

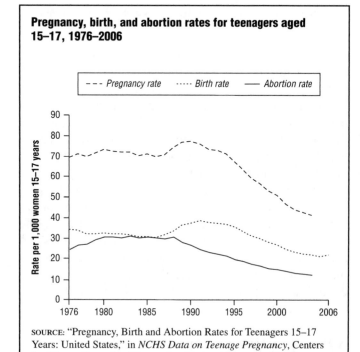

Pregnancy, birth, and abortion rates for teenagers aged 15–17, 1976–2006

– – – Pregnancy rate   ⋯⋯ Birth rate   —— Abortion rate

SOURCE: "Pregnancy, Birth and Abortion Rates for Teenagers 15–17 Years: United States," in *NCHS Data on Teenage Pregnancy*, Centers for Disease Control and Prevention, National Center for Health Statistics, October 2008, http://www.cdc.gov/nchs/data/infosheets/infosheet_teen_preg.htm (accessed May 11, 2009)

FIGURE 5.3

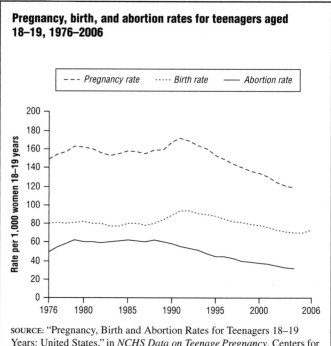

Pregnancy, birth, and abortion rates for teenagers aged 18–19, 1976–2006

– – – Pregnancy rate   ⋯⋯ Birth rate   —— Abortion rate

SOURCE: "Pregnancy, Birth and Abortion Rates for Teenagers 18–19 Years: United States," in *NCHS Data on Teenage Pregnancy*, Centers for Disease Control and Prevention, National Center for Health Statistics, October 2008, http://www.cdc.gov/nchs/data/infosheets/infosheet_teen_preg.htm (accessed May 11, 2009)

declined, falling to rates lower than the 1976 rates by 1996 for teens aged 15 to 17 and by 1997 for teens aged 18 to 19. By 2004 teen pregnancy rates were the lowest ever for each age group since 1976. Birthrates for young women in these age groups mimic the rising and falling patterns of pregnancy rates from 1976 to 2004.

Table 5.1 shows teen pregnancy rates by age and by year from 1990 to 2004. It includes the category of adolescents younger than 15 years of age as well as the 15- to 17- and 18- to 19-year-old groups. In 2004 the pregnancy rate for women aged 18 to 19 was the highest of the three age groups, at 118.6 pregnancies per 1,000 women. The pregnancy rate for 15- to 17-year-olds was dramatically less at 41.5 pregnancies per 1,000, and for female adolescents aged 14 and younger it was 1.6 pregnancies per 1,000.

A clear and steady decline in pregnancy rates from 1990 to 2004 within each of the three age groups can be seen in Table 5.1. For the 18- to 19-year-old group, the pregnancy rate declined from 167.7 per 1,000 in 1990 to 118.6 per 1,000 in 2004. For the 15- to 17-year-old group the pregnancy rate declined from 77.1 per 1,000 in 1990 to 41.5 per 1,000 in 2004. There are very few pregnancies in adolescents under the age of 15. Nevertheless, the pregnancy rate declined in this group as well, from 3.4 pregnancies per 1,000 in 1990 to 1.6 pregnancies per 1,000 in 2004.

The rest of Table 5.1 shows the outcomes of the pregnancies. For example, in 2004 there were 72.2 pregnancies per 1,000 teens aged 15 to 19. What happened with these

TABLE 5.1

Pregnancy, birth, abortion, and miscarriage rates, teenagers aged 15–19 and adolescents under 15 years, 1990–2004

[Rates are pregnancy outcomes per 1,000 women in specified group estimated as of April 1 for 1990 and 2000 and as of July 1 for all other years]

Pregnancy outcome, race, and Hispanic origin and year	Total[a]	Under 15 years[b]	15–19 years Total	15–17 years	18–19 years
All races[d]					
All pregnancies					
2004	103.0	1.6	72.2	41.5	118.6
2003	103.2	1.6	73.7	42.7	120.7
2002	101.9	1.7	76.0	44.1	124.4
2001	102.9	1.8	80.4	46.7	130.5
2000	104.1	2.0	84.8	50.8	134.5
1999	102.2	2.1	86.9	53.1	136.6
1998	102.2	2.3	90.1	56.7	140.3
1997	101.6	2.4	92.7	59.5	144.3
1996	102.8	2.7	97.0	63.4	149.0
1995	103.5	2.9	101.1	67.4	153.4
1994	106.1	3.2	106.1	71.1	159.6
1993	108.8	3.2	109.4	72.7	164.1
1992	111.1	3.3	112.3	73.5	169.3
1991	112.7	3.3	116.4	76.1	172.1
1990	115.8	3.4	116.8	77.1	167.7
Live births					
2004	66.3	0.7	41.1	22.1	70.0
2003	66.1	0.6	41.6	22.4	70.7
2002	64.8	0.7	43.0	23.2	72.8
2001	65.3	0.8	45.3	24.7	76.1
2000	65.9	0.9	47.7	26.9	78.1
1999	64.4	0.9	48.8	28.2	79.1
1998	64.3	1.0	50.3	29.9	80.9
1997	63.6	1.1	51.3	31.4	82.1
1996	64.1	1.2	53.5	33.3	84.7
1995	64.6	1.3	56.0	35.5	87.7
1994	65.9	1.4	58.2	37.2	90.2
1993	67.0	1.4	59.0	37.5	91.1
1992	68.4	1.4	60.3	37.6	93.6
1991	69.3	1.4	61.8	38.6	94.0
1990	70.9	1.4	59.9	37.5	88.6
Induced abortions					
2004	19.7	0.7	19.8	11.8	31.9
2003	20.2	0.7	20.7	12.5	33.0
2002	20.5	0.7	21.3	12.8	34.1
2001	20.9	0.8	22.6	13.5	36.3
2000	21.3	0.9	24.0	14.5	37.7
1999	21.4	0.9	24.7	15.2	38.6
1998	21.5	1.0	25.8	16.4	40.0
1997	21.9	1.0	27.1	17.2	42.6
1996	22.4	1.1	28.6	18.6	44.0
1995	22.5	1.2	29.4	19.5	44.8
1994	23.7	1.3	31.6	21.0	47.8
1993	25.0	1.4	33.9	22.2	51.2
1992	25.7	1.4	35.2	22.9	53.3
1991	26.2	1.4	37.4	24.2	55.7
1990	27.4	1.5	40.3	26.5	57.9

TABLE 5.1

Pregnancy, birth, abortion, and miscarriage rates, teenagers aged 15–19 and adolescents under 15 years, 1990–2004 [CONTINUED]

[Rates are pregnancy outcomes per 1,000 women in specified group estimated as of April 1 for 1990 and 2000 and as of July 1 for all other years]

Pregnancy outcome, race, and Hispanic origin and year	Total[a]	Under 15 years[b]	15–19 years Total	15–17 years	18–19 years
Fetal losses[e]					
2004	17.0	0.2	11.3	7.7	16.7
2003	16.9	0.2	11.4	7.8	16.9
2002	16.6	0.2	11.8	8.1	17.4
2001	16.7	0.3	12.4	8.6	18.2
2000	16.9	0.3	13.1	9.4	18.7
1999	16.5	0.3	13.5	9.8	18.9
1998	16.4	0.3	14.0	10.4	19.4
1997	16.2	0.4	14.3	10.9	19.6
1996	16.3	0.4	15.0	11.6	20.3
1995	16.3	0.5	15.7	12.3	21.0
1994	16.6	0.5	16.3	12.9	21.6
1993	16.7	0.5	16.5	13.0	21.8
1992	17.0	0.5	16.8	13.0	22.4
1991	17.1	0.5	17.2	13.4	22.5
1990	17.4	0.5	16.6	13.0	21.2

[a]Rates computer by relating the number of events to women of all ages to women aged 15–44 years.
[b]Rates computer by relating the number of events to women under age 15 years to women aged 10–14 years.
[c]Includes races other than white and black and origin not stated.
[d]Spontaneous fetal losses from recognized pregnancies of all gestational periods as estimated from reports from women in the National Surveys of Family Growth conducted by the National Center for Health Statistics. The rate of fetal loss depends on the degree to which losses at very early gestations are detected.
[e]Includes all persons of Hispanic origin of any race.
Notes: Rates for 2000–2002 for ages 15–19, 15–17 and 18–19 years, have been revised and may differ from rates previously published. Due to sample size limitations in any given year, fetal loss proportions for teenagers for 1990–2004 are based on cycles 3 through 6 of the National Survey of Family Growth (conducted 1982, 1988, 1995, and 2002). Rates for 1990–2000 have been revised for ages 10–14 and may differ from rates previously published.

SOURCE: Adapted from Stephanie J. Ventura et al., "Table 2. Pregnancy, Live Birth, Induced Abortion, and Fetal Loss Rates by Age, Race, and Hispanic Origin of Woman: United States, 1990–2004—Con.," in "Estimated Pregnancy Rates by Outcome for the United States, 1990–2004," *National Vital Statistics Reports*, vol. 56, no. 15, April 14, 2008, http://www.cdc.gov/nchs/data/nvsr/nvsr56/nvsr56_15.pdf (accessed June 5, 2009)

pregnancies? There were 41.1 births per 1,000 teens aged 15 to 19 in 2004, 19.8 abortions, and 11.3 fetal losses (miscarriages), making up the total outcomes for the 72.2 pregnancies per 1,000 teens.

Explaining the Decline in Teen Pregnancy Rates

In "Explaining Recent Declines in Adolescent Pregnancy in the United States: The Contribution of Abstinence and Improved Contraceptive Use" (*American Journal of Public Health*, vol. 97, no. 1, January 2007), John S. Santelli et al. use data from 1995 to 2002 concerning the effectiveness of contraceptive use among sexually active teens and self-reports of abstinence or sexual activity to help explain the decline in pregnancy rates in the United States in the past two decades. The researchers conclude, "The decline in U.S. adolescent pregnancy rates appears to be following the patterns observed in other developed countries, where improved contraceptive use has been the primary determinant of declining rates." Santelli et al. note that "although more adolescents in the United States are delaying initiation of sexual intercourse, the impact of this change on pregnancy risk is small and confined to younger teenagers (i.e., 15- to 17-year-olds)."

Variation in Teen Pregnancy Rates among Groups

Teen pregnancy rates vary among the major racial and ethnic groups in the United States. Figure 5.4 shows that in 2004 pregnancy rates were the highest for Hispanic female

FIGURE 5.4

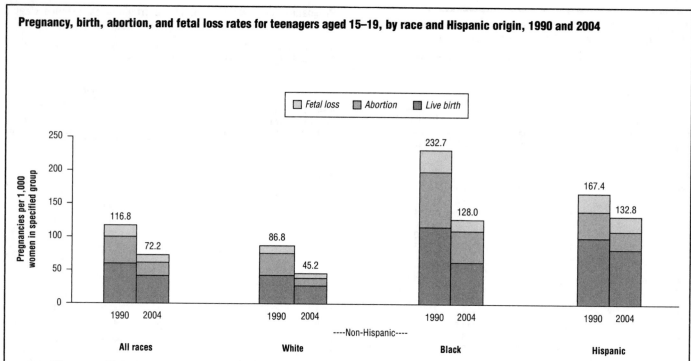

Pregnancy, birth, abortion, and fetal loss rates for teenagers aged 15–19, by race and Hispanic origin, 1990 and 2004

SOURCE: "Pregnancy, Birth, Abortion, and Fetal Loss Rates for Teenagers 15–19 Years, by Race and Hispanic Origin: United States, 1990 and 2004," in *NCHS Data on Teenage Pregnancy*, Centers for Disease Control and Prevention, National Center for Health Statistics, October 2008, http://www.cdc.gov/nchs/data/infosheets/infosheet_teen_preg.htm (accessed May 11, 2009)

teens (132.8 pregnancies per 1,000 women aged 15 to 19), closely followed by African-American female teens (128). In 1990, however, this picture was reversed, with African-American teens aged 15 to 19 having a much higher pregnancy rate (232.7 per 1,000) than Hispanic teens of the same age (167.4 per 1,000). Pregnancy rates fell for both African-American and Hispanic teens from 1990 to 2004. The lowest pregnancy rate in 2004 was for non-Hispanic white teens at 45.2 pregnancies per 1,000. This group showed a decline in pregnancy rates from 1990 as well.

Life Consequences of Teen Pregnancy

In the fact sheet "Why It Matters: Teen Pregnancy, Poverty, and Income Disparity" (May 2007, http://www.thenationalcampaign.org/why-it-matters/pdf/poverty.pdf), the National Campaign to Prevent Teen Pregnancy discusses the theme of poverty and how it is one consequence of teen pregnancy. The organization explains that teen mothers are less likely to obtain the education they need to get a good job—only 40% of teen mothers graduate from high school, compared with 75% of female teens of similar socioeconomic status who are not mothers. It also notes that "virtually all of the increase in child poverty between 1980 and 1996 was related to the increase in nonmarital childbearing, and half of never-married mothers begin their childbearing as teens."

David M. Fergusson, Joseph M. Boden, and L. John Horwood support in "Abortion among Young Women and Subsequent Life Outcomes" (*Perspectives on Sexual and Reproductive Health*, vol. 39, no. 1, March 2007) the assertion on educational outcomes noted in the National Campaign to Prevent Teen Pregnancy fact sheet. The researchers find that pregnant women under the age of 21 "who had abortions had higher levels of subsequent educational achievement than those who became pregnant but did not have abortions."

Poverty is not the only life consequence of teen pregnancy. The National Campaign to Prevent Teen Pregnancy notes in the fact sheet "Why It Matters: Teen Pregnancy and Other Health Issues" (February 2007, http://www.thenationalcampaign.org/why-it-matters/pdf/health.pdf) that the children of teenage mothers have lower birth weights, increasing the risk of infant death, blindness, deafness, chronic respiratory problems, mental retardation, mental illness, and cerebral palsy. Low birth weight also doubles the chances that a child will be diagnosed with dyslexia, hyperactivity, or another disability. Children of teenage mothers are also more likely to be abused and neglected and to perform poorly in school. The National Campaign to Prevent Teen Pregnancy also reports that the sons of teenage mothers are twice as likely to end up in prison than are the sons of older mothers and that the daughters of teen mothers are three times more likely to become teen mothers themselves than are the daughters born of older mothers.

Fergusson, Boden, and Horwood conclude, "In general, there is a clear need for further study of the social, educational and related outcomes of the decision to terminate a pregnancy so that women may be properly informed of the potential consequences of this [abortion] decision for their life course."

Teen Pregnancy Outcomes

Figure 5.5 shows that across ages and races, slightly over one out of four (27.4%) of teen pregnancies ended in abortion in 2004. More than one out of two (57%) teens who became pregnant gave birth, and about one out of six (15.6%) miscarried.

FIGURE 5.5

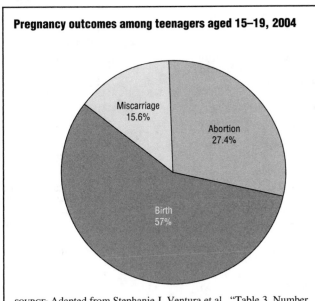

Pregnancy outcomes among teenagers aged 15–19, 2004

Miscarriage 15.6%

Abortion 27.4%

Birth 57%

SOURCE: Adapted from Stephanie J. Ventura et al., "Table 3. Number and Percent Distribution of Pregnancies by Outcome of Pregnancy by Age, Race, and Hispanic Origin of Woman: United States, 1990 and 2004," in "Estimated Pregnancy Rates by Outcome for the United States, 1990–2004," *National Vital Statistics Reports*, vol. 56, no. 15, April 14, 2008, http://www.cdc.gov/nchs/data/nvsr/nvsr56/nvsr56_15.pdf (accessed June 5, 2009)

Figure 5.6 shows pregnancy outcomes by age for selected years from 1990 to 2004. (The pregnancy rate—the number of pregnancies per 1,000 women of that age group—is shown at the top of each bar.) Over time, the pregnancy rate decreased for both age groups. However, what happened to the proportion (percentage) of the three possible pregnancy outcomes of fetal loss: miscarriage, abortion, and birth?

In the 15- to 17-year-old age group the percentage of pregnant teens having an abortion decreased from 34.5% in 1990 to 28.3% in 2004. (See Table 5.2.) A similar decrease occurred in the 18- to 19-year-old group, from about 34.5% in 1990 to about 26.9% in 2004.

If the proportion of abortions in both age groups decreased over time, then what increased? Table 5.2 shows that in the 15- to 17-year-old group both the percentage of fetal loss increased (16.9% in 1990 to 18.5% in 2004) as did the percentage of births (48.7% to 53.5%). In the 18- to 19-year-old group, the percentage of fetal loss increased only slightly (12.6% in 1990 to 14.1% in 2004), but the percentage of births increased dramatically (52.8% to 59%).

Table 5.2 shows the pregnancy outcomes by race and Hispanic origin for 1990 and 2004. The proportion of fetal losses for Hispanic teens aged 15 to 19 from 1990 to 2004 increased only slightly, from 16.8% to 17.3%. The proportion of fetal losses for white teens of the same age group increased more dramatically: 13.4% to 15.8%. Conversely, the proportion of fetal losses for African-Americans decreased from 14.2% to 13.7%. Thus, in 1990 the proportion of fetal losses was highest for Hispanic teens at 16.8% and lowest for white teens at 13.4%. In 2004 Hispanic teens still had the highest proportion of fetal losses (17.3%), but African-American teens had the lowest proportion of fetal losses (13.7%).

FIGURE 5.6

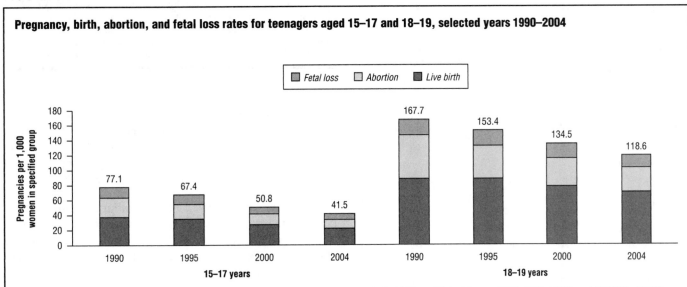

Pregnancy, birth, abortion, and fetal loss rates for teenagers aged 15–17 and 18–19, selected years 1990–2004

■ Fetal loss ☐ Abortion ■ Live birth

SOURCE: "Pregnancy, Birth, Abortion, and Fetal Loss Rates for Teenagers 15–17 and 18–19 Years: United States, 1990, 1995, 2000, and 2004," in *NCHS Data on Teenage Pregnancy*, Centers for Disease Control and Prevention, National Center for Health Statistics, October 2008, http://www.cdc.gov/nchs/data/infosheets/infosheet_teen_preg.htm (accessed May 11, 2009)

TABLE 5.2

Number and percent of pregnancies by outcome of pregnancy by race, teenagers aged 15–19 and adolescents under 15 years, 1990 and 2004

[Numbers in thousands]

Pregnancy outcome and race and Hispanic origin	Total	Under 15 years	15–19 years Total	15–17 years	18–19 years
2004					
All races[1]		**Number of pregnancies**			
All pregnancies	6,390	16	729	252	477
Live births	4,112	7	415	134	281
Induced abortions	1,222	7	200	71	128
Fetal losses[2]	1,056	2	114	47	67
Non-Hispanic white					
All pregnancies	3,355	4	289	86	204
Live births	2,322	1	171	46	125
Induced abortions	418	2	73	24	49
Fetal losses[2]	615	1	46	16	30
Non-Hispanic black					
All pregnancies	1,211	7	198	76	123
Live births	582	3	98	35	63
Induced abortions	453	4	73	29	45
Fetal losses[2]	176	1	27	12	15
Hispanic[3]					
All pregnancies	1,410	5	214	81	133
Live births	946	2	133	49	84
Induced abortions	269	1	44	16	28
Fetal losses[2]	194	1	37	17	20
All races[1]		**Percent distribution**			
All pregnancies	100.0	100.0	100.0	100.0	100.0
Live births	64.4	41.9	57.0	53.2	59.0
Induced abortions	19.1	43.6	27.4	28.3	26.9
Fetal losses[2]	16.5	14.5	15.6	18.5	14.1
Non-Hispanic white					
All pregnancies	100.0	100.0	100.0	100.0	100.0
Live births	69.2	40.3	59.0	53.5	61.4
Induced abortions	12.4	45.7	25.1	27.9	24.0
Fetal losses[2]	18.3	14.0	15.8	18.6	14.7
Non-Hispanic black					
All pregnancies	100.0	100.0	100.0	100.0	100.0
Live births	48.1	37.1	49.3	46.3	51.2
Induced abortions	37.4	50.0	37.0	37.7	36.6
Fetal losses[2]	14.5	12.9	13.7	16.1	12.2
Hispanic[3]					
All pregnancies	100.0	100.0	100.0	100.0	100.0
Live births	67.1	51.3	62.2	60.0	63.6
Induced abortions	19.1	31.0	20.4	19.1	21.2
Fetal losses[2]	13.8	17.8	17.3	20.8	15.2
1990					
All races[a]		**Number of pregnancies**			
All pregnancies	6,786	28	1,017	377	641
Live births	4,158	12	522	183	338
Induced abortions	1,609	13	351	130	221
Fetal losses[2]	1,019	4	145	64	81
Non-Hispanic white					
All pregnancies	4,242	8	527	177	350
Live births	2,711	3	259	79	180
Induced abortions	852	5	198	71	126
Fetal losses[2]	679	1	70	27	43
Non-Hispanic black					
All pregnancies	1,377	15	301	126	174
Live births	674	6	150	62	88
Induced abortions	507	7	108	42	65
Fetal losses[2]	196	2	43	22	21

TABLE 5.2

Number and percent of pregnancies by outcome of pregnancy by race, teenagers aged 15–19 and adolescents under 15 years, 1990 and 2004 [CONTINUED]

[Numbers in thousands]

Pregnancy outcome and race and Hispanic origin	Total	Under 15 years	15–19 years Total	15–17 years	18–19 years
Hispanic[c]					
All pregnancies	911	4	164	64	100
Live births	597	2	98	37	61
Induced abortions	195	1	38	14	24
Fetal losses[2]	119	1	27	13	15
All races[a]		**Percent distribution**			
All pregnancies	100.0	100.0	100.0	100.0	100.0
Live births	61.3	41.2	51.3	48.7	52.8
Induced abortions	23.7	44.5	34.5	34.5	34.5
Fetal losses[2]	15.0	14.3	14.2	16.9	12.6
Non-Hispanic white					
All pregnancies	100.0	100.0	100.0	100.0	100.0
Live births	63.9	32.8	49.1	44.3	51.6
Induced abortions	20.1	55.8	37.5	40.3	36.1
Fetal losses[2]	16.0	11.4	13.4	15.4	12.3
Non-Hispanic black					
All pregnancies	100.0	100.0	100.0	100.0	100.0
Live births	48.9	41.3	49.9	49.3	50.4
Induced abortions	36.8	44.3	35.9	33.5	37.6
Fetal losses[2]	14.2	14.4	14.2	17.1	12.1
Hispanic[c]					
All pregnancies	100.0	100.0	100.0	100.0	100.0
Live births	65.5	55.1	59.9	58.3	60.9
Induced abortions	21.4	25.8	23.4	21.5	24.5
Fetal losses[2]	13.1	19.1	16.8	20.2	14.6

[a]Includes races other than white and black and origin not stated.
[b]Spontaneous fetal losses from recognized pregnancies of all gestational periods as estimated from reports from women in the National Surveys of Family Growth conducted by the National Center for Health Statistics. The rate of fetal loss depends on the degree to which losses at very early gestations are detected.
[c]Includes all persons of Hispanic origin of any race.
Notes: Due to rounding, figures may not add to totals. Percent distributions based on unrounded frequencies. Due to sample size limitations in any given year, fetal loss proportions for teenagers for 2003 are based on cycles 3 through 6 of the National Survey of Family Growth (conducted 1982, 1988, 1995, and 2002).

SOURCE: Adapted from Stephanie J. Ventura et al., "Table 3. Number and Percent Distribution of Pregnancies by Outcome of Pregnancy by Age, Race, and Hispanic Origin of Woman: United States, 1990 and 2004," in "Estimated Pregnancy Rates by Outcome for the United States, 1990–2004," *National Vital Statistics Reports*, vol. 56, no. 15, April 14, 2008, http://www.cdc.gov/nchs/data/nvsr/nvsr56/nvsr56_15.pdf (accessed June 5, 2009)

Regarding abortion, the percentage of abortions for white teens aged 15 to 19 decreased substantially between 1990 and 2004, from 37.5% to 25.1%. (See Table 5.2.) Conversely, the proportion of births for white teens of that age group increased during that time, from 49.1% in 1990 to 59% in 2002.

Hispanic teens showed a trend similar to whites, but the percentage change was slight in comparison. Abortions in this group declined from 23.4% in 1990 to about 20.4% in 2004. (See Table 5.2.) Births in the Hispanic group increased from 59.9% to 62.2%.

In the African-American group, the pattern was reversed from Hispanics and whites, but the change over time was slight. The percentage of abortions for African-American teens aged 15 to 19 increased slightly from 35.9% in 1990 to nearly 37% in 2004. The percentage of births decreased from 49.9% to approximately 49.3%.

PREVENTING TEEN PREGNANCY

In "Sexual Health of Adolescents and Young Adults in the United States" (September 2008, http://www.kff.org/womenshealth/upload/3040_04.pdf), the Kaiser Family Foundation (KFF) indicates that the median age for first sex is in the mid- to late teens, at 16.9 years for boys and 17.4 years for girls. (Median in this case means that half have had sex and half have not.) In 2007 only 4% of female teens and 10.1% of male teens reported having their first sexual intercourse before age 13. (See Table 5.3.)

Table 5.3 also shows the percentage of ninth through 12th graders who had engaged in sexual intercourse by the time they were surveyed in 2007: 45.9% of high school girls and 49.8% of high school boys. This percentage has declined over time. According to the KFF, in the fact sheet "U.S. Teen Sexual Activity" (January 2005, http://www.kff.org/youthhivstds/upload/U-S-Teen-Sexual-Activity-Fact-Sheet.pdf), 50% of high school girls and 56% of high school boys responded that they had had sexual intercourse by the time they were surveyed in 1993.

Sex and Abstinence-Only Education

What methods can be used to prevent teen pregnancy from occurring as a result of these sexual encounters? What is the role of sex education and the availability of contraception? Countries such as France, Germany, and the Netherlands try to prevent teenage pregnancy through education about sexuality and contraception (birth control), whereas the United States places more emphasis on preventing teenage sex by encouraging abstinence.

The 1996 federal welfare reform law, the Personal Responsibility and Work Opportunity Reconciliation Act (Title V, Section 510), provided an annual $50 million allocation over a five-year period (1998 to 2002) to states for abstinence education programs. The purpose of these programs was "to enable the State to provide abstinence education, and at the option of the State, where appropriate, mentoring, counseling, and adult supervision to promote abstinence from sexual activity, with a focus on those groups which are most likely to bear children out-of-wedlock." Funded programs were prohibited from teaching birth control, although students requesting information could be given referrals. In addition, the law included an incentive provision, allotting $50 million to be distributed to the top five states that reduced their nonmarital births without increasing abortions during the previous two years. Congress then passed the Welfare Reform Extension Act of 2003, the Welfare Reform Extension Act of 2004, and the Welfare Reform Extension Act of 2005, which reauthorized and funded the abstinence education program in those years and through 2009.

POSITIONS OF MEDICAL SOCIETIES ON ABSTINENCE-ONLY EDUCATION. In 2006, in response to data showing that abstinence-only programs did not delay the age at which teenagers engaged in first sexual intercourse, provided misinformation and withheld needed information about contraception and protection from sexually transmitted infections (STIs), including the human immunodeficiency virus (HIV) and the acquired immunodeficiency syndrome (AIDS), and was ethically problematic in its coercive nature, the Society

TABLE 5.3

Percentage of high school students who ever had sexual intercourse and who had sexual intercourse for the first time before age 13 years, by sex, race/ethnicity, and grade, 2007

Category	Ever had sexual intercourse			Had first sexual intercourse before age 13 years		
	Female	Male	Total	Female	Male	Total
	%	%	%	%	%	%
Race/ethnicity						
White*	43.7	43.6	43.7	3.1	5.7	4.4
Black*	60.9	72.6	66.5	6.9	26.2	16.3
Hispanic	45.8	58.2	52.0	4.5	11.9	8.2
Grade						
9	27.4	38.1	32.8	4.9	13.5	9.2
10	41.9	45.6	43.8	4.7	9.1	6.9
11	53.6	57.3	55.5	3.4	9.9	6.6
12	66.2	62.8	64.6	2.4	6.7	4.5
Total	**45.9**	**49.8**	**47.8**	**4.0**	**10.1**	**7.1**

*Non-Hispanic.

SOURCE: Adapted from Danice K. Eaton et al., "Table 61. Percentage of High School Students Who Ever Had Sexual Intercourse and Who Had Sexual Intercourse for the First Time before Age 13 Years, by Sex, Race/Ethnicity, and Grade—United States, Youth Risk Behavior Survey, 2007," in "Youth Risk Behavior Surveillance—United States, 2007," *Morbidity and Mortality Weekly Report*, June 6, 2008, Vol. 57, no. SS-4, http://www.cdc.gov/HealthyYouth/yrbs/pdf/yrbss07_mmwr.pdf (accessed May 15, 2009)

for Adolescent Medicine (SAM) published the position paper "Abstinence-Only Education Policies and Programs: A Position Paper of the Society for Adolescent Medicine" (*Journal of Adolescent Health*, vol. 38). SAM documents the problems with abstinence-only sex education and states that it "supports a comprehensive approach to sexual risk reduction including abstinence as well as correct and consistent use of condoms and contraception among teens who choose to be sexually active.... Efforts to promote abstinence should be provided within health education programs that provide adolescents with complete and accurate information about sexual health, including information about concepts of healthy sexuality, sexual orientation and tolerance, personal responsibility, risks of HIV and other STIs and unwanted pregnancy, access to reproductive health care, and benefits and risks of condoms and other contraceptive methods."

SAM also states that "government policy regarding sexual and reproductive health education should be science-based" and that "current U.S. federal law and guidelines regarding abstinence-only funding are ethically flawed and interfere with fundamental human rights." Furthermore, SAM calls for the repeal of abstinence-only funding laws and the institution of funding that supports "comprehensive medically accurate sexuality education."

Other medical societies that have taken positions against abstinence-only education include the American Academy of Pediatrics, in "Sexuality Education for Children and Adolescents" (*Pediatrics*, vol. 108, no. 2, August 2001), and the American Public Health Association, in "Abstinence and U.S. Abstinence-Only Education Policies: Ethical and Human Rights Concerns Policy Statement" (November 8, 2006, http://www.apha.org/advocacy/policy/policysearch/default.htm?id=1334).

ABSTINENCE-ONLY VERSUS NO SEX EDUCATION. In *Impacts of Four Title V, Section 510 Abstinence Education Programs: Final Report* (April 2007, http://www.mathematica-mpr.com/publications/pdfs/impactabstinence.pdf), Christopher Trenholm et al. present the results of a multiyear study of four prominent Title V, Section 510 abstinence-only sex education programs. Nearly 59% (1,209) of the 2,057 students in the study were enrolled in one of the four abstinence-only programs and the remainder (848) were not enrolled in sex education. By the time the students were surveyed regarding their sex practices, those enrolled in abstinence-only education had completed their multiyear programs.

Trenholm et al. report no difference in abstinence between students enrolled in abstinence-only sex education programs and students not enrolled in sex education programs. Forty-nine percent of each group remained abstinent from sexual intercourse, and 55% to 56% had remained abstinent during the last 12 months before they were surveyed. In addition, the two groups did not differ in their rates of unprotected sex: 23% always used a condom, 17%

sometimes used a condom, and 4% never used a condom. The average age of first intercourse in both groups was 14.9 years. (The researchers note that this age may seem young, but these results are from a group consisting of only sexually experienced teens with an average age less than 17.)

The students in the study were also asked questions about their perceived effectiveness of condoms and birth control pills for pregnancy prevention. Slightly over half the students in both groups thought that—when used properly—condoms (51% and 52%, respectively) and birth control pills (56% and 55%, respectively) usually prevent pregnancy. Thirty-eight percent of both groups thought condoms sometimes prevent pregnancy, and 33% and 36%, respectively, thought birth control pills sometimes prevent pregnancy. Only 3% of both groups thought condoms or birth control pills never prevent pregnancy, and 7% of both groups were unsure if each type of contraception prevents pregnancy.

COMPARING ABSTINENCE-ONLY, COMPREHENSIVE, AND NO SEX EDUCATION. In 2008 Pamela K. Kohler, Lisa E. Manhart, and William E. Lafferty published "Abstinence-Only and Comprehensive Sex Education and the Initiation of Sexual Activity and Teen Pregnancy" (*Journal of Adolescent Health*, vol. 42), in which they compare abstinence-only education, comprehensive sex education, and no sex education regarding the effects of these programs on the initiation of sexual activity and teen pregnancy. Comprehensive sex education is a type of program that not only teaches the benefits of abstinence but also teaches contraceptive methods to avoid pregnancy and condoms to avoid STIs.

Kohler, Manhart, and Lafferty note that students who had completed abstinence-only programs did not have a reduction in the initiation of sexual activity or in their risk for teen pregnancy, compared with students who had comprehensive or no sex education programs. Moreover, when the researchers compare teens who had comprehensive sex education with those who had abstinence-only education, they find that "comprehensive sex education was associated with a 50% lower risk of teen pregnancy." In their discussion of the results, Kohler, Manhart, and Lafferty state, "Although future prospective studies expressly designed to evaluate the effects of formal sex education programs are required, these data suggest that formal comprehensive sex education programs reduce the risk for teen pregnancy without increasing the likelihood that adolescents will engage in sexual activity, and confirm results from randomized controlled trials that abstinence-only programs have a minimal effect on sexual risk behavior."

FUNDING FOR ABSTINENCE-ONLY SEX EDUCATION CUT. In "Just Say No to Abstinence Education" (*Newsweek*, October 18, 2008), Laura Beil reports that in 2008, 25 state health departments had rejected Title V, Section 510 funds for abstinence-only education, up from 11 state health departments in 2007. These health departments were influenced not only by research reports such as the ones previously described in this chapter but also by the report

"Births: Preliminary Data for 2006" (*National Vital Statistics Reports*, vol. 56, no. 7, December 5, 2007) by Brady E. Hamilton, Joyce A. Martin, and Stephanie J. Ventura of the National Center for Health Statistics (NCHS). This latter report showed that after 15 years of steady decline, the teen birthrate was on the rise again.

In his 2010 budget, President Barack Obama (1961–) eliminated funding for abstinence-only education. By doing so, he was able to provide $178 million for teen pregnancy prevention. Sharon Jayson reports in "Obama Budget Shifts Money from Abstinence-Only Sex Education: It's a Major Reversal from Bush's Policies" (*USA Today*, May 12, 2009) that about three-fourths of the funding would be used for community-based programs that have been shown to delay teens' first intercourse, increase contraceptive use for sexually active teens, and reduce teen pregnancy. The other one-fourth would be used for "innovative" programs.

NEED FOR SEX EDUCATION. A majority of adults and teens agree that teens should be given more information about both abstinence and contraception. Figure 5.7 shows that nearly three-fourths (73%) of adults and over half (56%) of teens surveyed in 2006 believed teens should be receiving more information about both of these methods rather than only one or the other.

A 2008 survey conducted by the National Campaign to Prevent Teen and Unplanned Pregnancy and *Self* magazine shows that young people need more education on contraceptive measures if they are to be well informed about a variety of methods of preventing pregnancy. (See Table 5.4.) Men and women aged 18 to 29 responded to questions asking whether they knew "everything" or "a lot" about certain contraceptive methods. Even though 90% of men and 86% of women responded that they knew everything or a lot about male condoms, large proportions of the survey population were lacking information about other means of contraception. For example, less than 17% of both young men and young women knew a lot about the rhythm method, vaginal ring, intrauterine device (IUD), diaphragm, female condom, and contraceptive implants.

State Sex Education Policy

As of June 2009, 20 states and the District of Columbia mandated sex education in public schools, and 35 states and the District of Columbia mandated STI/HIV education. (See Table 5.5.) Twenty-three states required that abstinence be stressed when taught as part of sex education, and 10 states required that it be only covered. Only 14 states and the District of Columbia required that sex education programs cover contraception, whereas 17 states required that STI/

FIGURE 5.7

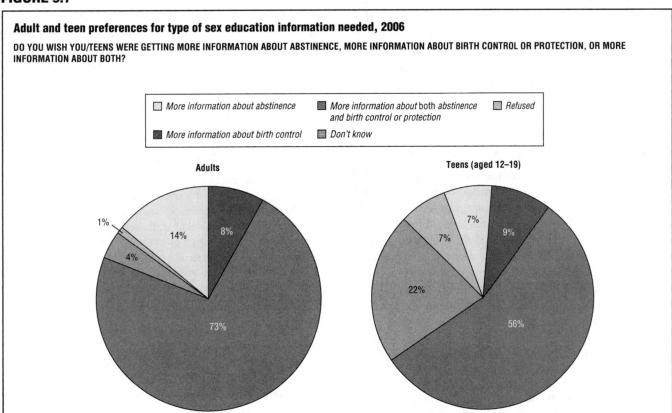

Adult and teen preferences for type of sex education information needed, 2006

DO YOU WISH YOU/TEENS WERE GETTING MORE INFORMATION ABOUT ABSTINENCE, MORE INFORMATION ABOUT BIRTH CONTROL OR PROTECTION, OR MORE INFORMATION ABOUT BOTH?

SOURCE: "Figure 3. Do You Wish You/Teens Were Getting More Information about Abstinence, More Information about Birth Control or Protection, or More Information about Both?" in *Science Says: American Opinion on Teen Pregnancy and Related Issues 2007*, no. 31, The National Campaign to Prevent Teen Pregnancy, May 2007, http://www.thenationalcampaign.org/resources/pdf/SS/SS31_AmericanOpinion.pdf (accessed June 10, 2009)

TABLE 5.4

Percentages of persons aged 18–29 years saying they know a lot about particular contraceptive methods, 2008

	All	Men	Women
Male condoms	88%	90%	86%
The pill	65%	52%	78%
Withdrawal	64%	66%	61%
The morning after pill/ emergency contraception	32%	30%	34%
The patch	21%	17%	26%
Rhythm method (natural family planning)	16%	16%	16%
Vaginal ring/NuvaRing	16%	14%	18%
IUD	13%	11%	15%
Diaphragm	11%	14%	9%
Female condom	11%	12%	11%
Contraception implants	10%	10%	9%

SOURCE: "1. Thinking about Birth Control/Contraception/Protection Methods, How Much Would You Say You Know about Each of the Following? (Percentage Answering That They Know 'Everything' or 'A Lot' about the Following Methods of Contraception.)" in *Magical Thinking: Young Adults' Attitudes and Beliefs about Sex, Contraception, and Unplanned Pregnancy, Results from a Public Opinion Survey*, The National Campaign to Prevent Teen and Unplanned Pregnancy, and Self Magazine, 2008, http://www.thenationalcampaign.org/resources/pdf/pubs/MagicalThinking.pdf (accessed May 16, 2009)

HIV programs cover contraception. No state required that contraception be stressed in either sex education classes or STI/HIV prevention classes.

Parental consent requirements or "opt-out" clauses, which allow parents to remove students from instruction the parents find objectionable, may restrict the information adolescents receive. Table 5.5 shows that as of June 2009 three states required parental consent for students to participate in sex or STI/HIV education, and 36 states and the District of Columbia allowed parents to remove their children from these classes.

Characteristics of Effective Sex Education Programs

In *What Works: Curriculum-Based Programs That Prevent Teen Pregnancy* (December 2007, http://www.thenationalcampaign.org/resources/pdf/pubs/WhatWorks_FINAL.pdf), the National Campaign to Prevent Teen Pregnancy provides an overview of the characteristics of sex education programs that "can delay sexual activity, improve contraceptive use among sexually active teens, and/or prevent teen pregnancy." This research-based report lists specific programs that have been shown to be effective, describes their effects, and provides other information specific to each. The report also lists general characteristics of effective sex education programs and notes that they:

- Convince teens that not having sex or that using contraception consistently and carefully is the *right* thing to do, as opposed to simply laying out the pros and cons of different sexual choices. That is, there is a clear message.

- Last a sufficient length of time (i.e., more than a few weeks).

- Select leaders who believe in the program and provide them with adequate training.

- Actively engage participants and have them personalize the information.

- Address peer pressure.

- Teach communication skills.

- Reflect the age, sexual experience, and culture of young people in the program.

Media Influences on Teenage Sex

SEXUAL RISK AND RESPONSIBILITY ON TELEVISION. According to Dale Kunkel et al., in *Sex on TV 2005: A Kaiser Family Foundation Report* (November 2005, http://www.kff.org/entmedia/upload/Sex-on-TV-4-Full-Report.pdf), the most recent study of the amount and nature of sexual material on television as of mid-2009, the number of television shows with sexual content increased significantly from 1998 to 2005.

Kunkel et al. looked at 1,154 programs and developed a composite week of television for each of the 10 of the most frequently viewed channels. The composite week was developed by randomly sampling the programs between October 2004 and April 2005. A summary of the sexual behavior shown on television compared with similar studies conducted in 1998 and 2002 showed that in 2005, 70% of the programs included sexual talk or behavior, up from 56% in 1998 and 64% in 2002. The researchers also determined that in 2005, 68% of shows had talk about sex, up from 54% in 1998 and 61% in 2002; and 35% showed sexual behavior, up from 23% in 1998 and 32% in 2002.

According to Kunkel et al.:

One of the most important factors likely to shape the socializing effects of sexual portrayals is the extent to which risk and responsibility concerns associated with sexual activity are included. In this study, we measured the presence of three types of themes involving the risks or responsibilities of sexual behavior: (1) *sexual patience*: waiting until a relationship matures and both people are equally ready to engage in sex; (2) *sexual precaution*: pursuing efforts to prevent HIV/AIDS, STDs, and/or unwanted pregnancy when sexually active; and (3) *depiction of risks and/or negative consequences* of irresponsible sexual behavior. Sexual encounters that are presented without any of these elements certainly convey a much different message to the audience, and in particular to young viewers, than portrayals that include them.

The results of the measurements of these themes revealed that the percentage of sexual scenes that contain risk/responsibility messages rose slightly in 2002, but that the percentage in 2005 was exactly the same as in 1998.

TABLE 5.5

State sex and Sexually Transmitted Infections/Human Immunodeficiency Virus (STI/HIV) education policy, 2009

State	Sex education Mandated	Abstinence	Contraception	STI/HIV Education Mandated	Abstinence	Contraception	Consent required	Opt-out permitted
		If taught, content required			If taught, content required		Parental role	
Alabama		Stress	Cover	X	Stress	Cover		X[a]
Arizona		Stress			Stress		X[b]	X[b]
Arkansas		Stress			Stress			
California		Cover	Cover	X	Cover	Cover		X
Colorado		Stress	Cover		Stress			X
Connecticut		Cover		X				X
Delaware	X	Cover	Cover	X	Cover	Cover		
Dist. of Columbia	X		Cover	X				X
Florida	X	Cover		X				X
Georgia	X	Cover		X	Cover			X
Hawaii	X	Stress	Cover	X	Stress	Cover		
Idaho								X
Illinois		Stress[c]			Stress[c]	Cover[c]		X
Indiana		Stress		X	Stress			
Iowa	X			X				X
Kansas	X			X				X
Kentucky	X	Cover		X	Cover			
Louisiana		Stress			Stress			X
Maine	X	Stress	Cover	X	Stress	Cover		X
Maryland	X	Cover	Cover	X	Cover	Cover		X
Massachusetts								X[a]
Michigan		Stress		X	Stress			X
Minnesota	X			X	Cover			X
Mississippi[d]		Stress			Stress			X
Missouri		Stress		X	Stress			X
Montana	X	Cover		X	Cover			X[b]
Nevada	X			X			X	
New Hampshire				X	Cover			X
New Jersey	X			X				X[a]
New Mexico				X	Stress	Cover		
New York				X	Stress	Cover		X[b]
North Carolina	X	Stress		X	Stress			
Ohio				X	Stress			X
Oklahoma		Stress		X	Cover	Cover		X
Oregon	X	Stress	Cover	X	Stress	Cover		X
Pennsylvania				X	Stress			X[a,b]
Rhode Island	X	Stress	Cover	X	Stress	Cover		X
South Carolina	X	Stress	Cover	X	Stress	Cover		X
South Dakota[e]								
Tennessee	X	Stress		X	Stress			X
Texas		Stress			Stress			X
Utah[f]	X	Stress		X	Stress		X	X
Vermont	X	Cover	Cover	X	Cover	Cover		X[a]
Virginia		Cover	Cover		Cover	Cover		X
Washington		Stress	Cover	X	Stress	Cover		X
West Virginia		Stress	Cover	X	Stress	Cover		X
Wisconsin		Stress		X	Stress			X
Total	**20 + DC**			**35 + DC**			**3**	**36 + DC**

[a]Parents' removal of student must be based on religious or moral beliefs.
[b]In AZ, MT, NY and PA, opt-out is only permitted for STI education, including instruction on HIV; in AZ, parental consent is required only for sex education.
[c]IL has a broad set of laws mandating general health education, including abstinence; a more specific second law requires a school district that provides sex education to stress abstinence and to provide statistics on the efficacy of condoms as HIV/STI prevention.
[d]Localities may override state requirements for sex education topics, including abstinence; state prohibits including material that "contradicts the required components."
[e]Abstinence is taught within state-mandated character education.
[f]State prohibits teachers from responding to students' spontaneous questions in ways that conflict with the law's requirements.

SOURCE: Guttmacher Institute, Community Health Centers and Family Planning, "State Sex and STD/HIV Education Policy," in *State Policies in Brief: Sex and STI/HIV Education*, New York: Guttmacher, June 1, 2009, http://www.guttmacher.org/statecenter/spibs/spib_SE.pdf (accessed June 8, 2009)

There does not appear to be an upward trend in the percentage of risk/responsibility messages in sexual portrayals on television.

SEX ON TELEVISION, TEEN SEXUAL BEHAVIOR, AND TEEN PREGNANCY. In November 2003 Rebecca L. Collins et al. of the Rand Corporation, a nonprofit research organization, published "Entertainment Television as a Healthy Sex Educator: The Impact of Condom-Efficacy Information in an Episode of *Friends*" (*Pediatrics*, vol. 112, no. 5). The results of this research study provide evidence that television causes changes in sexual activity and that change can be positive. The study reveals that American teenagers absorb sex education messages from television programs and that watching and discussing television programs with an adult reinforces the sex education messages.

In September 2004 Collins et al. published a subsequent study, the results of which did not show positive effects of television viewing on teen sex. In "Watching Sex on Television Predicts Adolescent Initiation of Sexual Behavior" (*Pediatrics*, vol. 114, no. 3), the researchers note that in spite of some of the positive references to safer sex and sexual responsibility on television as noted in the 2003 study, "watching sex on TV predicts and may hasten adolescent sexual initiation. Reducing the amount of sexual content in entertainment programming, reducing adolescent exposure to this content, or increasing references to and depictions of possible negative consequences of sexual activity could appreciably delay the initiation of coital and noncoital activities. Alternatively, parents may be able to reduce the effects of sexual content by watching TV with their teenaged children and discussing their own beliefs about sex and the behaviors portrayed."

In November 2008 Anita Chandra et al. of the Rand Corporation published "Does Watching Sex on Television Predict Teen Pregnancy? Findings from a National Longitudinal Survey of Youth" (*Pediatrics*, vol. 122, no. 5), a study that provided results that were even more specific regarding the link between teen viewing of sex on television and teen sexual behavior. The researchers find that there is a positive correlation between the viewing of sexual content on television and subsequent teen pregnancy. Chandra et al. explain the correlation, "Teens who were exposed to high levels of television sexual content (90th percentile) were twice as likely to experience a pregnancy in the subsequent 3 years, compared with those with lower levels of exposure (10th percentile)." Teens exposed to high levels of television sexual content means that 90% of teens watched less television sexual content than they did. Teens with lower levels of exposure means that 90% of teens watched more television sexual content than they did. The researchers conclude that "adolescents who view substantial televised sexual content have an increased risk of experiencing a pregnancy before age 20, compared with youths who view less sexual content on television."

POSITIVE MESSAGES REGARDING TEEN SEX AND PREGNANCY. Other television programming, some magazines, and some Web sites targeted to teens provide positive, educational messages regarding teen sex and pregnancy. For example, the award-winning ChannelOne.com (June 11, 2009, http://www-int.channelone.com/static/about/) reports that *Channel One Network*, a nationwide school-based news program that covers issues affecting American teens, is viewed by about 6 million students every school day. *Teen People* magazine and the National Campaign to Prevent Teen Pregnancy sponsor a contest each year asking teens to create a magazine advertisement with a message about preventing teen pregnancy. *Teen People* also provides continuing editorial coverage of issues surrounding teen pregnancy, and *Sports Illustrated* and BET's *Heart and Soul* magazine feature teen pregnancy prevention in their public service messages. Kiwibox.com features discussions on what it is like to be a teen mother, how to know when you are ready to have sex, and how to prevent pregnancy and STDs.

TRENDS IN SEXUAL RISK BEHAVIORS

Unprotected sexual intercourse and multiple sex partners place young people at risk for pregnancy as well as for HIV infection and other STDs. According to the CDC, from 1991 to 2007 the percentage of high school students who reported ever having sexual intercourse decreased, who had multiple sex partners (more than four) decreased, and who were currently sexually active decreased. (See Table 5.6.) Even though the percentages may seem to tell a different "story" than the CDC reports in some cases, the CDC is reporting increases, decreases, and no change based on statistical tests that reveal whether the differences (if any) in the percentages are sufficient to state that they are greater than expected by chance alone as populations are sampled.

Among currently sexually active high school students, condom use at last sexual intercourse increased from 1991 to 2003, and there was no change from 2003 to 2007. (See Table 5.6.) However, the percentage of these students who used alcohol or drugs before their last sexual intercourse increased from 1991 to 2003 and then decreased from 2003 to 2007. Birth control pill use from 1991 through 2007 saw no statistically significant change among these students.

Table 5.7 shows the results for 2007 on two of the trend questions concerning the use of birth control pills and condoms. The results are broken down by race, grade, and gender. In the high school population, condom use was highest for African-American males in 2007, with 74% of sexually active African-American boys reporting condom use during their last sexual intercourse. In surveying grade-level use, condom use was highest for ninth-grade boys. More high school males (68.5%) than females (54.9%) reported condom use. The use of birth control pills is not as prevalent among high school students as was condom use. The highest rate of use in 2007 was white females at 24%.

TEEN BIRTHRATES
International Comparisons

The U.S. birthrate for teens aged 15 to 19 is much higher than for other industrialized countries. This difference can be seen in the United Nations publication *World Fertility Patterns 2007* (March 2008, http://www.un.org/esa/population/publications/worldfertility2007/worldfertility2007.htm), which includes a detailed and extensive data table of age-specific fertility rates per 1,000 women, which are equivalent in this case to birthrates for each age group. The data table shows the U.S. teen birthrate to have been 43 births per 1,000 teens aged 15 to 19 in 2002. In 2007 the U.S. teen birthrate was 42.5 births per 1,000

TABLE 5.6

Trends in the prevalence of sexual behaviors among high school students, selected years 1991–2007

	1991	1993	1995	1997	1999	2001	2003	2005	2007	Changes from 1991–2007[a]	Changes from 2005–2007[b]
Ever had sexual intercourse	54.1	53.0	53.1	48.4	49.9	45.6	46.7	46.8	47.8	Decreased,1991–2007	No change
Had sexual intercourse with four or more persons during their life	18.7	18.7	17.8	16.0	16.2	14.2	14.4	14.3	14.9	Decreased, 1991–2007	No change
Currently sexually active (had sexual intercourse with at least one person during the 3 months before the survey)	37.5	37.5	37.9	34.8	36.3	33.4	34.3	33.9	35.0	Decreased, 1991–2007	No change
Used a condom during last sexual intercourse (among students who were currently sexually active)	46.2	52.8	54.4	56.8	58.0	57.9	63.0	62.8	61.5	Increased, 1991–2003 No change, 2003–2007	No change
Used birth control pills before last sexual intercourse (to prevent pregnancy, among students who were currently sexually active)	20.8	18.4	17.4	16.6	16.2	18.2	17.0	17.6	16.0	No change, 1991–2007	No change
Drank alcohol or used drugs before last sexual intercourse (among students who were currently sexually active)	21.6	21.3	24.8	24.7	24.8	25.6	25.4	23.3	22.5	Increased, 1991–2001 Decreased, 2001–2007	No change
Ever taught in school about AIDS or HIV infection	83.3	86.1	86.3	91.5	90.6	89.0	87.9	87.9	89.5	Increased, 1991–1997 Decreased, 1997–2007	No change

[a]Based on trend analyses using a logistic regression model controlling for sex, race/ethnicity, and grade.
[b]Based on t-test analyses.

SOURCE: "Trends in the Prevalence of Sexual Behaviors, National YRBS: 1991–2007," in *Healthy Youth! YRBSS National Trends in Risk Behaviors*, Centers for Disease Control and Prevention, National Center for Chronic Disease Prevention and Health Promotion, Division of Adolescent and School Health, 2008, http://www.cdc.gov/HealthyYouth/yrbs/pdf/yrbs07_us_sexual_behaviors_trend.pdf (accessed May 11, 2009)

TABLE 5.7

Percentage of high school students who used a condom during last sexual intercourse and who used birth control pills before last sexual intercourse[a, b], by sex, race/ethnicity, and grade, 2007

	Condom use			Birth control pill use		
	Female	Male	Total	Female	Male	Total
Category	%	%	%	%	%	%
Race/Ethnicity						
White[c]	53.9	66.4	59.7	24.0	17.0	20.8
Black[c]	60.1	74.0	67.3	12.1	6.3	9.1
Hispanic	52.1	69.9	61.4	9.1	9.0	9.1
Grade						
9	61.0	75.8	69.3	9.2	8.3	8.7
10	59.5	73.2	66.1	13.7	9.5	11.6
11	55.1	69.3	62.0	18.9	11.0	15.0
12	49.9	59.6	54.2	25.6	20.8	23.5
Total	**54.9**	**68.5**	**61.5**	**18.7**	**13.1**	**16.0**

[a]Among the 35.0% of students nationwide who were currently sexually active.
[b]To prevent pregnancy.
[c]Non-Hispanic.

SOURCE: Adapted from Danice K. Eaton et al., "Table 65. Percentage of High School Students Who Used a Condom during Last Sexual Intercourse and Who Used Birth Control Pills before Last Sexual Intercourse, by Sex, Race/Ethnicity, and Grade—United States, Youth Risk Behavior Survey, 2007," in "Youth Risk Behavior Surveillance—United States, 2007," *Morbidity and Mortality Weekly Report*, June 6, 2008, Vol. 57, no. SS-4, http://www.cdc.gov/HealthyYouth/yrbs/pdf/yrbss07_mmwr.pdf (accessed May 15, 2009)

teens. (See Table 5.8.) Compared with other industrialized countries, such as Japan (6 births per 1,000 teens aged 15 to 19 in 2004), the Netherlands (7 per 1,000 in 2003), Sweden (7 per 1,000 in 2002), France (8 per 1,000 in 2003), Canada (14 per 1,000 in 2003), the United Kingdom (27 per 1,000 in 2002), and the Russian Federation (28 per 1,000 in 2004), the United States' birthrate is between 1.5 and 7 times higher.

TABLE 5.8

Births and birth rates for adolescents and teenagers aged 10–19, by race, 2006 and 2007

[Data for 2007 are based on a continuous file of records received from the states. Figures for 2007 are based on weighted data rounded to the nearest individual, so categories may not add to totals. Rates are per 1,000 women in the specified age and race and Hispanic origin group]

Age and race and Hispanic origin of mother	2007 Number of births	2007 Rate	2006 Number of births	2006 Rate
All races and origins[a]				
Total[b]	4,317,119	69.5	4,265,555	68.5
10–14 years	6,218	0.6	6,396	0.6
15–19 years	445,045	42.5	435,436	41.9
15–17 years	140,640	22.2	138,943	22.0
18–19 years	304,405	73.9	296,493	73.0
Non-Hispanic white[c]				
Total[b]	2,312,473	60.1	2,308,640	59.5
10–14 years	1,269	0.2	1,267	0.2
15–19 years	173,104	27.2	169,729	26.6
15–17 years	45,144	11.8	45,260	11.8
18–19 years	127,960	50.5	124,469	49.3
Non-Hispanic black[c]				
Total[b]	627,230	71.6	617,247	70.6
10–14 years	2,326	1.5	2,462	1.6
15–19 years	106,224	64.3	103,725	63.7
15–17 years	36,266	35.8	36,365	36.2
18–19 years	69,958	109.3	67,360	108.4
American Indian or Alaska Native total[c, d]				
Total[b]	49,284	64.7	47,721	63.1
10–14 years	120	0.9	124	0.9
15–19 years	8,925	59.0	8,261	55.0
15–17 years	2,909	31.7	2,820	30.7
18–19 years	6,016	101.3	5,441	93.0
Asian or Pacific Islander total				
Total[b]	254,734	71.4	241,045	67.5
10–14 years	92	0.2	73	0.2
15–19 years	8,022	17.3	7,812	17.0
15–17 years	2,336	8.4	2,438	8.8
18–19 years	5,686	30.7	5,374	29.5

TABLE 5.8

Births and birth rates for adolescents and teenagers aged 10–19, by race, 2006 and 2007 [CONTINUED]

[Data for 2007 are based on a continuous file of records received from the states. Figures for 2007 are based on weighted data rounded to the nearest individual, so categories may not add to totals. Rates are per 1,000 women in the specified age and race and Hispanic origin group]

Age and race and Hispanic origin of mother	2007 Number of births	2007 Rate	2006 Number of births	2006 Rate
Hispanic[e]				
Total[b]	1,061,970	102.1	1,039,077	101.5
10–14 years	2,407	1.2	2,456	1.3
15–19 years	148,453	81.7	145,669	83.0
15–17 years	53,941	47.8	51,990	47.9
18–19 years	94,511	137.1	93,679	139.7

[a]Includes origin not stated.
[b]The total number includes births to women of all ages, 10–54 years. The rates shown for all ages is the fertility rate, which is defined as the total number of births (regardless of the mother's age) per 1,000 woman aged 15–44 years.
[c]Race and Hispanic origins are reported separately on birth certificates. Persons of Hispanic origin may be of any race. Race categories are consistent with the 1977 Office of Management and Budget (OMB) standards. In 2007, 27 states reported multiple-race data. The multiple-race for these states were bridged to the single-race categories of the 1977 OMB standards for comparability with other states. Multiple-race reporting areas vary for 2006–2007.
[d]Data for persons of Hispanic origin are included for this race group.
[e]Includes all persons of Hispanic orgin of any race.

SOURCE: Adapted from Brady E. Hamilton, Joyce A. Martin, and Stephanie J. Ventura, "Table 2. Births and Birth Rates, by Age and Race and Hispanic Origin of Mother: United States, Final 2006 and Preliminary 2007," in "Births: Preliminary Data for 2007," *National Vital Statistics Reports*, vol. 57, no. 12, March 18, 2009, http://www.cdc.gov/nchs/data/nvsr/nvsr57/nvsr57_12.pdf (accessed May 8, 2009)

Teen Birthrates Rise after 15 Years of Decline

Even though teen birthrates in the United States have been high compared with other developed countries, there have been positive statistics. The birthrate for adolescents aged 10 to 14 years decreased 50% between 1991 and 2005, from 1.4 births per 1,000 female teens to 0.7 per 1,000. (See Table 5.9.) In addition, the birthrate for teens aged 15 to 19 years decreased 34%, from 61.8 births per 1,000 in 1991 to 40.5 per 1,000 in 2005. Nonetheless, in 2006—for the first time in 15 years—birthrates in the United States rose for teens aged 15 to 19, from 40.5 births per 1,000 to 41.9 births per 1,000. In 2007 the birthrate for this age group rose again—to 42.5 births per 1,000. Table 5.9, Figure 5.2, and Figure 5.3 show that these increases occurred not only for teens aged 15 to 17 but also for teens aged 18 to 19.

In *NCHS Data on Teenage Pregnancy* (October 2008, http://www.cdc.gov/nchs/data/infosheets/infosheet_teen_preg.htm), the NCHS offers some insight for this increase.

Declines in teen pregnancy and birthrates through the first few years in the 21st century appear to be explained, in part, by reported declines between 1995 and 2002 in the percent of female teens who ever had intercourse and the percent who used contraception at last intercourse. Female teens reported these declines in the NCHS's 2002 National Survey of Family Growth. However, the CDC's Youth Risk Behavior Survey 2007 (YRBS) shows that both the reported increase in teen contraceptive use and reported decrease in female teen sexual intercourse changed direction after 2001. The NCHS expects new data and analyses of these data to be available by late 2009 to further explain the recent upward trend in teen births.

Births to Unmarried Teenagers

Table 5.10 shows the number and percentage of all births to unmarried women in age-specific groups. The data indicate that most of the births to teens were to those who were unmarried (because most teens are unmarried). In 2006, 84.4% of the births to women under the age of 20 were to unmarried teens. In 2007 that proportion rose to 85.7%. As the age groups ascend (with the exception of the 40 to 45 age group), the proportion of all births in each group to unmarried women descend, because in the older age groups more women are married so more births are to married women. Nonetheless, when looking

TABLE 5.9

Birth rates and percentage change in rates for teenagers aged 15–19, by age, race, and Hispanic origin, selected years 1991–2007

[Data for 2007 are based on a continuous file of records received from the states. Rates are per 1,000 women in the specified age and race and Hispanic origin group.]

Age and race and Hispanic origin of mother	Year				Percent change		
	2007	2006	2005	1991	2006–2007	2005–2007	1991–2005
10–14 years							
All races and origins[a]	0.6	0.6	0.7	1.4	0	−14	−50
Non-Hispanic white[b]	0.2	0.2	0.2	0.5	0	0	−60
Non-Hispanic black[b]	1.5	1.6	1.7	4.9	−6	−12	−65
American Indian or Alaska Native total[b, c]	0.9	0.9	0.9	1.6	0	0	−44
Asian or Pacific Islander total[b, c]	0.2	0.2	0.2	0.8	0	0	−75
Hispanic[d]	1.2	1.3	1.3	2.4	−8	−8	−46
15–19 years							
All races and origins[a]	42.5	41.9	40.5	61.8	1	5	−34
Non-Hispanic white[b]	27.2	26.6	25.9	43.4	2	5	−40
Non-Hispanic black[b]	64.3	63.7	60.9	118.2	1	6	−48
American Indian or Alaska Native total[b, c]	59.0	55.0	52.7	84.1	7	12	−37
Asian or Pacific Islander total[b, c]	17.3	17.0	17.0	27.3	2	2	−38
Hispanic[d]	81.7	83.0	81.7	104.6	−2	0	−22
15–17 years							
All races and origins[a]	22.2	22.0	21.4	38.6	1	4	−45
Non-Hispanic white[b]	11.8	11.8	11.5	23.6	0	3	−51
Non-Hispanic black[b]	35.8	36.2	34.9	86.1	−1	3	−59
American Indian or Alaska Native total[b, c]	31.7	30.7	30.5	51.9	3	4	−41
Asian or Pacific Islander total[b, c]	8.4	8.8	8.2	16.3	−5	2	−50
Hispanic[d]	47.8	47.9	48.5	69.2	0	−1	−30
18–19 years							
All races and origins[a]	73.9	73.0	69.9	94.0	1	6	−26
Non-Hispanic white[b]	50.5	49.3	48.0	70.6	2	5	−32
Non-Hispanic black[b]	109.3	108.4	103.0	162.2	1	6	−36
American Indian or Alaska Native total[b, c]	101.3	93.0	87.6	134.2	9	16	−35
Asian or Pacific Islander total[b, c]	30.7	29.5	30.1	42.2	4	2	−29
Hispanic[d]	137.1	139.7	134.6	155.5	−2	2	−13

[a]Includes origin not stated.
[b]Race and Hispanic origin are reported separately on birth certificates Persons of Hispanic origin may be of any race. Race categories are consistent with the 1977 Office of Management and Budget (OMB) standards. In 2007, 27 states reported multiple-race data. The multiple-race data for these states were bridged to the single-race categories of the 1977 OMB standards for comparability with other states. Multiple-race reporting areas vary for 2005–2007.
[c]Data for persons of Hispanic origin are included for this race group.
[d]Includes all persons of Hispanic origin of any race.

SOURCE: Brady E. Hamilton, Joyce A. Martin, and Stephanie J. Ventura, "Table 3. Birth Rates for Women Aged 15–19 Years, by Age and Race and Hispanic Origin of Mother: United States, Final 1991, 2005, and 2006, and Preliminary 2007; and Percentage Change in Rates, 1991–2005, 2005–2007, and 2006–2007," in "Births: Preliminary Data for 2007," *National Vital Statistics Reports*, vol. 57, no. 12, March 18, 2009, http://www.cdc.gov/nchs/data/nvsr/nvsr57/nvsr57_12.pdf (accessed May 8, 2009)

at age-specific populations of unmarried women alone, the birthrate in 2006 for unmarried women aged 20 to 29 was much higher than for unmarried teens (see Figure 3.8 in Chapter 3), because there were more births (see Table 5.10) to an age group having fewer unmarried women.

Race and Ethnicity

The decline of teen birthrates from 1991 through 2005 and the subsequent rise in 2006 and 2007 was not consistent across race and age. Regarding the decline, the CDC indicates that in the 10 to 14 age group the largest decline in birthrate from 1991 through 2005 was among Asian-American or Pacific Islander teens, followed by African-American teens. (See Table 5.9.) In all other age groups the largest decline for this time period was among African-American teens.

Even though teen birthrates in general rose in 2006 and 2007, there was no increase in the birthrate for teens aged 10 to 14 years. Conversely, there was a 14% decrease in the birthrate

for this age group. (See Table 5.9.) This decline was accounted for by a 12% decrease in the birthrates for African-American youth and an 8% decrease for Hispanic youth. Birthrates remained stable for white, Native American or Alaskan Native, and Asian-American or Pacific Islander young teens.

For teens aged 15 to 17 birthrates rose 4% from 2005 to 2007 and 1% from 2006 to 2007. All races showed increases in their birthrates of 2% to 4% from 2005 to 2007 with the exception of Hispanic youth, who showed a 1% decrease. In addition, birthrates in this age group in general declined or remained stable from 2006 to 2007 among all races with the exception of Native American or Alaskan Native teens, who showed an increase of 3% in their birthrate.

Older teens aged 18 to 19 showed the highest increase in birthrates, not only from 2005 to 2007 but also from 2006 to 2007. The greatest increase in birthrates was with older Native American or Alaskan Native teens who showed a

TABLE 5.10

Number and percent of births to unmarried women, 2006 and 2007

[Data for 2007 are based on a continuous file of records received from the states. Figures for 2007 are based on weighted data rounded to the nearest individual, so categories may not add to total.]

	Number of births		Percent	
Age of mother	2007	2006	2007	2006
All ages, unmarried	1,714,643	1,641,946	39.7	38.5
Under 20 years	386,702	372,876	85.7	84.4
Under 15 years	6,142	6,288	98.8	98.3
15–19 years	380,560	366,588	85.5	84.2
15–17 years	130,519	127,749	92.8	91.9
18–19 years	250,041	238,839	82.1	80.6
20–24 years	644,591	625,780	59.5	57.9
25–29 years	389,169	366,085	32.2	31.0
30–34 years	185,425	173,586	19.3	18.3
35–39 years	86,343	81,828	17.3	16.4
40–54 years	22,411	21,791	19.9	19.4

SOURCE: Brady E. Hamilton, Joyce A. Martin, and Stephanie J. Ventura, "Table 7. Number and Percentage of Births to Unmarried Women, by Age: United States, Final 2006 and Preliminary 2007," in "Births: Preliminary Data for 2007," *National Vital Statistics Reports*, vol. 57, no. 12, March 18, 2009, http://www.cdc.gov/nchs/data/nvsr/nvsr57/nvsr57_12.pdf (accessed May 8, 2009)

16% increase in birthrates from 2005 to 2007, and a 9% increase in 2006 to 2007 alone. The lowest increase was with Hispanic older teens, who showed a 2% increase from 2005 to 2007, but a 2% decrease from 2006 to 2007.

In summary, the increase in the teen birthrate from 2005 to 2007 appears to have been caused primarily by an increase in the birthrate of older teens aged 18 to 19, over both years, and by an increase in the birthrate of teens aged 15 to 17 from 2005 to 2006. There also appears to have been a substantial increase in the birthrate of Native American or Alaskan Native teens aged 15 to 19 from 2005 to 2007.

State-Specific Birthrates

In 2006 the birthrates for teens 15 to 19 years old ranged from a low of 18.7 births per 1,000 women in New Hampshire to a high of 68.4 births per 1,000 women in Mississippi. (See Table 5.11.) Other states with some of the lowest teen birthrates in 2006 were Vermont (20.8 teen births per 1,000), Massachusetts (21.3), and Connecticut (23.5). Other states with some of the highest teen birthrates in 2006 were New Mexico (64.1 teen births per 1,000), Texas (63.1), and Arkansas (62.3).

TEEN ABORTION

Figure 5.2 and Figure 5.3 visually show how abortion rates have dropped for female teens aged 15 to 19 from 1988 through 2004. The decline is clear for both age groups of teenagers shown—15 to 17 and 18 to 19.

Before 1988 the abortion rate for older teens aged 18 to 19 rose from 1976 to 1979 after the *Roe v. Wade* (410 U.S. 113) decision in 1973, and then it leveled out through 1988. (See Figure 5.3.) In 1988 there were about

TABLE 5.11

Birth rates for teenagers aged 15–19, by state and territory, 2006

[By place of residence. Birth rates by age are live births per 1,000 women in specified age group estimated in each area. Populations estimated as of July 1.]

	Teenage birth rate		
	15–19 years		
State	Total	15–17 years	18–19 years
United States*	41.9	22.0	73.0
Alabama	53.5	27.7	93.8
Alaska	44.5	19.2	92.7
Arizona	62.0	34.4	108.7
Arkansas	62.3	30.5	113.5
California	39.9	21.5	68.2
Colorado	43.8	24.2	76.2
Connecticut	23.5	12.3	40.9
Delaware	41.9	22.5	68.4
District of Columbia	48.4	39.1	56.5
Florida	45.2	23.0	82.3
Georgia	54.2	28.3	97.3
Hawaii	40.5	21.0	72.8
Idaho	39.2	17.9	72.3
Illinois	39.5	22.5	65.5
Indiana	43.5	20.7	79.8
Iowa	32.9	16.0	57.2
Kansas	42.0	19.5	76.4
Kentucky	54.6	25.8	102.5
Louisiana	53.9	28.2	90.8
Maine	25.8	9.9	51.7
Maryland	33.6	17.6	58.6
Massachusetts	21.3	10.7	35.9
Michigan	33.8	17.0	60.4
Minnesota	27.9	13.8	49.5
Mississippi	68.4	39.6	112.6
Missouri	45.7	22.7	83.1
Montana	39.6	17.7	76.2
Nebraska	33.4	16.3	58.8
Nevada	55.8	28.0	111.0
New Hampshire	18.7	7.6	36.2
New Jersey	24.9	12.1	46.7
New Mexico	64.1	36.0	108.5
New York	25.7	13.1	43.7
North Carolina	49.7	25.6	87.2
North Dakota	26.5	12.6	43.4
Ohio	40.0	19.8	72.4
Oklahoma	59.6	30.3	107.3
Oregon	35.7	17.5	65.8
Pennsylvania	31.0	16.7	51.6
Rhode Island	27.8	18.1	38.8
South Carolina	53.0	29.0	88.5
South Dakota	40.2	19.0	72.2
Tennessee	54.7	27.4	100.6
Texas	63.1	35.8	106.9
Utah	34.0	16.4	58.5
Vermont	20.8	8.1	38.7
Virginia	35.2	17.0	62.4
Washington	33.4	15.4	64.0
West Virginia	44.9	21.4	80.4
Wisconsin	30.9	15.5	54.8
Wyoming	47.3	18.3	91.8
Puerto Rico	60.0	39.3	91.7
Virgin Islands	49.6	20.0	114.4
Guam	58.7	31.8	102.4
American Samoa	37.1	16.9	73.0
Northern Marianas	31.6	19.2	45.7

*Excludes data for the territories.

SOURCE: Adapted from Joyce A. Martin et al, "Table 11. Number of Births, Birth Rates, Fertility Rates, Total Fertility Rates, and Birth Rates for Teenagers 15–19 Years, by Age of Mother: United States, Each State and Territory, 2006," in "Births: Final Data for 2006," *National Vital Statistics Reports*, vol. 57, no. 7, January 7, 2009, http://www.cdc.gov/nchs/data/nvsr/nvsr57/nvsr57_07.pdf (accessed May 8, 2009)

62 abortions per 1,000 older female teens. By 2004 the abortion rate for older teens had dropped by 49% to 31.9 abortions per 1,000. (See Table 5.1.)

The abortion rate for younger teens aged 15 to 17 followed a pattern similar to that of older teens. The abortion rate rose from 1976 to 1980, and then it leveled out through 1988. (See Figure 5.2.) In 1988 there were about 30 abortions per 1,000 younger female teens. By 2004 the abortion rate for younger teens had dropped by 61% to 11.8 abortions per 1,000.

Table 5.1 lists the abortion rates for the older and younger teen age groups as well as for adolescents aged 14 and younger from 1990 through 2004. Pregnancy, birth, and abortion rates are very low for this young age group. In 1990 the abortion rate for adolescents aged 14 and younger was 1.5 abortions for 1,000 adolescents and by 2004 it had dropped by 53% to 0.7 abortions per 1,000.

Race and Ethnicity

Table 5.2 shows the number and percent distribution of pregnancy outcomes by age and race for 1990 and 2004. In 2004 Hispanic teens had the lowest proportion of induced abortion in the 15- to 19-year-old age group. One out of five (20.4%) pregnancies of Hispanic teens resulted in abortion, and one out of four (25.1%) pregnancies of white teens of this age group ended in abortion. African-American teens of this age had the highest proportion of abortion—more than one out of three (37%) pregnancies of African-American teens aged 15 to 19 ended in abortion.

How do these pregnancy outcomes compare to those of 1990? In that year white teens had the highest proportion of abortions in the 15- to 19-year-old age group at 37.5%. (See Table 5.2.) By 2004 they had reduced this proportion to 25.1%. In 1990 African-American teens had the second highest proportion of abortion in this age group: 35.9%. The proportion of abortions for African-American teens rose to 37% by 2004. Hispanic teens in both 1990 and 2004 had the lowest proportion of abortions. In 1990, 23.4% of pregnancies of Hispanic teens aged 15 to 19 ended in abortion; by 2004 this percentage fell to 20.4%.

Susan A. Cohen reports in "Abortion and Women of Color: The Bigger Picture" (*Guttmacher Policy Review*, vol. 11, no. 3, Summer 2008) that many factors explain the high abortion rate of African-American women. One primary reason is that African-American women have a rate of unintended pregnancy three times that of white women. This high rate of unintended pregnancies is linked to disparities in access to and consistent use of effective contraceptives. Cohen determines that financial, geographic, educational, and personal issues contribute to using contraceptives less frequently and less consistently.

Abortion Ratios

As mentioned previously, an abortion rate is the number of abortions per 1,000 women in the category considered. An abortion ratio differs in that the number of abortions in a category (such as to teens aged 15 to 19) is compared with the number of live births in that same category rather than to the number of women in that category. Figure 4.5 in Chapter 4 shows abortion ratios by age group using CDC data and calculations from 1973 through 2005. The CDC defines the abortion ratio as the number of abortions per 1,000 live births. For example, the abortion ratio for adolescents younger than 15 was 800 abortions for every 1,000 live births in 2005.

The abortion ratio varies by age and was highest for female adolescents younger than 15 from 1973 through 2005. (See Figure 4.5.) The next highest abortion ratio in 2005 was for teens 15 to 19, but from 1973 on the abortion ratio of this group fluctuated slightly above and slightly below the abortion ratio for women aged 40 and older. The abortion ratio was lowest for women aged 20 to 39.

Relinquishment for Adoption

A teenager faced with an unintended pregnancy can choose parenthood (often obtaining help from relatives), relinquishing (giving up) the infant for adoption, or abortion. Most women of any age choose to keep their infant or to have an abortion. Table 5.12 shows that between 1996 and 2002 only 1% of all unmarried women under the age of 45 who gave birth relinquished their child for adoption.

Before 1973 relinquishment was more common than in recent years, with 8.7% of all unmarried women relinquishing their children for adoption. Very few African-American women (1.5%) gave up their children for adoption, whereas a large percentage of white women (19.3%) did. Table 5.12 shows that there has been a downward trend in relinquishment

TABLE 5.12

Percentage of children relinquished for adoption who were born to never-married women under age 45, before 1973 and 1973–2002

| Race | Year of child's birth | | | | |
	Before 1973[a]	1973– 1981[a]	1982– 1988[a]	1989– 1995[a]	1996– 2002[a]
All women[c]	8.7	4.1	2.0	0.9	1.0
Black or African American women[d]	1.5	0.2	1.1	—	*
White women[d]	19.3	7.5	3.2	1.7	1.3

—Quantity zero.
*Figure does not meet standards of reliability or precision.
[a]Infants relinquished at birth only.
[b]Infants relinquished at birth or within the first month of life.
[c]Includes women of other races, not shown separately.
[d]Includes women of Hispanic origin and women of multiple races who choose this as the single race that best describes them.

SOURCE: Jo Jones, "Table 16. Among Children Born to Never-Married Women under 45 Years of Age, Percentage Who Were Relinquished for Adoption, by Race, According to Year of Child's Birth: United States, Before 1973–2002," in "Adoption Experiences of Women and Men and Demand for Children to Adopt by Women 18–44 Years of Age in the United States, 2002," *Vital and Health Statistics*, series 23, no. 27, August 2008, http://www.cdc.gov/nchs/data/series/sr_23/sr23_027.pdf (accessed June 14, 2009)

of births occurring to never-married women. This decline parallels a steady increase in the rate of births to unmarried women. (See Figure 3.7 in Chapter 3.)

Recent declines in abortion rates (see Table 5.1) suggest that the choice of abortion over relinquishment is not a significant factor in the lower prevalence of relinquishment in recent years. In "Adoption Experiences of Women and Men and Demand for Children to Adopt by Women 18–44 Years of Age in the United States, 2002" (*Vital and Health Statistics*, series 23, no. 27, August 2008), Jo Jones of the NCHS notes that societal and legislative changes have affected the number of children available for adoption in the United States over the past 30 years. Not only did the birthrate decline steadily through 1990 to 2005 but also unmarried women more frequently wanted to keep and raise their children. In addition, the Adoption Assistance and Child Welfare Act of 1980 gave preference to the placement of children with relatives over adoption by others.

PARENTAL INVOLVEMENT IN ABORTION DECISIONS

Table 5.13 shows that in June 2009, 34 states had laws requiring some parental involvement before a minor had an abortion. As of October 31, 2006, Alaska,

TABLE 5.13

State policies on parental involvement in minors' abortions, June 2009

State	Required parental involvement: Consent only	Required parental involvement: Notification and consent	Required parental involvement: Notification only	Alternatives: Judicial bypass	Alternatives: Other adult relatives	Exceptions: Medical emergency	Exceptions: Abuse, assault, incest or neglect
Alabama	X			X		X	
Alaska	▼						
Arizona	X			X		X	X
Arkansas	X			X		X	X
California	▼						
Colorado			X	X		X	X
Delaware			X[a, b]	X[a, b]	X[b]	X[b]	
Florida			X	X		X	
Georgia			X	X		X	
Idaho	X			X		X	X
Illinois			▼				
Indiana	X			X		X	
Iowa			X	X	X	X	X
Kansas			X	X		X	X
Kentucky	X			X		X	
Louisiana	X			X		X	
Massachusetts	X			X		X	
Michigan	X			X		X	
Minnesota			Both parents	X		X	X
Mississippi	Both parents			X		X	
Missouri	X			X			
Montana			▼				
Nebraska			X	X		X	X
Nevada			▼			X	
New Jersey			▼			X	
New Mexico	▼						
North Carolina	X			X	X	X	
North Dakota	Both parents			X		X	
Ohio	X			X			
Oklahoma		X		X		X	X
Pennsylvania	X			X		X	
Rhode Island	X			X			
South Carolina	X[b]			X[b]	X[b]	X[b]	X[b]
South Dakota			X	X		X	
Tennessee	X			X		X	X
Texas	X			X		X	X[d]
Utah		X		X[c]		X	
Virginia	X			X	X	X	X
West Virginia			X[a]	X[a]			
Wisconsin	X[a]			X[a]	X	X	X
Wyoming	X			X		X	
Total	**22**	**2**	**10**	**34**	**6**	**33**	**14**

Note: Except where indicated, policies require the involvement of one parent.
▼Enforcement permanently enjoined (prohibited) by court order; policy not in effect.
[a]Allows specified health professionals to waive parental involvement in limited circumstances.
[b]While most states laws apply to all minors, Delaware's law applies to women under 16 and South Carolina's law applies to women under 17.
[c]The provision only applies to parental consent requirements.
[d]The provision only applies to the parental notice requirements.

SOURCE: Guttmacher Institute, Community Health Centers and Family Planning, "Parental Involvement in Minors' Abortions," in *State Policies in Brief: Parental Involvement in Minors' Abortions*, New York: Guttmacher, June 1, 2009, http://www.guttmacher.org/statecenter/spibs/spib_PIMA.pdf (accessed June 15, 2009)

California, Illinois, Montana, Nevada, New Jersey, and New Mexico had laws that had been prohibited by court order.

Parental consent or notification laws generally include judicial bypass (waiver) provisions if the young woman does not want to or cannot tell her parents of her decision. In a judicial bypass, the court decides if the minor is mature enough to make the decision on her own or if the abortion would be in her best interests. In 2009 all of the 34 states that had laws requiring some parental involvement before a minor had an abortion also had a judicial bypass provision. In addition, six states had laws in which a minor could involve a grandparent or other adult relative in the decision instead of a parent.

CHAPTER 6
ABORTION CLINICS

QUALITY OF ABORTION CLINIC SERVICES

The National Abortion Federation (NAF) is a professional association of abortion providers in the United States and Canada. The mission of the NAF is to promote and enhance the quality of abortion services. The federation has developed clinical policy guidelines to help ensure safe, high-quality abortion care.

In *2009 Clinical Policy Guidelines* (May 2009, http://www. prochoice.org/pubs_research/publications/downloads/professional_education/CPG2009.pdf), the NAF addresses three types of policies: standards, recommendations, and options. Standards are applied rigidly and include directives such as, "Abortion must be performed by licensed physicians or licensed/certified/registered midlevel clinicians trained in the provision of abortion care, in accordance with state law." Recommendations allow some flexibility in clinical management but must be justified when not followed. Recommendations include items such as, "Appropriate referrals should be available for patients who cannot be cared for at your facility." Options require no justification. For example, the option following the standard, "The clinician must ensure that accurate information is provided regarding the risks, benefits, and possible complications of abortion," is: "This information may be provided either on an individual basis or in group sessions."

More than 400 institutions across the United States and Canada are members of the NAF and work with the NAF's Clinical Services Department to help them comply with the *Clinical Policy Guidelines*. As part of their interaction with institutional members, the NAF makes site visits to determine guideline compliance. Member institutions also conduct annual self-evaluations. Those in compliance receive a certificate that is displayed to inform patients of their documented quality of abortion care.

ACTIONS AGAINST ABORTION CLINICS
Violence and Disruption

The NAF has tracked incidents of violence and disruption against abortion providers across the country since 1977. NAF members report incidents on a regular basis. Their reports are supplemented with information from newspaper reports, law enforcement agencies, and abortion provider organizations. A year-end survey is conducted to complete each year's presentation.

Over the years many abortion clinics throughout the nation have experienced violence. The most serious instances of clinic violence have been the murder and attempted murder of abortion doctors and clinic workers. The first clinic murder occurred in 1993, when Michael Griffin (1961–) shot and killed the physician David Gunn (1946–1993) in Pensacola, Florida. Four murders occurred the year after, and two happened in 1998. (See Table 6.1.) In May 2009 the Wichita, Kansas, physician George Tiller (1941–2009), one of only a few U.S. physicians who performed late-term abortions, was shot to death while in church. A few hours later police arrested the alleged gunman, Scott Roeder (1958–). Besides these murders, there have been 17 attempted murders of abortion providers since 1977, including one on Tiller in 1993, in which he was shot in both arms by the activist Rachelle Shannon (1956–).

Incidents of extreme violence against abortion providers, such as murder, bombing, arson, and acid attacks, decreased from about the mid-1990s on. (See Table 6.1.) The NAF credits the arrest and prosecution of Eric Rudolph (1967–), James Kopp (1954–), and Clayton Waagner (1956–), three antiabortion extremists, as key factors in the decline of severe forms of violence against abortion providers. However, other forms of violence still plague abortion clinics. Overall, in 2008 there were 237 identified acts of violence, down from the record high of 795 in 2001. The 2001 total is high as a result of the 554 hoax anthrax threat letters recorded that year in the aftermath of the

TABLE 6.1

Incidents of violence and disruption against abortion providers in the United States and Canada, 1977–2009

Violence	1977–93	1994	1995	1996	1997	1998	1999	2000	2001	2002	2003	2004	2005	2006	2007	2008	2009[a]	Total
Murder[b]	1	4	0	0	0	2	0	0	0	0	0	0	0	0	0	0	1	8
Attempted murder	3	8	1	1	2	1	0	1	0	0	0	0	0	0	0	0	0	17
Bombing[b]	28	1	1	2	6	1	1	0	1	0	0	0	0	0	0	0	0	41
Arson[b]	113	11	14	3	8	4	8	2	2	1	3	2	2	0	2	0	0	175
Attempted bomb/arson[b]	61	3	1	4	2	5	1	3	2	0	0	1	6	4	2	1	0	96
Invasion	345	2	4	0	7	5	3	4	2	1	0	0	0	4	7	6	0	390
Vandalism	543	42	31	29	105	46	63	56	58	60	48	49	83	72	59	45	11	1400
Trespassing	0	0	0	0	0	0	193	81	144	163	66	67	633	336	122	148	40	1993
Butyric acid attacks	72	8	0	0	0	19	0	0	0	0	0	0	0	0	1	0	0	100
Anthrax threats	0	0	0	0	0	12	35	30	554	23	0	1	0	0	1	3	0	659
Assault & battery	88	7	2	1	9	4	2	7	2	1	7	8	8	11	12	6	4	179
Death threats	166	59	41	13	11	25	13	9	14	3	7	4	10	10	13	2	6	406
Kidnapping	2	0	0	1	0	1	0	0	0	0	0	0	0	0	0	0	0	4
Burglary	31	3	3	6	6	6	4	5	6	1	9	5	11	30	12	7	6	151
Stalking[c]	188	22	61	52	67	13	13	17	10	12	3	15	8	6	19	19	0	525
Total	**1641**	**170**	**159**	**112**	**223**	**144**	**336**	**215**	**795**	**265**	**143**	**152**	**761**	**474**	**249**	**237**	**67**	**6143**
Disruption																		
Hate mail/harassing calls	1452	381	255	605	2829	915	1646	1011	404	230	432	453	515	548	522	396	1401	13995
Email/Internet harassment	0	0	0	0	0	0	0	0	0	24	70	51	77	25	38	44	10	339
Hoax device/susp. package	0	0	0	0	0	0	0	0	0	41	13	9	16	17	23	24	5	148
Bomb threats	297	14	41	13	79	31	39	20	31	7	17	13	11	7	6	13	3	642
Picketing	6361	1407	1356	3932	7518	8402	8727	8478	9969	10241	11348	11640	13415	13505	11113	12503	1922	141837
Total	**8110**	**1802**	**1652**	**4550**	**10426**	**9348**	**10412**	**9509**	**10404**	**10543**	**11880**	**12166**	**14034**	**14102**	**11702**	**12980**	**3341**	**156961**
Clinic Blockades																		
Number of incidents	609	25	5	7	25	2	3	4	2	4	10	34	4	13	7	8	1	763
Number of arrests[d]	33444	217	54	65	29	16	5	0	0	0	0	0	0	0	3	1	0	33834

[a]Through April 2009.

[b]Incidents recorded are those classified as such by the appropriate law enforcement agency. Incidents that were ruled inconclusive or accidental are not included.

[c]Stalking is defined as the persistent following, threatening, and harassing of an abortion provider, staff member, or patient away from the clinic. Tabulation of stalking incidents began in 1993.

[d]The "number of arrests" represents the total number of arrests, not the total number of persons arrested. Many blockaders are arrested multiple times.

Notes: All numbers represent incidents reported to or obtained by the National Abortion Federation (NAF). Actual incidents are likely much higher. Tabulation of trespassing began in 1999 and tabulation of email harassment and hoax devices began in 2002.

SOURCE: "NAF Violence and Disruption Statistics: Incidents of Violence & Disruption against Abortion Providers in the U.S. & Canada, 2009," National Abortion Federation, 2009," http://prochoice.org/pubs_research/publications/downloads/about_abortion/violence_stats.pdf (accessed July 1, 2009)

FIGURE 6.1

Extreme abortion clinic violence, by state, 1993–2008

[Total number of incidents = 128]

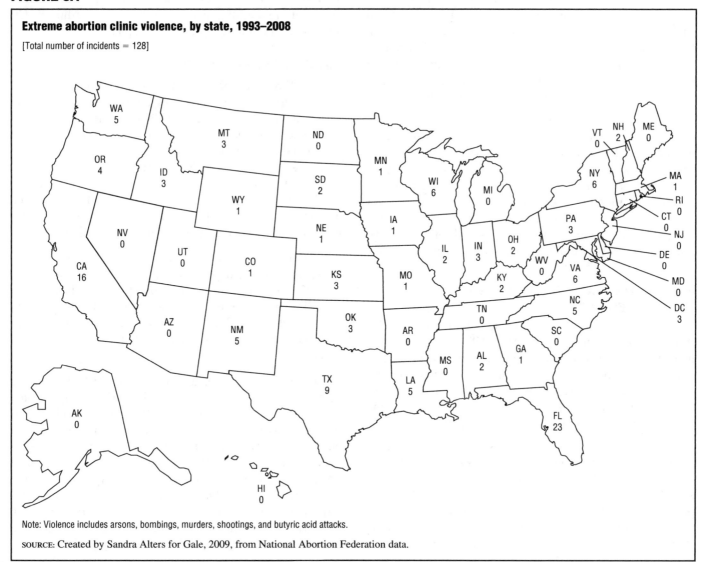

Note: Violence includes arsons, bombings, murders, shootings, and butyric acid attacks.

SOURCE: Created by Sandra Alters for Gale, 2009, from National Abortion Federation data.

September 11, 2001, terrorist attacks. (The 2009 statistics reflect data only from January through April 2009.)

As Table 6.1 shows, between 1994 and 2008, 1997 had the highest number of clinic bombings (six). During this same time span, 1995 had the highest number of arson-related fires (14). In recent years both types of incidents have decreased dramatically. There was one clinic bombing in 2001 and no bombings were reported from 2002 through April 2009. There was one arson-related fire in 2002, three in 2003, and two each year in 2004, 2005, and 2007.

Incidents of vandalism remained somewhat stable from 1998 through 2004, fluctuating from a low of 46 incidents to a high of 63 incidents, but these incidents increased somewhat in 2005 and 2006 to 83 and 72 incidents, respectively. The number fell again in 2007 and 2008 to 45. Between January and April 2009 there were 11 such incidents.

Death threats to abortion providers were relatively low after 2001: three in 2002, seven in 2003, and four in 2004. The number of death threats increased to 10 in 2005 and

2006, to 13 in 2007, but fell to 2 in 2008. In 2009, however, from just January through April, death threats totaled six. The next month, in May, Tiller was murdered.

Figure 6.1 shows abortion clinic violence by state. The numbers include arsons, bombings, murders, shootings, and butyric acid attacks. (Butyric acid is a liquid with a vomit-like odor and can cause thousands of dollars of damage, requiring clinics to conduct extensive cleanups.) Florida, California, and Texas (in that order) had the highest number of incidences from 1993 to 2008.

The NAF first collected data on stalking (the persistent following, threatening, and harassing of an abortion provider, staff member, or patient away from the clinic) in 1993, reporting a record high of 188 cases that year. (See Table 6.1.) Stalking cases dropped to about one-third or less of that amount through the mid-1990s. After 1997 the annual number of stalking cases dropped again; in 2003, 2005, and 2006 they numbered in the single digits. Nonetheless, 19 stalking cases were reported in 2007 and 2008.

Picketing is by far the major activity of pro-life activists. The number of incidents of picketing has increased each year since 2000, peaking at 13,505 incidents in 2006. (See Table 6.1.) According to reports from abortion clinics, picketing and various forms of harassment are becoming more intense, although Table 6.1 shows that the number of picketing incidents decreased somewhat after 2006.

Many protests at abortion clinics have been under the direction of Operation Rescue/Operation Save America, an organization that seeks to shut down clinics completely but denies promoting the use of violence. Operation Save America believes the United States, in permitting abortion, has lost its morality. Demonstrators claim they are not only saving the lives of the unborn but also preventing the judgment of God from being passed on the United States for murder committed through abortion.

FREEDOM OF ACCESS TO CLINIC ENTRANCES ACT

The Freedom of Access to Clinic Entrances (FACE) Act was signed into law in May 1994 in response to increasing violence against abortion clinic workers and clients. FACE prohibits physical attacks on clinic employees and patient escorts, attempted arson of clinic facilities, blockades of clinic entrances by people or vehicles, and threats of bodily harm to providers or recipients of services.

FACE's opponents challenge its constitutionality on a number of grounds. Some charge that FACE violates the freedom of speech and religion protections under the First Amendment, whereas others claim that Congress lacks the power to pass such a law under the commerce clause (to regulate interstate commerce) of the U.S. Constitution. Regardless, the U.S. Supreme Court has affirmed the constitutionality of FACE by refusing to hear challenges to the law. (For more information on court cases regarding FACE and abortion clinic violence, see Chapter 2.)

The Effectiveness of FACE

In "Freedom of Access to Clinic Entrances Act" (2009, http://www.prochoice.org/about_abortion/violence/FACE_act.html), NARAL Pro-Choice America states that "the FACE law has had a clear impact on the decline in certain types of violence against clinics and providers, specifically clinic blockades." Even though violence continues, the frequency of clinic blockades are at their lowest levels since blockades were first used. The federal statute has also spurred enhanced clinic protection by law enforcement and has withstood many constitutional challenges.

After the passage of FACE in 1994, the number of clinic blockades dropped sharply, from 25 in 1994 to five in 1995. (See Table 6.1.) In general, there have been only a few clinic blockades each year since the mid-1990s (except for 1997) through 2002. Clinic blockades increased to 10 in 2003 and to 34 in 2004. In 2008 there were eight clinic blockades.

Under FACE, states and the District of Columbia are able to protect access to clinics in various ways. Some states prohibit specific activities at abortion clinic facilities, such as blocking the entrance (obstruction), threatening clinic workers or patients, damaging property, making harassing telephone calls, creating excessive noise, releasing substances with noxious odors, or having access to weapons during demonstrations. Some states require a protected bubble zone around a person entering or leaving an abortion clinic. Table 6.2 lists the states that have enacted such laws and the acts they prohibit.

TABLE 6.2

States that prohibit specific actions against abortion clinics and the actions they prohibit, May 2009

State	Specific Prohibited Actions					Protected "bubble zone"
	Obstruction	Threat	Damage	Telephone harassment	Other	
California*	X	X	X			
Colorado						8-ft. zone within 100 ft. of door
Dist. of Columbia	X	X	X	X	Noise	
Kansas	X					
Maine	X			X	Noise, odor	
Maryland	X					
Massachusetts						35-ft. zone around entrances and walkways
Michigan		X				
Minnesota	X					
Montana	X					8-ft. zone within 36 ft. of door
Nevada	X					
New York	X	X	X			
North Carolina	X	X			Weapon	
Oregon	X		X			
Washington	X	X	X	X		
Wisconsin		X				
Total	**11+DC**	**6+DC**	**4+DC**	**2+DC**	**2+DC**	**3**

*Requires the collection and analysis of data by state attorney general's office and training for law enforcement officers by experts on clinic violence.

SOURCE: Guttmacher Institute, Community Health Centers and Family Planning, "Protecting Access to Clinics," in *State Policies in Brief: Protecting Access to Clinics*, New York: Guttmacher, May 1, 2009, http://www.guttmacher.org/statecenter/spibs/spib_PAC.pdf (accessed May 12, 2009)

FACE and the Internet

In February 1999 a federal jury in Portland, Oregon, unanimously ruled that it is illegal for pro-life activists to threaten abortion providers through Wild West–style "wanted posters" and the Web site "Nuremberg Files." The "Nuremberg Files" listed the names of abortion doctors accused of committing "crimes against humanity." The list included the doctors' addresses and other family information. Murdered doctors were listed with lines drawn through their names.

The jury ordered the defendants (American Coalition of Life Activists, Advocates for Life Ministries, and 12 individuals) to pay the plaintiffs (Planned Parenthood Federation of America, the Portland Feminist Women's Health Center, and four abortion doctors) more than $109 million in damages. The jury found all defendants guilty of violating or conspiring to violate FACE and all but two defendants of violating or conspiring to violate the Racketeer Influenced and Corrupt Organizations Act.

In March 2001 a three-judge panel of the Ninth Circuit Court of Appeals unanimously reversed the jury verdict and the injunction against continued publishing of the materials. Then in May 2002 an 11-judge panel of the Ninth Circuit U.S. Court of Appeals upheld the 1999 trial verdict, stating that the "Nuremberg Files" Web site and the wanted posters amounted to threats and intimidation that violated FACE as well as other laws. The NAF states in "Freedom of Access to Clinic Entrances (FACE) Act" (2009, http://www.prochoice.org/about_abortion/facts/face_act.html) that the U.S. Supreme Court has refused to hear the appeal of this or any other federal cases regarding FACE, "in essence affirming the Act's constitutionality."

CHAPTER 7
MEDICAL AND ETHICAL QUESTIONS CONCERNING ABORTION

ABORTION AND HEALTH

Abortion was widely practiced during the colonial period and early years of the United States but became less common between the early 1800s and 1973, when—under certain conditions—it was considered a criminal offense. After abortion was legally banned, women of means were generally able to find doctors willing to perform supposedly therapeutic (medically necessary) abortions allowed by law. Many poor women, however, died or developed medical complications from self-induced abortions or abortions performed by untrained people.

Since the 1973 U.S. Supreme Court ruling on the legality of abortion in *Roe v. Wade* (410 U.S. 113), a number of studies have been conducted on the physical, emotional, and psychological impact of abortion on women. For example, the Institute of Medicine concludes in *Legalized Abortion and the Public Health* (1975) that "evidence suggests that legislation and practices that permit women to obtain abortions in proper medical surroundings will lead to fewer deaths and a lower rate of medical complications than [will] restrictive legislation and practices."

Figure 7.1 shows the impact of the *Roe v. Wade* decision on the number of legal and illegal abortions in the United States just before and after that decision. In 1970, just before the *Roe v. Wade* decision, 15 states liberalized their abortion laws.

Willard Cates Jr., David A. Grimes, and Kenneth F. Schulz note in "The Public Health Impact of Legal Abortion: 30 Years Later" (*Perspectives on Sexual and Reproductive Health*, vol. 35, no. 1, January–February 2003) that the legalization of abortion not only led women to seek legal abortion but it also led women to seek abortions earlier in their pregnancies, which made the procedure safer by reducing the risk of complications. They conclude that "although the available medical evidence does not directly address society's moral issues, it allows an objective insight to the health effects of wider access to legal abortion."

Complications and Deaths

In the fact sheet "Safety of Abortion" (December 2006, http://www.prochoice.org/pubs_research/publications/downloads/about_abortion/safety_of_abortion.pdf), Susan Dudley and Beth Kruse of the National Abortion Federation indicate that "surgical abortion is one of the safest types of medical procedures. Complications from having a first-trimester aspiration abortion are considerably less frequent and less serious than those associated with giving birth. Early medical abortion (using medications to end a pregnancy) has a similar safety profile."

However, like any other surgical procedure, surgical abortion carries some risk of complications. In general, the earlier in pregnancy the abortion is performed, the less complicated and safer it is. Figure 4.3 in Chapter 4 shows that in 2005 slightly more than half of teens aged 15 to 19 who had abortions did so at eight weeks or less of gestation, as did about 60% of 20- to 24-year-olds, about 65% of 25- to 29-year-olds, and about 68% of women aged 30 and older. Over 90% of all these women had abortions at 15 weeks or less of gestation. Only a small percentage of women had abortions later in the pregnancy.

According to the Guttmacher Institute, in *In Brief: Facts on Induced Abortion in the United States* (July 2008, http://www.guttmacher.org/pubs/fb_induced_abortion.html), the risk of abortion complications is minimal; less than 0.3% of women having abortions require hospitalization because of complications. Nonetheless, the Guttmacher Institute emphasizes the difference in risk between earlier and later abortions, stating, "The risk of death associated with abortion increases with the length of pregnancy, from one death for every one million abortions at or before eight weeks to one per 29,000 at 16-20 weeks—and one per 11,000 at 21 or more weeks."

Besides the length of pregnancy, other factors that determine the likelihood of complications include the physician's skill and training, the use of general anesthesia, the abortion

FIGURE 7.1

Number of legal and illegal abortions, 1969–80

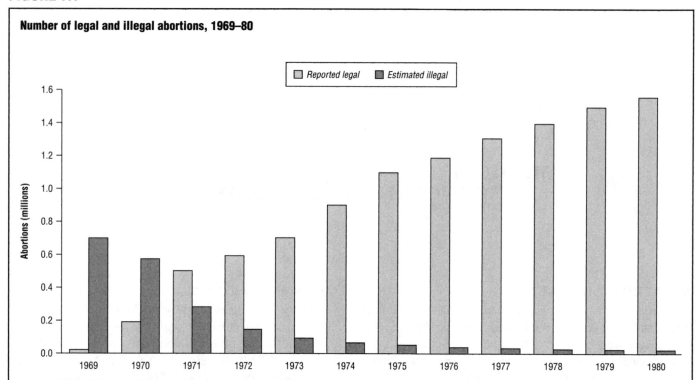

SOURCE: Willard Cates, Jr., "Figure 1. Number of Legal and Illegal Abortions in the United States, 1969–1980," in "Legal Abortion: the Public Health Record," *Science*, 1982, vol. 215, no. 4540. Reprinted with permission from AAAS. Data source for legal abortion data: L.B. Finer and S.K. Henshaw, "Estimates of U.S. Abortion Incidence, 2001–2003," The Alan Guttmacher Institute (AGI) New York 2006, http://www.guttmacher.org/pubs/2006/08/03/ab_incidence.pdf (accessed May 12, 2009)

method used, and the woman's overall health. However, most complications with abortion procedures occur when the procedure is performed by a person without the necessary medical skills, in an environment that does not meet minimum medical standards, or both. These conditions are generally found in developing countries where abortion is restricted by law and/or where safe abortions are not readily available. Abortions conducted under such conditions are called unsafe abortions. Table 7.1 shows that the greatest numbers of deaths due to unsafe abortion occur in Africa and Asia. Very few occur in Europe, Latin America and the Caribbean, Northern America, and Oceania (the islands of the Pacific and adjacent seas). Note that in Table 7.1 there are some numbers in parentheses. These numbers are calculations using data from only the countries in the region with evidence of unsafe abortion. The numbers adjacent to them but not in parentheses include data from all countries in the region.

David A. Grimes et al. indicate in "Unsafe Abortion: The Preventable Pandemic" (*Lancet*, vol. 368, no. 9550, November 25, 2006) that complications are a much more common consequence of unsafe abortion than death. Complications include severe bleeding; bloodstream infection; infection of the lining of the abdominal cavity; and trauma to the cervix (entrance to the womb), vagina, uterus (womb), and abdominal organs. The researchers note that

between 20% and 50% of women who have unsafe abortions are hospitalized for complications.

Psychological Effects

In 1987 President Ronald Reagan (1911–2004) promised the various right-to-life groups that he would investigate the health effects of abortion, including psychological stress. Many antiabortion groups claimed that for many women, having an abortion can lead to serious psychological problems, most notably postabortion syndrome. Some even compared this to the posttraumatic stress disorder suffered by many Vietnam War (1954–1975) veterans.

President Reagan instructed the U.S. surgeon general C. Everett Koop (1916–) to prepare the report. Martin Tolchin notes in "Koop's Stand on Abortion's Effect Surprises Friends and Foes Alike" (*New York Times*, January 11, 1989) that after meetings with experts and thorough reviews of many studies for almost a year and a half, Koop reported in a January 1989 letter to President Reagan that his investigation of the psychological effects of abortion was inconclusive because of methodological problems with the scientific studies he examined. Koop observed that "the data do not support the premise that abortion does nor does not cause or contribute to psychological problems."

TABLE 7.1

Global and regional estimates of annual incidence of unsafe abortion and death due to unsafe abortion, 2003

[Rates and ratios are calculated for all countries and, in parenthesis, only for countries with evidence of unsafe abortion[a]]

		Unsafe abortion		Mortality due to unsafe abortion		
	Number (rounded)[b]	Incidence rate (per 1000 women aged 15–44 years)	Incidence ratio (per 100 live births)	Number of deaths (rounded)[†]	% of all maternal deaths	Mortality ratio (per 100,000 live births) (rounded)[b]
World	19,700,000	14 (22)	15 (20)	66,500	13	50 (70)
Developed countries[c]	500,000	2 (6)	3 (13)	<60	4 (8)	(2)[d]
Developing countries	19,200,000	16 (24)	16 (20)	66,400	13	60 (70)
Least developed countries	4,000,000	25	15	24,000	10	90
Other developing countries	15,300,000	15 (23)	17 (22)	42,400	15 (16)	50 (60)
Sub-Saharan Africa	4,700,000	31	16	35,600	14	120
Africa	5,500,000	29	17	36,000	14	110
Eastern Africa	2,300,000	39	20	17,600	17	160
Middle Africa	600,000	26	12	5,000	10	100
Northern Africa	1,000,000	22 (23)	20 (21)	1,100	11	20
Southern Africa	200,000	18	18	300	9	20
Western Africa	1,500,000	28	14	11,900	13	110
Asia*	9,800,000	11 (20)	13 (18)	28,400	12 (13)	40 (50)
Eastern Asia[c]	d	d	d	d	d	d
South-central Asia	6,300,000	18	16	24,300	13	60
South-eastern Asia	3,100,000	23 (27)	27 (31)	3,200	14 (16)	30
Western Asia	400,000	8 (13)	7 (10)	1,000	11 (12)	20(30)
Europe	500,000	3 (6)	6 (13)	<60	6 (8)	1 (2)
Eastern Europe	400,000	5 (6)	13 (14)	<50	6 (7)	2
Northern Europe	2,000	0.1 (1)	0.1 (2)	d	3 (22)	(3)[d]
Southern Europe	100,000	3 (6)	7 (14)	d	11 (19)	1
Western Europe	d	d	d	d	d	d
Latin America and the Caribbean	3,900,000	29 (30)	33 (34)	2,000	11	20
Caribbean	100,000	16 (28)	19 (26)	200	12	30 (40)
Central America	900,000	25	26	300	11	10
South America	2,900,000	33	38	1,400	11	20
Northern America	d	d	d	d	d	d
Oceania[e]	20,000	11	8	<100	10	20

[a]Rates, ratios and percentages are calculated for all countries of each region, except Asia (which excludes Japan) and Oceania (which excludes Australia and New Zealand). Rates, ratios and percentages in parentheses were calculated exclusively for countries with evidence of unsafe abortion. Where the difference between the two calculations was less than 1 percentage point, only one figure is shown.
[b]Figures may not exactly add up to totals because of rounding.
[c]Japan, Australia and New Zealand have been excluded from the regional estimates, but are included in the total for developed countries.
[d]No estimates are shown for regions where the incidence is negligible.

SOURCE: Elisabeth Ahman and Iqbal Shah, "Table 2. Global and Regional Estimates of Annual Incidence of Unsafe Abortion and Associated Mortality in 2003," in *Unsafe Abortion: Global and Regional Estimates of the Incidence of Unsafe Abortion and Associated Mortality in 2003*, 5th ed., World Health Organization, September 25, 2007, http://whqlibdoc.who.int/publications/2007/9789241596121_eng.pdf (accessed August 3, 2009).

In response to Koop's inconclusive findings, Nancy E. Adler et al. conducted a study that reviewed published research having "the most rigorous research designs" and published their findings in "Psychological Responses after Abortion" (*Science*, vol. 248, no. 4951, April 6, 1990). The researchers found "consistent findings on the psychological status of women who have had legal abortions under nonrestrictive circumstances. . . . Although there may be sensations of regret, sadness, or guilt, the weight of the evidence from scientific studies indicates that legal abortion of an unwanted pregnancy in the first trimester does not pose a psychological hazard for most women." Adler et al. noted that "the time of greatest distress is likely to be before the abortion. Severe negative reactions after abortions are rare and can best be understood in the framework of coping with a normal life stress."

Since the time of Koop's findings and Adler et al.'s review, the psychological impact of abortion has been extensively and repeatedly examined. In *Report of the APA Task Force on Mental Health and Abortion* (August 13, 2008, http://www.apa.org/releases/abortion-report.pdf), the Task Force on Mental Health and Abortion (TFMHA) of the American Psychological Association analyzes and summarizes literature on mental health factors associated with abortion and its aftermath. The task force finds that many of the studies it examined were flawed methodologically (as had Koop 20 years earlier), so it emphasizes that its conclusions are formulated based on those it found to be the most methodologically rigorous.

In the executive summary of its 91-page report, the task force asserts, "The best scientific evidence published indicates that among adult women who have an *unplanned pregnancy* the relative risk of mental health problems is no greater if they have a single elective first-trimester abortion than if they deliver that pregnancy. The evidence regarding the relative mental health risks associated with multiple abortions is more equivocal. Positive associations observed between multiple abortions and poorer mental health may be linked to co-occurring risks that predispose a woman to both multiple unwanted pregnancies and mental health problems."

The task force also addresses women's psychological health after having an abortion later in pregnancy due to a finding of fetal abnormality. It indicates that "terminating a wanted pregnancy late in pregnancy due to fetal abnormality appears to be associated with negative psychological reactions equivalent to those experienced by women who miscarry a wanted pregnancy or who experience a stillbirth or death of a newborn, but less than those who deliver a child with life-threatening abnormalities." When compared with the results for women having unplanned pregnancies and single elective first-trimester abortions, these results suggest that "the differing patterns of psychological experiences observed among women who terminate an unplanned pregnancy versus those who terminate a planned and wanted pregnancy highlight the importance of taking pregnancy intendedness and wantedness into account when seeking to understand psychological reactions to abortion."

The task force concludes:

> None of the literature reviewed adequately addressed the prevalence of mental health problems among women in the United States who have had an abortion. In general, however, the prevalence of mental health problems observed among women in the United States who had a single, legal, first-trimester abortion for nontherapeutic reasons was consistent with normative [normal] rates of comparable mental health problems in the general population of women in the United States.

> Nonetheless, it is clear that some women do experience sadness, grief, and feelings of loss following termination of a pregnancy, and some experience clinically significant disorders, including depression and anxiety. However, the TFMHA reviewed no evidence sufficient to support the claim that an observed association between abortion history and mental health was caused by the abortion *per se*, as opposed to other factors.

ETHICAL QUESTIONS RELATED TO ABORTION

Scientific advances often raise ethical questions. Ethics is a branch of philosophy concerned with evaluating human action. Some distinguish ethics, what is considered right or wrong behavior based on reason, from morals, what is considered right or wrong behavior based on social custom.

Embryonic Stem Cell Research

WHAT ARE STEM CELLS? A fetus is a developing animal (in this case human) from the end of eight weeks after conception to birth. From conception through eight weeks, the developing organism is called a pre-embryo and then an embryo. The embryo and fetus are rich sources of cells that differentiate (turn into) the variety of cell types that make up the body. These cells are called stem cells. Multipotent stem cells can give rise to only certain types of cells. Pluripotent stem cells can develop into any of the more than 200 types of cells in the body.

To develop human stem cell lines for research, cells are harvested from the inner cell mass of a week-old embryo. If these stem cells are cultured properly, they can grow and divide indefinitely. The stem cell line is a mass of cells descended from an original stem cell. It shares the original cell's genetic characteristics. Groups of cells can be separated from the cell line and distributed to researchers.

Stem cells are important in medical research for a variety of reasons. One reason is that they hold the key to understanding how cells differentiate into a variety of specialized tissues during development. Understanding cell differentiation can help scientists better understand serious medical conditions linked to problems with cell differentiation, such as cancer and birth defects. Stem cells are also important to medical research because they can be used to make needed cells for medical treatment. For example, pluripotent stem cells could likely be used as a renewable source of replacement cells and tissues to treat diseases, conditions, and disabilities such as Parkinson's disease (a disorder that affects nerve cells in the part of the brain that controls muscle movement), Alzheimer's disease (a progressive neurological disease that causes impaired thinking, memory, and behavior), spinal cord injuries, burns, multiple sclerosis (a chronic progressive disorder in which the immune system destroys the myelin sheath that protects nerve fibers), heart disease, diabetes, and arthritis.

Fetal research and the use of fetal and embryonic tissue in research is not a recent medical development. It dates back to the 1930s and was responsible, in the mid-20th century, for the development of vaccines against poliomyelitis (a highly infectious viral disease that, in its severe form, affects the central nervous system and can lead to paralysis) and rubella (German measles), as well as the preventive treatment of Rh incompatibility (a condition in which a mismatch between the blood of a pregnant woman and that of her fetus can harm the fetus).

THE LINK TO ABORTION. Antiabortion groups oppose fetal/embryonic stem cell research because they believe it destroys human life and encourages abortion. Supporters say the embryos are going to be destroyed anyway and that research using the cells may be able to cure debilitating and lifelong diseases. Creating embryos intended for research raises additional ethical questions.

The controversy about the use of aborted fetuses for medical research erupted after the 1973 *Roe v. Wade* decision legalized abortion. Thus, shortly after this decision was announced, the U.S. Department of Health, Education, and Welfare (HEW; now the U.S. Department of Health and Human Services) placed a moratorium (a hold) on medical research using living embryos. The following year Congress added its own moratorium on all federally funded embryonic research, including research on infertility, prenatal diagnosis (determination of diseases or conditions while the fetus is still within the uterus), and in vitro fertilization (IVF; eggs are fertilized outside of the body and then implanted in the uterus). The purpose of both moratoriums was to provide time to study the issue and develop national guidelines.

HISTORICAL BACKGROUND. In 1974 Congress established the National Commission for the Protection of Human Subjects of Biomedical and Behavioral Research, and one of the topics that it had to address was fetal and embryonic tissue. The commission's first job was to develop ethical guidelines for research on fetal and embryonic tissue, which led to the HEW adopting regulations for such research based on the commission's recommendations. The commission then recommended the establishment of a national Ethics Advisory Board (EAB) to review research protocols (plans) for compliance with the ethical guidelines.

In 1975, with research regulations and the EAB in place, the moratorium was lifted on basic research that had no direct medical application. In 1979 the EAB recommended federal funding for research on IVF and embryo transfer up to 14 days, but the HEW rejected this recommendation. In the following year, funding for the EAB expired and was never reinstituted. Therefore, no body existed that could review and recommend embryo research protocols.

In October 1987 the National Institutes of Health (NIH), which is part of the U.S. Department of Health and Human Services (HHS), received a request to fund a research study in which fetal tissue would be transplanted into the brains of patients suffering from Parkinson's disease. The HHS is the primary federal agency that funds and supports medical research. The HHS denied the request and then in March 1988 it imposed a moratorium on the use of federal funds for fetal tissue transplantation research until an expert panel could study the ethical implications of such research. In November 1989, despite the panel's finding that the use of fetal tissue in research is acceptable public policy, the HHS secretary Louis W. Sullivan (1933–) continued the moratorium. Adam Clymer reports in "Bush Vetoes Bill to Lift Ban on Money for Fetal Research" (*New York Times*, June 24, 1992) that in 1992 President George H. W. Bush (1924–) vetoed Congress's efforts to restore public funding of fetal tissue research, fearing "its potential for promoting and legitimizing abortion."

When President Bill Clinton (1946–) took office in 1993, one of his first actions was to lift the ban on federally funded research using fetal tissue from induced abortion. That same year, the National Institutes of Health Revitalization Act legalized fetal tissue transplantation research. The law provided ethical guidelines that ensured informed consent, forbade payment for fetal tissue, and forbade altering the timing or method of abortion for the sake of research. In 1995, however, Congress banned the use of federal funds for research on embryos. In January 1999 the HHS ruled that stem cell research does not fall within the congressional ban on human embryo research. According to the HHS Office of the General Counsel, because stem cells alone are not capable of developing into a human, they could not be considered embryos.

The Clinton administration created rules for funding stem cell research, but they were never implemented. In 2000 the NIH announced that it would accept applications for stem cell projects that involved cells taken from frozen embryos developed in fertility treatments that were no longer needed. Shortly after taking office, however, President George W. Bush (1946–) put that plan on hold and began a review of the policy.

In August 2001 Bush announced his decision to allow federal funding for experiments involving stem cells already derived from embryos, but he would not allow federal funding for research that would cause the destruction of further embryos. The decision did not affect private-sector embryonic stem cell research. However, Bush placed certain restrictions on the research. At the same time that he announced his policy on embryonic stem cell research, Bush created the President's Council on Bioethics to monitor this research and recommend guidelines and regulations. The council included scientists, doctors, ethicists, lawyers, and theologians.

Some opposed to embryonic stem cell research support the idea of using stem cells extracted from human bone marrow for stem cell research. Bone marrow stem cells are those that develop into the various types of blood cells, such as red and white blood cells, repopulating the blood with these cells as they die. However, Manuel Alvarez-Dolado et al., in "Fusion of Bone-Marrow-Derived Cells with Purkinjue Neurons, Cardiomyocytes, and Hepatocytes" (*Nature*, vol. 425, no. 6961, October 30, 2003), and Yevgenia Kozorovitskiy and Elizabeth Gould of Princeton University, in "Stem Cell Fusion in the Brain" (*Nature Cell Biology*, vol. 5, no. 11, November 2003), indicate that only embryonic stem cells—not bone marrow stem cells—can differentiate into new cells of various types and regenerate diseased or dead tissue other than blood. In "Bone Marrow Research Is Questioned; Potential for Regeneration Overstated, Study Says" (*Washington Post*, October 13, 2003), Rick Weiss reports that results of this research suggest that previous studies regarding bone marrow stem cells are "overinterpreted." Alvarez-Dolado et al. explain that the adult stem cells often fuse with existing cells in the brain, liver, and heart, but there is no evidence that the cells then differentiate to become new brain, liver, or heart cells.

In the editorial "Embryonic Stem-Cell Research—The Case for Federal Funding" (*New England Journal of Medicine*, October 21, 2004), Jeffrey M. Drazen notes that "a critical point has been overlooked" in the embryonic stem cell research debate. According to Drazen:

> Research using this technology is strongly supported in a number of countries, including Australia, Israel, the Czech Republic, Singapore, Korea, and the United Kingdom. Others in the world appreciate the potential of this technology. If we continue to prevent federal funds from being used to support this research in the United States, the ability of our biomedical scientists to compete with other research teams throughout the world will be undermined. No matter how hard we try, we cannot legislate an end to a process of discovery that many in this country and elsewhere in the world consider ethically justifiable. The work will go on—but outside the United States.... If we fail to bring the necessary research technology into the mainstream now, our children and grandchildren may need to leave the United States to benefit from treatments other nations are currently developing. Our research scientists must be able to adopt and use embryonic stem-cell technology as they pursue its use in the treatment of many degenerative diseases. Such research has promise, but it must be nurtured to flourish.

In spite of the arguments of scientists concerning the need for embryonic stem cells for research and the need for new lines of embryonic stem cells, the Bush administration pushed forward with alternative sources. In December 2005 the Stem Cell Therapeutic and Research Act of 2005 was signed into law by Bush after its passage by Congress. This act provided for the collection and maintenance of human umbilical cord blood stem cells not only for the treatment of patients but also for research. The umbilical cord is made up of arteries and veins that shuttle blood to and from the developing fetus and the placenta of the mother. The placenta develops in the lining of the uterus and is where blood gases, nutrients, and wastes are exchanged. Cord blood is a source of stem cells for the treatment of a variety of conditions, diseases, and disorders and can be used for bone marrow transplantation.

The next year brought the passage of a bill that responded to fears that cells or tissues could be removed from fetuses that had been conceived solely for use in medical therapies or for research. Congress passed and Bush signed into law the Fetus Farming Prohibition Act of 2006, which prohibits the use of tissue from fetuses conceived for use in fetal tissue transplants or stem cell therapy.

In an effort to extend federal financing of embryonic stem cell research beyond previous limits set by President Bush, the U.S. Senate and the U.S. House of Representatives passed the Stem Cell Research Enhancement Act of 2007. Besides enhanced funding, the act would also give researchers access—with donor consent—to thousands of embryos that would otherwise be frozen or discarded by fertility clinics. The bill was vetoed by Bush in June 2007.

President Barack Obama (1961–) took office in January 2009 and began undoing many of the Bush-era policies. According to Jim Tankersley and Noam N. Levy, in "Barack Obama Lifts Restrictions on Federal Funding for Stem Cell Research Using Human Embryos" (*Chicago Tribune*, March 9, 2009), President Obama "made his most forceful break yet from his predecessor's controversial scientific agenda [by] opening the door to a major expansion of government-funded research on embryonic stem cells and ordering federal agencies to strengthen the role of science in their decision-making." He signed an executive order lifting the limitations and gave the NIH 120 days to develop new guidelines for funding embryonic stem cell research. In "Effect of Obama's Stem Cell Reversal Could Take Years" (*Daily Record* [Baltimore, MD], March 10, 2009), Liz Farmer notes that $8.2 billion became available in 2009 for embryonic stem cell research, but that actually evaluating and then funding grant proposals to get money to researchers would not occur until at least 2010.

Genetic Testing

GENDER SELECTION. Progress in prenatal testing has raised a number of questions about the possible reasons for obtaining an abortion. Ultrasonography (also called ultrasound scanning, in which images of the fetus are made using sound waves) and amniocentesis (removal of a small amount of amniotic fluid to gain information about the fetus) are able to determine the sex of a fetus.

In some countries, such as China and India, parents often prefer boys and sometimes use abortion to prevent the birth of girls. China has a one-child policy, which has resulted in many Chinese couples preferring to have their one child be male rather than female. A major consequence of this parental preference is that sex ratios at birth are skewed; that is, the ratio of males to females no longer approximates the worldwide average of 103 to 107 males born for every 100 females. Wei Xing Zhu, Li Lu, and Therese Hesketh note in "China's Excess Males, Sex Selective Abortion, and One Child Policy: Analysis of Data from 2005 National Intercensus Survey" (*British Medical Journal*, vol. 338, April 18, 2009) that China's sex ratio was 124 males to 100 females for births from 2000 to 2004 and then 119 males to 100 females for births in 2005. In the United States women generally do not have abortions for reasons of sex preference in a child.

A technology called sperm sorting has become popular with couples who want to choose the sex of a child. The techniques used in sperm sorting were developed by the

Genetics and IVF Institute, a fertility clinic in Fairfax, Virginia. The original purpose of the technology for human use was to increase significantly the chances of couples, in which the mother is a carrier of 350 X-linked genetic disorders, to produce daughters. Giving the "carrier" X chromosome to a daughter produces another carrier, whereas giving it to a son produces a child with the affliction. However, sperm sorting is now offered for "family balancing." According to the clinic, more daughters than sons have been selected.

Another technology for gender selection is the initiation of IVF with preimplantation genetic diagnosis (PGD). With this technique, eggs are fertilized outside of the mother's body and the gender of each embryo is determined. Only those embryos with the desired sex are used, and the others are discarded.

In response to these types of gender selection, the Ethics Committee of the American Society of Reproductive Medicine issued three reports over several years starting in 1994 and concluded that using medical technologies to prevent children being born with genetic disorders is acceptable, but that using these technologies for nonmedical reasons creates a variety of ethical questions.

In May 2001 the committee issued "Preconception Gender Selection for Nonmedical Reasons" (*Fertility and Sterility*, vol. 75, no. 5), which was reviewed and left unchanged in June 2006. The committee concludes:

> If ... methods of preconception gender selection are found to be safe and effective, physicians should be free to offer preconception gender selection in clinical settings to couples who are seeking gender variety in their offspring if the couples (1) are fully informed of the risks of failure, (2) affirm that they will fully accept children of the opposite sex if the preconception gender selection fails, (3) are counseled about having unrealistic expectations about the behavior of children of the preferred gender, and (4) are offered the opportunity to participate in research to track and assess the safety, efficacy, and demographics of preconception selection. Practitioners offering assisted reproductive services are under no legal or ethical obligation to provide nonmedically indicated preconception methods of gender selection.

However, the Center for Genetics and Society raises other issues about sex selection. In "About Sex Selection" (2009, http://geneticsandsociety.org/article.php?list=type &type=29), the center notes that "sex selection raises concerns about exacerbating sex discrimination and violence against women, and normalizing the 'selection' and 'design' of children. The use and marketing of sex selection technologies are largely unregulated in the United States. Although the ongoing attacks on abortion rights complicate efforts to address even pre-pregnancy methods, a number of countries—including Canada, Germany, and the

United Kingdom—prohibit 'social' sex selection without affecting abortion rights."

By June 2009 an at-home test to determine the sex of a fetus eight weeks into a pregnancy was available in Australia and New Zealand. The IntelliGender test claims to be 80% accurate and works somewhat like a home pregnancy test. A pregnant woman mixes her urine with the test's chemicals, and a color change signals the sex of the fetus. Briony Sowden and Martin Johnston report in "Gender Test Spurs Abortion Fears" (*New Zealand Herald* [Auckland, New Zealand], June 8, 2009) that the Royal Australian and New Zealand College of Obstetricians and Gynaecologists expressed concern that women would abort fetuses based on sex. The IntelliGender test has been available in the United States since 2006.

SCREENING FOR BIRTH DEFECTS AND HEREDITARY DISEASES. Prenatal testing through amniocentesis, ultrasound, or other methods may reveal severe defects in the fetus, such as anencephaly (absence of most of the brain), spina bifida (incomplete development of the back and spine), and Down syndrome (a genetic disorder that usually includes mental retardation).

In addition, genetic (hereditary) testing allows some parents to determine if the child they are carrying has the gene for certain diseases, such as Huntington's disease (an inherited disease that affects the functioning of both the body and brain), Tay-Sachs disease (a disease that is most common among people of Jewish descent and results in neurological disorders and death in childhood), cystic fibrosis (an inherited disease of the mucous glands that produces problems associated with the lungs and pancreas), or the genes BRCA1 and BRCA2, which increase a female's risk of breast and ovarian cancer. Women who discover that the fetuses they are carrying are seriously impaired or will develop debilitating diseases may face an agonizing decision about whether to have an abortion.

Some people have no problem with genetic testing if it makes possible the use of preventive therapy for a predisposed condition, or an acceptance of and preparation for the child who may be born with abnormalities that cannot be treated. However, because most genetic tests are for untreatable disorders, some fear that the screening techniques may be used for eugenic (selective breeding) purposes, preventing the birth of children affected by hereditary defects.

Many people who are handicapped take issue with those who advocate abortions in cases of fetal defects and potential diseases. They argue that had late-term abortions been available to their mothers during pregnancy, they might have never had the chance for life. Many disabled people say they resent those who feel one can mandate a certain quality of life or place an economic value on it. Some observers are also wary that the genetic information obtained from prenatal testing might eventually result in preventing the birth of children with certain traits or behavioral tendencies.

Infertility Treatments

MULTIPLE BIRTHS. Many women who are unable to conceive have turned to assisted reproductive technology (ART). There are several methods of ART, including IVF, gamete intrafallopian transfer, and zygote intrafallopian transfer. IVF is the most widely used method to help women achieve pregnancy. IVF is performed by removing the woman's eggs, fertilizing them in the laboratory, and transferring the resulting embryo or embryos back into her uterus. According to Saswati Sunderam et al. of the Centers for Disease Control and Prevention (CDC), in "Assisted Reproductive Technology Surveillance—United States, 2006" (*Morbidity and Mortality Weekly Report*, vol. 58, no. SS-5, June 12, 2009), in 2006, 44% of ART transfer procedures resulted in a pregnancy and 36% resulted in a live-birth delivery. In 2006, 54,656 infants were born as a result of ART; 48% were born in multiple-birth deliveries.

The pregnancy success rate in ART decreases as the woman's age increases. Therefore, to increase the chances of success in older women, doctors are likely to implant more embryos. In a number of cases, many well-publicized triplet and higher births have resulted. Table 7.2 shows the outcomes of ART using each technology.

The birth of the McCaughey septuplets in 1997 in Iowa, the Chukwu octuplets in 1998 in Texas, and the Suleman octuplets in 2009 in California brought criticism from many in the medical profession who thought the parents and their fertility doctors had acted irresponsibly. Some believed the mothers had taken a tremendous risk with their health and that of their children. Siblings in multiple births are at a high risk for prematurity, low birth weight, long-term mental and physical disabilities, and death.

Ethicists ask if it is justifiable behavior to abort some fetuses when a woman is pregnant with multiples to reduce the risks to the remaining ones. This process is called selective reduction. Some people believe the parents of multiples should employ selective reduction. Those who are against selective reduction warn that the acceptance of abortion in cases of multiple births will eventually make it too easy in the future to "selectively reduce" other members of society, such as the elderly or the disabled.

In the last several decades, the rate of triplet and higher births increased dramatically. (See Figure 7.2.) In "Births: Final Data for 2006" (*National Vital Statistics Reports*, vol. 57, no. 7, January 7, 2009), Brady E. Hamilton et al. of the CDC attribute this upsurge to two primary causes:

1. The birthrate of women over age 30 has increased significantly since the 1980s and women aged 30 and older are more likely than women under the age of 30 to conceive multiples spontaneously.

2. The use of fertility-enhancing therapies, which increase the probability of multiple births, has increased as well.

However, the rate of triplet and higher births declined 21% between 1998 and 2006. (See Figure 7.2.) This decline is thought be the result of a drop in the number of embryos implanted during ART procedures, as was suggested in published guidelines authored by the American Society of Reproductive Medicine in the late 1990s (and later updated). The guidelines were developed in response to the rise in triplet and high multiple births and the resultant poor outcomes.

TABLE 7.2

Outcomes of assisted reproductive technology (ART), by procedure type, 2006

Procedure type	No. procedures started	No. egg retrievals	No. embryo transfers	Pregnancies* No.	Pregnancies* (%)[a]	Live-birth deliveries No.	Live-birth deliveries (%)[a]	Singleton live-birth deliveries No.	Singleton live-birth deliveries (%)[a]	Multiple live-birth deliveries No.	Multiple live-birth deliveries (%)[a]	No. live-born infants
Patient's eggs used												
Fresh embryos	99,199	87,799	80,313	34,719	43.2	28,404	35.4	19,682	24.5	8,722	10.9	37,610
Thawed embryos	22,023	NA[b]	20,057	7,401	36.9	5,797	28.9	4,395	21.9	1,402	7.0	7,276
Donor eggs used												
Fresh embryos	10,984	10,391	10,049	6,315	62.8	5,393	53.7	3,286	32.7	2,107	21.0	7,572
Thawed embryos	5,992	NA[b]	5,456	2,136	39.1	1,749	32.1	1,326	24.3	423	7.8	2,198
Total	138,198[c]	NA[b]	115,875	50,571	43.6	41,343	35.7	28,689	24.8	12,654	10.9	54,656

[a]Number of outcomes per 100 embryo transfers.
[b]NA=Not applicable.
[c]This number does not include 69 cycles in which a new treatment procedure was being evaluated.

SOURCE: Saswati Sunderam et al., "Table 1. Number and Outcomes of Assisted Reproductive Technology (ART), by Procedure Type—United States, 2006," in "Assisted Reproductive Technology Surveillance—United States, 2006," *Morbidity and Mortality Weekly Report*, vol. 58, no. SS-5, June 12, 2009, http://www.cdc.gov/mmwr/PDF/ss/ss5805.pdf (accessed June 18, 2009)

FIGURE 7.2

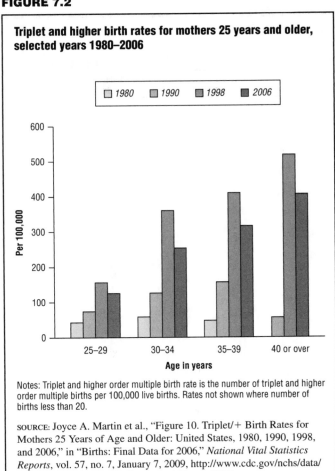

Triplet and higher birth rates for mothers 25 years and older, selected years 1980–2006

Notes: Triplet and higher order multiple birth rate is the number of triplet and higher order multiple births per 100,000 live births. Rates not shown where number of births less than 20.

SOURCE: Joyce A. Martin et al., "Figure 10. Triplet/+ Birth Rates for Mothers 25 Years of Age and Older: United States, 1980, 1990, 1998, and 2006," in "Births: Final Data for 2006," *National Vital Statistics Reports*, vol. 57, no. 7, January 7, 2009, http://www.cdc.gov/nchs/data/nvsr/nvsr57/nvsr57_07.pdf (accessed May 8, 2009)

Refusal of Abortion Treatment or Drugs

The Guttmacher Institute notes in *State Policies in Brief: Refusing to Provide Health Services* (August 1, 2009, http://www.guttmacher.org/statecenter/spibs/spib_RPHS.pdf) that most states have policies that allow some health care practitioners and institutions to refuse to provide abortion, contraception, or sterilization services. In states without such provisions, individual health care providers are often protected by law from being compelled to offer services in conflict with their religious beliefs. A few states have laws that allow pharmacists to refuse to fill prescriptions to which they object on moral or religious grounds.

Table 7.3 lists state policies that allow providers to refuse services. Forty-six states allow some health care providers to refuse to provide abortion services, and 43 states allow some institutions to refuse as well.

Some states have adopted restrictions on providing emergency contraception (called Plan B), which is a concentrated dose of the hormone found in birth control pills. Taken up to 72 hours after unprotected intercourse, Plan B can prevent unwanted pregnancy. In 2006 the U.S. Food and Drug Administration approved Plan B as an over-the-counter (OTC; without a prescription) medication for women aged 18 and older. In 2009 the drug was approved as OTC for women aged 17. Female teens younger than 17 need a prescription to buy the medication. However, states can pass laws that expand minors' access to emergency contraception. Table 7.4 lists states with emergency contraception policies. Some states allow pharmacists to dispense emergency contraceptive pills without a prescription. In addition, some states have laws requiring emergency rooms and pharmacists to fill valid prescriptions for emergency contraception; they cannot refuse on religious or other grounds.

Many leading professional associations have weighed in on the issue of health care providers' and pharmacists' refusal to provide abortion and contraception services and medications, balancing the provider's right to refuse with the responsibility to provide appropriate health care. Most professional association statements embody the idea that providers have the right not to perform services or provide medicines that may go against their moral or religious beliefs, but that they have a responsibility to refer the patient to a provider who can provide that service or medication.

FETAL RIGHTS

Fetal rights is the view that the unborn deserve the same legal protections as children. Since its 1973 decision in *Roe v. Wade*, the U.S. Supreme Court has consistently ruled that the woman's right to health and life outweighs the state's interest in the fetus, even after viability. In recent years, however, there have been a number of attempts to elevate the status of the fetus to that of a child.

In 2007 the Supreme Court ruled 5-4 in *Gonzales v. Carhart* (550 U.S. 124) that the federal Partial-Birth Abortion Ban Act of 2003 was constitutional (see Chapter 2). The act imposes civil and criminal penalties on physicians who knowingly perform the intact dilation and extraction abortion procedure, which can be used for abortions at 21 or more weeks of gestation. Justice Ruth Bader Ginsburg (1933–) noted in her dissenting opinion, "Today's decision is alarming.... It tolerates, indeed applauds, federal intervention to ban nationwide a procedure found necessary and proper in certain cases by the American College of Obstetricians and Gynecologists (ACOG).... For the first time since *Roe*, the Court blesses a prohibition with no exception safeguarding a woman's health." Thus, this ruling does not directly decree that the fetus is a child, but it does put the interests of the life of a fetus before the life of the women bearing the fetus.

THE FETUS AS A VICTIM OF A CRIME
Unborn Victims of Violence Act of 2004

The Unborn Victims of Violence Act of 2004 is the first federal law to recognize the fetus as a victim of a crime. The

TABLE 7.3

State policies allowing health care providers to refuse abortion, contraception, or sterilization, 2009

State	Abortion Individual providers	Institutions	Contraception Individual providers	Pharmacists	Pharmacies	Institutions	Sterilization Individual providers	Institutions
Alaska	X	Private						
Arizona	X	X						
Arkansas	X	X	X	X	a	Private	X	X
California	X	Religious		b				
Colorado	X	X	X	a	a	Private		
Connecticut	X							
Delaware	X	X						
Florida	X	X	X	a				
Georgia	X	X		X			X	X
Hawaii	X	X						
Idaho	X	X					X	X
Illinois	X	Private	X	a	c	X	X	X
Indiana	X	Private						
Iowa	X	Private						
Kansas	X	X					X	X
Kentucky	X	X					X	
Louisiana	X	X						
Maine	X	X	X	a	a	Private		
Maryland	X	X					X	X
Massachusetts	X	X				Private	X	Private
Michigan	X	X						
Minnesota	X	Private						
Mississippi	X	X	X	X	X	X	X	X
Missouri	X	X						
Montana	X	Private					X	Private
Nebraska	X	X						
Nevada	X	Private						
New Jersey	X	Private			d	Private	X	Private
New Mexico	X	X						X
New York	X							
North Carolina	X	X						
North Dakota	X	X						
Ohio	X	X						
Oklahoma	X	X						
Oregon	X	Private						
Pennsylvania	X	Private					X	Private
Rhode Island	X						X	
South Carolina	X	Private						
South Dakota	X	X		X				
Tennessee	X	X	X	a	a	Private		
Texas	X	Private						
Utah	X	Private						
Virginia	X	X						
Washington	X	X	X		e	X	X	X
West Virginia							X	X
Wisconsin	X	X					X	X
Wyoming	X	Private						
Total	**46**	**43**	**8**	**4**	**1**	**9**	**16**	**15**

Note: Unless indicated, the right to refuse applies to all institutions–private, religious and public.
^aA broadly worded refusal clause may apply.
^bPharmacists have a duty to dispense valid prescriptions and can only refuse to dispense a prescription, including contraceptives, when their employers approves the refusal and the woman can still access her prescription in a timely manner.
^cState regulation requires pharmacies to fill valid contraceptive prescriptions.
^dPharmacies have a duty to fill valid prescriptions.
^eThe policy in Washington that requires pharmacies dispense valid prescriptions and deliver FDA-approved drugs, such as Plan B, is not in effect pending the outcome of a court case.

SOURCE: Guttmacher Institute, Community Health Centers and Family Planning, "Policies Allowing Providers to Refuse," in *State Policies in Brief: Refusing to Provide Health Services*, New York: Guttmacher, May 1, 2009, http://www.guttmacher.org/statecenter/spibs/spib_RPHS.pdf (accessed May 13, 2009)

law makes it "a separate offense" to injure or cause the death of "a child, who is in utero [in the womb] at the time the conduct takes place." The act applies only to federal offenses, such as crimes committed on federal properties, against certain federal officials and employees, and by members of the military. It does not apply to crimes prosecuted by the individual states. Even though the law does not seek the prosecution of "conduct relating to an abortion," abortion advocates claim that this law sets the stage for dismantling the legal right to abortion.

The States and Unborn Victims

The National Right to Life Committee indicates in *State Homicide Laws That Recognize Unborn Victims* (June

TABLE 7.4

State policies on emergency contraception (EC), April 2009

	Expanding access						Restricting access			
	Emergency rooms required to:		Pharmacists may dispense EC without physician prescription under:		Pharmacy stocking birth control must dispense EC	Pharmacy must fill valid prescriptions	State law excludes EC from:		State law allows refusal to dispense EC by:	
State	Provide information about EC	Dispense EC upon request	Collaborative practice agreement	State-approved protocol			Medicaid family planning expansion	Contraceptive coverage mandate	Pharmacist	Pharmacy
Alaska			X[b]							c
Arkansas	X							X	X	c
California	X	X	X	X		X				
Colorado	X[d]	X[d]							c	c
Connecticut	X[d]									
District of Columbia	X	X							c	
Florida			X						c	
Georgia			X						X	
Hawaii									c	
Illinois	X				X				c	c
Indiana							e		c	
Maine			X	X						
Massachusetts	X	X	X							
Minnesota	X	X								
Mississippi									X	X
New Hampshire			X			X				
New Jersey	X	X								
New Mexico	X	X		X						
New York	X	X						X		
North Carolina										
Ohio	f	f								
Oregon	X	X[g]								
Pennsylvania	X									
South Carolina		X								
South Dakota									X[c]	c
Tennessee							e			
Texas	X									
Vermont			X			a				
Washington	X	X	X							
Wisconsin	X	X								
Total	**15+DC**	**11+DC**	**7**	**3**	**1**	**2**	**2**	**2**	**4**	**1**

[a]Policy is not in effect pending the outcome of a court case.

[b]Pharmacists may dispense any prescription drug, including emergency contraception.

[c]A broadly worded refusal policy may apply to pharmacists or pharmacies, but does not specifically include them.

[d]A hospital may contract with an independent medical professional in order to provide the emergency contraception services.

[e]Waiver application will exclude emergency contraception explicitly in Texas, implicitly in Indiana.

[f]Policy does not include an enforcement mechanism.

[g]A hospital may refuse based on religious or moral beliefs to provide emergency contraception when requested by a woman who has been sexually assaulted. However, a refusing hospital is then required to immediately transport the woman to the closest medical facility that will provide her with the medication.

SOURCE: Guttmacher Institute, Community Health Centers and Family Planning, "Emergency Contraception Policies," in *State Policies in Brief: Emergency Contraception*, New York: Guttmacher, April 1, 2009, http://www.guttmacher.org/statecenter/spibs/spib_EC.pdf (accessed May 13, 2009)

25, 2008, http://www.nrlc.org/Unborn_Victims/Statehomi cidelaws092302.html) that in 2008, 25 states had homicide laws that recognize unborn children as victims throughout the entire prenatal period. Another 10 states had homicide laws that recognize unborn children as victims during part of their prenatal development.

FETAL RIGHTS VERSUS PARENTS' RIGHTS

If a pregnant woman's behaviors during pregnancy are detrimental to the fetus, should this be considered child abuse? According to the Guttmacher Institute, in *State Policies in Brief: Substance Abuse during Pregnancy* (August 1, 2009, http://www.guttmacher.org/statecenter/spibs/spib _SADP.pdf), in 2009, 15 states answered "yes" to this question and had laws stating that substance abuse during pregnancy is considered child abuse. These laws were civil laws not criminal laws, except in South Carolina, where the state supreme court has held that a viable fetus is a person.

Opponents of fetal rights believe that if a fetus is granted the same legal rights traditionally granted to people, the law will be forced to embark on the "slippery slope" of what control the state should have over women (and men). If substance use can be prohibited, then everything a woman does that might potentially harm the fetus could be regulated. Her eating and drinking, her work, or her health habits could all be scrutinized by the courts. Could a woman who inadvertently harmed a fetus before she knew she was pregnant be held liable? Could a woman be criminally prosecuted for failing to seek prenatal care?

Results of medical research reveal increasing evidence that a woman's behavior is not the only influence on the fetus. Men who smoke, abuse drugs (including marijuana) and alcohol, or work with toxic chemicals may be damaging their sperm, thereby causing genetically defective fetuses. Men, however, have not yet been charged with abuse of the unborn.

CHAPTER 8
ABORTION AROUND THE WORLD

Throughout the world abortion is regularly used as a method of birth control. Because women are fertile for almost half of their lives, many have unwanted pregnancies at one time or another. Regardless of whether abortion is legal, women in all countries and cultures have relied on abortion to control childbirth. Abortion rates around the world generally reflect the religious and political power in the country, the cultural values, and the availability of contraception. An abortion rate is the number of abortions per 1,000 women aged 15 to 44.

The major organizations that compile international abortion statistics are the Guttmacher Institute, which supports a woman's right to choose abortion, and the World Health Organization (WHO) of the United Nations (UN). It is difficult for these organizations to obtain up-to-date worldwide abortion statistics for a variety of reasons. In countries where abortion is illegal or severely restricted, abortions are not a part of the medical record. In addition, it is impossible to know how many women get private abortions and how many of those who turn up at the hospital with a spontaneous abortion (miscarriage) actually induced the abortion through a home method. Many countries in which abortion is legal do not keep complete medical records; as a result, estimates often need to be made. Moreover, there are sometimes legal and confidentiality issues surrounding abortion data. The abortion and health data that are available for countries with these issues are generally neither as current nor as accurate as that for the United States.

The Guttmacher Institute and the WHO report in "Facts on Induced Abortion Worldwide" (October 2008, http:// www.guttmacher.org/pubs/fb_IAW.html) that each year approximately 205 million women throughout the world become pregnant. Twenty-three million of worldwide pregnancies occur in developed countries; 40% of them are unintended and 28% end in abortion. The remaining 182 million of worldwide pregnancies occur in developing countries; more than a third of them are unintended and 19% end in abortion.

ABORTION LAWS WORLDWIDE

The Center for Reproductive Rights, which supports a woman's right to choose, indicates in "The World's Abortion Laws 2008 Fact Sheet" (November 2008, http://repro ductiverights.org/en/document/world-abortion-laws-2008-fact-sheet) that over 60% of people live in countries where abortion is permitted for a wide range of reasons or without restriction. Another 26% of the world's population live in countries that generally forbid abortion. Countries are categorized based on the restrictiveness of abortion laws, as follows:

- Prohibited altogether or permitted only to save the woman's life: in 2008 there were 68 countries (25.7% of the world's population) in this category. (See Table 8.1.) As Figure 8.1 shows, in June 2007 most countries with highly restrictive laws were in Central and South America, Africa, the Middle East, and Indonesia.

- To preserve the woman's physical health (and to save her life): 35 countries (9.6% of the world's population) allow an abortion if it threatens a woman's physical health. These types of laws sometimes require that the potential injury be either serious or permanent.

- To preserve the woman's mental health (and to preserve her physical health and save her life): 23 countries (4.2% of the world's population) allow the termination of pregnancy if continuing it would jeopardize a woman's mental health. However, what constitutes a threat to mental health varies from country to country, from psychological distress caused by rape to mental anguish because the woman is carrying a fetus that might have abnormalities.

- Socioeconomic grounds (also to save the woman's life and physical and mental health: 14 countries (21.3% of the world's population) permit abortion, but consider a woman's economic resources, her age, whether she is married, and the number of children she already has. These laws are usually interpreted liberally.

TABLE 8.1

World abortion laws, May 2008

[Countries, by restrictiveness of abortion law, 2008. Categories from the most to least restrictive.]

I. To save the woman's life or prohibited altogether (countries printed in bold make an explicit exception to save a woman's life)		II. To preserve physical health (also to save the woman's life)	III. To preserve mental health (also to save the woman's life and physical health)	IV. Socioeconomic grounds (also to save the woman's life, physical health and mental health)	V. Without restriction as to reason
Afghanistan	Mauritius	Argentina-[l]	Algeria	Australia-[m]	Albania
Andorra	**Mexico**-[m, i, s]	Bahamas	Botswana-[i, p, s]	Barbados-[r, i, p, s]	Armenia
Angola	Micronesia-[k]	Benin-[i, p, s]	Colombia-[i, p, s]	Belize-[s]	Austria[d]
Antigua & Barbuda	Monaco	Bolivia-[r, p]	Gambia	Cyprus-[i, s]	Azerbaijan
Bangladesh	**Myanmar**	Burkina Faso-[i, p, s]	Ghana-[i, p, s]	Fiji	Bahrain
Bhutan-[l, n]	**Nicaragua**-[o]	Burundi	Hong Kong-[i, p, s]	Finland-[i, s, n] +	Belarus
Brazil-[l]	**Nigeria**	Cameroon-[i]	Israel-[i, p, s, n]	Great Britain-[s]	Belgium[d]
Brunei Darussalam	Oman	Chad-[s]	Jamaica-[r]	Iceland-[i, ps, n]	Bosnia-Herzegovina-[r]
Central African Rep.	Palau-[k]	Comoros	Liberia-[i, p, s]	India-[r, i, s]	Bulgaria
Chile-[o]	**Panama**-[r, i, s]	Costa Rica	Malaysia	Japan-[q]	Cambodia[d]
Congo (Brazzaville)	**Papua New Guinea**	Djibouti	Namibia-[i, p, s]	Luxembourg-[r, i, s]	Canada[h]
Côte d'Ivoire	**Paraguay**	Ecuador-[l]	Nauru	Saint Vincent &	Cape Verde
Dem. Rep. of Congo	Philippines	Equatorial	New Zealand-[p, s]	Grenadines-[i, p, s]	China[h-j]
Dominica	San Marino	Guinea-[q, r]	Northern Ireland	Taiwan-[q, r, p, s]	Croatia-[r]
Dominican Republic	Sao Tome & Principe	Eritrea-[p]	Saint Kitts & Nevis	Zambia-[s]	Cuba-[r]
Egypt	Senegal	Ethiopia-[i, p, s, n]	Saint Lucia-[i, p]		Czech Rep.-[r]
El Salvador-[o]	**Soloman Islands**	Grenada	Samoa	14 Countries, 21.3%	Dem. People's Rep.
Gabon	Somalia	Guinea-[i, p, s]	Seychelles-[i, p, s]	of World's Population	of Korea[h]
Guatemala	**Sri Lanka**	Jordan	Sierra Leone		Denmark-[r]
Guinea-Bissau	**Sudan**-[l]	Kuwait-[q, r, s]	Spain-[i, s]		Estonia
Haiti	Suriname	Liechtenstein-[b]	Swaziland-[i, p, s]		France[d]
Honduras	**Syria**-[q, r]	Maldives-[q]	Thailand-[i, s]		Fmr. Yugoslav Rep.
Indonesia	**Tanzania**	Morocco-[q]	Trinidad & Tobago		Macedonia-[r]
Iran-[s]	Tonga	Mozambique			Georgia-[r]
Iraq	**Tuvalu**	Niger-[s]	23 Countries, 4.2% of		Germany[d]
Ireland	**Uganda**	Pakistan	World's Population		Greece-[r]
Kenya	**United Arab**	Peru			Guyana[b]
Kiribati	**Emirates**-[q, r]	Poland-[r, i, p, s]			Hungary
Laos	**Venezuela**	Qatar-[F]			Italy[a-r]
Lebanon	**West Bank &**	Rep. of Korea[q, i, p, s]			Kazakhstan
Lesotho	**Gaza Strip**	Rwanda			Kyrgyzstan
Libya-[r]	**Yemen**	Saudi Arabia-[q, r]			Latvia-[r]
Madagascar		Togo-[i, p, s]			Lithuania
Malawi-[q]	68 Countries, 25.7%	Uruguay-[l]			Moldova
Mali-[l, p]	of World's Population	Vanuatu			Mongolia
Malta		Zimbabwe-[i, p, s]			Montenegro-[r]
Marshall Islands-[k]					Nepal-[j]
Mauritania		35 Countries, 9.6% of			Netherlands[g]
		World's Population			Norway-[r]
					Portugal[c-r]
					Puerto Rico [v]
					Romania[d]
					Russian Fed.
					Serbia-[r]
					Singapore[f]
					Slovak Rep.-[r]
					Slovenia-[r]
					South Africa
					Sweden[e]
					Switzerland
					Tajikistan
					Tunisia
					Turkey[c-q, r]
					Turkmenistan
					Ukraine
					United States[g-m, r]
					Uzbekistan
					Vietnam[o]
					56 Countries, 39.3% of World's Population

- Without restriction as to reason: 56 countries (39.3% of the world's population) allow abortion without limiting the reasons for pregnancy termination.

In addition, in some countries a woman may obtain a legal abortion based on "juridical grounds" (rape or incest) or "fetal impairment grounds" (probable genetic defects).

TABLE 8.1

World abortion laws, May 2008 [CONTINUED]

A note on terminology: "Countries" listed on the table include independent states and, where populations exceed one million, semi-autonomous regions, territories, and jurisdictions of special status. The table therefore includes Hong Kong, Northern Ireland, Puerto Rico, Taiwan, and the West Bank and Gaza Strip.

Gestational Limits Key: All countries in category V have gestational limits of 12 weeks unless otherwise indicated. Gestational limits are calculated from the first day of the last menstrual period, which is considered to occur two weeks prior to conception. Where laws specify that gestitional age limits are calculated from the date of conception, these limits have been extended by two weeks.

[a]Gestational limit of 90 days.
[b]Gestational limit of 8 weeks.
[c]Gestational limit of 10 weeks.
[d]Gestational limit of 14 weeks.
[e]Gestational limit of 18 weeks.
[f]Gestational limit of 24 weeks.
[g]Law does not limit pre-viability abortion.
[h]Law does not indicate gestational limit; regulatory mechanisms vary.

Indications:
[i]Abortion permitted in cases of rape.
[j]Sex selective abortion prohibited.
[k]Law unclear.
[l]Abortion permitted in the case of rape of a woman with a mental disability.
[m]Federal system in which abortion law is determined at state level; classification reflects legal status of abortion for largest number of people.
[n]Abortion permitted on additional enumerated grounds relating to such factors as the woman's age or capacity to care for a child.
[o]Recent legislation eliminated all exceptions to prohibit on abortion; availability of defense of necessity highly unlikely.
[p]Abortion permitted in cases of incest.
[q]Spousal authorization required.
[r]Parental authorization/notification required.
[s]Abortion permitted in cases of fetal impairment.

SOURCE: "The World's Abortion Laws," Center for Reproductive Rights, May 2008, http://reproductiverights.org/sites/crr.civicactions.net/files/pub_fac_abortionlaws2008.pdf (accessed June 27, 2009)

Countries that recognize these grounds for legal abortion may be classified under any of the five categories of restrictiveness. Access to abortion may also be limited by spousal or parental consent laws.

Abortion Limitations Even When Laws Are Liberal

In the countries where abortion is not restricted as to reason, and in the countries that allow abortion based on socioeconomic grounds, the laws usually mandate certain conditions for allowing the abortion. These countries may impose gestational limits; consent, counseling, and waiting-period requirements; fetal-age restrictions; limitations on advertising abortion services; and limitations on the place of abortion and the person performing the procedure. For example, a woman in Turkey must present her marriage certificate in most hospitals to get an abortion, and if she is married she must have her husband's permission. In Germany beginning in January 2010 a woman considering an abortion after 20 weeks' gestation must receive a psychological evaluation and counseling, and then must wait three days before the abortion can be performed. In Belgium the waiting period for any abortion is six days. Most countries set fetal age limits of seeking an abortion with the least restrictions at an upper limit of 12 to 14 weeks.

LEGAL AND SAFE WORLDWIDE ABORTION STATISTICS

According to Gilda Sedgh et al. of the Guttmacher Institute, in "Induced Abortion: Estimated Rates and Trends Worldwide" (*Lancet*, vol. 370, no. 9595, October 13, 2007), the WHO defines unsafe abortions as those "done either by people lacking the necessary skills or in an environment that does not conform to minimum medical standards, or both. These include (a) abortions in countries where the law is restrictive and (b) abortions that do not meet legal requirements in countries where the law is not restrictive." Safe abortions are defined as those "(a) in countries where abortion law is not restrictive, and (b) that meet legal requirements in countries where the law is restrictive." In essence, unsafe abortions largely correspond to illegal abortions and safe abortions to legal abortions.

Table 8.2 and Table 8.3 show legal abortion numbers, rates, and ratios for countries with populations exceeding 1 million. These data were compiled by Sedgh et al. from government statistics and nationally representative surveys and were the most recent data as of mid-2009.

The data in Table 8.2 are from countries where reporting is relatively complete. Because of their completeness and reliability, these data can be compared over time and among countries. Where abortion is legal and reporting is believed to be complete, Cuba (57 per 1,000 women aged 15 to 44), the Russian Federation (45), Estonia (36), and Belarus (35) had the highest abortion rates in 2003. Nepal (5 per 1,000 women), South Africa (6), Switzerland (7), Tunisia (7), Belgium (8), and Germany (8) had the lowest abortion rates in 2003.

The abortion ratio is the number of abortions per 100 known live births. Table 8.2 shows that in 2003 among countries where abortion is legal and reporting is believed to be complete, Cuba (109), the Russian Federation (104), and Belarus (91) had the highest abortion ratios. This means

FIGURE 8.1

Levels of abortion restriction worldwide, June 2007

Currently, over 60% of the world's people live in countries where induced abortion is permitted either for a wide range of reasons or without restriction as to reason. In contrast, about 26% of all people reside in countries where abortion is generally prohibited.

SOURCE: Adapted from "The World's Abortion Laws, May 2007," Center for Reproductive Rights, July 2007, http://reproductiverights.org/sites/crr.civicactions.net/files/documents/Abortion%20Map_FA.pdf (accessed June 8, 2009)

that slightly more pregnancies in Cuba and the Russian Federation were terminated by abortion than resulted in live births in 2003. In Belarus the ratio tipped in the other direction—slightly more pregnancies resulted in live births than were ended in abortion in 2003. Nepal had the lowest abortion ratio: for every 100 pregnancies that resulted in live birth in 2003, only four were terminated by abortion.

Table 8.3 lists abortion statistics in countries where reporting is incomplete. Sedgh et al. obtained abortion information for these countries using available government statistics and nationally representative surveys. Sometimes the data for the same country but from different sources are dramatically different. For example, Vietnam shows four rows of estimates: two for 2003 and two for 1996. The two sets of data

for each of the two years come from different sources. One set of data are from government statistics, and one set (denoted by the footnote) come from nationally representative surveys. The government statistics show a dramatic decrease in the number of abortions in Vietnam from 1996 to 2003. However, the survey data show a slight increase. Disparities such as these point out how difficult it is to draw conclusions from these data. There is no way to know which data, if any, are accurate or show a true picture of what is happening in that country. One possibility is that abortion has become increasingly private over the years and that the government statistics do not reflect many of these private procedures.

Using two sets of data such as these can also help investigators determine whether government reports of abor-

TABLE 8.2

Measures of legal abortion in countries where reporting is relatively complete, by country and year, 1996 and 2003

Country	No.[a] 2003	No.[a] 1996	Rate[b] 2003	Rate[b] 1996	Average annual % change	Ratio,[c] 2003	Total abortion rate,[d] 2003
Eastern Europe							
Belarus[e]	80,200	u	35	u	u	91	1.1[f]
Bulgaria	34,700	89,000	22	51	−11.7	52	0.6[f]
Czech Republic	27,100	46,500	13	21	−6.9	29	0.4
Hungary	53,800	76,600	26	35	−4.2	57	0.7
Russian Federation	1,504,000	2,284,600	45	69	−6.0	104	1.3
Slovakia	16,200	25,200	13	20	−6.1	31	0.4[f]
Northern Europe							
Denmark	15,600	18,100	15	16	−1.6	24	0.4
England and Wales[g]	181,600	167,900	17	16	0.9	29	0.5
Estonia	10,600	16,900	36	56	−6.1	82	1.1
Finland	10,700	10,400	11	10	1.1	19	0.3
Latvia	19,000	23,100	29	44	−6.0	69	0.9
Lithuania	11,500	27,800	15	34	−11.0	38	0.5
Norway	13,800	14,300	15	16	−0.5	25	0.5
Scotland[h]	12,600	12,300	12	11	0.5	23	0.4
Sweden	34,400	32,100	20	19	1.1	34	0.6
Southern Europe							
Italy	132,800	u	11	u	u	25	0.3
Slovenia	6,900	10,400	16	23	−5.2	40	0.5
Western Europe							
Belgium[i]	16,200	14,800	8	7	1.7	14	0.2
France	208,800	189,800	17	15	1.6	26	0.5[f]
Germany[j]	129,300	130,900	8	8	0.2	18	0.2
Netherlands[g]	28,800	22,400	9	7	4.0	14	0.3
Switzerland	10,500	u	7	u	u	15	0.2[f]
North America							
Canada[j]	104,200	111,800	15	16	−0.3	31	0.5
United States[k]	1,287,000	1,360,200	21	22	−1.2	31	0.6
Oceania							
Australia	84,500	89,100	20	22	−1.3	34	0.6[f]
New Zealand	18,500	14,800	21	17	2.8	33	0.7
South/Southeast Asia							
Nepal[l]	33,100	u	5	u	u	4	0.2[f]
Singapore	12,300	14,400	15	16	−0.9	31	0.4[f]
Western Asia							
Israel[m]	20,800	17,400	14	14	0.6	14	0.4

tions are complete. The data from Azerbaijan reflect such a situation. (See Table 8.3.) In 2001, 244,400 abortions were reported based on nationally representative surveys of women. In 2003 government statistics show only 12,000 abortions having taken place in that country that year. Did the number of abortions fall dramatically? Sedgh et al. suggest that this is not the case and that the more likely scenario is that the surveys simply show the dramatic underreporting of abortions in the government statistics.

Table 8.4 shows legal abortion rates by age for various countries. Across countries, women aged 20 to 29 generally had the highest abortion rates. Of the countries listed in Table 8.4, the Russian Federation had the highest abortion rates across all age groups in 1996. Its abortion rates fell considerably by 2003. Nonetheless, its rates were still the highest across countries and across age groups in that year except for women aged 19 and younger. Estonia, New Zealand, and Sweden had higher abortion rates than the Russian Federation in this age group.

Abortion Laws and Rates

Worldwide, women have abortions whether laws are restrictive or not, and the rate of abortion is not higher in countries where abortion is permitted. Table 8.5 compares the rate of abortion in six countries with liberal abortion laws to the rate of abortion in eight countries with severely restricted abortion laws. Among these countries, the rate of abortion is much higher in the countries with restrictive laws, compared with countries with more permissive laws, in spite of the fact that abortions in countries with restrictive abortion laws are generally illegal and often unsafe. As of mid-2009, these data were the most recent comparisons of this type.

ILLEGAL AND UNSAFE WORLDWIDE ABORTION STATISTICS
Regional Estimates of Unsafe Abortions

Table 7.1 in Chapter 7 uses data from *Unsafe Abortion: Global and Regional Estimates of the Incidence of Unsafe*

TABLE 8.2

Measures of legal abortion in countries where reporting is relatively complete, by country and year, 1996 and 2003 [CONTINUED]

Country	No.[a] 2003	No.[a] 1996	Rate[b] 2003	Rate[b] 1996	Rate[b] Average annual % change	Ratio,[c] 2003	Total abortion rate,[d] 2003
Caribbean							
Cuba[n]	151,500	209,900	57	78	−3.8	109	1.7[f]
Puerto Rico[o]	15,600	19,200	18	23	−2.2	28	0.5[f]
Africa							
South Africa	70,100	u	6	u	u	6	0.2[f]
Tunisia[p]	16,000	19,000	7	9	−6.1	9	0.2[f]

[a]Rounded to the nearest 100.
[b]Abortions per 1,000 women aged 15–44.
[c]Abortions per 100 live births.
[d]The number of abortions that the average woman would have during her reproductive lifetime, given present age-specific abortion rates.
[e]May include spontaneous abortions.
[f]Estimated by dividing the general abortion rate by 1,000 and multiplying by 30.
[g]Residents only.
[h]Includes abortions residents obtained in England or Wales.
[i]Includes abortions residents obtained in the Netherlands.
[j]Includes abortions residents obtained in selected U.S. states.
[k]Estimates are provisional and may change as more data become available.
[l]Abortions from March 2005 to February 2006.
[m]Abortion applications approved, as reported to the Central Bureau of Statistics.
[n]Estimates are for 1996 and 2004.
[o]Estimates are for 1991 and 2001.
[p]Estimates are for 1996 and 2000.
Note: u = unavailable.

SOURCE: Gilda Sedgh et al., "Table 1. Measures of Legal Abortion in Countries When Relatively Complete, by Country and Year," in "Legal Abortion Worldwide Recent Trends," *International Family Planning Perspectives*, vol. 33, no. 3, September 2007, http://www.guttmacher.org/pubs/journals/3310607.pdf (accessed June 5, 2009). Reprinted with permission of the authors.

Abortion and Associated Mortality in 2003 (September 25, 2007, http://who.int/reproductive-health/publications/unsafeabortion_2003/ua_estimates03.pdf) by Elisabeth Ahman and Iqbal Shah of the WHO. The table shows that the number of unsafe abortions performed in North America, eastern Asia, and western Europe is so low that no numbers are shown. Asia (without eastern Asia) accounted for the largest number of unsafe abortions in 2003 (9.8 million), which is 50% of all unsafe abortions worldwide. Africa had the second greatest number and percentage of unsafe abortions at 5.5 million or 28% worldwide. Latin America and the Caribbean had 3.9 million or 20%, and Europe (without western Europe) had 500,000 or 3%.

Deaths and Complications Due to Unsafe Abortion

Abortion is one of the safest medical procedures. However, as with most medical procedures it becomes unsafe if it is performed by untrained providers in unsanitary conditions. For many women with unwanted pregnancies, a safe abortion can be too expensive, unavailable, or illegal. Because of these limitations, a woman may delay getting an abortion until later in her pregnancy, when the risk of complications increases.

Table 7.1 gives estimates of deaths due to unsafe abortion. Ahman and Shah report that in 2003 an estimated 66,500 women died worldwide because of unsafe abortions. Unsafe abortions are performed primarily in developing countries, and most of the deaths occurred in Africa and Asia.

Up to half of all women who undergo unsafe abortions have complications. The most common complications include incomplete abortion, tears in the cervix, perforation of the uterus, fever, infection, septic shock (severe system-wide infection), and severe hemorrhaging. Other serious long-term health consequences may also affect women who have unsafe abortions. These problems may include chronic pelvic pain, problems getting and staying pregnant, infertility, blockage of a fallopian tube, and ectopic pregnancy (a pregnancy growing outside of the uterus, usually in a fallopian tube).

SAFE VERSUS UNSAFE WORLDWIDE ABORTION STATISTIC COMPARISONS

Table 8.6 and Table 8.7 use data from official national reporting systems, nationally representative surveys, and published studies on worldwide incidences of safe and unsafe abortions for 2003. Illegal abortion data are estimated using various types of information, such as the proportion of women hospitalized as a result of complications from abortions and surveys conducted by health care professionals. The tables compare safe and unsafe abortion rates, ratios, and percentages worldwide. As of mid-2009, these data were the most recent on this topic.

According to Table 8.6, an estimated 41.6 million abortions were performed around the world in 2003. Of these, 21.9 million were legal (safe) and 19.7 million were illegal (unsafe; as also reported in Table 7.1). The overall worldwide abortion rate was 29 abortions per 1,000 women aged 15 to 44, with the rate split between safe and unsafe abortions: 15 abortions per 1,000 women aged 15 to 44 were safe

TABLE 8.3

Measures of legal abortion in countries where reporting is incomplete or uncertain, by country and year, selected years 1996–2005

Country	Year	No.ᵃ	Rateᵇ	Ratioᶜ	Total abortion rateᵈ
Eastern Europe					
Moldova	2003	13,600	16	37	0.5ᵉ
	2005ᶠ	30,600	35	62	1.1ᵉ
Romania	2003ᶠ	166,700	35	78	1.0
	2004ᶠ	134,100	28ᵍ	64	0.8
	1999ᶠ	374,100	74	150	2.2ᵉ
Ukraine	2003	315,800	30	77	0.9ᵉ
	1999ᶠ	589,200	54	110	1.6
Northern Europe					
Irelandʰ	2003	6,300	7	10	0.2
Northern Irelandʰ	2003	1,300	4	6	0.1
Southern Europe					
Albania	2003	6,900	9	15	0.3ᵉ
Croatia	2003	5,900	7	15	0.2
Macedonia	2000ⁱ	11,400	25	39	0.7ᵉ
Serbia and Montenegro	2002	33,600	15	26ʲ	0.5ᵉ
Spain	2003	79,800	8	18	0.2ᵉ
Central Asia					
Kazakhstan	2003	127,200	35	51	1.0ᵉ
	1999ᶠ	176,100	47	76	1.4
Kyrgyzstan	2003ⁱ	19,200	15ʲ	17	0.5ᵉ
	1997ᶠ	54,300	51	27	1.5
Tajikistan	2003	10,500	7	7	0.2ᵉ
Turkmenistan	2000ᶠ	28,500	26	27	0.9
Uzbekistan	2003	27,700	4	5	0.1ᵉ
	2002ᶠ	166,200	28	28	0.9
East Asia					
China	2003	7,215,400	23	41	0.7ᵉ
	1996	8,834,200	29	44	0.9ᵉ
Hong Kong	2003	17,400	10	37	0.3
	1996	25,000	15	40	0.5
Japan	2003	319,800	13	28	0.4
	1996	338,900	13	28	0.4
Mongolia	2003	10,500	16	18	0.5ᵉ
South Korea	1999ᶠ	212,300	26ᵍ	38	0.7
South/Southeast Asia					
Bangladeshᵏ	2000	119,600	4	3	0.1ᵉ
India	2001	723,100	3	3	0.1ᵉ
	1996	570,900	3	2	0.1ᵉ
	2002ⁱ	2,400,000	10	9	0.3ᵉ
Vietnam	2003	540,400	26	33	0.8ᵉ
	1996	1,520,000	83	78	2.5ᵉ
	2002ᶠ	367,500	20ᵍ	22	0.6
	1997ᶠ	325,100	18ᵍ	17	0.5

and 14 per 1,000 women were unsafe. Latin America and the Caribbean, where abortions are generally illegal, had the highest abortion rate of any region—31 abortions per 1,000 women aged 15 to 44.

About one-fifth (20%) of all pregnancies in 2003 ended in abortion. (See Table 8.7.) Like the worldwide abortion rate, the worldwide percentage was split between safe and unsafe abortions. Europe, where abortion is generally legal, had the highest percentage of pregnancies ending in abortion in 2003: 32% compared with 22% in Latin America and the Caribbean, 22% in Asia, and 12% in Africa. Among the subregions, eastern Europe accounted for the highest proportion (45%) of pregnancies terminated by abortion.

ABORTION IN SELECTED COUNTRIES
Poland

The collapse of communism in Poland in 1989 led to the prohibition of abortion, which had been legal since 1956. As soon as the Solidarity Party gained control of Parliament, it amended the existing abortion law. Strongly supported by the Roman Catholic Church, the new statute severely restricted access to abortion, requiring a woman requesting a state-funded abortion to present written approval from three physicians and a psychologist from a state-approved list of doctors.

The new abortion provision granted physicians and hospital staffs in public hospitals the right to refuse to perform

TABLE 8.3

Measures of legal abortion in countries where reporting is incomplete or uncertain, by country and year, selected years 1996–2005 [CONTINUED]

Country	Year	No.[a]	Rate[b]	Ratio[c]	Total abortion rate[d]
Western Asia					
Armenia	2003	7,800	10	22	0.3[e]
	2000[g]	61,500	81	156	2.6[e]
Azerbaijan	2003	12,000	6	11	0.2[e]
	2001[g]	244,400	116	203	3.2
Georgia	2003[i]	13,800	14	30	0.4
	2005[g]	103,700	103[g]	224	3.1
	1999[g]	128,600	135	264	3.7
Turkey	2003[g]	146,800	12[g]	10[m]	0.4
	1998[g]	270,600	18[g]	19	0.4

[a]Rounded to the nearest 100.
[b]Abortions per 1,000 women aged 15–44.
[c]Abortions per 100 live births.
[d]The number of abortions that the average woman would have during her reproductive lifetime, given present age-specific abortion rates.
[e]Estimated by dividing the general abortion rate by 1,000 and multiplying by 30.
[f]Based on a nationally representative survey of all women aged 15–44, except in South Korea (married women aged 20–44), Vietnam (ever-married women aged 15–49) and Turkey (ever-married women aged 15–44). The estimated number of abortions in South Korea assumes that the rate for married women applies to all women aged 20–44. Data reflect average annual incidence and rates for the three years preceding the survey, except in South Korea, Vietnam and Turkey (preceding five years) and in Ukraine (preceding one year). Total number of abortions was calculated from the abortion rate and may include illegal abortions.
[g]Estimated by multiplying the total abortion rate by 1,000 and dividing by 30.
[h]Abortions in England and Wales obtained by women who gave Irish addresses.
[i]May include spontaneous abortions.
[j]Based on live births in 2001.
[k]Menstrual regulations.
[l]Based on a survey of health facilities.
[m]Abortions obtained by married women per 100 live births to all women.
Notes: Estimates are known to be incomplete for all countries except the following, for which the level of completeness is uncertain: Albania, China, Croatia, Japan, Macedonia, Moldova, Mongolia, Romania (2003), Serbia and Montenegro, Spain and Tajikistan. For each country, official statistics precede survey-based estimates where both are available.

SOURCE: Gilda Sedgh et al., "Table 2. Measures of Legal Abortion in Countries Where Reporting Is Incomplete or Uncertain by Country and Year," in "Legal Abortion Worldwide: Incidence and Recent Trends," *International Family Planning Perspectives*, vol. 33, no. 3, September 2007, http://www.guttmacher.org/pubs/journals/3310607.pdf (accessed June 5, 2009). Reprinted with permission of the authors.

abortions. In addition, the state stopped funding contraceptives for the poor, and funding was reduced for the Polish affiliate of the International Planned Parenthood Association, resulting in the closing of half of its offices.

In March 1993 a new antiabortion law, granting protection to a fetus from the moment of conception, went into effect. The law allowed abortion only if the pregnancy seriously threatened a woman's life or health, in cases of rape or incest, or if the fetus had irreparable abnormalities. Private clinics were forbidden to perform abortions, and physicians performing illegal abortions could be imprisoned for up to two years. If the woman died of complications, a physician could face up to 10 years' imprisonment. Women who had abortions were not punishable.

In "The Church Wins, Women Lose" (*The Nation*, April 26, 1993), Ann Snitow explains that the new law also required that the Catholic Church be involved in reproductive services and that sex education be based "on family and conceived life values, as well as, on methods and means of conscious procreation." "Conscious procreation" meant contraception, but little information on contraception was delivered by health professionals, other than information on natural family planning methods, which are accepted by the Catholic Church. Natural family planning encompasses a group of birth control techniques, such as a couple abstaining from sexual intercourse during the time of the month when a woman is most likely to conceive. Another technique is withdrawal, or coitus interruptus, in which the man removes his penis from his partner's vagina and genital area before ejaculation.

In November 1996 the Polish government again legalized abortion, but in May 1997 Poland's highest court, the Constitutional Tribunal, struck down the 1996 abortion law. In December 1997 the newly elected Parliament, which was dominated by pro–Catholic Church legislators, reinstated the strict 1993 antiabortion law. Under this law abortions are allowed only in cases of life endangerment, rape, or incest or if the fetus is damaged irreparably.

During the campaign for the 2001 general election, the Democratic Left Alliance promised to liberalize abortion. Even though the party won the election, laws were not changed because Poland sought the support of the Catholic Church to join the European Union, which the church would offer only if the existing abortion law remained in place.

In late 2004 the UN Human Rights Committee concluded a review on Poland's compliance with the International Covenant on Civil and Political Rights, demanding that the nation liberalize its abortion laws. However, in the 2005 elections, the conservative Law and Justice Party was voted into power. The party proposed a range of constitutional amendments, from

TABLE 8.4

Legal abortion rates by age of woman at termination, by country and year, 1996 and 2003

Country	Year	≤19[a]	20–24	25–29	30–34	35–39	≥40[b]
Eastern Europe							
Czech Republic	2003	8	14	15	16	13	7
	1996	12	27	31	28	19	10
Hungary	2003	20	33	33	31	24	9
	1996	30	47	49	44	31	13
Russian Federation	2003	25	69	70	58	38	15
	1996	44	144	145	94	55	31
Northern Europe							
Denmark	2003	15	21	18	17	13	6
	1996	15	23	21	20	13	6
England and Wales[c]	2003	23	31	22	15	10	4
	1996	22	28	20	14	9	3
Estonia	2003	28	53	51	43	32	14
	1996	43	93	83	63	43	19
Finland	2003	15	17	12	11	8	3
	1996	11	15	14	11	7	3
Latvia	2003	17	42	42	37	26	11
Lithuania	2003	7	21	23	21	15	7
Norway	2003	16	27	19	15	11	4
	1996	16	26	21	16	10	4
Scotland	2003	20	23	15	9	5	2
	1996	18	21	14	9	5	2
Sweden	2003	25	31	24	21	16	7
	1996	18	28	25	21	15	7
Southern Europe							
Italy	2003	7	15	14	12	10	5
Slovenia	2003	9	18	21	21	19	9
	1996	11	26	28	32	27	15
Western Europe							
Belgium	2003	8	13	11	9	6	2
	1996	7	11	10	8	5	2
Germany	2003	7	13	11	9	6	3
	1997	6	11	11	9	7	3
Netherlands[c]	2003	9	14	12	9	7	3
	1996	5	9	9	8	5	2
North America							
Canada	2003	17	31	21	14	9	3
	1996	23	34	23	14	8	3
United States	2003	22	43	31	19	10	4
	1996	29	49	32	18	10	3
Oceania							
New Zealand	2003	27	41	26	18	12	5
	1996	22	31	23	15	9	4
Western Asia							
Israel[d]	2003	11	15	15	16	15	9
	1996	10	16	17	17	16	10

[a]Based on abortions obtained by women aged 19 or younger and the female population aged 15–19.
[b]Based on abortions obtained by women aged 40 or older and the female population aged 40–44.
[c]Residents only.
[d]Based on abortion applications approved, as reported to the Central Bureau of Statistics.

SOURCE: Gilda Sedgh et al., "Table 3. Age-Specific Legal Abortions Rates, by Country and Year," in "Legal Abortion Worldwide: Incidence and Recent Trends," *International Family Planning Perspectives*, vol. 33, no. 3, September 2007, http://www.guttmacher.org/pubs/journals/3310607.pdf (accessed June 5, 2009). Reprinted with permission of the authors.

those banning abortion to those making it harder to weaken existing antiabortion legislation. In April 2007 the Parliament rejected these amendments. Nonetheless, Poland still has some of the strictest abortion laws in Europe.

Table 8.8 shows that from 1999 to 2004 there were fewer than 200 legal abortions performed in Poland each year. That number rose to 225 in 2005 and to 339 in 2006. Thus, many Polish women who wanted safe abortions had to obtain them elsewhere. Emma Morton notes in "10,000 Poles in UK for Free Abortions" (*The Sun* [London, England], December 15, 2008) that 10,000 Polish women traveled to the United Kingdom in 2007 for that purpose.

Romania

During the rule of the communist dictator Nicolae Ceausescu (1918–1989), abortion was banned (beginning

TABLE 8.5

Abortion rates worldwide, permissive vs. restrictive countries, selected countries and years 1989–2004

Country and year	Abortions per 1,000 women aged 15–44
Abortion is broadly permitted	
Belgium, 2003*	8
England/Wales, 2003	17
Finland, 2003	11
Germany, 2003	8
Netherlands, 2004	9
United States, 2002	21
Abortion is severely restricted	
Brazil, 1991	41
Chile, 1990	50
Colombia, 1989	36
Dominican Republic, 1990	47
Mexico, 1990	25
Nigeria, 1996	25
Peru, 1989	56
Philippines, 2000	27

Note: *Includes abortions obtained in the Netherlands.

SOURCE: Heather D. Boonstra et al., "Table 1.2. Abortion Rates Are Often Far Higher in Countries Where Abortion Is Illegal Than in Countries Where It Is Legal," in *Abortion in Women's Lives*, Guttmacher Institute, May 2006, http://www.guttmacher.org/pubs/2006/05/04/AiWL.pdf (accessed May 14, 2009)

in 1967), except for women who were older than 45 years and had at least five children. Modern contraception was also severely restricted. Ceausescu had hoped to build his country into a powerful nation based on population growth. Birthrates increased initially and then declined. The UN Department of Economic and Social Affairs (UNDESA) indicates in *World Fertility Report 2003* (March 12, 2004, http://www.un.org/esa/population/publications/worldfer tility/World_Fertility_Report.htm) that the 1968 total fertility rate of 3.6 lifetime births per woman nearly doubled the 1966 level, but that the fertility rate declined to 2.9 in 1970, fell to 2.1 by 1984, and remained at about 2.3 births per woman from 1985 through the end of communism and Ceausescu's rule in 1989.

Patricia Stephenson et al. note in "Commentary: The Public Health Consequences of Restricted Induced Abortion—Lessons from Romania" (*American Journal of Public Health*, vol. 82, no. 10, October 1992) that it was only after Ceausescu's regime was overthrown that the situation in Romania was revealed to the world. Many parents could not support their children because of poverty, so the children were placed in state care. Without contraception, women often resorted to illegal abortion to prevent unwanted births. During Ceausescu's rule an estimated 10,000 women died from illegal abortions, either self-induced or induced by untrained people. Between 1979 and 1989, when Ceausescu fell from power, Romania had the highest maternal mortality rate in Europe—10 times higher than any other European country. Many women also suffered permanent disfigurement.

After the revolution Romania's interim government made abortion available on request through the 12th week of pregnancy. Abortions up to the 24th week of pregnancy were permitted in cases of rape, incest, and endangerment of the woman's life if she were to carry her pregnancy to term. According to the UNDESA, in *World Fertility Report 2003*, after abortion was legalized the total fertility rate declined from 2 live births in 1990 to 1.4 live births per woman in 1993. Cynthia Dailard of the Guttmacher Institute explains in *Issues in Brief: Abortion in Context—United States and Worldwide* (May 1999, http://www.guttmacher.org/pubs/ ib_0599.html) that when abortion became legal in Romania in 1990, abortion-related mortality fell to one-third of its highest level, which had occurred the previous year.

With the shift in policy allowing abortion on demand, Romanians resorted to abortion as a principal method of birth control. According to the article "Romania: Abortions Continue to Exceed Live Births" (February 10, 2004, http:// www.lifesitenews.com/ldn/2004/feb/04021008.html), in 2003 Romania had the second-highest abortion rate in Europe (after Russia). However, the article "Newborns Exceed Abortions in Romania First Time since 1989" (Agence France Presse, March 29, 2006) reports that by 2005, for the first time since the fall of the communist regime, the number of newborns in Romania exceeded the number of abortions. Even though Romania was still among the top three countries for abortion rates world-wide in 2006, the number of abortions in Romania decreased 57% in less than a decade, from 347,126 in 1997 to 150,246 in 2006. (See Table 8.8.)

Russia

Abortion was first legalized in Russia in 1920 to make the procedure safe and reduce maternal mortality. Many women had abortions because contraception was not widely available and abortion was the primary method of family planning. By the mid-1930s there were three abortions for every birth, so Joseph Stalin (1879–1953) banned abortions to encourage more births. In 1955, two years after Stalin's death, abortion law was liberalized in Russia to once again make the procedure safe and reduce maternal mortality. Abortions were allowed on demand through the 12th week of pregnancy and for medical and social reasons through the 22nd week. Because modern methods of contraception were still not available in Russia at that time and for many years beyond, most women once again relied on abortion to control childbirth. A Russian woman who did not want more than two children would likely have as many as four or more abortions in her lifetime.

In the late 1960s contraceptive methods such as the intra-uterine device became available in Russia, but the quality of contraceptives was poor and the side effects from high-dosage hormonal methods were many. Even though the abortion rate fell, many women still relied on abortion as a method of birth control. In *Dire Demographics: Population Trends in*

TABLE 8.6

Estimated number and rate of safe and unsafe abortions worldwide, by region and subregion, 2003

	Number of abortions (millions)			Abortion rate[a]		
	Total	Safe	Unsafe	Total	Safe	Unsafe
Total						
World	41.6	21.9	19.7	29	15	14
Developed countries	6.6	6.1	0.5	26	24	2
Developing countries	35.0	15.8	19.2	29	13	16
Estimates by region						
Africa	5.6	0.1	5.5	29	c	29
Eastern Africa	2.3	b	2.3	39	c	39
Middle Africa	0.6	b	0.6	26	c	26
Northern Africa	1.0	b	1.0	22	c	22
Southern Africa	0.3	0.1	0.2	24	5	18
Western Africa	1.5	b	1.5	27	c	28
Asia	25.9	16.2	9.8	29	18	11
Eastern Asia	10.0	10.0	b	28	28	c
South-Central Asia	9.6	3.3	6.3	27	9	18
Southeastern Asia	5.2	2.1	3.1	39	16	23
Western Asia	1.2	0.8	0.4	24	16	8
Europe	4.3	3.9	0.5	28	25	3
Eastern Europe	3.0	2.7	0.4	44	39	5
Northern Europe	0.3	0.3	b	17	17	c
Southern Europe	0.6	0.5	0.1	18	15	3
Western Europe	0.4	0.4	b	12	12	c
Latin America and the Caribbean	4.1	0.2	3.9	31	1	29
Caribbean	0.3	0.2	0.1	35	19	16
Central America	0.9	b	0.9	25	c	25
South America	2.9	b	2.9	33	c	33
Northern America	1.5	1.5	b	21	21	c
Oceania	0.1	0.1	0.02	17	15	3[d]

[a]Abortions per 1000 women aged 15–44.
[b]Less than 0.05.
[c]Less than 0.5.
[d]The World Health Organization (WHO) published rate of 11 refers to developing regions of Oceania and does not include populations in Australia and New Zealand.

SOURCE: Gilda Sedgh et al., "Table 2. Estimated Number of Safe and Unsafe Induced Abortions and Abortion Rates by Region and Subregion, 2003," in "Induced Abortion: Estimated Rates and Trends Worldwide," *The Lancet*, vol. 370, no. 9595, October 13, 2007

the Russian Federation (2001, http://www.rand.org/pubs/monograph_reports/2007/MR1273.pdf), Julie DaVanzo and Clifford Grammich note that in 1970 Russia had 275 abortions for every 100 live births; this ratio fell to 235 abortions per 100 live births in 1993 and 175 abortions for every 100 live births in 1997. According to Robert Greenall, in "Russia Turns Spotlight on Abortion" (BBC News, September 16, 2003), by 2003 Russia's abortion ratio had dropped to 130 abortions for every 100 live births, but its abortion rate was still the highest in Europe after Romania. The dramatic drop in abortions in the Russian Federation can also be seen in the data reported in Table 8.2 and Table 8.4.

Greenall notes that in August 2003—for the first time since abortion laws were liberalized in 1955—the Russian government tightened abortion laws in the country in an effort to further reduce the abortion ratio. The new law involved restrictions on women's access to abortion after 12 weeks. Greenall notes that previously, "women in Russia could receive an abortion between 12 and 22 weeks of pregnancy by citing 13 special circumstances, including divorce, pov-

erty and poor housing." The 2003 resolution reduced these to four circumstances: rape, imprisonment, death or severe disability of the husband, or a court ruling removing the woman's parental rights.

Svetlana Osadchuk reports in "Simply an Issue of Control" (*Moscow Times*, April 16, 2008) that by 2008 Russian women were using various forms of contraception, although sales of "the pill" were low; the high-dose hormone pills of Russia's past had biased women against this method of contraception. The number of abortions fell through 2006, but many women still used early abortion as their method of birth control. (See Table 8.8.)

Ireland

Ireland is the only west European country that still bans abortion except in cases where the mother's life is threatened. (See Table 8.1.) Both the Republic of Ireland and Northern Ireland, which is part of the United Kingdom and separate governmentally from the rest of Ireland (the Republic of Ireland), ban abortion.

TABLE 8.7

Estimated ratios and percentages of safe and unsafe abortions worldwide, by region and subregion, 2003

	Abortion ratio[a]			% pregnancies ending in abortion[b]		
	Total	Safe	Unsafe	Total	Safe	Unsafe
Total						
World	31	16	15	20	11	10
Developed countries	50	46	3	28	26	2
Developing countries	29	13	16	19	9	11
Estimates by region						
Africa	17	c	17	12	c	12
Eastern Africa	20	c	20	14	c	14
Middle Africa	12	c	12	9	c	9
Northern Africa	21	c	20	15	c	14
Southern Africa	24	5	18	16	4	13
Western Africa	14	c	14	10	c	10
Asia	34	21	13	22	13	8
Eastern Asia	51	51	c	29	29	c
South-Central Asia	24	8	16	17	6	11
Southeastern Asia	45	19	27	27	11	16
Western Asia	22	14	7	15	10	5
Europe	59	53	6	32	29	3
Eastern Europe	105	92	13	45	39	5
Northern Europe	31	31	c	20	20	c
Southern Europe	38	31	7	24	19	4
Western Europe	23	23	c	16	16	c
Latin America and the Caribbean	35	2	33	22	1	21
Caribbean	42	23	19	25	14	11
Central America	26	c	26	18	c	18
South America	38	c	38	23	c	23
Northern America	33	33	c	21	21	c
Oceania	22	19	4d	15	13	3

[a]Per 100 births.
[b]Estimated pregnancies including livebirths, induced abortions, spontaneous abortions, and stillbirths.
[c]Less than 0.5.
[d]The World Health Organization (WHO) published ratio of 8 refers to developing regions of Oceania and does not include births in Australia and New Zealand.

SOURCE: Gilda Sedgh et al., "Table 3. Global, Regional, and Subregional Estimated Abortion Ratios and Percentages of Pregnancies That Ended in Abortion, 2003," in "Induced Abortion: Estimated Rates and Trends Worldwide," *The Lancet*, vol. 370, no. 9595, October 13, 2007

In 1983 the constitution of the Republic of Ireland was amended to ban abortion. However, in 1992 the Irish Supreme Court ruled that an Irish woman could legally obtain an abortion in another country if there was a threat to her life, including the threat of suicide. Shortly after this law was established, Irish voters approved a law giving women the right to obtain information regarding abortion services abroad and allowing women to travel abroad to get abortions. In May 1995 the Irish Supreme Court ruled constitutional a measure allowing doctors and clinics to provide women with information about foreign abortion clinics. According to the article "Main Parties Unwilling to Grab Nettle of Abortion" (*Irish Times* [Dublin, Ireland], May 10, 2007), an Irish poll found that 77% of respondents believed abortion should be allowed. Nevertheless, most Irish political parties are against legalizing abortion within Ireland.

The article "Q&A: Abortion in NI" (BBC News, June 13, 2001) explains that the ban on abortion in Northern Ireland began in 1861, much earlier in history than in the Republic of Ireland. That same year the Offenses against the Person Act made abortion illegal in all of the United Kingdom. This law was amended in Northern Ireland in 1945 to allow abortion in cases in which the mother's life, physical health, or mental health was in danger. In 1967 abortions became legal in England and Wales, but not in Northern Ireland. In 2008 an amendment was added to the Human Fertilization and Embryology Bill that would legalize abortion in Northern Ireland, but it was withdrawn in response to pressure from antiabortion groups. The BBC article notes that every year approximately 1,500 women from Northern Ireland travel to England to obtain abortions.

China

In China abortion is allowed without restriction as to reason. (See Table 8.1.) In the 1970s China initiated a stringent family planning program that has resulted in one of the fastest fertility declines in the world. The program promotes one-child families in urban areas and two-child families in rural areas and for ethnic minorities. In *Low Fertility in Urban China* (March 2001, http://dspace.anu.edu.au/bitstream/1885/41475/2/PaperZhao.pdf), Zhongwei Zhao notes that between 1975 and 1998 the total fertility rate declined by about two children, from 3.6 to 1.5 lifetime

TABLE 8.8

Number of legally induced abortions worldwide by country, 1997–2006

Continent and country or area	Number									
	1997	1998	1999	2000	2001	2002	2003	2004	2005	2006
Africa										
Réunion	4,729	4,652	4,522	4,404	4,339	4,385	—	—	—	—
Seychelles	362	411	536	495	461	460	440	435	413	443
South Africa[a]	—	28,978	—	—	—	—	—	—	—	—
America, North										
Anguilla	—	—	—	—	—	27	24	26	21	—
Canada	111,709	110,331	105,666	105,427	106,418	105,154[b]	103,768[b]	100,039[b]	96,815[b]	—
Costa Rica	8,705	8,850	9,160	9,711	8,220	8,332	8,967	8,074	7,974	—
Cuba	80,097	75,109	80,037	76,293	69,563	70,823[c]	65,628[c]	67,277[c]	62,530[c]	—
Dominican Republic	22,911	31,068	—	—	20,187	28,091	24,899	26,438	29,167	—
Greenland	843	915	842	944	809	821	869	—	899	—
Mexico[d]	561	595	614	541	571	591	676	752	735	799
Panama[e]	—	—	—	11	—	—	—	—	—	—
Puerto Rico	—	—	—	—	1,229	—	7,781	9,215	6,713	—
Turks Caicos Islands[f]	—	—	—	—	—	39	32	43	32	—
Asia										
Armenia	25,266	18,286	14,403	11,769	10,419	9,372	10,290	10,487	10,925	11,132
Azerbaijan	25,182	24,914	20,878	17,501	18,332	16,606	16,903	19,798	—	—
Bahrain	1,592	1,680	1,658	1,655	1,747	1,749	—	—	—	—
China: Hong Kong SAR (Special Administration Region):	23,939	22,086	20,891	21,375	20,235	18,651	17,420	15,880	14,190	—
Israel[g]	19,210	18,500	18,372	18,689	19,131	19,126	19,671	19,712	19,090	19,452
Japan[h]	337,799	333,220	337,288	341,146	341,588	329,326	319,831	301,673	289,127	276,352
Kazakhstan	156,222	148,799	137,808	—	—	—	—	—	—	—
Kyrgyzstan[i]	31,598	28,090	25,790	22,044	23,390	18,995	19,225	19,984	20,035	14,914
Mongolia	12,870	9,135	9,200	11,837	12,056	9,977	10,472	8,919	9,064	12,594
Qatar	97	71	124	177	127	121	131	172	169	—
Singapore	13,827	13,838	13,753	13,734	13,140	12,749	12,272	12,070	11,482	12,032
Tajikistan	—	—	21,234	22,066	19,087	21,104	18,822	20,500	19,400	17,500
Europe										
Åland Islands[j]	57	64	76	59	59	61	70	59	68	53
Albania	22,103	18,944	19,930	21,004	17,125	17,500	12,087	10,517	9,403	9,552
Belarus	152,660	145,339	135,824	121,895	101,402	89,895	80,174	71,700	64,655	58,516
Belgium	—	11,999	12,734	13,762	14,775	14,791	15,595	—	—	—
Bulgaria	87,896	79,842	72,382	61,378	51,165	50,824	48,035	47,223	41,795	37,272
Channel Islands: Guernsey	57	104	92	89	—	—	—	—	—	—
Croatia	10,036	8,907	8,064	7,534	6,574	6,191	5,923	5,232	4,563	4,733
Czech Republic	45,022	42,959	39,382	34,623	32,528	31,142	29,298	27,574	26,453	25,352
Denmark[k]	17,152	16,592	16,271	15,681	15,315	14,991	15,622	14,674	15,103	15,053
Estonia[l]	16,615	15,798	14,503	12,743	11,653	10,834	10,619	10,074	9,610	9,378
Faeroe Islands	38	59	47	49	42	49	37	44	29	41
Finland[m]	10,250	10,751	10,837	10,932	10,738	10,974	10,767	11,162	10,969	10,645
France[n]	188,477	195,368	196,295	—	201,434	204,931	202,594	209,907	—	—
Germany	130,890	131,795	130,471	134,609	134,964	130,387	128,030	129,650	124,023	119,710
Greece	12,853	11,838	11,824	18,015	22,223	16,173	15,782	—	—	—
Hungary	74,564	68,971	65,981	59,249	56,404	56,075	53,789	52,539	48,689	46,324
Iceland	921	—	935	987	984	926	951	889	867	—
Italy	140,166	138,354	138,708	—	132,073	131,039	124,118	—	—	—
Latvia	21,768	19,964	18,031	17,240	15,647	14,685	14,508	13,723	12,785	11,825
Lithuania[o]	22,680	21,022	18,846	16,259	13,677	12,495	11,513	10,644	9,972	9,536
Moldova	—	31,293	27,908	20,395	16,028	15,739	17,551	17,965	16,642	15,742
Montenegro	—	—	—	—	—	—	—	—	1,952	—
Netherlands	—	24,141	—	—	—	—	—	—	—	—
Norway[p]	—	14,028	14,251	14,635	13,887	13,557	13,888	14,071	13,989	14,132

births per woman for China countrywide, and declined by about half of a child in urban China, from 1.8 to 1.1. According to the Population Reference Bureau, in *2008 World Population Data Sheet* (August 2008, http://www.prb.org/pdf08/08WPDS_Eng.pdf), in 2008 China's total fertility rate remained low; countrywide it was at 1.6 lifetime births per woman. Nonetheless, in 2008 China was the most populous country in the world with over 1.3 billion inhabitants.

Critics of China's family planning laws feel that a pervading cultural preference for boys in China, coupled with the limitation on the number of births per family, endangers females. Every year, many girls are abandoned, killed, aborted, or hidden from family planning authorities.

In *The World Factbook* (2009, https://www.cia.gov/library/publications/the-world-factbook/geos/xx.html), the Central Intelligence Agency (CIA) estimates that in 2009, 107 boys were born for every 100 girls worldwide. This statistic—the sex ratio at birth—indicates the number of male births for every 100 female births. The CIA

TABLE 8.8

Number of legally induced abortions worldwide by country, 1997–2006 [CONTINUED]

Continent and country or area	Number									
	1997	1998	1999	2000	2001	2002	2003	2004	2005	2006
Europe										
Poland[q]	3,171[r]	312	151	138	123	159	174	199	225	339
Romania	347,126	271,496	259,888	257,865	254,855	247,608	224,807	191,038	163,359	150,246
Russian Federation	—	—	—	—	2,014,710	1,944,481	1,864,647	1,797,567	1,732,289	1,582,398
Serbia[s]	—	—	—	—	—	30,794[t]	—	29,856[t]	26,645[t]	25,665
Slovakia	—	21,109	19,949	—	18,026	17,382	16,222	15,307	14,427	14,243
Slovenia	9,712	9,116	8,707	8,429	7,799	7,327	6,873	6,403	5,851	5,632
Spain	46,902	53,847	58,399	63,756	69,857	77,125	79,788	84,985	91,664	
Sweden	31,443	31,008	30,712	30,980	31,772	33,365	34,473	34,454	34,978	36,045
The Former Yugoslav Rep. of Macedonia	12,028	—	—	—	—	—	—	—	—	—
Ukraine	596,740	525,329	495,760	434,223	369,750	345,967	315,835	289,065	263,590	229,618
United Kingdom[u]	191,855	199,887	195,394	197,366	197,913	—	—	—	—	—
Oceania										
New Caledonia	1,528	1,466	—	—	—	—	—	—	—	—
New Zealand	15,208	15,029	15,501	16,103	16,410	17,380	18,511	18,211	17,531	17,934

Notes
*Provisional.
[a]Data refer to both 1997 and 1998.
[b]Data excludes abortions performed on non-Canadian residents.
[c]Late foetal death is indicated by the fact that the foetus is at least 500 grams or more in weight.
[d]Excluding abortions to mothers living abroad which occurred in the country.
[e]Data refer to abortions granted for medical reasons by the Comision Multidisciplinaria Nacional de Aborto Terapéutico.
[f]For abortions performed in hospitals at Grand Turk and Providenciales.
[g]Legally induced abortions are applications to commissions for termination of pregnancy and not authorizations. Including data for East Jerusalem and Israeli residents in certain other territories under occupation by Israeli military forces since June 1967.
[h]Data refer to Japanese nationals in Japan only.
[i]Data on abortions are based on administrative reporting of Ministry of Health.
[j]Also included in Finland.
[k]Excluding Faeroe Islands and Greenland shown separately, if available.
[l]Data refer to the legally induced abortions if the woman's place of residence is in Estonia.
[m]Including Aland Islands.
[n]Excluding Overseas Departments, namely, French Guiana, Guadeloupe, Martinique and Reunion, shown separately, if available. Total only contains women between 15 and 49 years old.
[o]Data refer to requested abortions only and exclude abortions due to therapeutic reasons.
[p]Excluding Svalbard and Jan Mayen Island shown separately, if available.
[q]Based on hospital and polyclinic records.
[r]From 1993, a restrictive legal adjustment binds in Poland. In 1997 regulations were moderated briefly and only that year women were able to have an abortion if they had difficult life conditions.
[s]Without data for Kosovo and Metohia.
[t]Data refer to institutions included in the Health Institutions Network Plan in the Republic of Serbia.
[u]Excluding Channel Islands and Isle of Man, shown separately, if available. For resident population only.

SOURCE: "Table 13. Legally Induced Abortions: 1997–2006," in *United Nations Demographic Yearbook 2006*, United Nations Department of Economic and Social Affairs, Statistics Division, July 21, 2008, http://unstats.un.org/unsd/demographic/products/dyb/dyb2006/Table13.pdf (accessed May 13, 2009). The United Nations is the author of the original material.

calculates that the sex ratio at birth in China was 110 boys per 100 girls in 2009. Population data show that in China males outnumber females by 38.1 million.

India

There are many similarities with family planning policies in China and those in India. When the Indian government started providing family planning services in 1952, it became one of the first developing countries to promote population control. However, the policy was not aggressive (unlike China's), and the population continued to grow. In 1971 India legalized abortion with the enactment of the Medical Termination of Pregnancy Act as part of a national population policy to help control this population growth. Education about India's population problem became part of the school curriculum and in the 1980s an increased number of family planning programs were implemented, including financial assistance for those families in need of such help. Farina Gul Abrejo, Babar Tasneem Shaikh, and Narjis Rizvi of Aga Khan University indicate in "'And They Kill Me Only Because I Am a Girl' … a Review of Sex-Selective Abortions in South Asia" (*European Journal of Contraception and Reproductive Health Care*, vol. 14, no. 1, February 2009) that government programs promote two children as an "ideal" total number (unlike one for China), but many Indian couples, especially those in rural areas where they work the land, continue having children until two sons have been born. A high rate of sex-selective abortion occurs in India as well, although the government condemns this practice.

The preference for sons in India is also strongly influenced by the custom of providing a suitable dowry (money or property brought by a bride to her husband at marriage), which puts a great financial burden on the bride's parents. In addition, sons customarily live with their parents after marriage, providing both financial and emotional support to them, especially as the parents grow older. Due to this strong cultural and socioeconomic preference for sons in India, the sex ratio at birth is skewed as in China. The CIA estimates in *World Factbook* that the Indian sex ratio at birth in 2009 was 112 boys per 100 girls. Population data show that in India males outnumber females by 35.7 million.

Abortion is permitted for a wide range of reasons in India and no spousal consent is required. (See Table 8.1.) However, abortions must be performed within the first 20 weeks of pregnancy and must be done by a gynecologist or by a medical practitioner who has been trained at a government-approved training facility to provide abortions. There are other technical constraints as well, including the types of facilities at which abortions may be legally performed. In "Unsafe Abortion: The Preventable Pandemic" (*Lancet*, vol. 368, no. 9550, November 25, 2006), David A. Grimes et al. note that fewer than 20% of primary health care centers provide abortion services, and at times service is sporadic due to shortages of adequately trained physicians and functioning equipment. Therefore, abortions are legal in India, but safe legal abortions are difficult to obtain.

Overall, the total fertility rate in India has been declining. The UN reports in *World Fertility Patterns 2007* (2008, http://www.un.org/esa/population/publications/worldfertility2007/worldfertility2007.htm) that in 1981 the total fertility rate was 4.9 lifetime births per woman, but by 2004 that rate had dropped to 2.8 lifetime births per woman. In *World Factbook*, the CIA estimates the total fertility rate was 2.7 in 2009. Despite these efforts to control population growth, India has seen its population nearly triple between 1960 and 2009. According to the U.S. Census Bureau, in *Global Population Profile: 2002* (March 2004, http://www.census.gov/ipc/prod/wp02/wp-02.pdf), the population of India in 1960 was 445.9 million. The CIA estimates in *World Factbook* that India's population was nearly 1.2 billion in 2009. The Population Reference Bureau predicts in *2008 World Population Data Sheet* that India will become more populous than China—the most populous country in 2008—by 2050.

Latin America

Latin America consists of the Spanish-, Portuguese-, and French-speaking countries of the Western Hemisphere that lie south of the United States. In most countries of Latin America abortion is illegal except in cases of endangerment of the woman's life, rape, incest, and fetal abnormality. However, women rarely seek legal abortions using these exceptions because they do not know they are eligible, nor do they know the legal requirements for obtaining an abortion. In addition, they may not be able to afford a legal abortion. Hence, abortions have become secret and generally unsafe in Latin America.

According to Jean Friedman-Rudovsky, in "Abortion under Siege in Latin America" (*Time*, August 9, 2007), there are many reasons for Latin America's strict abortion laws. The Catholic Church certainly has a negative influence on liberalizing abortion laws as do "macho attitudes" in Latin America that view women's issues as unimportant. There is also a cultural view that abortion upsets the balance of nature. Many view abortion rights as part of a Western imperialist agenda.

In "Mexico's High Court Says Will Hear Case against Abortion Law" (Associated Press, May 30, 2007), Ioan Grillo indicates that in April 2007 the Mexico City assembly passed a law allowing abortion there in the first 12 weeks of pregnancy. The law was quickly challenged but still stood as of mid-2009. Abortion is banned in other parts of Mexico except in the previously mentioned situations. Fatima Juarez et al. note in "Estimates of Induced Abortion in Mexico: What's Changed between 1990 and 2006?" (*International Family Planning Perspectives*, vol. 34, no. 4, December 2008) that despite these legal restrictions, abortions performed in Mexico increased by one-third between 1990 and 2006, from 533,098 to 874,747.

Table 8.6 shows that of the 19.7 million unsafe abortions performed worldwide in 2003, an estimated 3.9 million were performed in Latin America. According to Dailard, unsafe abortion is the cause of as many as 21% of maternal deaths in Latin America. Antonio Bernabé-Ortiz et al. find in "Clandestine Induced Abortion: Prevalence, Incidence and Risk Factors among Women in a Latin American Country" (*Canadian Medical Association Journal*, vol. 180, no. 3, February 3, 2009) that 49% of sexually active women interviewed in Peru in late 2005 did not use contraception. The prevalence of abortion in sexually active women aged 18 to 29 years was 13.6% with an annual incidence of abortion of 3.3%.

South Africa

When South Africa was under apartheid (1948–1991—the system of racial segregation that involved discrimination against nonwhites), abortion was illegal except in cases where the pregnancy threatened the woman's mental health. The government, fearing that black people would outnumber white people, used tax credits to encourage white women to have children. Nonetheless, many upper- and middle-income women with unwanted pregnancies sought abortions in private physicians' offices or abroad. Many poor women with unwanted pregnancies, however, either terminated their own pregnancies or used the services of unqualified abortionists.

Reacting to pressures from the medical profession and women's groups, the legislature enacted the Abortion and Sterilization Act of 1975, which legalized abortion. Nonetheless, because of the stringent provisions of the law, such as requiring the approval of two physicians and a psychiatrist, many women continued seeking illegal abortions.

In November 1996 South Africa's first democratically elected Parliament passed a new abortion law—the most liberal abortion law in Africa—the Choice of Termination of Pregnancy Act. Under the law, women and adolescents can receive state funding for abortions up to the 12th week of pregnancy. From the 13th up to and including the 20th week of pregnancy, abortion is legal in cases of danger to the mother's physical or mental health, rape, incest, and fetal defect. The law also allows abortion if continuing the pregnancy would affect the woman's social or economic circumstances. Abortion after 20 weeks of pregnancy is allowed if a physician or trained midwife finds that continuation of the pregnancy would threaten the woman's health or result in fetal abnormality. Even though adolescents are counseled to consult their parents, the law allows them to have an abortion without parental knowledge. Nonetheless, access to abortion, especially in rural areas, is not always available.

Both houses of Parliament passed an amendment to the 1996 law—the Choice of Termination of Pregnancy Amendment Bill, which was implemented in 2003. This legislation designated facilities to provide abortion services to women, decentralized and improved the efficiency of the abortion process, and allowed registered nurses and midwives who have undergone appropriate training to perform abortions. However, the bill encountered a massive groundswell of public opinion against abortion.

In an effort to quantify public sentiment on this issue, the Human Sciences Research Council questioned approximately 5,000 adults for the South African Social Attitudes Survey (2004, http://www.hsrc.ac.za/Media_Release-225.phtml). The results reveal that 70% of the South African adult respondents opposed abortion, even if the family concerned is poor and cannot afford more children. The other key finding is that 56% were against ending the pregnancy of a woman whose child may be "deformed."

In 2006 the South African Constitutional Court ruled that Parliament had not sufficiently involved the public when it passed the abortion law amendment bill and stated that it would nullify the amendment unless Parliament conducted public hearings within 18 months. In "Call for Better Abortion Services for HIV-Positive Women" (*Business Day* [South Africa], August 10, 2007), Tamar Kahn reports that researchers determined that since the implementation of the amendment there had been a 91% decline in deaths from abortion-related causes. Parliament held the hearings and the bill was finally passed in January 2008.

A WORLDWIDE PLAN FOR REPRODUCTIVE HEALTH

At the landmark International Conference on Population and Development (ICPD) in Cairo, Egypt, in September 1994, 179 nations reached consensus on a 20-year plan to achieve reproductive health and rights for all. The plan was wide ranging and included ideas about increased contraceptive services, fewer maternal deaths, better education for girls, and greater equality for women. The Cairo conference was the first in which the pervasiveness of abortions throughout the world was openly discussed.

According to the UN Population Fund (UNFPA), in "Background Information on Key International Agreements" (2006, http://www.unfpa.org/mothers/consensus.htm), the international community agreed on a common position regarding abortion, which states, "In no case should abortion be promoted as a method of family planning. All Governments and relevant intergovernmental and nongovernmental organizations are urged to strengthen their commitment to women's health, to deal with the health impact of unsafe abortion as a major public health concern and to reduce the recourse to abortion through expanded and improved family-planning services. Prevention of unwanted pregnancies must always be given the highest priority and every attempt should be made to eliminate the need for abortion. Women who have unwanted pregnancies should have ready access to reliable information and compassionate counselling."

In July 1999, 179 countries met to assess the progress of the Programme of Action. The five-year review process, known as ICPD+5, found that nations implementing the program recommendations had improved conditions within their countries. For example, the UNFPA (July 31, 2003, http://www.un.org/popin/unpopcom/32ndsess/gastatements.htm) reports that more than 40 countries had introduced reproductive health services, and nearly half the countries had addressed the issue of adolescent reproductive health needs. Furthermore, in *Report of the 1998 UNFPA Field Inquiry: Progress in the Implementation of the ICPD Programme of Action* (January 1999, http://www.unfpa.org/upload/lib_pub_file/239_filename_icpd+5_report.pdf), the UNFPA indicates that almost all Latin American countries had introduced policies or laws to safeguard women's rights, and more than half the Asian countries and some African countries had protected women's rights in areas such as inheritance, property, and employment. Nonetheless, the delegates agreed that much work still needed to be done.

In 2004 a 10-year review of the Programme of Action took place. Progress toward goals was seen to be impressive; however, there were also mixed results. For example, the UNFPA reports in *ICPD at Ten: The World Reaffirms Cairo—Official Outcomes of the ICPD at Ten Review* (2005, http://www.unfpa.org/upload/lib_pub_file/404_filename_reaffirming_cairo.pdf) that even though "the level of contraceptive use in Asia has risen considerably ... a large number of individuals and couples still lack access to high-quality reproductive health information and services, a situation that leads to maternal mortality and morbidity, unwanted pregnancies, unsafe abortion and HIV/AIDS." The attendees at the ICPD at 10 meetings declared the need to continue addressing major issues such as gender equality, reproductive health and family planning, safe motherhood, and safe abortion.

The 15th anniversary of the first ICPD conference was celebrated in 2009. The scope and depth of the Cairo Consensus, although implemented primarily by the UNFPA, required broad participation from nongovernmental organizations, research institutions, regional associations, and international agencies. Therefore, forums and events for the 15th anniversary took place throughout the world in 2009, ending in December of that year. Various aspects of the ICPD were addressed at these meetings. The goals for the year's interactions were to celebrate accomplishments, consolidate lessons learned, strengthen partnerships, broaden the ownership of the ICPD agenda, and develop recommendations to accelerate progress.

CHAPTER 9
PUBLIC ATTITUDES TOWARD ABORTION

Like all statistics, public opinion polls should be viewed cautiously. The way a question is phrased influences the respondents' answers. Many other factors may also influence a response in ways that are difficult to determine. For example, a respondent might never have thought of the issue until asked, or he or she might be giving the pollster the answer he or she thinks the pollster wants to hear. Organizations that survey people's opinions do not claim absolute accuracy; their findings are approximate snapshots of the attitudes of the nation at a given time. The surveys presented here have been selected from many polls taken on abortion. A typical, well-conducted survey claims accuracy to about plus or minus three percentage points.

PRO-CHOICE/PRO-LIFE IDENTIFICATION

From 1995 to 2009 the Gallup Organization has examined trends on pro-choice/pro-life identification using the consistent stand-alone question: "With respect to the abortion issue, would you consider yourself to be pro-choice or pro-life?" According to Lydia Saad of the Gallup Organization, in *More Americans 'Pro-Life' Than 'Pro-Choice' for First Time* (May 15, 2009, http://www.gallup.com/poll/118399/More-Americans-Pro-Life-Than-Pro-Choice-First-Time.aspx), those identifying themselves as pro-choice ranged from a low of 46% in 2001 to a high of 56% in 1995. Those responding that they were pro-life ranged from a low of 33% in 1995 to a high of 46% in 2001. Thus, the proportion of those considering themselves pro-choice was always larger than the proportion of those considering themselves to be pro-life with the exception of 2001, in which the proportion of both groups was the same. In 2009, for the first time ever, the proportion of those identifying themselves as pro-life became larger than those identifying themselves as pro-choice. Those considering themselves to be pro-choice dipped to an all-time low of 42%. Conversely, the proportion of those identifying themselves as pro-life rose to an all-time high of 51% in that year.

MORAL ACCEPTABILITY OF ABORTION

Table 9.1 shows how adult Americans felt about the morality of abortion from 2001 through 2008. A larger proportion of respondents to Gallup polls have consistently felt that abortion was morally wrong, compared with those who felt it was morally acceptable. Only 1% to 2% of respondents had no opinion on this subject, and virtually none thought it was not a moral issue. Over the years between 7% and 11% believed the morality of abortion depended on the situation.

In *Moral Issues Divide Westerners from Muslims in the West* (May 23, 2008, http://www.gallup.com/poll/107512/Moral-Issues-Divide-Westerners-From-Muslims-West.aspx), Magali Rheault and Dalia Mogahed of the Gallup Organization compare differences in the proportions of residents living in key Western countries who view abortion to be morally acceptable and the proportions of Muslims living in three European capitals who also view abortion to be morally acceptable. A much higher proportion of the general population of the United States (40%), Germany (52%), the United Kingdom (58%), and France (77%) believe abortion is morally acceptable, compared with religious Americans (22%) and Muslims living in London, England (10%), Paris, France (24%), and Berlin, Germany (34%). (See Figure 9.1.) This poll suggests that general populations from various locations in the world, which include those who profess no religious affiliation, are more likely to view abortion as morally acceptable than those who identify themselves as belonging to spiritual groups from various locations in the world.

WHEN DOES LIFE BEGIN?

Bob Unruh reports in "Majority Voters Bash Obama 'Family' Values" (August 25, 2008, http://www.worldnetdaily.com/index.php?fa=PAGE.view&pageId=73430) that according to a Zogby International poll 59% of the 1,099 adults surveyed responded they believe human life begins

TABLE 9.1

Public opinion on morality of abortion, 2001–09

REGARDLESS OF WHETHER OR NOT YOU THINK IT SHOULD BE LEGAL, PLEASE TELL ME WHETHER YOU PERSONALLY BELIEVE THAT IN GENERAL ABORTION IS MORALLY ACCEPTABLE OR MORALLY WRONG.

	Morally acceptable	Morally wrong	Depends on situation (vol.)	Not a moral issue (vol.)	No opinion
	%	%	%	%	%
2009 May 7–10	36	56	6	*	1
2008 May 8–11	40	48	10	*	2
2007 May 10–13	40	51	7	*	1
2006 May 8–11	43	44	11	*	2
2005 May 2–5	40	51	8	—	1
2004 May 2–4	40	50	8	*	2
2003 May 5–7	37	53	9	*	1
2002 May 6–9	38	53	8	*	1
2001 May 10–14	42	45	11	1	1

*Less than 0.5%
(vol.) = Volunteered response

SOURCE: "Regardless of Whether or Not You Think It Should Be Legal, for Each One, Please Tell Me Whether You Personally Believe That in General It Is Morally Acceptable or Morally Wrong. How about Abortion?" in *Moral Issues*, The Gallup Organization, May 2009, http://www.gallup.com/poll/1681/Moral-Issues.aspx (accessed August 19, 2009). Copyright © 2009 by The Gallup Organization. Reproduced by permission of The Gallup Organization.

FIGURE 9.1

Public opinion on morality of abortion by religious preference and country or city of residence, 2008

ABORTION?

Percentage of respondents who say it is "morally acceptable"

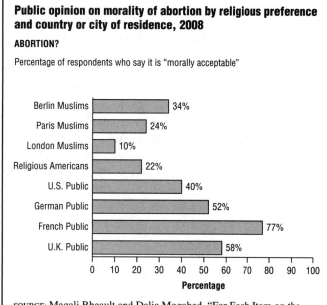

SOURCE: Magali Rheault and Dalia Mogahed, "For Each Item on the List, Please Tell Me Whether You Personally Believe That It Is Morally Acceptable or Morally Wrong: Abortion," in *Moral Issues Divide Westerners from Muslims in the West*, The Gallup Organization, May 23, 2008, http://www.gallup.com/poll/107512/Moral-Issues-Divide-Westerners-From-Muslims-West.aspx (accessed June 27, 2009). Copyright © 2008 by The Gallup Organization. Reproduced by permission of The Gallup Organization.

at conception. Of those polled, 16.8% said life begins when the fetus can survive outside the uterus with medical assistance, and 17.2% said life begins at birth.

SHOULD ABORTION BE LEGAL?

In 1973, a few months after the *Roe v. Wade* (410 U.S. 113) decision by the U.S. Supreme Court, Harris Interactive asked: "In 1973, the U.S. Supreme Court decided that states laws which made it illegal for a woman to have an abortion up to three months of pregnancy were unconstitutional, and that the decision on whether a woman should have an abortion up to three months of pregnancy should be left to the woman and her doctor to decide. In general, do you favor or oppose this part of the U.S. Supreme Court decision making abortions up to three months of pregnancy legal?" (See Table 9.2.) Half (52%) of the respondents favored the Supreme Court decision and 42% opposed it.

Every few years Harris Interactive asked the same question. During the two decades from 1976 to 1996 support rose and fell, but in 1996 support for the Supreme Court decision was the same as in 1973 at 52%. (See Table 9.2.) In 1998, on the 25th anniversary of *Roe v. Wade*, the proportion of those who supported the decision was higher than in 1973, at 57%, whereas the proportion of those against the decision was about the same, at 41%.

In recent years support for *Roe v. Wade* has declined. In a 2006 Harris poll the percentage of those favoring the ruling dropped below the 1972 level at 49%, and the proportion who opposed the ruling rose to 47%, which was higher than the 42% opposition in 1973 and the 41% in 1998. (See Table 9.2.) However, in 2007 the percentage of those favoring the ruling rose again, this time to 56%, with those opposed at 40%.

Asking the question about support for *Roe v. Wade* in a different way yields slightly different results, showing a bit more support for this law. In 2005, when Gallup asked "Would you like to see the Supreme Court overturn its 1973 *Roe versus Wade* decision concerning abortion, or not?" an overwhelming majority (63%) of respondents did not want to see the Supreme Court overturn its decision. (See Table 9.3.) Only 28% did. By 2008 there was more support for overturning the decision: 33% wanted the law overturned; nonetheless, 52% did not.

According to Nate Silver, in "CNN Poll: Record Support for Roe v Wade?" (May 24, 2009, http://www.fivethirtyeight.com/2009/05/cnn-poll-record-support-for-roe-v-wade.html), results of a CNN poll in 2009 showed a higher level of support for *Roe v. Wade* than did the 2008 Gallup poll and the 2007 Harris poll. Respondents to the CNN poll were asked: "Would you like to see the Supreme Court completely overturn its *Roe versus Wade* decision, or not?" Sixty-eight percent said they would not like to see this Supreme Court decision overturned and 30% said they would. No matter which poll is used, results show that the majority of Americans do not want the *Roe v. Wade* decision overturned.

TABLE 9.2

Public opinion on *Roe v. Wade*, selected years 1973–2007

"IN 1973, THE U.S. SUPREME COURT DECIDED THAT STATES LAWS WHICH MADE IT ILLEGAL FOR A WOMAN TO HAVE AN ABORTION UP TO THREE MONTHS OF PREGNANCY WERE UNCONSTITUTIONAL, AND THAT THE DECISION ON WHETHER A WOMAN SHOULD HAVE AN ABORTION UP TO THREE MONTHS OF PREGNANCY SHOULD BE LEFT TO THE WOMAN AND HER DOCTOR TO DECIDE. IN GENERAL, DO YOU FAVOR OR OPPOSE THIS PART OF THE U.S. SUPREME COURT DECISION MAKING ABORTIONS UP TO THREE MONTHS OF PREGNANCY LEGAL?"

Base: All adults

	1973 %	1976 %	1979 %	1981 %	1985 %	1989 %	1991 %	1992 %	1993 %	1996 %	1998 %	2005 %	2006 %	2007 %
Favor	52	59	60	56	50	59	65	61	56	52	57	52	49	56
Oppose	42	28	37	41	47	37	33	35	42	41	41	47	47	40
Not sure/Refused	7	13	3	3	3	4	4	4	3	7	2	1	4	4

Note: Percentages may not add up exactly to 100% due to rounding.

SOURCE: "Table 1. Attitudes toward Roe V. Wade," in "Support for Roe v. Wade Increases Significantly, Reaches Highest Level in Nine Years," *The Harris Poll*, no. 111, November 9, 2007, http://www.harrisinteractive.com/harris_poll/index.asp?PID=830 (accessed May 14, 2009).

TABLE 9.3

Public opinion on whether *Roe v. Wade* decision concerning abortion should be overturned, July 2005–May 2008

WOULD YOU LIKE TO SEE THE SUPREME COURT OVERTURN ITS 1973 *ROE V. WADE* DECISION?

	Yes, overturn	No, not overturn	No opinion
2008 May 8–11	33%	52	15
2007 May 10–13	35%	53	12
2006 May 8–11	32%	55	13
2006 Jan 20–22	25%	66	9
2005 Jul 7–10*	28%	63	9

*Asked of a half sample

SOURCE: "Would You Like to See the Supreme Court Overturn Its 1973 *Roe v. Wade* Decision Concerning Abortion, or Not?" in *Abortion*, The Gallup Organization, 2008, http://www.gallup.com/poll/1576/Abortion.aspx#1 (accessed June 27, 2009). Copyright © 2008 by The Gallup Organization. Reproduced by permission of The Gallup Organization.

During Which Stage of Pregnancy Should Abortion Be Legal?

The Supreme Court's decision in *Roe v. Wade* permits abortion throughout pregnancy, but it allows restrictions to be put on its use in the second and third trimesters. In 2005 Harris Interactive surveyed Americans to find out when they thought abortions should be illegal and reported the results in "Only a Small Majority Still Supports *Roe v. Wade* and Opposition Is at Its Highest in 20 Years" (March 3, 2005, http://www.harrisinteractive.com/harris_poll/index.asp?PID=547). Respondents were asked: "In general, do you think that abortion should be legal or illegal during the following stages of pregnancy?" (As of mid-2009, this was the most recent Harris poll that asked this question.) In 2005, 60% said abortion should be legal during the first three months of pregnancy. A similar proportion (63%) of those surveyed in 1998 responded the same way. A much smaller percentage of respondents in both polls said abortion should be legal during the second trimester of pregnancy—26% in both 2005 and 1998. Only 12% in 2005 and 13% in 1998 thought abortion should be legal in the last trimester of pregnancy.

Under What Circumstances Should Abortion Be Legal?

For many people abortion is a difficult issue—one that is permissible in some situations but not in others. Each year or two from 1975 to 2009, the Gallup Organization asked Americans: "Do you think abortions should be legal under any circumstances, legal only under certain circumstances, or illegal in all circumstances?" Over this 34-year span American responses to this question have varied somewhat, but in 2009 they were close to 1975 levels. (See Figure 9.2.)

In 1975, 21% of adult Americans thought abortions should be legal under any circumstances. (See Figure 9.2.) After peaking at 34% in 1992, support for this idea fell to about the 1975 level at 23% in 1998, but then rose again to 30% by 2006. By 2009 this support declined to 22% of Americans.

In 1975 about half (54%) of respondents thought abortions should be legal only under certain circumstances. (See Figure 9.2.) In 1998, 61% supported this idea, but support fell after that to a low of 51% in 2002. In 2009, 53% of Americans thought abortions should be legal only under certain circumstances—one percentage point less than in 1975.

In 1975, 22% of respondents thought abortions should be illegal. (See Figure 9.2.) After vacillating between a high of 22% and a low of 12% over more than three decades, in 2009 the proportion of those who thought abortion should be illegal in all circumstances was at 23%.

The Pew Research Center for the People and the Press has probed this same aspect of the abortion question since 1995 by using only two questions rather than three as Gallup

FIGURE 9.2

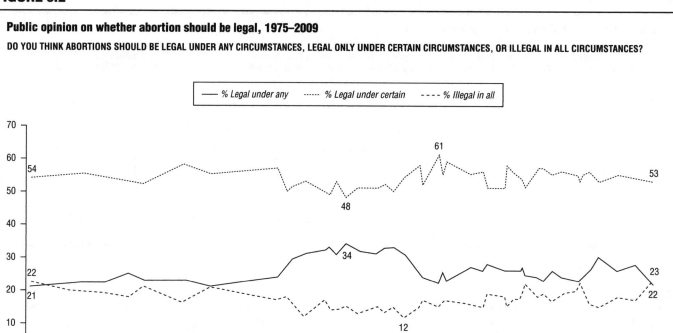

Public opinion on whether abortion should be legal, 1975–2009

DO YOU THINK ABORTIONS SHOULD BE LEGAL UNDER ANY CIRCUMSTANCES, LEGAL ONLY UNDER CERTAIN CIRCUMSTANCES, OR ILLEGAL IN ALL CIRCUMSTANCES?

SOURCE: Lydia Saad, "Do you think abortions should be legal under any circumstances, legal only under certain circumstances, or illegal in all circumstances?" in *More Americans "Pro-Life" Than "Pro-Choice" for First Time*, The Gallup Organization, May 15, 2009, http://www.gallup.com/poll/118399/More-Americans-Pro-Life-Than-Pro-Choice-First-Time.aspx?version=print © 2009 by The Gallup Organization. Reproduced by permission of The Gallup Organization.

does. Pew asks whether abortion should be legal in all or most cases, or should be illegal in all or most cases. In "Public Takes Conservative Turn on Gun Control, Abortion" (April 30, 2009, http://pewresearch.org/pubs/1212/abortion-gun-control-opinion-gender-gap), Pew indicates that in 1995 well over half of all respondents said abortion should be legal in all or most cases. That support dropped to 54% in 2008 and then to 46% in 2009. In addition, in 1995 far less than half of all respondents said abortion should be illegal in all or most cases. That support increased to 44% in 2009. Thus, in 2009 the proportion of adult Americans who thought abortion should be legal in all or most cases (46%) was only slightly higher than the proportion who thought abortion should be illegal in all or most cases (44%).

OPINIONS ON ABORTION POLICY OF THE OBAMA ADMINISTRATION

One of the first items on the presidential agenda of Barack Obama (1961–) when he took over the office in January 2009 was to rescind the Mexico City Policy, which had been put into place by President Ronald Reagan (1911–2004). This policy had been enforced by executive order for almost a decade, was rescinded by President Bill Clinton (1946–), and was reinstated by George W. Bush (1946–). The Mexico City Policy stated that the United States would no longer financially support private family planning

groups overseas that performed or promoted abortion. By reversing this policy, Obama made his pro-choice stance on abortion clear. (See Chapter 3.)

Shortly thereafter, between January 30 and February 1, 2009, the Gallup Organization asked over 1,000 adult Americans whether they approved or disapproved of certain actions Obama had taken as president, including "allowing funding for overseas family planning groups that provide abortions." Jeffrey M. Jones reports in *Americans Approve of Most Obama Actions to Date* (February 2, 2009, http://www.gallup.com/poll/114091/Americans-Approve-Obama-Actions-Date.aspx) that only 35% of respondents approved of this action. It was the least popular action among seven actions about which pollsters asked, including ordering the closure of the Guantánamo Bay prison. The abortion decision was most unpopular among Republicans—only 8% approved—whereas 33% of Independents and 59% of Democrats approved.

In May 2009, after Obama had been in office for 100 days, CNN and the Opinion Research Corporation conducted a poll on the new president's performance and reported the findings in "CNN Poll: Abortion Not Hurting Obama" (May 18, 2009, http://politicalticker.blogs.cnn.com/2009/05/18/cnn-poll-abortion-not-hurting-obama/). Pollsters asked 1,010 adult Americans whether Obama's views on abortion changed their view of him and the job he was doing as president. A majority (57%) of respondents answered that the president's pro-choice stance had no effect on their opinion of him. Twenty-seven percent said his views on abortion made them think less favorably of him, whereas 15% said his views made them think more favorably of him. When Catholics alone were polled on this question, they responded in the same proportions as did the general public.

OPINIONS ON PARTIAL-BIRTH ABORTION

President Bush signed the Partial-Birth Abortion Ban Act into law in November 2003. However, legal challenges to the law's constitutionality postponed its implementation. The issue was brought to the Supreme Court, and in April 2007 the high court ruled 5-4 in *Gonzales v. Carhart* (550 U.S. 124) that the act was constitutional. The act imposes civil and criminal penalties on physicians who knowingly perform the intact dilation and extraction (intact D&X) abortion procedure, which is called "intact D&E" in the act and in the court ruling because it is a variation of the dilation and evacuation (D&E) procedure. The intact D&X (intact D&E) can be used for abortions at 21 or more weeks of gestation.

Shortly after the Supreme Court ruling, Gallup conducted a poll to determine public opinion on whether partial-birth abortion should be legal. Jones notes in *Slim Majority Approves of Supreme Court Following Partial-Birth Ruling* (May 15, 2007, http://www.gallup.com/poll/27592/Slim-Majority-Approves-Supreme-Court-Following-PartialBirth-Ruling.aspx) that 36% of respondents thought late-term abortion should be legal, whereas 56% thought it should not. Thus, a majority of Americans agreed with the Supreme Court ruling, even though it did not have an exception to safeguard a woman's health.

ABORTION STANCE BASED ON PERSONAL CHARACTERISTICS

Age and Attitude toward Abortion

According to the Pew Research Center for the People and the Press, in "Public Takes Conservative Turn on Gun Control, Abortion," older Americans (those aged 65 and older) are less likely than younger Americans to support legal abortion. In addition, the proportion of the older age group that supports abortion appears to be shrinking.

In August 2008 those aged 65 and older (46%) had the lowest proportion of respondents of any other age group saying they thought abortion should be legal in all or most cases. However, the greatest support came from those aged 50 to 64 years at 58%, and then this support declined with age: 55% of those aged 30 to 49 thought abortion should be legal in all or most cases, as did 52% of those aged 18 to 29. By April 2009 support for legal abortion declined in all age groups, but the declines were greatest in the older

age groups. Support for legal abortions dropped by 10 percentage points to 36% for those 65 years and older, by 11 percentage points to 47% for those aged 50 to 64, by 5 percentage points to 50% for those aged 30 to 49, and by 5 percentage points to 47% for those aged 18 to 29.

Education Level and Attitude toward Abortion

In "Public Takes Conservative Turn on Gun Control, Abortion," the Pew Research Center for the People and the Press indicates that better-educated Americans are more likely to support legal abortion than less-well-educated Americans. In addition, declines in support for legal abortion from 2008 to 2009 were inversely proportional to the level of education. That is, the declines increased as the level of education decreased. Specifically, in April 2008, 64% of college graduates, 57% of those with some college, and 47% of those with a high school education or less supported legal abortion. By April 2009 support for legal abortion declined by six percentage points to 58% for college graduates, by eight percentage points to 49% for those with some college, and by nine percentage points to 38% for those with a high school education or less.

Religious Beliefs/Affiliation and Attitude toward Abortion

The Pew Research Center for the People and the Press notes in "Public Takes Conservative Turn on Gun Control, Abortion" that Americans who profess no religious affiliation are more likely to support legal abortion than Americans who identify themselves as belonging to a spiritual group. In August 2008, 49% of both Protestants and Catholics supported legal abortion, compared with 72% of those with no religious affiliation. Even though support for legal abortion declined in all groups, it declined by only one percentage point to 71% in the unaffiliated group, by two percentage points to 47% in the Catholic group, and by 11 percentage points to 38% in the Protestant group.

These statistics are consistent with results that Saad reports, which indicate that a greater proportion of Protestants than Catholics considered themselves to be pro-life in 2009. In that year 59% of Protestants/other Christians used the pro-life label to describe their choice, 52% of Catholics responded in this way, and only 31% of people professing other religions or no religion said they were pro-life.

Political Affiliations and Attitude toward Abortion

According to the Pew Research Center for the People and the Press, in "Public Takes Conservative Turn on Gun Control, Abortion," members of the opposing political parties are also opposed in their views on whether abortion should be legal and generally available. In April 2009, 63% of Republicans believed abortion should be illegal in all or most cases, whereas only 27% of Democrats thought the same. In the middle of these two groups are the Independents—those who identify themselves as neither Republican nor Democrat. In April 2009, 45% of Independents believed abortion should be illegal in all or most cases.

These statistics are consistent with the 2009 results that Saad reports. According to Saad, 70% of Republicans and those who "lean" toward a Republican political stance were pro-life, whereas only 33% of Democrats and those who lean toward a Democratic political stance were pro-life.

Gender and Attitude toward Abortion

A person's age, education level, religious beliefs, and political affiliation play a major role in his or her opinions about abortion. Those who are older, less educated, devoutly religious, and politically conservative are more likely to believe that abortion should be restricted. However, differences in opinions between men and women about abortion are not as clear cut.

Historically, men and women have been evenly divided on the abortion issue. However, Saad indicates that in 2009 the proportion of both men and women who were pro-life significantly overtook the proportion of those who were pro-choice. In 2008, 50% of women were pro-choice and 43% were pro-life, which was similar to the proportions in men: 49% were pro-choice and 46% were pro-life. By 2009, 49% of women were pro-life and 44% were pro-choice, and 54% of men were pro-life and 39% were pro-choice.

This widening gap between men and women on the abortion issue and the change within each gender group is also reflected by the Pew Research Center for the People and the Press in "Public Takes Conservative Turn on Gun Control, Abortion." Support for legal abortion among both groups declined from 2008 to 2009, but it fell more precipitously for men than for women. In August 2008, 53% of men responded that abortion should be legal and 42% that it should be illegal. In April 2009 only 43% of men responded that abortion should be legal and 46% that it should be illegal—a 10-percentage-point drop in support in less than a year. In August 2008, 54% of women responded that abortion should be legal and 42% that it should be illegal. In April 2009, 49% of women responded that abortion should be legal and 42% that it should be illegal, a five-percentage-point drop in support.

CHAPTER 10
THE *ROE V. WADE* DECISION SHOULD BE RECONSIDERED

On January 22, 1973, the U.S. Supreme Court handed down a landmark decision in the now famous *Roe v. Wade* (410 U.S. 113) legal battle. The ruling made it legal for a woman and her doctor to choose abortion without restrictions in the earlier months of pregnancy and with restrictions in the later months.

Thirty years later, Congress passed the Partial-Birth Abortion Ban Act of 2003 (see Chapters 2, 12, and 13). On November 5, 2003, President George W. Bush (1946–) signed it into law, becoming the first U.S. president to ever place a federal ban on abortion. The constitutionality of the act was heard in the Supreme Court as *Gonzales v. Carhart* (550 U.S. 124). In April 2007 the high court ruled in a 5-4 decision that the act was constitutional. The act imposes civil and criminal penalties on physicians who knowingly perform the intact dilation and extraction abortion procedure.

Justice Anthony M. Kennedy (1936–) delivered the opinion of the court. Those who applaud the high court's decision in upholding the federal Partial-Birth Abortion Ban Act not only expect state late-term abortion bans to be revived but also see the possibility of adding more restrictions on late-term abortion procedures and possibly reopening the discussion on the *Roe v. Wade* decision. The excerpts in this chapter reflect the position that the *Roe v. Wade* decision should be reconsidered.

Justice Ruth Bader Ginsburg (1933–) wrote the dissenting opinion in the court ruling in which she expressed concern about a future attack on the *Roe v. Wade* decision and a woman's right to choose abortion. The quotations in Chapter 11 mirror this concern.

The following is a portion of "The Third Presidential Debate" (*New York Times*, October 15, 2008), a transcript of the third and final presidential debate at Hofstra University between Senator John McCain (1936–; R-AZ) and Senator Barack Obama (1961–; D-IL). The moderator was

Bob Schieffer (1937–), the chief Washington correspondent for CBS.

SCHIEFFER: Senator McCain, you believe *Roe v. Wade* should be overturned.... Could ... you ever nominate someone to the Supreme Court who disagrees with you on this issue?

MCCAIN: I would never and have never in all the years I've been there imposed a litmus test on any nominee to the court. That's not appropriate to do.

SCHIEFFER: But you don't want *Roe v. Wade* to be overturned?

MCCAIN: I thought it was a bad decision. I think there were a lot of decisions that were bad. I think that decisions should rest in the hands of the states. I'm a federalist. And I believe strongly that we should have nominees to the United States Supreme Court based on their qualifications rather than any litmus test....

I will find the best people in the world—in the United States of America who have a history of strict adherence to the Constitution. And not legislating from the bench.

SCHIEFFER: But even if it was someone—even someone who had a history of being for abortion rights, you would consider them?

MCCAIN: I would consider anyone in their qualifications. I do not believe that someone who has supported *Roe v. Wade* that would be part of those qualifications. But I certainly would not impose any litmus test....

Let me talk to you about an important aspect of this issue. We have to change the culture of America. Those of us who are proudly pro-life understand that. And it's got to be courage and compassion that we show to a young woman who's facing this terribly difficult decision....

Of course, we have to come together. Of course, we have to work together, and, of course, it's vital that we do so and help these young women who are facing such a difficult decision, with a compassion, that we'll help them with the adoptive services, with the courage to bring that child into this world and we'll help take care of it.

The following is a portion of "The Republicans' First Presidential Candidates Debate" (May 3, 2007, http://www.nytimes.com), a transcript of the first 2008 Republican primary presidential debate that asked candidates about their views on the possible repeal of the *Roe v. Wade* decision. The presidential primary candidates in the debate were Senator Sam Brownback (1956–; R-KS), former Virginia governor James S. Gilmore III (1949–), former New York City mayor Rudolph Giuliani (1944–), former Arkansas governor Mike Huckabee (1955–), Representative Duncan L. Hunter (1948–; R-CA), Senator McCain, Representative Ron Paul (1935–; R-TX), former Massachusetts governor Mitt Romney (1947–), Representative Thomas G. Tancredo (1945–; R-CO), and former Wisconsin governor Tommy G. Thompson (1941–). The moderator was the MSNBC news commentator Chris Matthews (1945–) and the other questioners were John F. Harris (1963–), the editor in chief of Politico.com, and Jim VandeHei (1971–), the executive editor of Politico.com.

MR. MATTHEWS: Starting with you, Governor. Would the day that *Roe v. Wade* is repealed be a good day for Americans?

MR. ROMNEY: Absolutely.

MR. MATTHEWS: Senator.

SEN. BROWNBACK: Be a glorious day of human liberty and freedom.

MR. MATTHEWS: Governor.

MR. GILMORE: Yes, it was wrongly decided.

MR. MATTHEWS: Governor.

MR. HUCKABEE: Most certainly.

(Cross talk.)

MR. MATTHEWS: Congressman.

REP. HUNTER: Yes.

MR. MATTHEWS: Governor.

MR. THOMPSON: Yes.

MR. MATTHEWS: Senator.

SEN. MCCAIN: Repeal.

MR. MATTHEWS: Mayor.

MR. GIULIANI: It would be okay.

MR. MATTHEWS: Okay to repeal?

MR. GIULIANI: It would be okay to repeal. Or it would be okay also if a strict constructionist judge

viewed it as precedent, and I think a judge has to make that decision.

MR. MATTHEWS: Would it be okay if they didn't repeal it?

MR. GIULIANI: I think that—I think the court has to make that decision, and then the country can deal with it. We're a federalist system of government, and states could make their own decisions.

MR. MATTHEWS: Congressman?

REP. TANCREDO: After 40 million dead because we have aborted them in this country, I say that that would be the greatest day in this country's history when that is in fact overturned.

MR. MATTHEWS: We're looking for nuance here. Governor Gilmore, you have said in the past that you believe in the first eight to 12 weeks of pregnancy, that a woman should have the right to have an abortion. Do you still stick with that exception?

MR. GILMORE: I do, Chris. My views on this, my beliefs on this are a matter of conviction. And they've always been the same, and they've never changed the entire time that I've been in public life.

However, my record as governor of Virginia, I think, has been one that the pro-life community, of which I am a part, would be very proud—passing a 24-hour waiting period, passing informed consent, passing parental notification, signing the partial-birth abortion law in Virginia. So I think the record is there. But my views—my views are strongly and fundamentally believed, and been held that way.

MR. MATTHEWS: Governor Thompson, do you have any nuance on this, or you're just happy with the repeal of *Roe v. Wade*?

MR. THOMPSON: I believe it should be left up to the states. That was what was originally implied in the Constitution and was changed when the Supreme Court made the decision.

I, like a lot of people up here, have made a record of pro-life for a long time, signing the partial-birth abortion, pre-notification for parents and so on. I think it's imperative that states have the responsibility for making these laws.

MR. MATTHEWS: John.

MR. HARRIS: Governor Romney, in recent months you've said you were, quote, "always for life," but we've also heard you say you were once, quote, "effectively pro-choice." Which is it?

MR. ROMNEY: Well, I've always been personally pro-life, but for me there was a great question about whether or not government should intrude in that decision. And when I ran for office, I said I'd protect the law as it was, which is effectively a pro-choice position.

About two years ago when we were studying cloning in our state, I said, look, we have gone too far; it's a brave new world mentality that *Roe v. Wade* has given us; and I change my mind.

I took the same course that Ronald Reagan and George Herbert Walker Bush and Henry Hyde took. And I said I was wrong and changed my mind and said I'm pro-life. And I'm proud of that and I won't apologize to anybody for becoming pro-life.

MR. HARRIS: Governor, with respect, some people are going to see those changes of mind as awfully politically convenient.

MR. ROMNEY: You know, I told you that I studied at great length this issue. When I ran, I—for the very first time, I told you that I was personally pro-life but that I would protect a woman's right to choose as the law existed. And that stayed the same until two years ago, as I indicated, and at that time, as a result of the debate we had, the conclusion I reached was that we had gone too far, that cloning and that creating new embryos was wrong, and that we should therefore allow our state to become a pro-life state.

I believe states should have the right to make this decision, and that's a position I indicated in an op-ed to the *Boston Globe* two years ago.

MR. HARRIS: Senator Brownback, this is an important issue for you.

SEN. BROWNBACK: It is.

MR. HARRIS: Could you support a nominee of your party who is not pro-life?

SEN. BROWNBACK: I could because I believe in the Ronald Reagan principle that somebody that's with you 80 percent of the time is not your enemy; that's your friend and that's our ally. And this is a big coalition party, and it's a coalition party that's governed for a number of years in this country. And it governs because it governs with a coalition of economic and social conservatives and people that want to be strong for the United States.

But I want to emphasize, I believe life is one of the central issues of our day, and I believe that every human life at every phase is unique, is beautiful, is a child of a loving God period.

TESTIMONY OF M. EDWARD WHELAN, PRESIDENT OF THE ETHICS AND PUBLIC POLICY CENTER, BEFORE THE SENATE JUDICIARY SUBCOMMITTEE ON THE CONSTITUTION, CIVIL RIGHTS, AND PROPERTY RIGHTS, HEARING ON SUPREME COURT ABORTION CASES, JUNE 22, 2005

Why re-examine *Roe v. Wade*? Why are we here today addressing a case that the Supreme Court decided 32 years ago, that it ratified 13 years ago, and that America's cultural elites overwhelmingly embrace? The answer, I would submit, is twofold.

First, *Roe v. Wade* marks the second time in American history that the Supreme Court has invoked "substantive due process" to deny American citizens the authority to protect the basic rights of an entire class of human beings. The first time, of course, was the Court's infamous 1857 decision in the *Dred Scott* case (*Dred Scott v. Sandford*, 60 U.S. 393 [1857]). There, the Court held that the Missouri Compromise of 1820, which prohibited slavery in the northern portion of the Louisiana Territories, could not constitutionally be applied to persons who brought their slaves into free territory. Such a prohibition, the Court nakedly asserted, "could hardly be dignified with the name of due process."…. Thus were discarded the efforts of the people, through their representatives, to resolve politically and peacefully the greatest moral issue of their age. Chief Justice Taney and his concurring colleagues thought that they were conclusively resolving the issue of slavery. Instead, they only made all the more inevitable the Civil War that erupted four years later.

Roe is the *Dred Scott* of our age. Like few other Supreme Court cases in our nation's history, *Roe* is not merely patently wrong but also fundamentally hostile to core precepts of American government and citizenship. *Roe* is a lawless power grab by the Supreme Court, an unconstitutional act of aggression by the Court against the political branches and the American people. *Roe* prevents all Americans from working together, through an ongoing process of peaceful and vigorous persuasion, to establish and revise the policies on abortion governing our respective states. *Roe* imposes on all Americans a radical regime of unrestricted abortion for any reason all the way up to viability—and, under the predominant reading of sloppy language in *Roe*'s companion case, *Doe v. Bolton*, essentially unrestricted even in the period from viability until birth. *Roe* fuels endless litigation in which pro-abortion extremists challenge modest abortion-related measures that state legislators have enacted and that are overwhelmingly favored by the public—provisions, for example, seeking to ensure informed consent and parental involvement for minors and barring atrocities like partial-birth abortion. *Roe* disenfranchises the millions and millions of patriotic American citizens who believe that the self-evident truth proclaimed in the Declaration of Independence—that all men are created equal and are endowed by their Creator with an unalienable right to life—warrants significant governmental protection of the lives of unborn human beings.

So long as Americans remain Americans—so long, that is, as they remain faithful to the foundational principles of this country—I believe that the American body politic will never accept *Roe*.

The second reason to examine *Roe* is the ongoing confusion that somehow surrounds the decision. Leading political and media figures, deliberately or otherwise, routinely misrepresent and understate the radical nature of the abortion regime that the Court imposed in *Roe*. And, conversely, they distort and exaggerate the consequences of reversing *Roe* and of restoring to the American people the power to determine abortion policy in their respective States. The more that Americans understand *Roe*, the more they regard it as illegitimate.

Reasonable people of good will with differing values or with varying prudential assessments of the practical effect of protective abortion laws may come to a variety of conclusions on what abortion policy ought to be in the many diverse states of this great nation. But, I respectfully submit, it is well past time for all Americans, no matter what their views on abortion, to recognize that the Court-imposed abortion regime should be dismantled and the issue of abortion should be returned to its rightful place in the democratic political process....

Myths about *Roe* abound, and I will not strive to dispel all of them here. One set of myths dramatically understates the radical nature of the abortion regime that *Roe* invented and imposed on the entire country. *Roe* is often said, for example, merely to have created a constitutional right to abortion during the first three months of pregnancy (or the first trimester). Nothing in *Roe* remotely supports such a characterization.

A more elementary confusion is reflected in the commonplace assertion that *Roe* "legalized" abortion. At one level, this proposition is true, but it completely obscures the fact that the Court did not merely legalize abortion—it constitutionalized abortion. In other words, the American people, acting through their state legislators, had the constitutional authority before *Roe* to make abortion policy. (Some States had legalized abortion, and others were in the process of liberalizing their abortion laws.) *Roe* deprived the American people of this authority.

The assertion that *Roe* "legalized" abortion also bears on a surprisingly widespread misunderstanding of the effect of a Supreme Court reversal of *Roe*. Many otherwise well-informed people seem to think that a reversal of *Roe* would mean that abortion would thereby be illegal nationwide. But of course a reversal of *Roe* would merely restore to the people of the States their constitutional authority to establish—and to revise over time—the abortion laws and policies for their respective States.

This confusion about what reversing *Roe* means is also closely related to confusion, or deliberate obfuscation, over what it means for a Supreme Court Justice to be opposed to *Roe*. In particular, such a Justice is often mislabeled "pro-life." But Justices like Rehnquist, White, Scalia, and Thomas who have recognized that the Constitution does not speak to the question of abortion take a position that is entirely neutral on the substance of America's abortion laws. Their modest point concerns process: abortion policy is to be made through the political processes, not by the courts. These Justices do not adopt a "pro-life" reading of the Due Process Clause under which permissive abortion laws would themselves be unconstitutional.

STATEMENT OF JEAN A. WRIGHT, M.D., M.B.A, BEFORE THE SUBCOMMITTEE ON THE CONSTITUTION, FEDERALISM, AND PROPERTY RIGHTS, SENATE JUDICIARY COMMITTEE, HEARING ON "THE 25TH ANNIVERSARY OF *ROE V. WADE*: HAS IT STOOD THE TEST OF TIME?" JANUARY 21, 1998

I would like to focus my remarks on the changes we have seen in the field of pediatrics, particularly the areas of neonatology, surgery, anesthesia, and intensive care. Medical knowledge in those areas provide a new standard of science, upon which, a very different conclusion might be reached if *Roe v. Wade* were decided in 1998, rather than the limited information that was available in 1973....

In 1973, the scientific discussion heavily focused on the issues of fetal viability. At that time, the common understanding was that infants born before 28 weeks could not survive. Today, that age of viability has been pushed back from 28 weeks to 23 and 24 weeks. And some investigators are working on an artificial placenta to support those even younger.

In fact, while the number of children that are born and survive at 23–28 weeks gestation [is] still a minority of the infants in a NICU [Neonatal Intensive Care Unit], they are common enough that the colloquial term "Micro-premie" has been coined to describe them, and an additional body of neonatal science has grown to support the care of the very premature infant. So in 25 years, we have gone from a practice in which those infants once thought to be nonviable, are now beneficiaries of medical advances in order to provide them with every opportunity to survive.

... Very preterm neonates [newborns] have the neuroanatomic substrate and functional physiologic and chemical processes in the brain responsible for mediating pain or noxious stimuli (known as nociception)....

Anatomic studies have shown that the density of cutaneous nociceptive nerve endings in the late fetus and newborn infant equal or exceed that of adult skin....

... A controlled study of intrauterine blood sampling and blood transfusions in fetuses between 20 and 34 weeks of gestation showed that hormonal responses that were consistent with fetal perception of pain....

Preterm neonates born at 23 weeks gestation show highly specific and well-coordinated physiologic and behavioral responses to pain, similar to those seen in full-term neonates, older infants, and small children....

All of the scientific references I have just made, are from research breakthroughs in the last 10 years. This information was not available in 1973. As a result of this newly emerging understanding of fetal pain development, Anand and Craig, in a 1996 Editorial in the Journal *PAIN*, called for a new definition of Pain, a definition that is not subjective, and that is not dependent on the patient's ability to provide a self-report.

...Today, we are the beneficiaries of an enormous fund of new medical knowledge, and I believe we should incorporate that into our approach to protecting the life of the unborn.

Furthermore, places such as the University of California, with its Fetal Surgery Center, are doing just that. Exciting surgical advances which allow for the surgeon to partially remove the fetus through an incision in the womb, fix the congenital defect, and then slip the "pre-viable" infant back into the womb should make us reconsider the outcome and viability of many pre-term infants, particularly those with challenging congenital defects....

Today we are hearing evidence, both medical and legal, that was not available to our counterparts in 1973. We cannot change the ramifications of their decision; but we can make better and more informed decisions today. Just as the incoming tide raises the level of the water in the harbor, and in doing so, all the boats rise to the same new level; so should we allow the tide of new medical and legal information serve as a tide to raise both our medical and legal understanding of the unborn. And in doing so, lead us to making better decisions for this vulnerable population.

STATEMENT OF SENATOR JOHN P. EAST (1931–1986; R-NC), JANUARY 16, 1986

Regarding abortion, the source of the current controversy over abortion, of course, is the 1973 *Roe v. Wade* decision of the United States Supreme Court. The *Roe* ruling made two principal determinations. First, *Roe* recognized a federal constitutional right to an abortion throughout pregnancy for virtually any reason. Second, *Roe* determined that the unborn child is not a "person" under the Fourteenth Amendment to the U.S. Constitution, which guarantees a right to life. I disagree with both of these aspects of the *Roe* decision.

The Constitution does not make any explicit or implicit reference to abortion, much less guarantee a right to it. Hence, the *Roe* decision, which invalidated the duly enacted abortion laws of all 50 states, was an unconstitutional act on the part of the Court. It is incumbent upon the Court to recognize its error and overrule the *Roe* recognition of a right to abortion....

Legislative history reveals that the framers of the Fourteenth Amendment clearly intended for its provisions to protect all human beings. Since unborn children are human beings, I believe that the Fourteenth Amendment protects their right to live. The Court ought to overrule *Roe* in this regard as well. Until it does so, I will continue to support congressional initiatives to provide unborn children with a constitutionally guaranteed right to life.

STATEMENT OF PROFESSOR LYNN WARDLE, BRIGHAM YOUNG UNIVERSITY SCHOOL OF LAW, BEFORE THE SUBCOMMITTEE ON THE CONSTITUTION, SENATE JUDICIARY COMMITTEE, FEBRUARY 28, 1983

I appear before the subcommittee today to recommend that it propose and the Senate pass an amendment to the Constitution that would reverse *Roe v. Wade*....

I would like to rephrase the issue. I think the question is whether the right of the people to protect human life is to be abridged. A decade has passed since *Roe v. Wade* was decided, a decade in which federal courts have faced a flood of abortion litigation, in which Congress has faced a deluge of abortion proposals, and in which the number of abortions performed annually has reached in excess of 1.5 million, a total approaching 15 million since *Roe v. Wade*.

Moreover, as many commentators had predicted, since *Roe*, there has been a profound and appalling increase in the kinds of inhumane acts that manifest a disregard for and involve even the destruction of other forms of unwanted, defenseless human life. Not only are human beings who bear the stigma of being labeled defective because of some potential physical or mental condition being ruthlessly destroyed before birth, but since *Roe*, they have increasingly become the victims of infanticide and selective non-treatment, to use the euphemism.

...While these practical and doctrinal excesses are approaching shocking extremes, the Supreme Court has refused to reconsider *Roe v. Wade*. Thus, at this time, 10 years after that disaster, I feel the sentiments of the English statesman and orator, Edmund Burke, who is reported to have said, "An event is happening about which it is difficult to speak, but about which it is impossible to remain silent." I believe the time has come for Congress to restore the right of the people to protect all human life.

It is now painfully apparent that the constitutionalization of abortion is a slippery slope, leading ever downward into increasingly more detailed technical questions. As the courts have become increasingly more involved in supervising the enactment and enforcement of abortion regulations, the fundamental question keeps reappearing—why should the courts, rather than state legislatures, be deciding these issues? The answer, of course, is that they should not.

The exercise of judicial power to invalidate legislation affects the relationship between the coequal branches of government. The assumption by the judiciary of a major role in supervising abortion regulation represents a substantial shift in the delicate balance of power.

I believe that the issue of abortion is the type of issue that should appropriately be left to legislative resolution.

When employed unwisely or unnecessarily, the Supreme Court's power to declare legislative acts unconstitutional constitutes a threat to the continued effectiveness of the federal courts as well as to the stability of our democratic system. After all, there is some irony that a people who are self-governing cannot establish the laws dealing with such a fundamental question as the regulation and legality of abortion.

CHAPTER 11
THE *ROE V. WADE* DECISION SHOULD NOT BE RECONSIDERED

The following is a portion of "The Third Presidential Debate" (*New York Times*, October 15, 2008), a transcript of the third and final presidential debate at Hofstra University between Senator Barack Obama (1961–; D-IL) and Senator John McCain (1936–; R-AZ). The moderator was Bob Schieffer (1937–), the chief Washington correspondent for CBS.

SCHIEFFER: Senator Obama, you believe [*Roe v. Wade*] shouldn't [be overturned]. Could…you ever nominate someone to the Supreme Court who disagrees with you on this issue?…

OBAMA: Well, I think it's true that we shouldn't apply a strict litmus test and the most important thing in any judge is their capacity to provide fairness and justice to the American people.

And it is true that this is going to be, I think, one of the most consequential decisions of the next president. It is very likely that one of us will be making at least one and probably more than one appointments and *Roe versus Wade* probably hangs in the balance.

Now I would not provide a litmus test. But I am somebody who believes that *Roe versus Wade* was rightly decided. I think that abortion is a very difficult issue and it is a moral issue and one that I think good people on both sides can disagree on.

But what ultimately I believe is that women in consultation with their families, their doctors, their religious advisers, are in the best position to make this decision. And I think that the Constitution has a right to privacy in it that shouldn't be subject to state referendum, any more than our First Amendment rights are subject to state referendum, any more than many of the other rights that we have should be subject to popular vote.

… So this is going to be an important issue. I will look for those judges who have an outstanding judicial

record, who have the intellect, and who hopefully have a sense of what real-world folks are going through.…

I think that it's important for judges to understand that if a woman is out there trying to raise a family, trying to support her family, and is being treated unfairly, then the court has to stand up, if nobody else will. And that's the kind of judge that I want.…

The last point I want to make on the issue of abortion. This is an issue that—look, it divides us. And in some ways, it may be difficult to—to reconcile the two views.

But there surely is some common ground when both those who believe in choice and those who are opposed to abortion can come together and say, "We should try to prevent unintended pregnancies by providing appropriate education to our youth, communicating that sexuality is sacred and that they should not be engaged in cavalier activity, and providing options for adoption, and helping single mothers if they want to choose to keep the baby."

Those are all things that we put in the Democratic platform for the first time this year, and I think that's where we can find some common ground, because nobody's pro-abortion. I think it's always a tragic situation.

… We should try to reduce these circumstances.

The following is a portion of "South Carolina Democratic Debate Transcript" (April 26, 2007, http://www.msnbc.msn.com/id/18352397/), a transcript of the first 2008 Democratic primary presidential debate that asked candidates questions concerning *Roe v. Wade*. The presidential primary candidates in the debate were Senator Joseph R. Biden (1942–; D-DE), Senator Hillary Rodham Clinton (1947–; D-NY), Senator Christopher J. Dodd (1944–; D-CT), former vice presidential candidate and senator from North Carolina John Edwards (1953–), former congressman and senator Mike Gravel (1930–), Representative Dennis J. Kucinich (1946; D-OH), Senator Obama, and New Mexico governor Bill Richardson (1947–). The moderator was the NBC news anchorman Brian Williams (1959–).

MR. WILLIAMS: Senator Biden, as president would you have a specific litmus test question on *Roe versus Wade* that you would ask of your nominees for the high court?

BIDEN: I strongly support *Roe v. Wade*. I wouldn't have a specific question but I would make sure that the people I sent to be nominated for the Supreme Court shared my values; and understood that there is a right to privacy in the United States Constitution.

That's why I led the fight to defeat [Robert H.] Bork. Thank God he is not in the court or *Roe v. Wade* would be gone by now.

Number two, that's why I was so outspoken and have been criticized for being outspoken and leading the effort to try to defeat [John G.] Roberts [Jr.] and [Samuel A.] Alito [Jr.]. That's why I opposed, the other, [Clarence] Thomas on the court.

The truth of the matter is that this decision [on partial-birth abortion] was intellectually dishonest. I think it is a rare procedure that should only be available when the woman's life and health is at stake.

But, what this court did is it took that decision, and it said—put a Trojan horse in—through dishonest reasoning, laid the groundwork for undoing *Roe v. Wade*.

That's the danger of this decision. Not the specific procedure, but the rationale offered to justify, I think, the next step they're going to try to take.

WILLIAMS: Senator, thank you. Congressman Kucinich, same question. Would you ask a litmus test, *Roe versus Wade* question of high-court nominees?

KUCINICH: Any of my appointments to the high court would necessarily reflect my thinking. I don't know how it could be otherwise. I intend to be a president who's a healer, who understands that this country has been put in a debate that has torn it apart.

But the truth of the matter is, it's possible, I believe, to take a course of action where you can get all the people of America in support of a culture of life which includes prenatal care, postnatal care, child care, universal health care, a living wage, all those things that give support to life.

And we also need to listen carefully to those who are concerned about abortion.

At the same time, a healer as president would help reconcile this nation, and cause a woman's right to privacy to be protected unquestioningly, protect *Roe v. Wade*, but also go out and listen to people and engage people and open up hearts—because this is an issue that requires an enormous amount of compassion, and that's the approach I would take.

WILLIAMS: Congressman, thank you. Senator Dodd, you were the only senator on this stage to vote to confirm Chief Justice Roberts. Do you regret your vote?

SENATOR DODD: No. I'm disappointed terribly by the decision that he reached the other day [on partial-birth abortion], because he did something he said he wouldn't do. He said during his confirmation hearings that he would uphold precedent. That was a very important answer he gave to me. I did not have the same degree of satisfaction when Justice Alito made a similar statement.

And what he did, of course, is walk away from the woman's health. For 34 years, the woman's health has been a major consideration on this issue since *Roe versus Wade* was first decided.

And to deviate from that, to me, was a major, major setback here. I happen to believe a woman has a right to choose. I've voted that way and done that, supported that for the 26 years I've been in the United States Senate.

But I also think what Dennis just said is extremely important. Abortions ought to be rare, safe and legal. And I think all of us here, regardless of your views on the question, would like to see national leadership in the country that would start providing additional choices so that women aren't faced with just the choice they have today.

Supporting expanding adoption, children's health issues....

REMARKS DELIVERED BY SENATOR DIANNE FEINSTEIN (1933–; D-CA) AT THE LOS ANGELES COUNTY BAR ASSOCIATION AND PUBLIC COUNSEL LUNCHEON AT THE BILTMORE HOTEL, LOS ANGELES, CALIFORNIA, AUGUST 24, 2005

In 1992, I was elected as a Democratic pro-choice woman to represent the State of California. In poll after poll, Californians are consistently and overwhelmingly pro-choice. In fact, the most recent Field Poll, conducted in May, 2004, 71 percent of California voters support maintaining the current level of access to abortion services, or lessening existing restrictions. So do a majority of all Americans.

It would be very difficult for me to vote to confirm someone to the Supreme Court whom I knew would overturn *Roe*, and return our country to the days of the 1950s.

I remember what it was like then, when abortion was illegal. When I was a college student, I watched the passing of the plate to collect money so young women could go to Tijuana for an abortion. I knew a woman who ended her life because she was pregnant.

In the 1960s I served on the California Women's Board of Terms and Parole. California had an indeterminate sentence law then, and we actually sentenced women convicted of felonies in the State, and I sentenced women who were convicted of the crime of performing an illegal abortion. I saw what they did. I saw how they did it. And I saw the morbidity they left in their wake. I don't want to go back to those days.

Today we are faced with a divided court and a polarized country. It's clear the American people are divided about the course this country has taken. However, it is also clear, that Americans overwhelmingly believe that the government should not interfere with personal family decisions—especially decisions about life and death.

These are private matters. They represent the most personal, moral, and spiritual choices an individual or family must make. It may be fruitful for some on the extremes to reduce these issues to rhetorical slogans for their own political advantage, but how the Court decides future cases could determine whether both the beginning-of-life and the end-of-life decisions remain private, or whether they could be subject to expensive litigation or perhaps the risk of prison.

I believe the choice is clear. Government should not be allowed to interfere in personal family decisions and overrule the most difficult choices a family can make.

STATEMENT OF SENATOR TOM HARKIN (1939–; D-IA) REGARDING A RESOLUTION TO THE PARTIAL-BIRTH ABORTION BAN ACT, WHICH HE SPONSORED WITH SENATOR BARBARA BOXER (1940–; D-CA), APRIL 25, 2000

Last October 21, during debate on the so-called partial-birth abortion bill in the Senate, I, along with Senator Boxer, offered a resolution to this so-called partial-birth abortion bill. Our resolution was very simple. It stated that it was the sense of the Senate that *Roe v. Wade* was an appropriate decision and should not be repealed....

Our amendment barely passed, 51-47. Fifty-one said yes, *Roe v. Wade* was a good decision, it should not be overturned. Forty-seven Senators voted against that resolution, basically saying they did not agree with *Roe v. Wade* and that it should be overturned.

... Every time the so-called partial-birth abortion bill, or any other antichoice legislation, comes to the Senate floor, I will offer my amendment, and there will be another vote on the *Roe v. Wade* resolution. People in the leadership know that. That is why they have not bothered to bring up any of their antichoice legislation since the last vote on October 21. They know I will offer my amendment every single time to lift their veil of moderation. So today I am challenging the House Republican leadership to allow a vote on our amendment. Let's let people know where their representatives stand on the basic issue of choice, the basic issue of *Roe v. Wade*. Because *Roe v. Wade* is the moderate, mainstream policy on which American women have come to rely. The *Roe v. Wade* vote in the Senate should

send a wakeup call to all Americans that this policy is in jeopardy. They need to act to maintain it.

In this most personal of decisions, we need to trust women, not politicians, to make the choice.... Whether it is the case in front of the Supreme Court or whether it is the vote in the Senate, the issue is simply this: Do you trust politicians, whether they are in a State government or in the Federal Government, to make this decision for women or do you trust women?

... The bottom line is this: *Roe v. Wade* was an enlightened decision. It is moderate. It puts the basic decisions on reproductive health where it belongs, with the woman and not with the Government.

Today, as the Supreme Court, across the street, listens to the arguments on the Nebraska partial-birth abortion law, let us resolve that we are going to maintain a woman's basic right to choose, that we will not let the politicians take it over, that we will not return to the dark days of back-alley abortions and the criminalization of a woman's own right to choose her reproductive health.

That is what this issue is about.

STATEMENT OF RONALD M. GREEN, JOHN PHILIPS PROFESSOR OF RELIGION, DARTMOUTH COLLEGE, AND DIRECTOR OF DARTMOUTH'S ETHICS INSTITUTE, BEFORE THE SUBCOMMITTEE ON THE CONSTITUTION, HOUSE JUDICIARY COMMITTEE, APRIL 22, 1996

In considering the question of abortion more than 23 years ago, the Supreme Court had to face an extremely difficult set of questions. Among these were the question[s] of how we are to assess the legal and moral claims of prenatal life, and how we are to balance the claims of the embryo or fetus against a woman's rights of autonomy and privacy in reproductive decision-making.

The issue of the moral or legal status of prenatal human life is particularly difficult. In approaching this issue, the court noted the wide diversity of philosophical and religious views on when life begins....

... Obviously the Court could not privilege any one position ... and chose instead to look at the discernible interests of women and society in the matter of state involvement in regulating abortion and protecting prenatal life.

... The Court also acted in the best positive American traditions of separation of church and state by allowing individuals and religious groups the freedom to determine how they themselves view and will decide to treat prenatal human life.

... The justices ... made the decision ... that questions affecting the basic rights of women and involving a determination of the moral and legal status of prenatal life could not be left to the jurisdiction of local communities or the states. It is unthinkable that one state could come to a ruling on this matter, for example, not to protect the fetus, while another could rule differently....

The Court ruled properly, I believe, when it concluded that during the early phases of a pregnancy, maternal privacy and autonomy should take priority over any state interests in prenatal life.

[Some people] argue that even if the early embryo or fetus lacks many of the qualities we normally associate with full humanness, it possesses a unique genetic identity and potential and should be respected for this. However ... it is now known that, following conception, the embryo can spontaneously fission into two distinct persons, each having an identical genome or genetic blueprint. This is the way that identical twins develop in nature. More surprisingly, during the early phases of development, two distinct embryos can fuse together to create a single individual, with each genetic cell line integrating itself successfully in the resulting bodily structure.... So it is not true that a unique human genetic identity is forged at conception or that we can unambiguously speak of individual persons as beginning at this time.

After the time of viability, when a fetus can live on its own in the world as a distinct and recognizable human being, the justices believed that it is reasonable to place greater restrictions on a woman's autonomy and privacy in the name of this growing human potential. [But] in cases of conflicts between the life and health of the mother and the life of the fetus, her well-being, as determined by competent medical authority, must come first.

... After more than two decades the basic framework of *Roe* still makes sense.

As a society we will continue to argue about the specifics of abortion law and policy within this reasonable framework. My own personal view is that we should continue to adhere to the lines drawn by the Court in *Roe*, including the specific application of the trimester approach adopted there. I hold this view because I believe that nothing has happened since 1973 that compels us to change this approach. The age of viability has not changed dramatically during this period and medical technology has not advanced to the point that we can avoid the occasional need for tragic later-term decisions about the woman's health or the health of her child.

STATEMENT OF WALTER DELLINGER, PROFESSOR OF LAW, DUKE UNIVERSITY SCHOOL OF LAW, DURHAM, NORTH CAROLINA, BEFORE THE SUBCOMMITTEE ON CIVIL AND CONSTITUTIONAL RIGHTS, HOUSE JUDICIARY COMMITTEE, OCTOBER 2, 1990

There is no doubt that a woman's right to decide whether or not to terminate a pregnancy is, at a minimum, a liberty interest protected by the due process clause. Any other conclusion would require the Court to overrule *Griswold v. Connecticut* [381 U.S. 479] protecting the right of married couples to use birth control.... Restrictive abortion laws give the state control over a woman's basic choices about reproduction and family planning, an intrusion utterly incompatible with any meaningful concept of individual liberty.

It is no exaggeration to say ... that mandatory childbearing is a totalitarian intervention into a woman's life.

Congress could, moreover, conclude that restrictive abortion regulations have a clearly disproportionate impact on the equality and liberty interest of poor women, young women, and women of color. The kinds of restrictions that states are enacting even now, while *Roe* still hangs by a thread, are restrictions that have devastating consequences for women who are hostage to youth, poverty, and geography.

... The fact is that in a federal system of open borders and freedom of interstate travel, no state can, in fact, enforce its restrictive abortion policy against its affluent and well-educated residents. What states may do is to enforce restrictive policy against those many of its residents who are vulnerable.

The notion of returning the abortion issue to the states would not actually result in different rules for residents of different states, as much as it would functionally produce different abortion policies for different economic and social classes.

The Congress can clearly take into account the fact that separate state policies would produce a national double standard for rich and poor, wholly incompatible with basic principles of justice. A woman's right to choose would be determined by the fortuitous happenstance of where she lived and whether she had the information and money to travel elsewhere, sometimes to a distant location, to obtain an abortion.

STATEMENT OF RHONDA COPELON, CENTER FOR CONSTITUTIONAL RIGHTS, BEFORE THE SUBCOMMITTEE ON THE CONSTITUTION, SENATE JUDICIARY COMMITTEE, MARCH 7, 1983

No decision of the Supreme Court of the United States has meant more to the lives, the health, the well-being, the freedom and the dignity of women in this country than the decisions in *Roe v. Wade*.

Roe v. Wade ranks with other landmark decisions that have moved this nation on the path toward liberty and equality....

Roe v. Wade is not ... a departure from constitutional tradition, rather it applied to women some of the basic concepts upon which this nation was founded, and that is one of the reasons it is so difficult to undo.

It repudiated the historic disregard for the dignity and full personhood of women and the relegation of women to a separate sphere and second class citizenship. It brought legal theory, developed by and for men, closer to encompassing the existence of women.

Consider for a moment the relation of some of our most fundamental constitutional principles to the issue of compulsory pregnancy and childbearing.

We all hold as sacred the physical privacy of our homes. If we guard so jealously our physical environment and possession from intrusion by the state, how can we accord lesser status to the dominion and control over the physical self?

The First Amendment protects our thoughts, our beliefs, our verbal as well as symbolic expression. We can neither be restrained from speech nor forced to break silence. The Constitution protects these rights not only because of a utilitarian view that a marketplace of ideas served the public good but also because of the place of expression in the development of individual identity and the fulfillment of human aspirations.

Is not the commitment to bring a child into the world and to raise it through daily love, nurture and teaching an awesome form of expression, a reflection of each individual's beliefs, thoughts, identity, and the notion of what is meaningful? Men and women speak with their bodies on picket lines and in demonstrations. Women likewise speak in childbearing.

The First Amendment also demands that the state respect diverse beliefs and practices that involve worship, ritual, and decisions about everyday life. We recognize as religious, matters of life and death and of ultimate concern. The decision whether or not to bear a child—like objection to military service—is a matter of conscientious dimension.

The religions and the people of this country are deeply divided over the propriety and, indeed, the necessity of abortion. While for some, any consideration of abortion is a grave evil, others hold that a pregnant woman has a religious and moral obligation to make a decision and to consider abortion rather than sacrifice her well-being, that of her family, or that of the incipient life. The right to abortion is thus rooted in the recognition that women, too, make conscientious decisions.

We deem fundamental also the principle enshrined in the Thirteenth Amendment that no person should be forced into involuntary servitude as a result either of private conspiracy or public law. Does this right not extend to women entitling her to say "no" to the unparalleled labor demanded by pregnancy, childbirth, and childbearing—to say "no" to the expropriation of her body and service for the sake of another? If we strip away the sentimentalism that has rendered invisible the work of childbearing and childrearing, forced pregnancy must surely be recognized as a form of involuntary servitude.

What of the equality of women? Not to apply the foregoing fundamental constitutional principles to the question of the liberty to choose abortion is to deny women equal personhood and dignity in the most fundamental sense.

At the same time, to deny the right to abortion ensures that women will be excluded from full participation in society. Unexpected pregnancy and involuntary motherhood can preclude education, shatter work patterns and aspirations, and make organizational and political involvement impossible. A woman is no more biologically required to remain pregnant than a cardiac patient is to die of a treatable condition.

In sum, the criticism of *Roe v. Wade* has less to do with judicial excess than it does with a view of woman as less than a whole person under the Constitution, as someone whose self and aspirations can and should be legally subordinated to the service of others. The criticism reflects a failure to understand the gravity with which women view the responsibility of childbearing and the violence of forced pregnancy to human dignity.

CHAPTER 12
CERTAIN TYPES OF LATE-TERM ABORTIONS SHOULD BE ILLEGAL

On October 2, 2003, the U.S. House of Representatives voted 281-142 to approve a bill that would ban certain types of late-term abortions—those that proponents of the measure call partial-birth abortions. The bill defines partial-birth abortion as a procedure in which a fetus is partially delivered alive and a physician performs "an overt act that the person knows will kill the partially delivered living fetus." The ban, which does not include a health exception, would apply when "the entire fetal head is outside the body of the mother, or, in the case of breech presentation, any part of the fetal trunk past the navel is outside the body of the mother." Doctors who perform the procedure could face fines and prison sentences of up to two years. On October 21, 2003, the U.S. Senate voted 64-34 to approve the bill. The version passed by the House and the Senate omits a nonbinding resolution expressing support for the *Roe v. Wade* (410 U.S. 113 [1973]) decision, which was included in the original Senate version of the bill. The measure was signed by President George W. Bush (1946–) on November 5, 2003, making the Partial-Birth Abortion Ban Act the first federal law criminalizing an established abortion procedure.

Hours after the president signed the bill, however, a federal judge in Nebraska placed a temporary restraining order on it, preventing the U.S. Department of Justice from enforcing the new law. The next day, two more judges in California and New York followed, questioning the bill's constitutionality. Three organizations that support a woman's right to choose—the American Civil Liberties Union, the National Abortion Federation, and the Planned Parenthood Federation of America—filed the lawsuits, seeking an injunction to bar its enforcement, relying in part on the legislation's failure to allow such an abortion to protect a woman's health, as required by earlier court decisions (such as *Stenberg v. Carhart* [530 U.S. 914 (2000)]). The lawsuits challenged the constitutionality of the Partial-Birth Abortion Ban Act of 2003.

The federal judge in San Francisco, the first to render a decision, ruled that the act was unconstitutional in three

ways: it places an undue burden on women seeking abortions, its language is vague, and it lacks a required exception for medical actions needed to preserve the woman's health. In 2004 federal judges in all three states ruled the legislation as unconstitutional. In July 2005 a federal appeals court in St. Louis, Illinois, upheld the Nebraska ruling.

The constitutionality of the 2003 Partial Birth Abortion Ban Act was heard in the U.S. Supreme Court as *Gonzales v. Carhart* (550 U.S. 124). On April 18, 2007, the high court ruled 5-4 that the Partial-Birth Abortion Ban Act is constitutional. The act imposes civil and criminal penalties on physicians who knowingly perform the procedure. Excerpts of the majority and dissenting opinions of the case can be found in Chapter 2.

COMMENT OF SENATOR BARACK OBAMA (1961–; D-IL) ON THIRD-TRIMESTER AND PARTIAL-BIRTH ABORTIONS DURING AN INTERVIEW WITH CAMERON STRANG, "Q&A WITH BARACK OBAMA," *RELEVANT MAGAZINE*, JULY 1, 2008

STRANG: Based on emails we received, another issue of deep importance to our readers is a candidate's stance on abortion. We largely know your platform, but there seems to be some real confusion about your position on third-trimester and partial-birth abortions. Can you clarify your stance for us?

OBAMA: I absolutely can, so please don't believe the emails. I have repeatedly said that I think it's entirely appropriate for states to restrict or even prohibit late-term abortions as long as there is a strict, well-defined exception for the health of the mother. Now, I don't think that "mental distress" qualifies as the health of the mother. I think it has to be a serious physical issue that arises in pregnancy, where there are real, significant problems to the mother carrying that child to term. Otherwise, as long as there is such a medical exception in place, I think we can prohibit late-term abortions.

STATEMENT OF PRESIDENT GEORGE W. BUSH ON THE SUPREME COURT DECISION THAT THE FEDERAL PARTIAL-BIRTH ABORTION BAN ACT OF 2003 IS CONSTITUTIONAL, APRIL 18, 2007

I am pleased that the Supreme Court has upheld a law that prohibits the abhorrent procedure of partial birth abortion. Today's decision affirms that the Constitution does not stand in the way of the people's representatives enacting laws reflecting the compassion and humanity of America.

The Supreme Court's decision is an affirmation of the progress we have made over the past six years in protecting human dignity and upholding the sanctity of life. We will continue to work for the day when every child is welcomed in life and protected in law.

STATEMENT OF SENATOR RICK SANTORUM (1958–; R-PA), INTRODUCING THE PARTIAL-BIRTH ABORTION BILL ON THE SENATE FLOOR, MARCH 10, 2003

Mr. President, we are now on a piece of legislation known as the partial-birth abortion bill. It is a bill we have debated in the Senate in two previous Congresses on four different occasions. We debated it the first time and passed it. It was vetoed by the President, President Clinton at the time, back in 1996. Then we attempted to override the President's veto and fell just a few votes short.

We came back the next session, went through the same process, sent the bill to the President, he vetoed it again, and we came closer but we still failed in overriding the President's veto.

Subsequently, there were a whole series—actually, concurrent with that debate—of States, over half the States in the Union, that passed bans on this horrific partial-birth abortion procedure. That is the procedure where the baby is delivered—this is a baby at over 20 weeks gestation; in other words, halfway through the pregnancy. The gestational period is 40 weeks. This procedure is only performed on babies in utero after 20 weeks. So these are late-term abortions.

The process is as follows: A woman shows up and decides she wants to have an abortion after 20 weeks. A doctor decides to use this methodology. The woman is given a drug to dilate her cervix. She is sent home. Two days later she returns, and the baby is then delivered in a breech position. Under the definition of this act as currently constituted, the baby has to be alive when it is brought in through the birth canal, the baby has to be in a breech position, has to be outside the mother at least past the navel, and be alive. Then the baby is killed in a fashion that I will describe in more detail later.

That procedure, as I said, was banned by over 25 States. It was brought, obviously, to the courts by many in those States. There were a couple of circuit courts that

found this to be constitutional, one that did not. The Supreme Court took one of those cases, the Nebraska case that was appealed to the circuit, and made a decision which I think was in error. It was a horrible decision, but a decision I think we need to contemplate here. It is a decision that said that an abortion past 20 weeks of a child that would otherwise be born alive is now encompassed by *Roe v. Wade*.

You hear a lot of comments about *Roe v. Wade*, that *Roe v. Wade* only allows legal abortions within the first trimester and under limited circumstances in the second trimester. These are babies in the second and third trimester, where the courts have basically said, as many of us who have been studying this issue for a long time have said, that there is no limitation on the right to abortion. Abortion is a right that is absolute in America. There are no limitations, as a result of court decisions, on the right to an abortion.

So they held, in this case, that the language of the statute was too vague, and that the description of the procedure was too vague, and that there needed to be a health exception to this procedure; in other words, to preserve the health of the mother.

We have responded to that with a bill we introduced last year, in the last session of Congress. In the last session of Congress, we introduced a piece of legislation in the House that was passed. Steve Chabot, at the time chairman of the Constitution Subcommittee on the Judiciary Committee, passed a piece of legislation in the House that banned this procedure. It is identical to the bill that is on the floor today....

We believe the issues the Supreme Court brought up with respect to the infirmities in the Nebraska statute have been addressed by this legislation. First, we have gone into much greater detail in describing this procedure, and either later tonight or tomorrow I will read the text of the bill and I will provide graphic illustration as to how this procedure is conducted.

Second, we dealt with the issue of health. *Roe v. Wade* requires a health exception when the health of the mother is potentially in danger. We have included in this legislation a voluminous amount of material that shows clearly, without dispute, in my ·mind—without dispute, period, not just in my mind—without any medical dispute, that there are no reasons this procedure has to be available for the health of the mother because there are no instances in which this procedure is required for the health of the mother. There is no medical organization out there that believes that to be the case.

While some do not support the legislation or have a neutral position, nobody has come forward and said this is medically necessary to protect the health of the mother, much less, by the way, the life of the mother.

So, since there is no reason for a health exception because there are no instances where a health exception is needed, then *Roe* does not apply. So we have laid that out very clearly in this legislation. We believe as a result of that, Congress has the right—because we do a heck of a lot more exhaustive study, in our deliberations with hearings and other testimony, than the Supreme Court can. They have to rely on the record of the lower court and the arguments made to that lower court.

In the case of Nebraska, frankly, the arguments were not particularly well put and the evidence was not particularly robust for either side. It was a very weak record, and the court made a decision based on that record. They will have a different record before them in this case when it is brought up to the court, and I believe the record will be clear and dispositive that no health exception is necessary.

We have dealt with the constitutional issues. Now we are back to the focus of this legislation. Do you want to allow a horrific procedure that is not medically necessary, never medically indicated, not taught in any medical school in this country, not recommended, and which, in fact, major health organizations of this country have said is bad medicine, contra-indicated, that is so brutal in the way it is administered to a baby that otherwise would be born alive?

Let me emphasize that it is a baby fetus—some will refer to it as the child in utero—that would otherwise be born alive. You don't want to allow this child to be brutally killed by thrusting a pair of scissors into the back of its skull and suctioning its brains out.

This goes on in America thousands of times a year. The number of partial-birth abortions has tripled, according to the abortion industry that doesn't keep very good records. They admit that. It has tripled, they say, to 2,200. Oddly enough, back in 1997 when we were debating this, the *Bergen County Record* took the bother of asking the local abortion clinic how many they did just in Bergen County. The partial-birth abortion national number at that time was 600. In Bergen County, they did 1,500. I guess they dismissed that.

The bottom line is that this goes on an enormous amount of times and they call it a rare procedure. If we had a procedure that killed 2,200 children in America every single year, we would not be saying it is a rare procedure in America. If we had a disease that affected 2,200 little babies every year, we wouldn't say this is a rare thing when we know, by the way, that the number is multiples of that. The people we have to rely on for that information are the people who want this to be legal and who don't tell us about the abortions they perform.

This is something that needs to be done. I am hopeful that we can deal with this issue in an expeditious fashion, get this over in the House of Representatives and have them pass it, and have the President sign it, because he will sign it.

I think there is broad bipartisan support for this legislation as there has been in the past. It is overwhelmingly supported by the American people. A very large majority support this legislation. Even those who do not consider themselves pro-life believe that at some point we have to draw the line on the brutal killing of a child literally inches from constitutional protection—inches from being born and being completely separated from the mother, being held in the birth canal and executed, having scissors thrust into the base of its skull and then to have a suction catheter inserted and the "cranial content" removed.

Just to describe it here sends chills down your back. Yet people will defend this procedure and say that a civilized nation such as America believes this is proper medicine. Medicine, healing? I, frankly, don't know who is healed in that situation. I do not know who is protected in that situation when every credible medical core organization says it is not medically necessary; in fact, it is "bad medicine," and it is harmful to the woman. I have just described how harmful it is to the little child.

I ask my colleagues to join me in passing this piece of legislation and ending this outrageous procedure.

STATEMENT OF MARK G. NEERHOF, MD, BEFORE THE SENATE COMMITTEE ON THE JUDICIARY, SUBCOMMITTEE ON THE CONSTITUTION, MARCH 25, 2003

My name is Mark Neerhof. I am an associate professor of Obstetrics and Gynecology at Northwestern University Medical School. I am an attending physician in the Department of Obstetrics and Gynecology, Division of Maternal-Fetal Medicine at Evanston Northwestern Healthcare in Evanston, Illinois. I have been practicing Maternal-Fetal Medicine for 14 years. I am very familiar with fetal anomalies of all sorts, and am familiar with the options available for termination of pregnancy. I have done many deliveries at the gestational ages where an intact D&X [the medical term for a so-called partial-birth abortion] is performed, and as a consequence, I am very familiar with the mechanism of delivery, including at these early gestational ages. I came here today to express my support for a ban on intact D&X. I will divide my reasons into 3 categories: maternal, fetal, and ethical.

Maternal Considerations

There exist no credible studies on intact D&X that evaluate or attest its safety. The procedure is not recognized in medical textbooks. Intact D&X poses serious medical risks to the mother. Patients who undergo an intact D&X are at risk for the potential complications associated with any surgical mid-trimester termination, including hemorrhage, infection, and uterine perforation. However, intact

D&X places these patients at increased risk of 2 additional complications. First, the risk of uterine rupture may be increased. An integral part of the D&X procedure is an internal podalic version, during which the physician instrumentally reaches into the uterus, grasps the fetus' feet, and pulls the feet down into the cervix, thus converting the lie to a footling breech. The internal version carries risk of uterine rupture, abruption, amniotic fluid embolus, and trauma to the uterus.

The second potential complication of intact D&X is the risk of iatrogenic laceration and secondary hemorrhage. Following internal version and partial breech extraction, scissors are forced into the base of the fetal skull while it is lodged in the birth canal. This blind procedure risks maternal injury from laceration of the uterus or cervix by the scissors and could result in severe bleeding and the threat of shock or even maternal death. These risks have not been adequately quantified.

None of these risks are medically necessary because other procedures are available to physicians who deem it necessary to perform an abortion late in pregnancy. As ACOG [American College of Obstetricians and Gynecologists] policy states clearly, intact D&X is never the only procedure available. Some clinicians have considered intact D&X necessary when hydrocephalus is present. However, a hydrocephalic fetus could be aborted by first draining the excess fluid from the fetal skull through ultrasound-guided cephalocentesis. Some physicians who perform abortions have been concerned that a ban on late abortions would affect their ability to provide other abortion services. Because of the proposed changes in federal legislation, it is clear that only intact D&X would be banned. It is my opinion that this legislation will not affect the total number of terminations done in this country, it will simply eliminate one of the procedures by which termination can be accomplished.

Fetal Considerations

Intact D&X is an extremely painful procedure for the fetus. The majority of intact D&X are performed on periviable fetuses. Fetuses or newborns at these gestational ages are fully capable of experiencing pain. The scientific evidence supporting this is abundant. If one still has a question in one's mind regarding this fact, one simply needs to visit a Neonatal Intensive Care Unit, and your remaining doubts will be short-lived. When infants of similar gestational ages are delivered, pain management is an important part of the care rendered to them in the intensive care nursery. However, with intact D&X, pain management is not provided for the fetus, who is literally within inches of being delivered. Forcibly incising the cranium with a scissors and then suctioning out the intracranial contents is certainly excruciatingly painful. I happen to serve as chairman of the Institutional Animal Care and Use Committee at my hospital. I am well aware of the

federal standard regulating the use of animals in research. It is beyond ironic that the pain management practiced for an intact D&X on a human fetus would not meet federal standards for the humane care of animals used in medical research. The needlessly inhumane treatment of periviable fetuses argues against intact D&X as a means of pregnancy termination.

Ethical Considerations

Intact D&X is most commonly performed between 20 and 24 weeks and thereby raises the question of the potential viability of the fetus. Recent unpublished data from my institution indicates an 88% survival rate at 24 weeks. These numbers will undoubtedly continue to improve over time.

Beyond the argument of potential viability, many pro-choice organizations and individuals assert that a woman should maintain control over that which is part of her own body (i.e., the autonomy argument). In this context, the physical position of the fetus with respect to the mother's body becomes relevant. However, once the fetus is outside the woman's body, the autonomy argument is invalid. The intact D&X procedure involves literally delivering the fetus so that only the head remains within the cervix. Based on my own experience, I can tell you that if the fetal head remains in the cervix, insertion of scissors into the base of the skull is, by necessity, a blind procedure, and consequently, potentially hazardous. If, as I suspect, the head is out of the cervix and in the vagina, that fetus is essentially delivered because there is nothing left to hold the fetal head in. At this juncture, the fetus is merely inches from being delivered and obtaining full legal rights of personhood under the US Constitution. What happens when, as must occasionally occur during the performance of an intact D&X, the fetal head inadvertently slips out of the mother and a live infant is fully delivered? For this reason, many otherwise pro-choice individuals have found intact D&X too close to infanticide to ethically justify its continued use.

In summary, the arguments for banning this procedure are based on maternal safety, fetal pain, and ethical considerations. I regret the necessity to support the development of legislation which will regulate medical care because, in general, that is not desirable. However, in this case, it is born out of the reluctance of the medical community to stand up for what is right.

STATEMENT OF CURTIS COOK, MD, BEFORE THE HOUSE JUDICIARY COMMITTEE, SUBCOMMITTEE ON THE CONSTITUTION, JULY 9, 2002

My name is Dr. Curtis Cook and I am a board-certified Maternal-Fetal Medicine specialist (perinatologist) practicing and teaching in the state of Michigan. I provide care exclusively to women experiencing complicated pregnancies. These include women with preexisting medical conditions such as diabetes, hypertension and even cardiac disease and cancer. This group of complicated pregnancies also entails those with suspected fetal abnormalities including lethal fetal anomalies such as anencephaly (absent brain) and renal agenesis (absent kidneys). Additionally, this group of complicated pregnancies includes those women who have developed obstetrical complications during the course of their gestation. This would include situations such as the premature onset of labor or early leaking of the amniotic fluid.

Never in the ten years I have been providing perinatal care to women with complicated pregnancies have I ever experienced a clinical situation where the late-term abortion procedure being considered before this committee (partial-birth abortion) has ever been required or even considered as a clinically superior procedure to other well-known and readily available medical and surgical options....

As part of my professional responsibilities, I also teach medical students and residents the clinical management of pregnant women. This includes the various medical and surgical options for facilitating a birth or emptying a uterus in all three trimesters of pregnancy. I have never encountered teaching materials on this technique (PBA) except for the information presented by Dr. Haskell at a National Abortion Federation seminar. I am also a fellow of both the American College of Obstetricians and Gynecologists and the Society of Maternal-Fetal Medicine as well as a member of the Association of Professors of Gynecology and Obstetrics. I am not aware of any educational materials from any one of these groups discussing the specific technique of partial-birth abortion (or D&X/intact D&E), the appropriate clinical use of this procedure or even clinical reports of its use. This also leads me to believe this is a rogue procedure with no role in modern obstetrics.

Frankly, I am appalled that any physician is providing such "services" given the gruesome nature of this inhumane procedure. By their own admission these procedures are being performed primarily between 20-28 weeks gestation and sometimes beyond on mostly healthy mothers carrying healthy babies. The current survivability of infants born at 23 weeks is greater than 30% and at 24 weeks it is almost 70%. By 28 weeks the survival rate exceeds 95%! Many of these infants are literally inches away from enjoying the full rights afforded any American citizen including the rights to life, liberty and the pursuit of happiness....

... This procedure does not protect the life nor preserve the health of pregnant women. It also does not enhance the ability of women to have successful pregnancies in the future and may even hinder such efforts. I am at a loss to think of any benefit of this procedure other than the guarantee of a dead baby at the time of the completed delivery.

In summary, I feel this procedure (PBA) is unnecessary, unsavory and potentially unsafe for women. Unfortunately it is still being perpetuated upon thousands of innocent partially-born children in this country every year. As I did before this committee five years ago, again I urge you to act quickly to prohibit this abomination of American medicine.

CHAPTER 13
NO NEW LIMITATIONS SHOULD BE PLACED ON LATE-TERM ABORTION PROCEDURES

RESPONSE OF ELIZABETH WEIL, CONTRIBUTING WRITER TO *NEW YORK TIMES MAGAZINE*, TO AYELET WALDMAN, AUTHOR OF *BAD MOTHER: A CHRONICLE OF MATERNAL CRIMES, MINOR CALAMITIES, AND OCCASIONAL MOMENTS OF GRACE* (2009), JUNE 4, 2009

Waldman: Do you, personally, have a place that you draw the line? Or are you comfortable in saying that the only line we are allowed to draw is our own?

Weil: Ah, the line, deciding when it's OK to stop a pregnancy and when doing so is tantamount to killing a baby. That is the truly difficult part of this debate. When I'm really honest with myself, I'm not sure where that line is. . . .

Still, the line, the limitations. Like most of the left I'm hesitant to pull out a pen and a ruler and draw. I can form a nebulous cloud around where I think it should be. . . . The outer contours of that cloud are easiest to sketch in, of course—first-trimester abortions, abortions for victims of abuse. The next level is straightforward for me, too—women carrying babies with known and serious fetal anomalies, babies that can't live outside the womb, no matter how late in the pregnancy such problems are detected. The tough zone starts for me with the horrible question of which babies . . . have defects so serious we think it's OK to decide they can't live? What do you think about a baby with cystic fibrosis? What about a blind or a deaf one? We all know great people born in horrible bodies. Should we be allowed to say, no thanks, I'd rather try again for a better-formed kid? . . .

I think part of the public discussion we need to have is about the link between abortion and prenatal testing. Why are we doing all this testing if we don't condone women acting on the results?

STATEMENT OF SENATOR CHRIS DODD (1944–; D-CT) REGARDING THE U.S. SUPREME COURT'S RULING THAT THE PARTIAL BIRTH ABORTION BAN ACT OF 2003 IS CONSTITUTIONAL, APRIL 18, 2007

Throughout my career I have believed that abortion should be safe, legal, and rare. I am deeply troubled by today's Supreme Court decision upholding the constitutionality of the Partial Birth Abortion Act of 2003, a decision which will needlessly endanger women's health throughout the country. I voted against this legislation in 2003 because it did not include an exception to allow this type of medical procedure when a mother's health is at risk. In overturning long-standing Supreme Court precedent, today's decision will create uncertainty throughout the country for women and doctors on what medical procedures are legal, and will undermine their ability to decide what is most appropriate for a patient's health, free from politics. While I am disappointed by today's decision by the Supreme Court, it has renewed my pledge to continue to support a woman's right to reproductive choice.

STATEMENT OF REPRESENTATIVE FRANK PALLONE JR. (1951–; D-NJ) REGARDING THE U.S. SUPREME COURT'S RULING THAT THE PARTIAL BIRTH ABORTION BAN ACT OF 2003 IS CONSTITUTIONAL, APRIL 18, 2007

I am extremely disappointed with the Supreme Court's decision today to abandon 30 years of rulings that protected a woman's right to make private health care decisions with her doctor. Instead, they have put our judicial system on a disconcerting downward slope of limiting civil liberties.

I agree with Justice [Ruth Bader] Ginsburg's dissenting opinion that this "alarming decision" is an effort to "chip away" at a woman's right to abortion and "blesses a prohibition with no exception safeguarding a woman's health."

The Partial Birth Abortion Ban, which was signed into law in 2003 by President Bush, had until today been struck down by every court that had examined it because it fails to provide an exception allowing the procedure to protect the life and health of the mother. It is no wonder, then, that the American College of Obstetricians and Gynecologists, the American Nurses Association, and many other medical groups oppose the federal ban.

By narrowly deciding to uphold this dangerously restrictive law, the Court has failed to protect women's health and has taken the process of making life or death decisions out of the hands of medical professionals.

STATEMENT OF FORMER SENATOR JOHN EDWARDS (1953–) REGARDING THE U.S. SUPREME COURT'S RULING THAT THE PARTIAL BIRTH ABORTION BAN ACT OF 2003 IS CONSTITUTIONAL, APRIL 18, 2007

I could not disagree more strongly with today's Supreme Court decision. The ban upheld by the Court is an ill-considered and sweeping prohibition that does not even take account for serious threats to the health of individual women. This hard right turn is a stark reminder of why Democrats cannot afford to lose the 2008 election. Too much is at stake—starting with, as the Court made all too clear today, a woman's right to choose.

OPINION OF RICHARD G. KOPF (1946–), CHIEF U.S. DISTRICT JUDGE, IN THE DECISION FOR *CARHART V. ASHCROFT* (331 F. SUPP. 2D 805 [2004]), U.S. DISTRICT COURT FOR THE DISTRICT OF NEBRASKA, SEPTEMBER 8, 2004, AFFIRMED BY *CARHART V. GONZALES* (413 F.3D 791), U.S. COURT OF APPEALS FOR THE EIGHTH CIRCUIT, JULY 8, 2005

Like giving birth to a child, when a woman ends her pregnancy during or after the second trimester, she confronts a serious problem. Her cervix will frequently be too small to allow the skull of the human fetus to pass through it. Although terminating a pregnancy in America is safer than childbirth, this "skull-is-too-large" difficulty makes the abortion of a human fetus, like the birth of a human baby, potentially very dangerous to both the life and health of the woman. Our elected representatives have decided that it is never necessary to use a specific surgical technique—"partial-birth abortion"—to deal with this concern during an abortion. On the contrary, they have banned the procedure.

After giving Congress the respectful consideration it is always due, I find and conclude that the ban is unreasonable and not supported by substantial evidence. In truth, "partial-birth abortions," which are medically known as "intact D & E" or "D & X" procedures, are sometimes necessary to preserve the health of a woman seeking an abortion.

While the procedure is infrequently used as a relative matter, when it is needed, the health of women frequently hangs in the balance.

Four examples, out of many, illustrate this point:

- During the 17th week of gestation, before many physicians are comfortable inducing fetal death by injection prior to beginning a surgical abortion, one of Mr. [John D.] Ashcroft's expert witnesses conceded that it would be consistent with the standard of care at the University of Michigan Medical School, where she practices, to crush the skull of the living fetus when the body was delivered intact outside the cervix and into the vaginal cavity if the skull was trapped by the cervix and the woman was hemorrhaging. (Tr. 1598–1602, Test. Dr. Shadigian.)

- Another of Mr. Ashcroft's expert witnesses, the head of obstetrics and gynecology at Yale, testified on direct examination, and confirmed again on cross-examination, that there are "compelling enough arguments as to [the banned technique's] safety, that I certainly would not want to prohibit its use in my institution." (Tr. 1706 & 1763, Test. Dr. Lockwood.)

- Another physician, Dr. Phillip D. Darney, the Chief of Obstetrics and Gynecology at San Francisco General Hospital, a major metropolitan hospital that performs 2,000 abortions a year, provided Congress with two very specific examples of abortions at 20 weeks and after (one case presenting with a bleeding placenta previa and clotting disorder and the other with a risk of massive hemorrhage) "in which the 'intact D & E' technique was critical to providing optimal care" and was the "safest technique of pregnancy termination" in those situations. (Ct.'s Ex. 9, Letter to Sen. Feinstein from Dr. Darney, at 100–01.)

- Still another doctor, who had served on the committee of physicians designated by the American College of Obstetricians and Gynecologists (ACOG) to look into this issue and who holds certifications in biomedical ethics, obstetrics and gynecology, and gynecologic oncology, Dr. Joanna M. Cain, testified that in the case "of cancer of the placenta often diagnosed in the second trimester," where "the least amount of instrumentation possible of the uterine wall is desirable[,] . . . it is much safer for the woman to have an intact D & X to remove the molar pregnancy." (Pls.' Ex. 115, Dep. Dr. Cain, at 177.)

Therefore, I declare the "Partial-Birth Abortion Ban Act of 2003" unconstitutional because it does not allow, and instead prohibits, the use of the procedure when necessary to preserve the health of a woman. In addition, I decide that the ban fails as a result of other constitutional imperfections. As a result, I will also permanently enjoin enforcement of the ban. Importantly, however, because the evidence was sparse regarding postviability, I do not decide whether the law is unconstitutional when the fetus is indisputably viable.

TEXT OF A MARCH 25, 2003, LETTER FROM LYNN EPSTEIN, MD, PRESIDENT OF THE AMERICAN MEDICAL WOMEN'S ASSOCIATION INC., TO REPRESENTATIVE JERROLD NADLER (1947–; D-NY), U.S. HOUSE OF REPRESENTATIVES, EXPRESSING OPPOSITION TO THE PARTIAL-BIRTH ABORTION BAN ACT OF 2003

The American Medical Women's Association (AMWA) strongly opposes HR 760, the "Partial-Birth Abortion Ban Act of 2003." While the Association has high respect for each member and their right to hold whatever moral, religious and philosophical beliefs his or her conscience dictates, as an organization of 10,000 women physicians and medical students dedicated to promoting women's health and advancing women in medicine, we believe HR 760 is unconscionable.

AMWA has long been an advocate for women's access to reproductive health care. As such, we recognize this legislation as an attempt to ban a procedure that in some circumstances is the safest and most appropriate alternative available to save the life and health of the woman. Furthermore, this bill violates the privilege of a patient in consultation with her physician to make the most appropriate decisions regarding her specific health circumstances.

AMWA opposes legislation such as HR 760 as inappropriate intervention in the decision-making relationship between physician and patient. The definition of the bill is too imprecise and it includes non-medical terminology for a procedure that may ultimately undermine the legality of other techniques in obstetrics and gynecology used in both abortion and non-abortion situations. At times, the use of these techniques is essential to the lives and health of women. The potential of this ban to criminalize certain obstetrics and gynecology techniques ultimately interferes with the quality of health and lives of women. Furthermore, the current ban fails to meet the provisions set forth by the Supreme Court in *Stenberg v. Carhart*, a ruling that overturned a Nebraska statute banning abortion because it contained no life and health exception for the mother.

AMWA's position on this bill corresponds to the position statement of the organization on abortion and reproductive health services to women and their families.

AMWA believes that the prevention of unintended pregnancies through access to contraception and education is the best option available for reducing the abortion rate in the United States. Legislative bans for procedures that use recognized obstetrics and gynecological techniques fails to protect the health and safety of women and their children, nor will it improve the lives of women and their families.

TEXT OF A MARCH 31, 2003, LETTER FROM GEORGE C. BENJAMIN, MD, EXECUTIVE DIRECTOR OF THE AMERICAN PUBLIC HEALTH ASSOCIATION, TO THE U.S. HOUSE OF REPRESENTATIVES URGING OPPOSITION TO THE PARTIAL-BIRTH ABORTION BAN ACT OF 2003

On behalf of the American Public Health Association (APHA)[,] the largest and oldest organization of public health professionals in the nation, representing more than 50,000 members from over 50 public health occupations, I write to urge your opposition to H.R. 760, the Partial-Birth Abortion Ban Act of 2003.

APHA has [a] long-standing policy regarding the sanctity of the provider-patient relationship and has long advocated for a woman's right to choose from a full range of reproductive health options. We believe that a physician in consultation with the patient should make the decision regarding what method should be used to terminate a pregnancy.

We are opposed to H.R. 760 because we believe this and other legislative and judicial restrictions to safe, medically accepted abortion procedures severely jeopardize women's health and well-being. APHA also opposes the bill because it fails to include adequate health exception language in instances where certain procedures may be determined by a physician to be the best or most appropriate to preserve the health of the woman. We urge members of the House of Representatives to oppose this legislation.

TEXT OF A MARCH 10, 2003, LETTER FROM NATALIE E. ROCHE, MD, AND GERSON WEISS, MD, TO SENATOR BARBARA BOXER (1940–; D-CA), U.S. SENATE, REGARDING THE PARTIAL-BIRTH ABORTION BAN ACT OF 2003

We are writing to urge you to stand in defense of women's reproductive health and vote against S. 3, legislation regarding so-called "partial birth" abortion.

We are practicing obstetrician-gynecologists, and academics in obstetrics, gynecology and women's health. We believe it is imperative that those who perform terminations and manage the pre- and post-operative care of women receiving abortions are given a voice in a debate that has largely ignored the two groups whose lives would be most affected by this legislation: physicians and patients.

It is misguided and unprincipled for lawmakers to legislate medicine. We all want safe and effective medical procedures for women; on that there is no dispute. However, the business of medicine is not always palatable to those who do not practice it on a regular basis. The description of a number of procedures—from liposuction to cardiac surgery—may seem distasteful to some, and even repugnant to others. When physicians analyze and debate surgical techniques among themselves, it is always for the best interest of the patient. Abortion is proven to be one of the safest procedures in medicine, significantly safer than childbirth, and in fact has saved numerous women's lives.

While we can argue as to why this legislation is dangerous, deceptive and unconstitutional—and it is—the fact of the matter is that the text of the bill is so vague and misleading that there is a great need to correct the misconceptions around abortion safety and technique. It is wrong to assume that a specific procedure is never needed; what is required is the safest option for the patient, and that varies from case to case....

(1) So-called "partial birth" abortion does not exist. There is no mention of the term "partial birth" abortion in any medical literature. Physicians are never taught a technique called "partial birth" abortion and therefore are unable to medically define the procedure.

What is described in this legislation, however, could ban all abortions. "What this bill describes, albeit in non-medical terms, can be interpreted as any abortion," stated one of our physician members. "Medicine is an art as much as it is a science; although there is a standard of care, each procedure—and indeed each woman—is different. The wording here could apply to any patient." The bill's language is too vague to be useful; in fact, it is so vague as to be harmful. It is intentionally unclear and deceptive.

(2) Physicians need to have all medical options available in order to provide the best medical care possible. Tying the hands of physicians endangers the health of patients. It is unethical and dangerous for legislators to dictate specific surgical procedures. Until a surgeon examines the patient, she does not necessarily know which technique or procedure would be in the patient's best interest. Banning procedures puts women's health at risk.

(3) Politicians should not legislate medicine. To do so would violate the sanctity and legality of the physician-patient relationship. The right to have an abortion is constitutionally-protected. To falsify scientific evidence in an attempt to deny women that right is unconscionable and dangerous.

The American College of Obstetricians and Gynecology, representing 45,000 ob-gyns, agrees: "The intervention of legislative bodies into medical decision making is inappropriate, ill advised, and dangerous."

The American Medical Women's Association, representing 10,000 female physicians, is opposed to an abortion ban because it "represents a serious impingement on the rights of physicians to determine appropriate medical management for individual patients." ...

We know that there is no such technique as "partial birth" abortion, and we believe this legislation is a thinly-veiled attempt to outlaw all abortions. Those supporting this legislation seem to want to confuse both legislators and the public about which abortion procedures are actually used. Since the greatest confusion seems to center around techniques that are used in the second and third trimesters, we will address those: dilation and evacuation (D&E), dilation and extraction (D&X), instillation, hysterectomy and hysterotomy (commonly known as a c-section).

Dilation and evacuation (D&E) is the standard approach for second-trimester abortions. The only difference between a D&E and a more common, first-trimester vacuum aspiration is the cervix must be further dilated. Morbidity and mortality studies indicate that this surgical method is preferable to labor induction methods (instillation), hysterotomy and hysterectomy.

From the years 1972–76, labor induction procedures carried a maternal mortality rate of 16.5 (note: all numbers listed are out of 100,000); the corresponding rate for D&E was 10.4. From 1977–82, labor induction fell to 6.8, but D&E dropped to 3.3. From 1983–87, induction methods had a 3.5 mortality rate, while D&E fell to 2.9. Although the difference between the methods shrank by the mid-1980s, the use of D&E had already quickly outpaced induction, thus altering the size of the sample.

Morbidity trends indicate that dilation and evacuation is much safer than labor induction procedures, and for women with certain medical conditions, e.g., coronary artery disease or asthma, labor induction can pose serious risks. Rates of major complications from labor induction were more than twice as high as those from D&E. There are instances of women who, after having failed inductions, acquired infections necessitating emergency D&Es, which ultimately saved her fertility and, in some instances, her life. Hysterotomy and hysterectomy, moreover, carry a mortality rate seven times that of induction techniques and ten times that of D&E.

There is a psychological component which makes D&E preferable to labor induction; undergoing difficult, expensive and painful labor for up to two days is extremely emotionally and psychologically draining, much more so than a surgical procedure that can be done in a few hours under general or local anesthesia. Furthermore, labor induction does not always work: Between 15 and 30 percent of cases require surgery to complete the procedure. There is no question that D&E is the safest method of second-trimester abortion.

There is also a technique known as dilation and extraction (D&X). D&X is merely a variant of D&E. There is a dearth of data on D&X as it is an uncommon procedure. However, it is sometimes a physician's preferred method of termination for a number of reasons: it offers a woman the chance to see the intact outcome of a desired pregnancy, thus speeding up the grieving process; it provides a greater chance of acquiring valuable information regarding hereditary illness or fetal anomaly; and there is a decreased risk of injury to the woman, as the procedure is quicker than induction and involves less use of sharp instruments in the uterus, providing a lesser chance of uterine perforations or tears and cervical lacerations.

It is important to note that these procedures are used at varying gestational ages. Neither a D&E nor a D&X is equivalent to a late-term abortion. D&E and D&X are used solely based on the size of the fetus, the health of the woman, and the physician's judgment, and the decision regarding which procedure to use is done on a case-by-case basis....

Because this legislation is so vague, it would outlaw D&E and D&X (and arguably techniques used in the first-trimester). Indeed, the Congressional findings—which go into detail, albeit in non-medical terms—do not remotely correlate with the language of the bill. This legislation is reckless. The outcome of its passage would undoubtedly be countless deaths and irreversible damage to thousands of women and families. We can safely assert that without D&E and D&X, that is, an enactment of S. 3, we will be returning to the days when an unwanted pregnancy led women to death through illegal and unsafe procedures, self-inflicted abortions, uncontrollable infections and suicide.

The cadre of physicians who provide abortions should be honored, not vilified. They are heroes to millions of women, offering the opportunity of choice and freedom. We urge you to consider scientific data rather than partisan rhetoric when voting on such far-reaching public health legislation. We strongly oppose legislation intended to ban so-called "partial birth" abortion.

IMPORTANT NAMES
AND ADDRESSES

American Association of University Women
1111 16th St. NW
Washington, DC 20036
(202) 785-7700
1-800-326-2289
FAX: (202) 872-1425
E-mail: connect@aauw.org
URL: http://www.aauw.org/

American Civil Liberties Union
125 Broad St., 18th Floor
New York, NY 10004
(212) 549-2500
URL: http://www.aclu.org/

**American College of Obstetricians
and Gynecologists**
409 12th St. SW
PO Box 96920
Washington, DC 20090-6920
(202) 638-5577
URL: http://www.acog.org/

American Life League
PO Box 1350
Stafford, VA 22555
(540) 659-4171
FAX: (540) 659-2586
E-mail: info@all.org
URL: http://www.all.org/

American Medical Association
515 N. State St.
Chicago, IL 60654
1-800-621-8335
URL: http://www.ama-assn.org/

Catholics for Choice
1436 U St. NW, Ste. 301
Washington, DC 20009-3997
(202) 986-6093
FAX: (202) 332-7995
URL: http://www.catholicsforchoice.org/

Center for Reproductive Rights
120 Wall St.
New York, NY 10005
(917) 637-3600

FAX: (917) 637-3666
E-mail: info@reprorights.org
URL: http://www.reproductiverights.org/

**Centers for Disease Control and Prevention
Division of Reproductive Health**
1600 Clifton Rd.
Atlanta, GA 30333
(404) 639-3534
1-800-232-4636
URL: http://www.cdc.gov/
reproductivehealth/index.htm

Christian Coalition of America
PO Box 37030
Washington, DC 20013-7030
(202) 479-6900
URL: http://www.cc.org/

Concerned Women for America
1015 15th St. NW, Ste. 1100
Washington, DC 20005
(202) 488-7000
FAX: (202) 488-0806
URL: http://www.cwfa.org/

Family Research Council
801 G St. NW
Washington, DC 20001
1-800-225-4008
URL: http://www.frc.org/

Feminist Majority Foundation
1600 Wilson Blvd., Ste. 801
Arlington, VA 22209
(703) 522-2214
FAX: (703) 522-2219
URL: http://www.feminist.org/

Guttmacher Institute
125 Maiden Ln., Seventh Floor
New York, NY 10038
(212) 248-1111
1-800-355-0244
FAX: (212) 248-1951
URL: http://www.guttmacher.org/

Human Life International
4 Family Life Ln.
Front Royal, VA 22630
1-800-549-5433
FAX: (540) 622-6247
E-mail: hli@hli.org
URL: http://www.hli.org/

Institute of Medicine
500 Fifth St. NW
Washington, DC 20001
(202) 334-2352
FAX: (202) 334-1412
E-mail: iomwww@nas.edu
URL: http://www.iom.edu/

**International Planned Parenthood
Federation**
4 Newhams Row
London, SE1 3UZ United Kingdom
(011-44) (0)20-7939-8200
E-mail: info@ippf.org
URL: http://www.ippf.org/

Kaiser Family Foundation
2400 Sand Hill Rd.
Menlo Park, CA 94025
(650) 854-9400
FAX: (650) 854-4800
URL: http://www.kff.org/

**Medical Students for
Choice**
PO Box 40188
Philadelphia, PA 19106
(215) 625-0800
FAX: (215) 625-4848
URL: http://www.ms4c.org/

NARAL Pro-Choice America
1156 15th St. NW, Ste. 700
Washington, DC 20005
(202) 973-3000
FAX: (202) 973-3096
URL: http://www.prochoiceamerica.org/

National Abortion Federation
1660 L St. NW, Ste. 450
Washington, DC 20036
(202) 667-5881
Hotline: 1-800-772-9100
FAX: (202) 667-5890
E-mail: naf@prochoice.org
URL: http://www.prochoice.org/

National Campaign to Prevent Teen Pregnancy
1776 Massachusetts Ave. NW, Ste. 200
Washington, DC 20036
(202) 478-8500
FAX: (202) 478-8588
URL: http://www.teenpregnancy.org/

National Center for Health Statistics
3311 Toledo Rd.
Hyattsville, MD 20782
1-800-232-4636
E-mail: cdcinfo@cdc.gov
URL: http://www.cdc.gov/nchs

National Institutes of Health
9000 Rockville Pike
Bethesda, MD 20892
(301) 496-4000
E-mail: NIHinfo@od.nih.gov
URL: http://www.nih.gov/

National Organization for Women
1100 H St. NW, Third Floor
Washington, DC 20005
(202) 628-8669
FAX: (202) 785-8576
URL: http://www.now.org/

National Right to Life Committee
512 10th St. NW
Washington, DC 20004
(202) 626-8800

E-mail: NRLC@nrlc.org
URL: http://www.nrlc.org/

National Women's Health Network
1413 K St. NW, Fourth Floor
Washington, DC 20005
(202) 682-2640
FAX: (202) 682-2648
E-mail: nwhn@nwhn.org
URL: http://www.nwhn.org/

National Women's Political Caucus
PO Box 50476
Washington, DC 20091
(202) 785-1100
FAX: (202) 370-6306
E-mail: info@nwpc.org
URL: http://www.nwpc.org/

Pan American Health Organization
525 23rd St. NW
Washington, DC 20037
(202) 974-3000
FAX: (202) 974-3663
URL: http://www.paho.org/

Planned Parenthood Federation of America
434 W. 33rd St.
New York, NY 10001
(212) 541-7800
FAX: (212) 245-1845
URL: http://www.plannedparenthood.org/

Population Action International
1300 19th St. NW, Ste. 200
Washington, DC 20036
(202) 557-3400
FAX: (202) 728-4177
E-mail: pai@popact.org
URL: http://www.populationaction.org/

Population Council
1 Dag Hammarskjold Plaza
New York, NY 10017
(212) 339-0500
FAX: (212) 755-6052
E-mail: pubinfo@popcouncil.org
URL: http://www.popcouncil.org/

Population Reference Bureau
1875 Connecticut Ave. NW, Ste. 520
Washington, DC 20009-5728
1-800-877-9881
FAX: (202) 328-3937
E-mail: popref@prb.org
URL: http://www.prb.org/

Religious Coalition for Reproductive Choice
1025 Vermont Ave. NW, Ste. 1130
Washington, DC 20005
(202) 628-7700
FAX: (202) 628-7716
E-mail: info@rcrc.org
URL: http://www.rcrc.org/

United Nations Population Fund
220 E. 42nd St.
New York, NY 10017
(212) 297-5000
FAX: (212) 370-0201
E-mail: hq@unfpa.org
URL: http://www.unfpa.org/

U.S. Conference of Catholic Bishops
Committee for Pro-Life Activities
3211 Fourth St. NE
Washington, DC 20017-1194
(202) 541-3000
URL: http://www.nccbuscc.org/prolife

RESOURCES

The three primary sources of abortion statistics used in this book are from the Centers for Disease Control and Prevention (CDC), the Guttmacher Institute, and NARAL Pro-Choice America. The CDC annually publishes its "Abortion Surveillance." The most current information on abortion data from the CDC used in the preparation of this book was "Abortion Surveillance—United States, 2005" (Sonya B. Gamble et al., November 2008).

The CDC also published "Births: Preliminary Data for 2007" (Brady E. Hamilton, Joyce A. Martin, and Stephanie J. Ventura, March 2009), "Births: Final Data for 2006" (Joyce A. Martin et al., January 2009), "Youth Risk Behavior Surveillance—United States, 2007" (Danice K. Eaton et al., June 2008), "Assisted Reproductive Technology Surveillance—United States, 2006" (Saswati Sunderam et al., June 2009), "Estimated Pregnancy Rates by Outcome for the United States, 1990–2004" (Stephanie J. Ventura et al., April 2008), "Adoption Experiences of Women and Men and Demand for Children to Adopt by Women 18–44 Years of Age in the United States, 2002" (Jo Jones, August 2008), "Changing Patterns of Nonmarital Childbearing in the United States" (Stephanie J. Ventura, May 2009), *NCHS Data on Teenage Pregnancy* (October 2008), and *Healthy Youth! YRBSS National Trends in Risk Behaviors* (2008).

Other government publications used in this book include "Funding History" (2009) by the U.S. Department of Health and Human Services' Office of Family Planning, and *Fertility of American Women: 2006* (August 2008) by the U.S. Census Bureau.

The Guttmacher Institute, which strongly supports abortion as an option, is the major nongovernmental source of abortion statistics in the world. The Guttmacher Institute publishes *Perspectives on Sexual and Reproductive Health*, a quarterly journal that provides research and analysis on sexual and reproductive health and rights in the United States and other developed countries. The *Perspectives on Sexual and Reproductive Health* articles used in this pub-

lication include Rachel K. Jones et al.'s "Abortion in the United States: Incidence and Access to Services, 2005" (March 2008) and Carolyn B. Sufrin, Mitchell D. Creinin, and Judy C. Chang's "Incarcerated Women and Abortion Provision: A Survey of Correctional Health Providers" (March 2009).

The Guttmacher Institute also publishes *International Family Planning Perspectives*, a quarterly journal that provides research on sexual and reproductive health and in Africa, Latin America, the Caribbean, and Asia. Gilda Sedgh et al.'s "Legal Abortion Worldwide: Incidence and Recent Trends" (September 2007) is an *International Family Planning Perspectives* article that was used in this publication.

The Guttmacher Institute offers many reports and fact sheets on family planning issues. Among the Guttmacher Institute publications that provided helpful information were *In Brief: Facts on Induced Abortion in the United States* (July 2008), *State Policies in Brief: An Overview of Abortion Laws* (May 2009), *State Policies in Brief: Sex and STD/HIV Education* (June 2009), *State Policies in Brief: Protecting Access to Clinics* (May 2009), *State Policies in Brief: Emergency Contraception* (April 2009), *State Policies in Brief: Minors' Access to Contraceptive Services* (August 2009), *State Policies in Brief: Parental Involvement in Minors' Abortions* (June 2009), *State Policies in Brief: State Funding of Abortion under Medicaid* (May 2009), *State Policies in Brief: Bans on "Partial-Birth" Abortion* (May 2009), *State Policies in Brief: State Policies on Later-Term Abortions* (May 2009), *State Policies in Brief: State Policies on Later-Term Abortions* (May 2009), and *Abortion in Women's Lives* (Heather D. Boonstra et al., May 2006).

NARAL Pro-Choice America publishes information on the status of abortion in the individual states in *Who Decides? The Status of Women's Reproductive Rights in the United States* (January 2009). This document was an excellent source of statistics and information for this book.

The National Campaign to Prevent Teen and Unplanned Pregnancy provides a wealth of information on teen pregnancy, including *Magical Thinking: Young Adults' Attitudes and Beliefs about Sex, Contraception, and Unplanned Pregnancy, Results from a Public Opinion Survey* (2008). This survey was conducted and published in conjunction with *Self* magazine.

Additional information on international abortion statistics was provided by the World Health Organization in *Unsafe Abortion: Global and Regional Estimates of the Incidence of Unsafe Abortion and Associated Mortality in 2003* (Elisabeth Ahman and Iqbal Shah, September 2007).

The National Abortion Federation (NAF), a national association of abortion providers and a strong abortion advocate, tabulates statistics on incidents of violence against abortion providers. The NAF publishes a wide range of consumer education materials on abortion and operates a nationwide toll-free consumer hotline to answer questions and make referrals to qualified abortion providers throughout the United States and Canada. "NAF Violence and Disruption Statistics: Incidents of Violence & Disruption against Abortion Providers in the U.S. & Canada" (2009) was particularly helpful.

Harris Interactive and the Gallup Organization publish surveys on American attitudes toward abortion, as do various news media. Particularly helpful were the Harris poll "Support for *Roe v. Wade* Increases Significantly, Reaches Highest Level in Nine Years" (November 2007) and the Gallup polls *More Americans "Pro-Life" Than "Pro-Choice" for First Time* (Lydia Saad, May 2009), *Abortion* (2008), *Moral Issues* (May 2008), and *Moral Issues Divide Westerners from Muslims in the West* (Magali Rheault and Dalia Mogahed, May 2008).

INDEX

Page references in italics refer to photographs. References with the letter t *following them indicate the presence of a table. The letter* f *indicates a figure. If more than one table or figure appears on a particular page, the exact item number for the table or figure being referenced is provided.*

Abortion